A History of Anthropological Theory

A History of Anthropological Theory

third edition

Paul A. Erickson & Liam D. Murphy

Originally published by Broadview Press 2008

Library and Archives Canada Cataloguing in Publication

Erickson, Paul A.
A history of anthropological theory / Paul A. Erickson and Liam D. Murphy.—3rd ed.

Includes bibliographical references and index.
ISBN 978-1-44260-110-9
(Previous ISBN 978-1-55111-871-0)
1. Anthropology—Philosophy. 2. Anthropology—History. I. Murphy, Liam Donat II. Title.

GN33.E74 2008 301.01 C2007-907594-0

We welcome comments and suggestions regarding any aspect of our publications—please feel free to contact us at the addresses below or at news@utphighereducation.com

www.utphighereducation.com

NORTH AMERICA
5201 Dufferin Street,
North York, Ontario
Canada M3H 5T8
Tel: (416) 978-2239
Fax: (416) 978-4738
customerservice
@utphighereducation.com

2250 Military Road,
Tonawanda, New York
USA 14150

UK, IRELAND, AND CONTINENTAL EUROPE
NBN International
Estover Road
Plymouth, United Kingdom
PL6 7PY
Tel: +44 (0) 1752 202300
Fax: +44 (0) 1752 202330
enquiries@nbninternational.com

Higher Education University of Toronto Press acknowledges the financial support of the Government of Canada throughthe Book Publishing Industry Development Program (BPIDP) for our publishing activities.

Cover design, photograph, and typeset by Zack Taylor.
Edited by Betsy Struthers.

This book is printed on paper containing 100% post-consumer fibre.

Printed in Canada

For Dawn

For Stephanie and Siobhan

Contents

List of Illustrations

Preface

In 1995, Paul Erickson organized a session of papers presented at the annual meeting of the American Anthropological Association exploring the theme "Teaching the History of Anthropological Theory: Strategies for Success." His own paper was a survey of courses in the history of anthropological theory taught at colleges and universities throughout Canada and the United States. The survey revealed that such courses were widespread in both graduate and undergraduate curricula. It also revealed that, owing to the diversified nature of anthropology, there was considerable variation in the scope of the courses and the way they were taught. Especially noteworthy were the great variation in texts and professors' serious dissatisfaction with their suitability. A recurring complaint of professors was, "We *need* a suitable textbook."

Two years later, in 1997, Erickson and Liam Murphy began a rich conversation concerning the history of anthropological theory that marked the beginning of a sustained "dialogue with the ancestors." Appropriately, this dialogue has been mirrored in the relations between the authors themselves: Erickson, the professor, and Murphy, the erstwhile student, himself turned professor. To date, this conversation has yielded the twin successes of two editions of *A History of Anthropological Theory* (1998, 2003) and its companion volume, *Readings for a History of Anthropological Theory* (2001, 2006).

In the beginning, *A History of Anthropological Theory* was generally based on a senior-level undergraduate course that Erickson had been teaching at Saint Mary's University for many years, a course in which Murphy himself was enrolled while a student there. As with any university course, this one had evolved through the incorporation of elements of various texts used on and off for years. These included Paul Bohannan and Mark Glazer's *High Points in Anthropology* (1989), Peter Bowler's *Evolution* (1989), Annemarie de Waal Malefijt's *Images of Man* (1974), Bruce Trigger's *A History of Archaeological Thought* (1990), and Marvin Harris's *The Rise of Anthropological Theory*

(1968) and *Cultural Materialism* (1979). The second, and now the third, editions of *A History of Anthropological Theory* have incorporated more of Murphy's bibliographic sources, especially pertaining to the end of the twentieth century, when he joined the profession. Although the book has not been written from any of these other authors' theoretical perspectives, its presentation and interpretation in places may be similar. Therefore, we are indebted to the authors for inspiration and for an organization of material that, in the classroom, works. If certain theories or theoreticians appear to have been "left out," the reason is not disrespect, but a desire to keep the book brief.

In the main, our third edition adopts the North American, "four field," framework for anthropology as a general discipline with specialized subdisciplines of linguistic, archaeological, physical, and cultural anthropology. Most North American anthropology is cultural anthropology, so the book concentrates on this subdiscipline—but not exclusively. It includes key sections on linguistic, archaeological, and physical anthropology that can be read with profit by all anthropology students. Unlike many comparable texts, which begin in the eighteenth or nineteenth century, our book begins in antiquity, in the understanding that all subdisciplines of anthropology are deeply rooted in Western experience.

This third edition of *A History of Anthropological Theory* incorporates many improvements to the first two editions. A major improvement is its reorganization to make the order of presentation of theorists parallel to the order in *Readings for a History of Anthropological Theory 2/e*. Accordingly, the sections on Sigmund Freud, Émile Durkheim, and Max Weber now appear at the end of Part One, followed by a new section on Ferdinand de Saussure. This reorganization will allow teachers and students to use both books in tandem more easily. Additional improvements to the third edition are a new section on public anthropology and revised, expanded, rearranged, and updated sections on Durkheim, Weber, Marxism, Charles Darwin and Darwinism, American cultural anthropology, French structural anthropology, feminism and anthropology, and postmodernity. We have also updated the conclusion, review questions, glossary, and suggested readings; added new illustrations; and edited the book throughout to improve its coherence and intellectual "flow." We are especially pleased to welcome to this third edition guest essays, Speaking About Anthropological Theory, by distinguished contemporary theorists Lila Abu-Lughod, Lee D. Baker, and Janice Boddy, who, drawing on personal experiences, explain why studying the history of anthropological theory is worthwhile.

Readers will observe that many sections of the book are subdivided to reflect the influence of particular individuals and "schools." Our choice to present our discussion in this way is no accident. It reflects a consensus that in university courses on the history of anthropology and anthropological theory, the "founding fathers" (and mothers) and "important" theories and theorists generally receive expanded coverage. As we explain in our updated Conclusion, these "ancestors" merit special focus in texts such as this one, insofar as their ideas continue to provide a degree of intellectual coherence and historical point of reference for students entering the discipline.

A History of Anthropological Theory 3/e is designed to serve as an introductory text, which users may wish to supplement with lengthier, more detailed, and special-interest texts, including primary-source "readers" such as our own *Readings for a History of Anthropological Theory 2/e*.

Experience has led us to believe that students in history of anthropological theory courses are usually prepared with background in one or more of the anthropology subdisciplines, but rarely in them all. For this reason, we have attempted to write *A History of Anthropological Theory 3/e* in straightforward, non-polemical, and jargon-free prose. The book is also largely free of elaborate references to the voluminous history of anthropological theory scholarship, and there are no footnotes or endnotes, only a list of follow-up sources and recommended readings. We have, however, included birth and death dates for key historical figures, where such dates were obtainable. The majority of students in history of anthropological theory courses are there not by choice, but because the course is a departmental major requirement. A common lament of these students is the challenging vocabulary of theoretical "-isms" and "-ologies." To help ease their pain, we have attempted to define each challenging word or phrase the first time it is used meaningfully in the text, and at the end of the text we have appended a glossary of boldfaced terms. An added list of review questions should also help. Still, students should not be lulled into complacency. Learning (and teaching) the history of anthropological theory is usually difficult, although ultimately highly intellectually rewarding.

Producing the third edition of *A History of Anthropological Theory* has been extremely gratifying to us, personally as well as professionally. As has previously been the case, we would not have enjoyed the process nearly as much were it not for the moral and professional support of many people. Erickson wishes to thank his wife Dawn for her invaluable advice and support. Murphy's outstanding debt of thanks must be to Paul and Dawn Erickson for their ongoing encouragement and friendship. His deepest thanks are also extended to his wife Dr. Stephanie M. Seery-Murphy, whose sweet disposition, wisdom, and gentle humour have been an ongoing inspiration. This third edition is dedicated to her and to their beautiful daughter, Siobhan.

Both authors are also indebted to guest essayists Abu-Lughod, Baker, and Boddy for their knowledge and insights and to the staff of Broadview Press, primarily for being such enthusiastic supporters of our work, but also for being extremely helpful and accommodating at all stages of the revision process. Special mention is due executive editor Anne Brackenbury and her associates, who have always been "in our corner," as well as the numerous anonymous reviewers who provided valuable advice on how to improve the book. Finally, Erickson and Murphy are very grateful to colleagues, students, and interested readers who gave us feedback. After almost a decade, *A History of Anthropological Theory* appears to still "have legs." We hope that this third edition finds new users to join loyal continuing users, allowing it to walk for some time to come.

Paul A. Erickson
Halifax, Nova Scotia

Liam D. Murphy
Sacramento, California

Timeline

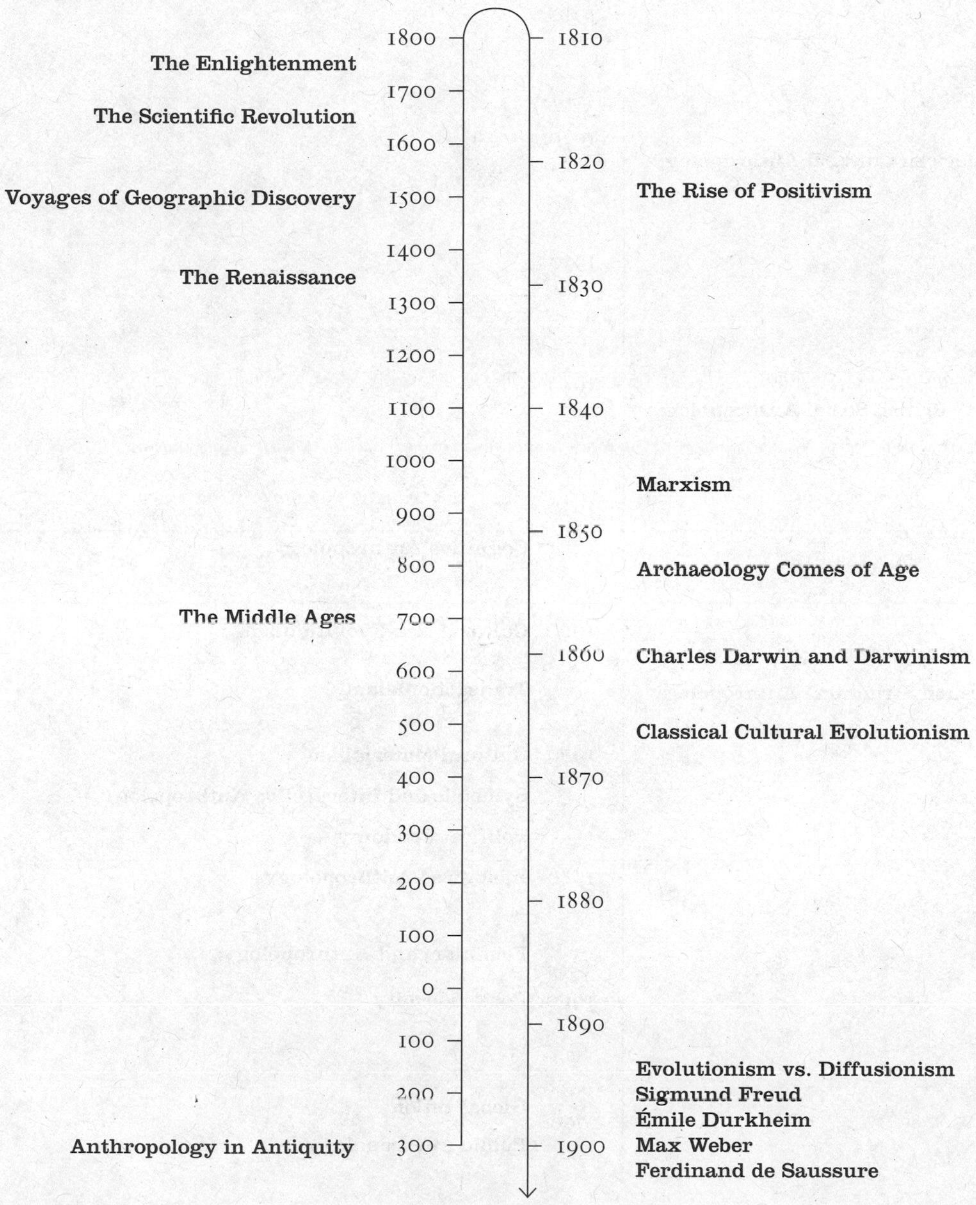

1800
1810
The Enlightenment
1700
The Scientific Revolution
1600
1820
Voyages of Geographic Discovery
1500
The Rise of Positivism
1400
The Renaissance
1830
1300
1200
1100
1840
1000
Marxism
900
1850
800
Archaeology Comes of Age
The Middle Ages
700
1860
Charles Darwin and Darwinism
600
500
Classical Cultural Evolutionism
400
1870
300
200
1880
100
0
1890
100
Evolutionism vs. Diffusionism
200
Sigmund Freud
Émile Durkheim
Anthropology in Antiquity
300
1900
Max Weber
Ferdinand de Saussure

A HISTORY OF ANTHROPOLOGICAL THEORY

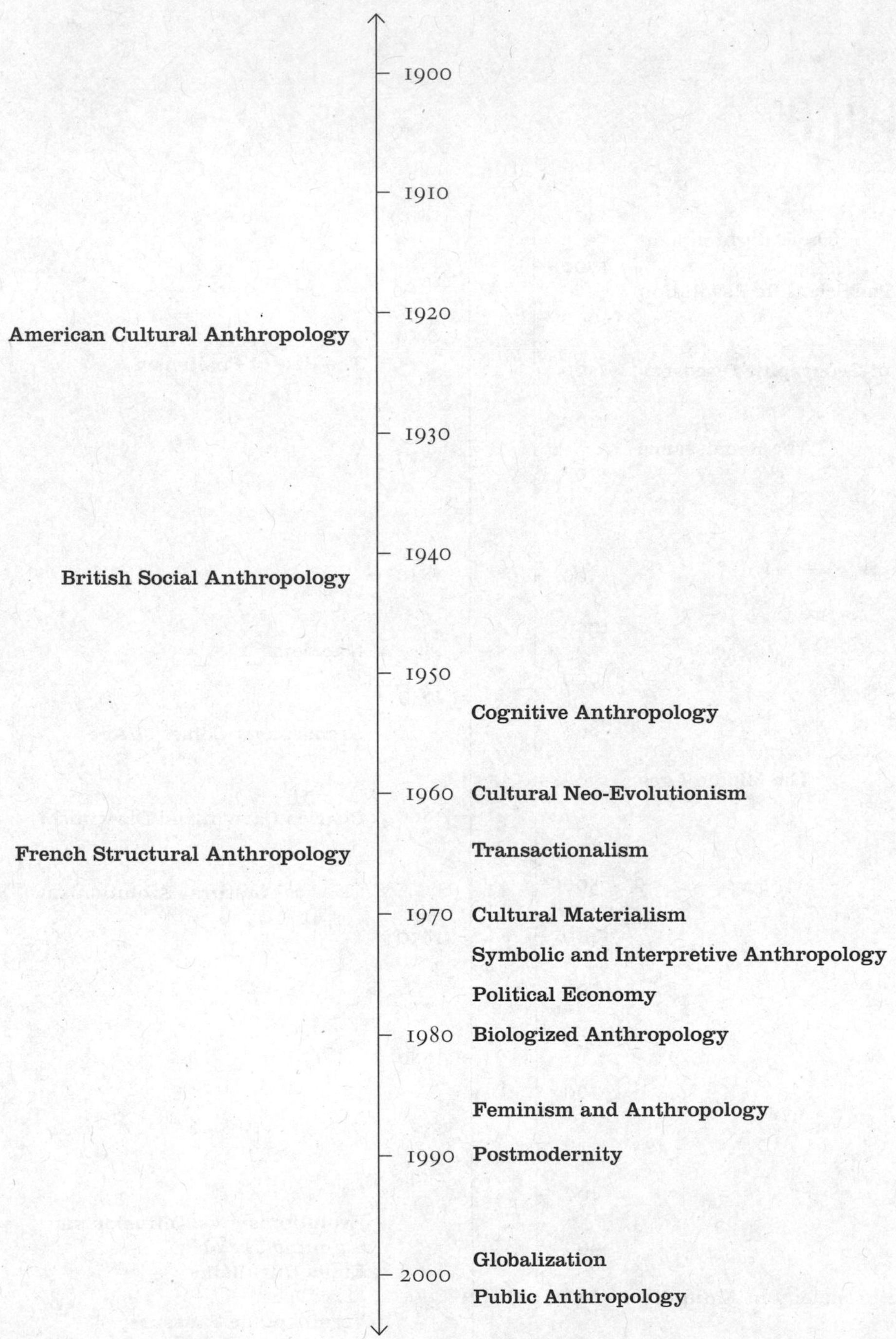

Introduction

Anthropology is a fascinating field of study of all peoples past and present. Traditionally in North America, the field has been divided into four subfields. The first subfield, physical, or biological, anthropology is concerned with the evolutionary origins and diversity of the species *Homo sapiens*. Physical anthropologists include paleoanthropologists, who study human fossils; primatologists, who study our monkey, ape, and related evolutionary "cousins"; and human geneticists. The second subfield, archaeological anthropology, is the study of artifacts, or the material remains of past human activity. Prehistoric archaeologists specialize in studying the artifacts of peoples without written records, while historical archaeologists specialize in studying the artifacts of peoples with written records. Archaeologists cooperate with a wide range of other specialists, including geologists, biologists, and historians. The third subfield, linguistic anthropology, is concerned with the nature of language and with the nature, history, and social function of the multitude of particular languages spoken and written around the world. The fourth subfield, cultural, or sociocultural, anthropology is the study of human lifeways and thoughts, often summed up simply as "culture." Cultural anthropologists, the most numerous in the field, specialize in studying one or more cultural groups and domains, such as Inuit art, Hopi religion, or Australian Aboriginal kinship. Taken together, these four subfields have given anthropology a uniquely "holistic," or broad-based and overarching, world view. Anthropologists are quick to assert that any statement about "human nature" must pertain to the biological and cultural nature of *everybody*.

A conspicuous trend in late twentieth-century anthropology, at least in North America, was the diversification of the traditional subfields into an increasing number of special interest groups. Arguably, this trend began with the addition of a "fifth" subfield, applied anthropology, which is designed to accommodate the interests of anthropologists finding employment outside universities and museums.

The trend has continued to the point where, in 2007, the American Anthropological Association, the largest association of professional anthropologists in the world, was divided into some 38 special-interest sections. These sections have interests as diverse as those represented, for example, by the Association for Feminist Anthropology, Society for the Anthropology of Food and Nutrition, Society for Visual Anthropology, Society for the Anthropology of Europe, and Society for the Anthropology of Consciousness. Under circumstances of such diversity, anthropology, prone to introspection anyway, was bound to question its holistic world view and intensify its efforts to understand just what it stands for theoretically.

"Theory" in anthropology stands for different things in different anthropological circles. By invoking broad, often unstated, definitions such as "general orientation," "guiding principle," and "intellectual framework," anthropologists have been able to discuss theory without always having to articulate just what it means to themselves or to others. This is particularly true in the "history of anthropological theory," an established topic of anthropological discussion in which "original," "important," and "influential" theories and theorists are identified relatively easily in hindsight. Such theories and theorists become "canonized" simply by being referred to as original, important, and influential by a sufficient number of anthropologists over a sufficient period of time. They then form lineages of theoretical ancestors in which descendants position themselves to gain theoretical identity.

In most North American colleges and universities, undergraduate anthropology majors and graduate students complete a course or course unit in the history of anthropological theory. The main manifest, or explicit, function of this experience is to enhance the theoretical sophistication of students and to introduce them to theories and theorists with whom they might not otherwise become acquainted. Its latent, or implicit, function is to serve as a rite of passage, in which new generations of anthropologists "join the club" by recapitulating its intellectual history. Unfortunately, many students regard the study of past anthropology as a mere backdrop to "real" research. Still others dismiss it as a collection of erroneous perspectives or cautionary tales about people who never *really* understood human life. Approached as a "dialogue with the ancestors," however, rather than "one dead guy a week" (these felicitous phrases come from William

Fowler and Julia Harrison), the history of anthropological theory can be exciting, thought-provoking, and moving. It can also be humbling and nurture respect, as "younger" anthropologists realize that they are heirs to an anthropological legacy that is time-honoured and, in the main, noble.

Any history of anthropological theory is written by a particular historian at a particular time and in a particular place. A respectable historian aims to be truthful but cannot, of course, expect to achieve "*the* truth, the whole truth, and nothing but the truth." This is because the historian must select elements from the past and put them together in a way that makes sense in the present, which is always changing. The inevitable result is that the historian's analytical categories may seem "imposed" on the past, rendering, for example, certain early figures and ideas as "unfairly" proto-anthropological. By selecting certain past figures and their ideas and by interpreting them in light of subsequent events to which we know they (often unwittingly) contributed, the historian can help us understand where anthropology came from and, therefore, what it really is.

In the analytical perspective adopted in this book, anthropological theory can be considered to be a branch of science, humanism, or religion. The differences among science, humanism, and religion have to do with how these three systems of thought treat the relationship among nature, people, and a cosmological order of existence frequently conceived of as "God." In science, people and God are treated as secondary to nature, which is paramount in the sense that nature encompasses people and God. In the science of biology, for example, people are considered to be composed of pre-existing natural elements like carbon and water, while in the science of psychiatry, or at least some versions of it, God is considered to be created by a pre-existing human brain. In humanism, God and nature are treated as secondary to people, who are paramount in the sense that people encompass both God and nature. Examples of humanism can be found in literature and philosophy, where "Man is the measure of all things" and "human nature," especially creatively expressed, is the central fact of existence. Finally, in religion, nature and people are treated as secondary to God, who is paramount in the sense that God encompasses nature and people. A familiar example of religion is the Judeo-Christian belief, expressed in the Bible, that God created "Heaven and Earth" and, within a few days, Adam and

Eve. Throughout its history, anthropology has been, in terms of these definitions, variously scientific, humanistic, and religious.

Beneath these theoretical complexities, anthropology can be seen to be searching for answers to fundamental questions asked by people everywhere, such as: "Where did we come from?," "Why do we differ?," and "How does the world work?" Confronting an avalanche of technical information in books, articles, and reports, anthropologists sometimes forget that these questions are universal and, therefore, that all peoples have their own versions of anthropology. The version relevant to most readers of this book is the one that developed in the history of Western civilization.

PART ONE

The Early History of Anthropological Theory

Perhaps more than any other Western academic discipline, anthropology embodies the ambition of scholarship to understand the character of humanity in all its diversity and complexity. Such an understanding can hardly be achieved without an appreciation for the rich history of thought that is the foundation upon which various contemporary perspectives and theoretical orientations have been erected.

For this reason, any thorough discussion of the origins of anthropology must begin long before the formal emergence of the discipline in the late nineteenth century. In common with all Western academic disciplines, the roots of anthropology lie grounded in the intellectual traditions of the Greco-Roman "ancient" world. Traced by the historian, this world reveals the first contours of what, in hindsight, can be called a nascent anthropological perspective.

Anthropology in Antiquity

In the West, beginning in Antiquity a few centuries before the birth of Christianity, Greco-Roman civilization produced several Classical intellectual traditions. Today, following the account of Annemarie de Waal Malefijt in *Images of Man,* some of these traditions seem scientific, or at least quasi-scientific, while others, such as the epic poetry of Homer (*c.*8th century B.C.) and Virgil (70-19 B.C.), appear more humanistic or religious. The roots of what most of us today would call anthropology can be found in the efforts at early Classical science.

The first group of Classical thinkers with a semblance of science were those philosophers whose thought predates that of Socrates, teacher of Plato. The pre-Socratics were really cosmologists, who speculated on the origin and nature of the cosmos, or embodied world. Some of these speculations were materialistic, meaning that they invoked natural rather than supernatural causes. One such pre-Socratic was the Greek philosopher Thales (*c*.640-*c*.546), who speculated that everything in the world came from water. Another was Anaximander (*c*.622-*c*.547), a pupil of Thales, who said that the original substance of the cosmos was not a known element but "something boundless" and undifferentiated. A third pre-Socratic was Empedocles (*c*.490-*c*.430), sometimes called an ancient precursor of Darwin. Empedocles believed that the cosmos evolved as different constituent elements encountered one another and formed larger bodies that survived if they were useful, a process vaguely resembling natural selection. Finally, an extreme version of pre-Socratic materialism is represented by Democritus (*c*.460-*c*.370), who proposed that human bodies, minds, and behaviour derived from changes in the shape, size, and velocity of constantly moving universal particles, or "atoms." Like other pre-Socratics, Democritus opposed the idea of a human "Golden Age," from which people had allegedly deteriorated. Instead, he saw progress and betterment in the working of natural forces.

Pre-Socratic science was not modern, of course, but it *was* different from ancient humanism and from the religion in ancient Greek myths like that of Prometheus, a primordial deity said to have made people out of clay and stolen fire for them from Mount Olympus. Pre-Socratic philosophers saw people created by nature, not gods.

Another ancient Greek tradition more scientific than religious was the tradition of travel writing, best represented by Herodotus (*c*.484-*c*.425), the "Father of History." In his travels beyond the limited world of ancient Greece, Herodotus observed diversity in race, language, and culture. He explained this diversity in a relatively objective, or non-ethnocentric, way by correlating it with geography, climate, and other features of the natural world. Herodotus was also humanistic because he stressed how human differences were caused by human, not divine, acts. This combination of science and humanism, as opposed to religion, makes his writing a kind of ancient precursor of ethnography.

In the fifth century B.C., there was a major change in Greek life when democracy in the city-state of Athens superseded the older political system based on kinship. This fundamental shift in politics was accompanied by a shift in thought, leading to new philosophical schools. One new school was Sophistry, which taught that practical skills and social effectiveness were goals more important than the search for objective knowledge or absolute truth. The Sophist Protagoras (*c.*481-*c.*411), to whom some attribute the phrase "Man is the measure of all things," believed that human behaviour is not influenced by gods but by life circumstances. Behaviour, then, is really cultural convention and should be seen as such—a doctrine not unlike the twentieth-century doctrine of **cultural relativism**. Protagoras also explained how various cultural conventions may have come about through an evolutionary-like process. For some Sophists, relativism led to Nihilism, the doctrine that nothing exists or is knowable. They became Nihilists because they felt that virtues were not absolute and that knowledge was merely what was said to be true by people in power—an idea that foreshadows a key part of the nineteenth-century doctrine of Marxism. Even in the fifth century B.C., broad anthropological ideas had begun to take root.

CULTURAL RELATIVISM The proposition that cultural differences should not be judged by absolute standards.

Some important Athenian philosophers were opposed to Sophistry. Socrates (*c.*469-399) taught that there *were* universal values, even though they were difficult to perceive and express. People had to train their minds for these tasks. Education was important, according to Socrates, because it enabled people to see through their cultural conventions, not merely manipulate them, as the Sophists advocated. Plato (*c.*427-347), the famous student of Socrates, agreed with his teacher that there were such universal values, which existed because they were innate in the human mind. According to Plato, people recognize objects because, before they perceive them, they have the *idea* of them. His *Republic* (360) was a dialogue about an ideal society constructed on the basis of people's perceptions of flaws in real societies. He reconstructed the development of society through time in order to show what had changed and what had not. What had remained the same were the transcendental "essences" of things. For more than two millennia, the enduring legacy of thinking in terms of Platonic essences encouraged physical anthropologists to view species and "races" as distinct and unchanging. Overcoming this legacy became a major challenge for twentieth-century evolutionists.

The philosopher Aristotle (384-322), Plato's student, agreed that society had developed over time, but he was much more empirical than Plato, examining the development of society in its own right rather than trying to pierce through it to a universal, transcendental realm. Aristotle was curious about the relationships among natural and social objects, which he assumed existed and were knowable. Contrasted with Plato, whose idea of transcendental essences became incorporated into religion, the legacy of Aristotle included science, inherited through Alexander the Great (356-323), whom Aristotle tutored. When Alexander the Great conquered the Greek city-states and the Persian Empire from India to Asia Minor and Egypt, founding the Egyptian city of Alexandria in 332 B.C., the scientific teachings of Aristotle spread.

Socrates, Plato, and Aristotle lived in the "Golden Age of Greece." After Alexander the Great died, the unity of Greek life and thought declined, and competing schools of thought emerged. Epicurus (*c*.342-270) pursued Empedocles' belief that people comprised atoms, which were dissolved at death and reabsorbed into nature. Epicurus was an extreme utilitarian in that he considered society to be a mechanical extension of humanity and therefore subservient to humanity. Later, the Roman poet Lucretius (*c*.96-*c*.55) expressed these views more forcefully in his materialistic poem *On The Nature of Things* (*c*.50).

Meanwhile, the Stoics, like the Epicureans, wanted a correct and happy life, but, unlike the Epicureans, they believed that nature and society were highly orderly. According to the Stoic philosopher Zeno (*c*.336-*c*.264), this order was not created by people or gods but was a natural cosmic order, sometimes called Logos. This concept was later co-opted by early Christian theologians seeking to defend their beliefs against various schools of Greek philosophy. Belief in a universal social order made it possible to compare and contrast particular social orders, a fundamental task of what today we call social science. Furthermore, according to the Stoics, matter, not mind, is real; matter can be perceived; and learning is the perception of matter. Therefore, contrary to Plato, the Stoics believed in what was later called ***tabula rasa***, or "blank slate," meaning a mind that acquires knowledge through experience rather than recognizes knowledge that is innate.

TABULA RASA Translated "blank slate," the idea that the mind acquires knowledge through experience rather than recognizes knowledge that is innate.

Stoicism was the philosophical bridge between the Greeks and the Romans, forming the philosophical basis for Rome's great advances in political organization and theory. In Rome, the idea of a natural order was developed into the concept of cosmopolis, or world citizenry, by statesman and orator Marcus Tullius Cicero (106-43). At the same time, other Roman writers like Seneca (4 B.C.-65 A.D.) and Marcus Aurelius (121-180 A.D.) used the concept to explore humanistic and religious themes, paving the way for its eventual attachment to Christianity. In both realms, secular and religious, Stoicism encouraged people to make their particular thoughts and actions accord with something universal while telling them that, as rational beings, they were capable of this achievement. Such a philosophy is one of the great legacies of Antiquity.

Toward the end of the Roman Empire, social conditions deteriorated, and several religions competed for appeal to the socially oppressed, all building on the Stoic idea of an overarching supernatural order in the universe. At first, these religions, or sects, were outlawed because they preached obedience to divine rather than civil law. Prominent among them were Mithraism; Orphism; the cults of Cybele, Isis, and Osiris—and Christianity. Outpacing the competition, Christianity gained converts and (ironically for a religion of the oppressed) became the state religion of Rome under Emperor Constantine I (Constantine "The Great," *c.*288-337). This action led in the fourth century A.D. to the Patristic period of Church history, during which time orthodox Church doctrine was established by Church "Fathers."

For anthropology, the most consequential Church Father was the Bishop of Hippo in northern Africa, Saint Augustine (354-430), author of *Confessions* (397) and *The City of God* (*c.*425). The Augustinian version of Christianity was the version that prevailed when the Roman Empire declined and Europe entered the Middle Ages.

Major tenets of Augustinian Christianity were not conducive to science, especially social, or human, science. According to Augustine, God was perfect and human nature was sinful. The cosmos and humanity were not in harmony. The cosmos had been created by an omnipotent, or all-powerful, God who was inscrutable, or unknowable. Therefore, it was pointless for people to study God or nature. Human behaviour was to be judged not by people or nature but by God. Finally, everything people could know about themselves, nature, and God was revealed in Scripture. These tenets, designed to account for the mystery of God, had the effect of smothering human curiosity and the sense that nature, too, is mysterious. Without mysteries and the curiosity to solve them, why bother to develop science?

On the positive side for science, and later for anthropology, Augustinian Christianity did stress the importance of history because it was from history, as revealed in Scripture, that Christians could learn at least something about God. Furthermore, Augustinian history was lineal, not cyclical or recurrent, and it was a universal history, not just the history of "nations." These tenets laid the broad foundation for the temporal and spatial, or cross-cultural, perspectives of anthropology.

The legacy of Antiquity to anthropology, then, was the establishment of the humanistic, religious, and scientific intellectual outlooks. In various guises, and in different times and places, these outlooks have persevered in anthropology ever since.

The Middle Ages

In the period following Augustine's death, the Western Roman Empire declined and was occupied by non-Christian "barbarians" and "pagans." The Christian tradition continued to flourish, however, in the Eastern Roman, or Byzantine, Empire, with its capital at Constantinople, founded by Constantine I in 330 A.D. There, and in pockets elsewhere, monastic Christian historians and encyclopedists like Isidore of Seville (*c.*560-636) denounced non-Christians while they kept the teachings of Augustine alive.

Meanwhile, the pre-Christian intellectual traditions of Antiquity were sustained by Middle Eastern Semitic peoples who, following the birth of the prophet Mohammed (*c.*570 A.D.), spread the Islamic religion out of Arabia, across northern Africa, and all the way to Spain. Contrasted with early Christians, who embraced the transcendental and otherworldly qualities of Platonism, Arab intellectuals like Ibn Khaldûn (1332-1406) had great respect for Aristotelian logic and science. More forcefully than Plato, Aristotle counteracted Augustine's scientifically negative attitude that people were incapable of knowing nature and that nature, except through God, was incapable of being known. When Islam and Augustinian Christianity interacted, Christian theology changed.

The critical interaction between Islam and Christianity occurred in the eighth century when Islamic Moors invaded Christian Spain. Afterward, Christian theology became increasingly "rational," meaning that human reason was brought to bear on theological issues. This trend culminated in the theology of Thomas Aquinas (*c.*1225-1274), author of *Summa Theologica* (1267-1273), one of the great treatises of the Roman Catholic Church. Thomistic Christianity (as the theology of Thomas Aquinas is called) differed radically from Augustinian Christianity. Unlike Augustine, Aquinas reasoned that people could, and should, know God through knowing nature. The true essence of humanity was not only sin but also the kernel of the divinity created within each human being. Human reason was a gift of God, and people were morally responsible to use this gift to glorify God by learning about God's creation, the natural world. Human reason could even be used to prove the existence of God. In Thomistic Christianity, God, people, and nature were harmonized into a self-contained intellectual system without internal contradictions. Nothing people discovered about nature through the exercise of their God-given reason could cast doubt on the credibility and authority of God or on his representative Church on Earth—or so it was asserted.

In order to keep Thomistic Christianity intact, it was necessary to ensure that science remained consistent with the Word of God. This was the job of numerous scholarly "commentators," who interpreted the writings of Aristotle and Church Fathers opportunistically. Scholasticism, as the doctrine supporting this activity came to be called, predominated in the Middle Ages. It has been caricatured as "seeing how many angels can be fitted onto the head of a pin." Inevitably, cracks in the whole system surfaced, and when it became impossible, or simply too difficult, to reconcile science and religion, scholars began to choose one over the other. Once this happened, the door was open for anthropology to develop, by contemporary standards, along more scientific lines.

The intellectual unity achieved by Thomistic Christianity was a kind of "medieval synthesis," which unified the three elements whose varied relationships define science, humanism, and religion, that is, nature, people, and God. Intellectually precarious from the start, it did not last long. Three complex events produced knowledge that, outside Thomistic circles, made the synthesis unravel. These events were the Renaissance, voyages of geographical discovery, and the Scientific Revolution, each of which shaped modern anthropology in critically important ways.

The Renaissance

The Renaissance, a revival of interest in ancient learning, marks the transition from the medieval to the modern world. The key developments took place from the fourteenth through the sixteenth centuries in the nuclear city-states of Western Europe, especially northern Italy. There, wealthy mercantilists and other members of the prospering middle class began to spend their money as "patrons" of artists and scientists who were unwilling to accept limits placed on their intellectual and creative freedom by the Church. The archetypical "Renaissance Man" was the Italian painter, sculptor, architect, musician, engineer, and mathematician Leonardo da Vinci (1452-1519). Like other creative geniuses of the Renaissance, da Vinci was enamoured of the ancient world because it represented a pre-Christian source of knowledge and values. Curiosity about the ancient world also produced classical archaeology, which developed during the Renaissance as an effort to use classical artifacts to supplement what was written in classical texts. In Italy, the rediscovery of Roman Antiquity was especially exhilarating because Rome was part of Italy's own "glorious past." Renaissance thinkers came to realize that the Ancients possessed a fuller and more satisfying grasp of human nature than did the austere Christians of the Middle Ages.

Renaissance interest in the ancient world produced a new sense of time, which no longer seemed static, but capable of producing change—change as dramatic as that represented by the difference between the ancient and medieval worlds. This realization led to a systematic contrast of ancient and medieval ways of life and, in turn, to a questioning of the authority of the medieval Catholic Church based on a preference for secular alternatives from the past. In the history of religion, this trend contributed to the Protestant reform movements of the sixteenth century, many of which stressed the "priesthood of all believers" and the importance of rationality in religious experience and practice. In the histories of humanism and science, the trend continued to broaden the secularization of thinking, paving the way for the emergence of the modern tradition of scholarly social criticism and analysis.

Three influential social critics and analysts inspired by the Renaissance outlook were Desiderius Erasmus (*c.*1466-1536), Thomas More (1478-1535), and Niccolò Machiavelli (1469-1527). In *The Praise*

Adam and Eve
This Renaissance engraving by Albrecht Dürer depicts Adam and Eve being expelled from the Garden of Eden, an act of profound consequence in the Judeo-Christian account of human creation.

of Folly (1509), Dutchman Erasmus opposed the idea of **original sin**, arguing that Greek virtues incorporated into early Christianity were superior to virtues espoused by later Christianity, which had grown excessively formal, bureaucratic, and corrupt. His highly irreverent book poked fun at the perceived stupidity, greed, and hypocrisy of priests and monks. In *Utopia* (1516), Englishman More contrasted the evils of contemporary society with the virtues of a society constructed on secular principles and based on ethnographic accounts of "simpler"

ORIGINAL SIN The Christian idea that early sin resulted in the expulsion of humanity from the Garden of Eden.

peoples, whose lives were happier because they lacked private property, money, and crime. In *The Prince* (1513), Italian Machiavelli described the qualities of an effective political ruler, who must be strong, intelligent, and wise enough to understand the good and bad parts of human nature. All three of these influential Renaissance thinkers show that by the early sixteenth century there had emerged a strong tradition of secular social analysis that later, in anthropology, would become **cross-cultural analysis**. The main Renaissance legacy to anthropology was this secular, critical approach.

CROSS-CULTURAL ANALYSIS Analysis of cultural similarities and differences.

Voyages of Geographical Discovery

During the late Roman Imperial period, Saint Augustine pronounced that "No antipodes exist." **Antipodes** were places on opposite sides of the world, together with the people who lived there. In making this pronouncement, Augustine was expressing the view, widely held at the time, that most parts of the world had already been discovered and that nothing dramatically different remained to be found. He was mistaken. Between Roman and early modern times, enough geographical exploration had taken place to bring Europeans into contact with peoples sufficiently different from themselves so as to raise the question of whether they were even human.

ANTIPODES Opposites, or peoples on opposite sides of the world.

European exploration began in earnest with the eleventh-century Christian crusades to Africa and parts of the Middle East. Exploration expanded in the thirteenth century when the Mongols conquered much of the Holy Roman Empire in central and eastern Europe. One of the most famous European explorers was the Venetian, Marco Polo (*c.*1254–*c.*1324), who spent 17 years in China at the court of the Mongol ruler Kublai Khan. Intense competition for profitable trade routes to Asia spurred further exploration by Portugal and Spain. By 1499, Vasco da Gama (*c.*1469–1524) found his way around Africa to India, while a few years earlier, in 1492, seeking the same destination, Christopher Columbus (*c.*1446–1506) discovered the "New World." When Vasco Núñez de Balboa (*c.*1475–1517) sailed around South America and discovered the Pacific Ocean in 1513, it became clear that the New World was in fact new (to Europeans). The first round of European exploration was concluded by Ferdinand Magellan (*c.*1480–1521), one of whose ships circumnavigated the globe in 1522.

The New World
This seventeenth-century map depicts the New World as the Island of Atlantis.

Initially, European opinions of non-European Native peoples presented a major challenge to the medieval synthesis of God, people, and nature. To Europeans, the Native peoples, especially the "Indian" Natives of the New World, appeared extraordinarily different, far too primitive and savage to belong to a single family of God's creation. Thomas Aquinas, who knew something about human diversity, had pronounced that Native peoples were imperfect humans and, therefore, **natural slaves** to Europeans. At the time, this pronounce-

NATURAL SLAVES The early theological conception of "primitive" peoples as innately imperfect and subservient to European Christians.

ment seemed plausible, but problems with it quickly arose. Imperfect natural slaves lacked the mental and moral capacity for free agency, or the ability to make a conscious choice. Without free agency, Native peoples could not make a valid conversion to Christianity as a means of achieving salvation. Therefore, they were denied the kingdom of God, rendering the efforts of missionaries futile.

NATURAL CHILDREN The early theological conception of "primitive" peoples as capable of "improvement" and conversion to Christianity.

Christian theology had to change, and it did. Influential Spanish theologians Bartolomé de Las Casas (1474-1566) and José de Acosta (*c.*1539-1600) redefined natural slaves as **natural children**, allowing benevolence to "save" them and make them civilized Christians. An important consequence of this redefinition, in theological terms, was to bring the human family closer together. But if all the peoples of the world were to belong to the same family, should they not be historically connected? The Protestant Reformation had made the Bible the sole authority on history for much of Christian Europe. A few Biblical passages did imply historical connections among different peoples, for example, through Adam and Eve, the sons of Noah, and tribes dispersed after destruction of the Tower of Babel. By and large, however, Biblical support for the idea that *all* the peoples of the world were God's children was scant and, in some circles, insufficient. Additional support was needed.

MONOGENESIS The doctrine that human races constitute a single biological species with a common origin and with differences produced over time; contrasted with polygenesis.

POLYGENESIS The doctrine that human races constitute separate species with separate origins and innate differences; contrasted with monogenesis.

In the period from the sixteenth through the eighteenth centuries, several ingenious schemes were designed to show that Europeans were historically connected to non-Europeans, especially to American Native peoples, with whom, following the colonization of America, Europeans were forced to interact. According to one scheme, Native peoples were descendants of survivors of the sunken continent of Atlantis, a relationship purportedly demonstrated by cultural similarities between Europeans and the Incas and Aztecs. Another scheme made Native peoples one of the ten Lost Tribes of Israel, while yet another, foreshadowing the modern scientific view, had them immigrating to America from northern Asia across the Bering Strait. Gradually, these schemes, inspired by the desire to reconcile natural observations with Christian theology, became more "scientific." In anthropology, they led to **monogenesis**, the doctrine that human "races" constitute a single biological species with a common origin and physical differences produced by natural agents over time. Later, monogenesis faced stiff competition from **polygenesis**, the doctrine that human races constitute distinct species with separate

The Old World Meets the New

Early sixteenth-century Spanish soldiers besiege the Aztec capital of Tenochtitlán.

origins and physical differences that are unalterable and racially innate. Debate between monogenesists and polygenesists was at times intense, reaching its peak in the heyday of classical nineteenth-century anthropology. In the twentieth century, use of the terms monogenesis and polygenesis declined, but anthropologists continued—and continue to this day—to debate the significance of human physical similarities and differences.

No other event in Western history has been as significant for anthropology as the voyages of geographical discovery. These voyages brought Europeans into contact with the different kinds of people anthropologists now study, creating what has been called the anthropological "Other." They also launched the era of European global domination of Native peoples by means of slavery, colonialism, imperialism, and "globalization." In the late twentieth century, anthropologists began to recognize their complicity in this domination and agonize over ways to "decolonialize" anthropology and give Native peoples "voice." This movement would have profound implications for anthropological theory.

The Scientific Revolution

A paramount reason for the change of medieval into modern times was the Scientific Revolution, meaning the invention of modern science as a method of intellectual investigation and the growth of specialized sciences and their accumulated bodies of knowledge about the natural world. Because most anthropologists have embraced some version of science, contrasted with humanism or religion, anthropology today is rooted in these momentous events.

There are two parts to the Scientific Revolution: the growth of scientific epistemologies and the accumulation of scientific knowledge. **Epistemology** is the branch of philosophy that explores the nature of knowledge. In the post-medieval era, when the intellectual authority of the Church was eroding, new epistemologies for science were required. Two major epistemologies emerged, both of which are employed by the practicing scientist today. One is **deduction,** the use of logic to reason from general to particular statements, or, defined more broadly, the process of drawing a conclusion from something known or assumed. Deduction is used in all sciences, especially the formal science of mathematics. The most famous intellectual architect of deduction was French mathematician René Descartes (1596-1650), who reasoned, "I exist, therefore God exists, therefore the real world exists." The **Cartesian** (the adjective derived from Descartes) version of deduction laid the foundation for the scientific tradition of **French rationalism**. A central tenet of Cartesian thought, one that would become pivotal in late twentieth-century critiques of **positivism**, is that it assumes the essential duality of a world divided into objects and subjects, the rational and the irrational, and the cultural and the natural.

The second epistemology of the Scientific Revolution is **induction**, the process of discovering general explanations for particular facts by weighing the observational evidence for propositions that make assertions about those facts. The most famous intellectual architects of induction were English philosophers Francis Bacon (1561-1626) and John Locke (1632-1704), whose ideas formed an important part of the eighteenth-century Enlightenment. Baconian and Lockean versions of induction laid the foundation for the scientific tradition of **British empiricism**. Both French rationalism and British empiricism have had followers in anthropology, leading to anthropological

EPISTEMOLOGY The branch of philosophy that explores the nature of knowledge.

DEDUCTION In scientific epistemology, the use of logic to reason from general to particular statements; contrasted with induction.

CARTESIAN The adjective derived from the name of philosopher René Descartes labeling a radical dualism between mind and matter, body and soul, and subject and object.

FRENCH RATIONALISM The intellectual tradition associated with René Descartes and the scientific epistemology of deduction.

POSITIVISM The view that science is objective and value-free.

INDUCTION In scientific epistemology, the process of arriving at generalizations about particular facts; contrasted with deduction.

BRITISH EMPIRICISM The scientific epistemology of induction fashioned by philosophers Francis Bacon and John Locke.

schools of thought with fundamentally different, and sometimes opposing, epistemologies.

From the thirteenth through the seventeenth centuries, increasingly powerful applications of scientific epistemologies supplanted medieval ways of thinking to produce a series of scientific discoveries culminating in the revolutionary scientific synthesis of Sir Isaac Newton. The story of this revolution begins with **mechanics**, the science of motion, and with **cosmology**, a branch of philosophy concerned with the origin and structure of the universe.

MECHANICS The medieval science of motion.

COSMOLOGY The branch of philosophy concerned with the origin and structure of the universe.

Medieval mechanics and cosmology derived from a combination of Christian theology and Aristotelian science. In the medieval world view, the Earth was the centre of the universe, and all bodies moved to its centre in a form of motion that was considered natural. All other motion was considered unnatural and needed a mover to be explained. In unnatural motion, if a body ceased being moved, it would stop, or come to rest. The speed of a moving body depended on the force of the mover, with a constant force producing a constant speed. When a moving body met resistance, its speed would decrease. If the resistance decreased, its velocity would increase proportionately so that, in a vacuum, where there is no resistance at all, its speed should be instantaneous. To medieval scientists, the concept of instantaneous speed seemed absurd. Therefore, there *was* no vacuum. Besides, God would abhor a vacuum anyway!

In this system, naturally falling bodies should not accelerate, or pick up speed. But they did. The solution to this problem, devised by medieval commentators, was to posit that air rushed in behind falling bodies, forcing them downward. As the height of the air beneath falling bodies decreased, they met less resistance and accelerated. This solution worked well for a while, then became unconvincing. There was the added problem of projectiles, or bodies impelled forward through the air. Why did projectiles slow down? According to a theory developed in the 1300s, projectiles were given the property of impetus, which spent itself in flight. By the same token, naturally falling bodies *acquired* impetus, which made them accelerate. The theory of impetus, a classic *ad hoc* explanation, was a bridge between medieval theories and the modern theory of inertia.

Medieval mechanics was an integral part of medieval cosmology. In medieval cosmology, the earthly domain was cut off from the celestial, or spiritual, domain by the four elements of earth, water, air, and fire, which covered the Earth in layered orbs, or spheres. The celestial orbs comprised a fifth element, something unchanging and eternal. There were ten celestial orbs, the outer one the empyrean heaven. Aristotle had proclaimed these orbs real, although frictionless. Ptolemy (87-150), the great Greek astronomer at Alexandria, was forced to add almost 80 additional orbs with epicycles, smaller circles moving around the circumference of larger circles, to account for "irregularities" in planetary motion. This solution created a major new problem: the orbs, supposedly real, intersected.

In 1543, Polish astronomer Nicholaus Copernicus (1473-1543) helped launch the Scientific Revolution by announcing that the Earth moved around the Sun, not the other way around, and that the Earth revolved on its own axis. Copernicus intended his action, which reduced the number of required orbs to 34, to be conservative, bolstering the Ptolemaic system by salvaging elements of it that still worked. But the implications were ominous. If the Earth was not the centre of the universe, how could it be special? How could God have created it for the glorification of people? Were there other worlds? Moreover, this solution created new technical problems and was beset by new nonconforming observations. If the Earth was rotating on its axis, why did falling bodies not land *behind* where they were dropped? Also, in the late 1500s, new stars and comets appeared, and their paths of movement, especially those of the comets, cut through the celestial orbs. To solve this problem, Danish astronomer Tycho Brahe (1546-1601) took the next bold step by announcing that the orbs did not exist. Then, in the early 1600s, German astronomer Johann Kepler (1571-1630), freed from the constraints of orbs, described planetary orbits as ellipses rather than perfect circles. Kepler's laws of planetary motion had planets moving around the Sun and sweeping equal areas in equal time, implying that planets closer to the Sun moved faster.

Meanwhile, Italian physicist and astronomer Galileo Galilei (1564-1642) used the telescope to observe sun spots and other "blemishes" on heavenly bodies. Reflecting on the revolutionary views of his predecessors, Galileo, in *Dialogue Concerning the Two Chief Systems of the World* (1632), systematically contrasted the Ptolemaic and Copernican world views. In the process, he solved the problem of falling bodies not landing behind where they were dropped by reasoning that everything on the Earth rotates with it; in other words, "behind" does not really exist. Still, two huge interrelated problems remained: what *caused* motion on Earth, now that the Earth was no longer the centre of the universe, and what *caused* celestial bodies to move, now that there were no orbs?

These remaining problems were solved by British scientist Isaac Newton (1642-1727), who, in *Principles of Mathematics* (1687), showed that one law, the **law of universal gravitation**, accounted for the motion of bodies both on the Earth and in the celestial realm. Newton showed that all bodies move by being attracted to one another with a force proportional to the square of the distance between them. Bodies on the Earth move because they are attracted to the Earth (and the Earth to them), and celestial bodies move because they are attracted to one another in patterns consistent with Kepler's laws of planetary motion. Contrasted with the medieval system, Newton's system maintains that inertia keeps bodies moving unless they are affected by new forces, rendering it unnecessary to keep bodies moving by constantly applying the same force. Moreover, a constant force produces constant acceleration, not speed. The Newtonian cosmos is one law-bound system of matter in motion, with the Earth and its inhabitants careening through empty space in a way that scientists do not have to invoke God to explain. For his intellectual achievements, Isaac Newton was knighted and buried in Westminster Abbey. Many years later, Charles Darwin—"the Newton of biology"—was buried nearby.

LAW OF UNIVERSAL GRAVITATION Isaac Newton's scientific explanation of universal planetary and earthly motion.

The significance of the Scientific Revolution for anthropology is twofold. First, the physical universe conceived by Newton is the universe most modern anthropologists accept. Second, Newton's accomplishments in natural science inspired similar efforts in the social sphere. The result was that in the century following Newton, the eighteenth-century Enlightenment, the seeds of social science were planted, took root, and flourished. In the late twentieth-century, however, many anthropologists began to question the efficacy of science, ushering in an era of self-doubt and, in some quarters, outright rejection of science as traditionally conceived.

The Enlightenment

The **Enlightenment** is the name given to the intellectual history of Europe in the eighteenth century, from the time of Newton's

ENLIGHTENMENT The period of eighteenth-century intellectual history preceding the French Revolution.

Principles of Mathematics to the time of the French Revolution, beginning in 1789. During this period, following fast on the Scientific Revolution, intellectual attitudes coalesced to produce key concepts of social science. In anthropology, the most important of these concepts was culture.

MECHANICAL PHILOSOPHY The philosophy inspired by the law of universal gravitation, portraying the universe as a complex machine with fine-tuned, interacting parts.

DEISTIC Pertaining to deism, the view that God created the universe but remains relatively uninvolved in its day-to-day operations; contrasted with theistic.

THEISTIC Pertaining to theism, the view that God created the universe and remains active in its day- to- day operations; contrasted with deistic.

In a way, the Enlightenment was a continuation of the Scientific Revolution because Enlightenment intellectuals were so enamoured of the philosophy of Newton that they extended it from the natural into the social realm. Newton's philosophy was called the **mechanical philosophy**, referring to his image of the universe as a complex machine with fine-tuned interacting parts. The machine was always moving, and the job of the scientist was to learn just how. Because Newton believed that God had *created* the universe, his philosophy was also called **deistic**; unlike a **theistic** philosopher, he did not invoke God to account for its day-to-day machinations. Metaphorically, the Newtonian universe was a clock, God the clockmaker.

Another major figure in the Enlightenment was British philosopher John Locke (1632-1704), who in *An Essay Concerning Human Understanding* (1690) expanded the scientific epistemology of British empiricism. The most important part of Locke's epistemology for anthropology was his idea, resurrected from the ancient Stoics, that the mind of each newborn person is a *tabula rasa*, or "blank slate," which is "written on" by life. What made this philosophy so important is that it was a philosophy of experience, in which human thoughts and behaviour were understood to be acquired rather than inherited or in some other way innate. Such an understanding was indispensable for the emergence of the concept of culture, which can be defined here as the accumulated way of living created and acquired by people and transmitted from one generation to another extrasomatically, other than through genes. Culture is the central concept of American anthropology. Its emergence during the Enlightenment is the reason why American anthropologist Marvin Harris argues in *The Rise of Anthropological Theory* (1968) that before the Enlightenment, anthropology did not really exist.

During the Enlightenment, a number of intellectuals used the philosophies of Newton and Locke to organize and analyze data on human diversity generated by the voyages of geographical discovery. One such intellectual was Jesuit Father Joseph Lafitau (1671-1746), who in *Customs of American Savages Compared with Those of Earliest*

Times (1724) created an inventory of culture traits and categories considerably less **ethnocentric**, or culturally biased, than those of his predecessors. Lafitau was one of several Jesuit missionaries whose eighteenth-century accounts of North American Native peoples are still consulted by ethnohistorians. Another Enlightenment figure was French social reformer Jean Jacques Rousseau (1712-1778), who in *Discourse on the Origin and Foundation of Inequality among Men* (1751) speculated on how and why human differences had developed over time. Rousseau sought to counteract what he considered to be overly intellectualized Enlightenment formulations by emphasizing human pathos and emotion. His speculations led him to conclude in *The Social Contract* (1762) that humanity had been happier in the past and that **noble savagery** was a condition whose disappearance ought to be lamented. In their speculative reconstructions of the past, both Lafitau and Rousseau used living Native peoples as models for past "savages." This was an early application of what in nineteenth-century anthropology would be called the **comparative method.**

ETHNOCENTRIC Pertaining to ethnocentrism, or cultural bias.

NOBLE SAVAGERY The romanticization of "primitive" life.

COMPARATIVE METHOD The use of extant primitive peoples to represent extinct primitive peoples, as in classical cultural evolutionism.

Aping the accomplishments of Newton, some Enlightenment intellectuals sought to discover "laws" of human history. These so-called **universal historians** proposed stages of human development during which, according to the philosophy of Locke, human experience was understood to have accumulated as culture. A prime example was Italian philosopher Giambattista Vico (1668-1744), who in *The New Science* (1725) described how humanity had passed through the three stages of gods, heroes, and men. These stages were secular and, according to Vico, the product of human, not divine, action. Another universal historian was the Baron de la Brède et de Montesquieu (1689-1755), who in *The Spirit of Laws* (1748) attempted to show how rules governing human conduct have always been correlated with culture. More radical was French philosopher François Marie Arouet de Voltaire (1694-1778). In his *Essay on the Customs and Spirit of Nations* (1745), Voltaire actively attacked the theological view of history and traced the growth of Christianity in secular terms. British historian Edward Gibbon (1737-1794) used the same approach more subtly in *The Decline and Fall of the Roman Empire* (1776-1778).

UNIVERSAL HISTORIANS Enlightenment thinkers who promulgated laws of human history.

Some universal historians of the Enlightenment stand out as more recognizably anthropological than others. One was French statesman Anne Robert Jacques Turgot (1727-1781), who in *Plans for Two Discourses on Universal History* (1750) described the passage of humanity through the three stages of hunting, pastoralism, and farming. Another was French philosopher Marie Jean de Condorcet (1743-1794), who in *Outline of the Intellectual Progress of Mankind* (1795) added more stages, for a total of ten, the last of which he predicted to be the future. Prediction, he urged, was based on his confidence in laws about the past. Scottish historians Adam Ferguson (1728-1816), John Millar (1735-1801), and William Robertson (1721-1793) stressed the importance of technology and economy in defining stages of universal history. Robertson even used the schema **savagery, barbarism, and civilization**, which became commonplace in the nineteenth century. In fact, from the perspective of nineteenth-century anthropology, the Scottish Enlightenment appears more theoretically sophisticated than the French.

SAVAGERY, BARBARISM, AND CIVILIZATION Lewis Henry Morgan's tripartite schema for the universal evolution of humanity.

Enlightenment schemes of universal history were united by the common ideals of human reason, progress, and perfectibility. Reason referred to the exercise of human intellect unfettered by authoritarian faith, including faith in religion. Progress referred to the resulting positive direction of historical change, opposite the direction presupposed by medieval Christianity, which considered humanity degenerate and fallen from the grace of God. Perfectibility referred to the final outcome of reason and progress, which, according to Enlightenment thinkers, would lead to steady improvement of human conditions on the Earth. Linked as it was to science, the intellectual agenda of the Enlightenment prevailed in anthropology for more than 100 years. In the early twentieth century, influential anthropological theorists began to question some of its ideals as unattainable, and in the later twentieth century, other influential theorists offered a more strident critique of those ideals as undesirable. Meanwhile, toward the end of the eighteenth century, the ideals became slogans for social reform, then rallying cries for the French Revolution.

The Rise of Positivism

The French Revolution was a political movement that overthrew the absolute monarchy of the Bourbon regime and its associated system of upper-class privilege, unleashing a new middle class, the **bourgeoisie**. Beginning in 1789, the Revolution lasted for a protracted, bloody decade before Napoleon Bonaparte (1769-1821) assumed control of France in 1799. In a move widely considered to be a betrayal of

BOURGEOISIE In Marxism, the middle class.

revolutionary ideals, Bonaparte made himself Emperor and plunged France into a series of expansionist wars that lasted until he was defeated at the Battle of Waterloo in 1815. Afterward, all of Europe needed a rest from political turmoil.

The Revolution was fought on the basis of Enlightenment ideals that insisted on the human capacity for moral and intellectual progress and, ultimately, perfection. When the Revolution turned out badly, European intellectuals turned their backs on these ideals. The result was a rise in conservative attitudes aimed at maintaining, or regaining, the political status quo. Conservatism appeared in a number of guises. One was fundamentalist Christianity, which condemned social science as excessively materialistic, atheistic, and amoral. Many new Christian denominations developed, espousing "evangelical" or **pietistic** perspectives. In this new theology, Newton's clockmaker God was replaced by a God of divine intervention, miracles, and punishment for those who strayed from the teachings of the Bible and its latter-day interpretations. Elsewhere, citizens fed up with radical "social engineering" established utopian, or visionary, socialist communities where they could live and do as they pleased. A strong reaction to Napoleon's vision of empire was nationalism, which promoted the ideology and mythology of particular peoples rather than a universal outlook on humankind. In Germany, which struggled to achieve nationhood, there was a revival of faith in predestination and a longing to return to past glory, resulting in a retreat from the idea of progress. This development had a noticeable effect on German ethnology, which embraced the idea of the ***volksgeist***, or special spirit, of Germans. Another guise of conservatism was Romanticism, a movement in art, literature, and even science that glorified the idiosyncratic, non-rational, and emotional sides of human nature and denied the primacy of Cartesian thought. Finally, there was racism, which was linked to all other guises of conservatism and which flourished in the nineteenth century.

PIETISTIC Pertaining to piety, or religious reverence and devotion.

VOLKSGEIST Translated "spirit of the people," according to some early theorists, the ethnographic essence of a people.

Conservatism also affected social science, which developed during the Enlightenment when principles of Newtonian science were used to investigate social change. In the early nineteenth century, social scientists also felt that it was time to put more emphasis on stability. The result was the all-encompassing philosophy of **Positivism**.

POSITIVISM The scientific philosophy of Auguste Comte.

Positivism (with a capital "P") was the creation of French philosopher Auguste Comte (1798-1857), an intellectual descendant of Marie Jean de Condorcet through intermediary Claude Henri, Comte de Saint-Simon (1760-1825). Comte's views are contained in his multi-volume work *Course of Positive Philosophy* (1830-1842), in which he described how almost all branches of knowledge have passed through three stages: theological, metaphysical, and positive. According to Comte, in the theological stage, phenomena were explained in terms of deities; in the metaphysical stage, in terms of abstract concepts; and in the positive stage, in terms of other phenomena. Starting with astronomy and physics in the Scientific Revolution, the natural sciences had already passed through the theological and metaphysical stages to become positive, meaning truly scientific. The social sciences, however, lagged behind. It was Comte's job to help them catch up. The social sciences had already passed out of the theological stage, where social phenomena had been explained in terms of God during the Middle Ages, well into the metaphysical stage, where they had been explained in terms of the abstract concept of reason during the Enlightenment. Now, Comte urged, social science should enter the positive phase, in the post-Enlightenment nineteenth century.

SOCIAL DYNAMICS In Positivism, the study of social change.

SOCIAL STATICS In Positivism, the study of social stability.

In Comte's scheme, science involved the search for generalizations. In positive social science, these would be of two kinds. **Social dynamics** (named after a branch of physics) would search for generalizations about social change, while **social statics** (physics again) would search for generalizations about social stability. Comte maintained that the French Revolution had gone too far in attempting to promote dynamic change and that its excesses needed to be tempered with social statics. Together, social dynamics and social statics offered a comprehensive scientific perspective on social phenomena.

As the creator of Positivism, Comte was one of the founding fathers of modern social science, in particular sociology, which was built on the foundation of his pronouncement that social phenomena are to be explained in their own terms. At the same time, positivism (with a small "p") underwent several philosophical transformations, so that by the middle of the twentieth century it had become synonymous with an outlook that promoted detached, value-free science as the model for social scientific inquiry. By the end of the century, anthropologists of various persuasions had begun to realize that, far from being detached, science is permeated by values, even if those values are not always explicit. They had also begun to understand how science functions in a social context and to argue that scientists bear responsibility for the detrimental social uses of science. Opposed to the traditional scientific model, these anthropologists began to cite positivism as a source of theoretical misguidance.

Marxism

As the nineteenth century progressed, in the wake of the French Revolution, the middle classes of Europe prospered. Meanwhile, the working classes grew restless and agitated for reform. Where the Industrial Revolution took hold, mainly in Britain, radical intellectuals rallied to support the growing labour movement. The most radical of these were Karl Marx and Friedrich Engels, co-creators of the theory of **dialectical materialism**, commonly called **Marxism**. Marxism has had a profound effect on the real world of politics. It has also affected anthropology, not only for this reason but also because aspects of Marx's thought have been elaborated and formally incorporated within anthropological theory, even by anthropologists whose "allegiance" is not explicitly Marxist.

DIALECTICAL MATERIALISM The philosophy of Karl Marx and Friedrich Engels, commonly called Marxism.

MARXISM A collection of views derived from Karl Marx and Friedrich Engels and their theory of dialectical materialism.

Karl Marx (1818-1883) was born in Prussia (now part of northern Germany), studied philosophy at the University of Berlin, then law at the University of Bonn. He became interested in the relationship between politics and economics, turning to the utopian variety of socialism in 1843. Early on, he decided that utopian socialism was ineffective and that, to become effective, socialism would have to be made "scientific." Friedrich Engels (1820-1895) was the son of a German textile manufacturer who spent several years in the English cities of Manchester and Liverpool as the agent of a textile firm. England had already experienced the undesirable effects of industrialization and was debating parliamentary measures to improve the poor conditions of urban workers. Engels analyzed these conditions in *The Condition of the Working-Class in England* (1844) and then expanded his analysis in collaboration with Marx. The result was their landmark treatise *The Communist Manifesto* (1848).

MATERIALISM In dialectical materialism, the belief that human existence determines human consciousness; in cultural materialism, the equivalent of the principle of infrastructural determinism.

The essential ingredients of dialectical materialism can be found in *The Communist Manifesto* and the much larger work *Capital* (1867). Marx and Engels began with the premise of **materialism**, meaning their belief that human existence determines human consciousness, contrasted with the idealist belief that human consciousness determines human existence. More specifically, they believed that human thoughts, actions, and institutions are determined by their relationship to the **means of production**, meaning how people make a living in the material world. This relationship is always changing because the means of production are always changing as people change their adaptations to physical conditions. In prehistory, according to Marx and Engels, who drew this part of their analysis from contemporary anthropology, people lived in a socio-economic system with material goods belonging to all, no private property, and equality under the "law." In civilization, however, powerful individuals gained control of land, the basic source of wealth. Thus, **primitive communism** was superseded by a system of unequal classes and the exploitation of one class by another.

MEANS OF PRODUCTION In dialectical materialism, how people make a living in the material world.

PRIMITIVE COMMUNISM In some versions of Marxism, the view that past primitive peoples lived in a state to which future communism will, in a fashion, return.

RULING CLASS In the theory of dialectical materialism, the class that controls the means of production.

DIALECTICAL In the Marxist theory of dialectical materialism, philosopher Friedrich Hegel's formulation of historical change as proceeding in the form of thesis-antithesis-synthesis.

THESIS-ANTITHESIS-SYNTHESIS In dialectical materialism, Friedrich Hegel's form for dialectical change.

Marx and Engels maintained that all modern societies are based on class distinctions. These distinctions become institutionalized in church and state, which function to keep the **ruling class**, the class that controls the means of production, in power. As the means of production change, the nature of classes, which "organize" the means of production, also changes. Eventually, the means of production outgrow their form of organization, which is "overthrown" in a social revolution, from which a new social system emerges. In classical Marxism, the sequence of social revolutions is **dialectical**, according to a revised version of the philosophy of Georg Wilhelm Friedrich Hegel (1770-1831). Hegel, an extreme idealist, described a world spirit manifesting itself in history through dialectical transformations of the form **thesis-antithesis-synthesis**. The thesis came first, followed by its opposite, the anti-thesis, which was then followed by a combination of the thesis and antithesis, the synthesis. Marx and Engels were attracted to Hegel's philosophy but felt that it needed to be epistemologically up-ended. Therefore, they "stood Hegel on his head" and moved the dialectic from the ideal to the material world. In the resulting theory of dialectical materialism, social transformations assume a dialectical form, with one social stage, the thesis, inevitably "sowing the seeds of its own destruction" by harbouring its opposite, the antithesis, which manifests itself in social revolution. This stage is followed by a third social stage, the synthesis, that retains elements of the preceding two. Marx and Engels's main focus was materialism rather than dialectics. Their primary interest in revising Hegel's philosophy was to use it to explain what had happened in world history and, through a communist revolution, what would happen in the future.

Although Marx and Engels were aware of prehistory, ancient history, and non-Western history, they began their account with the Middle Ages and feudalism, a system of agricultural economics with classes consisting of ruling-class lords and a ruled-class of unfree labourers, the serfs. During feudal times, a new manufacturing class emerged, the capitalists, whose power rested on money rather than land. The capitalist means of production was manufacturing, which, because of what it could produce, was superior to agriculture and eventually replaced it. For Marx and Engels, the triumph of capitalism over feudalism was the French Revolution, after which lords and serfs were superfluous, and the new classes became the ruling-class bourgeoisie and a ruled-class of urban workers, the **proletariat**.

PROLETARIAT In the lexicon of Marxism, the working class.

Marx and Engels did not spend too much time analyzing feudalism and how it gave rise to capitalism. They were much more anxious to analyze capitalism and how it would give rise to communism. Their analysis was based on the **labour theory of value**, the materialist premise that goods and services should be valued in terms of the human labour required to produce them. According to this theory, the value of a good or service, a commodity, is directly related to the amount of labour put into it. Exploitation occurs when capitalists "expropriate" some of this value as profit. Moreover, capitalists buy and sell labour itself as a commodity, valuing it according to wages determined by the labour "market." The result is that workers are alienated from the product of their labour and, therefore, from themselves.

LABOUR THEORY OF VALUE The proposition of Karl Marx that commodities should be valued in terms of the human labour required to produce them.

The disintegration of capitalism was the focus of the work *Capital*. In it, Marx explained how at first capitalism was progressive, opening up new markets as an efficient way of producing goods. But capitalism became regressive and less efficient, as competition among manufacturers decreased and economic power was concentrated in fewer and fewer hands. The growth of monopolies was inevitable, Marx observed, because competition produced winners as well as losers. Soon the monopoly system outgrew the original capitalist system of product diversity. Rich monopolists got richer by increasing profits, and poor workers got poorer because profit was taken from their wages. The proletariat became pauperized, and, as small business people were squeezed out by competition, they swelled its ranks. Under free market conditions, a glut of labourers caused a decrease in wages, intensifying poverty. Because of cheaper labour, profits increased. For a while, profits were reinvested in production, but eventually production generated more and more goods able to be bought by fewer and fewer people. This downward spiral of events led to economic recession, depression, and labour unrest. Soon the capitalist world was ripe for revolution.

In the mature phase of capitalism, the means of production would already be concentrated in a few locations. Workers could easily seize them in the name of the proletariat and nationalize them in the name of a nation governed by workers. The first stage of the revolution would be a temporary **dictatorship of the proletariat**, whose job would be to destroy the bourgeoisie as a class and eliminate private profit by putting it to public use. The result would be a classless society in which the state, formerly serving the interests of a few capitalists, would become agents of all workers. Eventually, the state would "wither away" and the final stage would emerge, the true stage of communism, in which workers would work according to their ability and receive compensation according to their needs. Final communism would represent a return to primitive communism with the technology of the industrial age.

DICTATORSHIP OF THE PROLETARIAT In the theory of dialectical materialism, the temporary phase of political organization leading to permanent communism.

Marxism achieved major political victories in the Soviet and Chinese revolutions of the twentieth century, which led to the installation of Marxist dogma and its modification by powerful politicians like Vladimir Lenin (1870-1924), Joseph Stalin (1879-1953), and Mao Tse-tung (1893-1976). Marxism also took root outside politics in academic disciplines such as anthropology.

Beginning in earnest in the 1930s, a minority of anthropologists embraced one or more of the tenets of Marxism. A few turned to Marxism in support of the fledgling communist regime in the Soviet Union, or in rejection of the capitalist system held responsible for the Great Depression. Since then, Marxist anthropologists have grown theoretically diverse and sometimes divergent from one another. Some, such as **structural Marxists** and political economists, have stressed how a given economic system is constrained by its ruling ideology. Others, such as some feminist anthropologists, have looked to Marxism as a means of understanding and combating the economic subjugation of women. Few Marxist anthropologists have accepted the entire theory of dialectical materialism, which history

STRUCTURAL MARXISTS Proponents of a theoretical blend of Marxism, dialectical philosophy, and French structural anthropology.

has helped refute. But they have demonstrated a personal commitment to help economically disadvantaged people and have been willing to use anthropology professionally for that purpose. Most Marxist anthropologists, including Marxist archaeologists, have preferred materialist over idealist explanations of culture change and historical over ahistorical approaches to cultural analysis. They have emphasized "class" because Marxism implies that different classes have different ideologies and "consciousnesses." In Marxist circles there have been disputes between so-called **vulgar materialists**, said by their detractors to be simple-minded materialists, and Marxist anthropologists who have embraced one form or another of dialectics. This latter group includes the structural Marxists, who blend classical Marxism with the twentieth-century anthropology of Claude Lévi-Strauss. Marxist anthropologists, vulgar and structural alike, join forces in criticizing anthropologists who promote "value-free" science—so-called positivist anthropologists. All science, they say, is value-laden, and those who deny this truth, naïvely or intentionally, perpetuate social inequities.

VULGAR MATERIALISTS A label for cultural materialists who, according to their critics, ignore dialectical thinking.

In the era of the Cold War, several Marxist and other politically left-leaning anthropologists came under scrutiny by the American government. Anthropologist David Price has explored this episode in his 2004 book *Threatening Anthropology: McCarthyism and the FBI's Investigation of American Anthropologists*. Citing documents obtained under the *Freedom of Information Act*, Price shows how in the early 1950s, using secret informants, the Federal Bureau of Investigation (FBI) compiled a dossier on University of Michigan anthropologist Leslie White. Meanwhile, anthropologist Melville Jacobs was forced to appear before a Washington State committee of the House Un-American Activities Committee, and anthropologist Gene Weltfish, who lost her job at Columbia University, was forced to testify before Senator Joseph McCarthy's Committee on Government Operations. According to Price, these and other such anthropologists came under suspicion less for their possible (or actual) membership in the Communist Party than for their "radical" politics and social activism, which were aimed at correcting the perceived social inequities of capitalism.

Price asserts that in 1951, Frederick Johnson and William W. Howells, the Executive Secretary and the President of the American Anthropological Association, sponsored a proposal, approved by the Association's Executive Board, to have the Central Intelligence

Agency (CIA) compile a comprehensive roster of Association members, identifying their areas of cultural, linguistic, and geographical expertise. On the questionnaire designed to elicit this information, involvement of the CIA was kept secret. Such an action would probably be unthinkable today, but at the time, the attitude of American anthropologists toward government espionage was more favourable. Just a few years earlier, during World War II, American anthropologists had worked willingly, even enthusiastically, with the government to help defeat fascist Germany and Japan, and during both world wars, American archaeologists patriotically provided cover for government intelligence-gathering overseas. This whole shadowy wartime era, when the government "spied" on anthropologists and anthropologists spied for the government, gives pause for thought during the twenty-first century "War on Terror."

Classical Cultural Evolutionism

The word evolution means transformation of forms, a process in which something changes while remaining partially the same. Evolution is associated most closely with biology, but it can also apply to any natural or social science attempting to reconstruct the past. The Marxist theory of dialectical materialism and the Enlightenment schemes of universal history were evolutionary. So was the first major cultural anthropological "ism": the **classical cultural evolutionism** of the nineteenth century.

CLASSICAL CULTURAL EVOLUTIONISM The theoretical orientation of nineteenth-century cultural evolutionists who used the comparative method.

PREHISTORY The period of human existence before writing.

Classical cultural evolutionism represents a continuation of Enlightenment universal historicism—with one important difference. While eighteenth-century universal historians concentrated on modern Western history, nineteenth-century cultural evolutionists concentrated on the history of non-Western peoples in **prehistory**, the time before writing. This difference derived from expanded ethnographic understanding of Native peoples and convincing new archaeological evidence that there *was* a prehistory. Taken together, ethnography and archaeology allowed nineteenth-century anthropologists to construct cultural evolutionary schemes in which descriptions of prehistoric artifacts were "fleshed out" with descriptions of present-day "primitive" peoples whose artifacts looked similar. This use of ethnography to supplement archaeology was called the "comparative method." In the early twentieth century, influential anthropologists criticized the comparative method as too speculative, and cultural evolutionism fell out of favour as an anthropological theory. In the late 1940s, it was revived by another group of anthropologists who called themselves **neo-evolutionists** and labeled their nineteenth-century predecessors "classical."

NEO-EVOLUTIONISTS
Twentieth-century anthropologists who revived and reformulated nineteenth-century classical cultural evolutionism.

The heyday of classical cultural evolutionism was the period from the 1860s through the 1890s. Although this followed publication of Charles Darwin's *Origin of Species* (1859), cultural evolutionism does *not* represent an application of Darwin's biological ideas to the realm of culture. Cultural evolutionists were far more interested in ethnography, archaeology, and an expanded view of universal history than in Darwin's theory of evolution by natural selection. It would be historically inaccurate to label cultural evolutionists "social" or "cultural" Darwinists.

Classical cultural evolutionists fall into "major" and "minor" categories. Major figures were more original, influential, and productive as authors. Minor figures published less, had less influence, and commented more on the ideas of others. The major classical cultural evolutionists were Herbert Spencer (1820-1903), John Lubbock (1834-1913), Lewis Henry Morgan (1818-1881), Edward Burnett Tylor (1832-1917), and James Frazer (1854-1941). Minor classical cultural evolutionists included Henry Maine (1822-1888), Johann Bachofen (1815-1887), and John McLennan (1827-1881). With the exception of Bachofen, a German, and Morgan, an American, all of them were British. The effect of their work was to reinforce the prevailing attitude of smug Victorian superiority by demonstrating how modern civilization had evolved from primitive cultures in the direction of "progress."

These classical cultural evolutionists were interested in an array of cultural institutions and beliefs. One group, led by Morgan, was interested in marriage, family, and sociopolitical organization. Another group, led by Tylor, was interested in religion, magic, and other ideological systems. With the exception of Spencer, a philosopher or sociologist more than an anthropologist, and Lubbock, an archaeologist as much as a cultural anthropologist, the classical cultural evolutionists "specialized" in one or the other of these interest groups.

Lewis Henry Morgan, an unlikely candidate for future anthropological fame, grew up in and around Rochester, New York, where he later practiced law. He belonged to a fraternal order known as the League of the Iroquois and, in order to authenticate the order's rituals, began to study nearby Iroquois tribes, eventually becoming adopted by them and helping them press their Native land-claims cases in court. In his studies, Morgan relied heavily on his bilingual Native assistant Ely Parker (1823-1859), probably the first significant **informant** in the history of American ethnography. Morgan took a keen interest in kinship, the study of how people are related to one another formally. This interest led to his first major book, *League of the Ho-de-no-sau-nee, or Iroquois* (1851), a study of Iroquois social organization. He expanded his studies with information gathered from travels throughout the United States and Canada and from responses to questionnaires distributed around the world by the Smithsonian Institution. This information was incorporated into his more comprehensive books, *Systems of Consanguinity and Affinity of the Human Family* (1870) and his magnum opus *Ancient Society* (1877).

INFORMANT In anthropological fieldwork, someone who provides information.

In *Ancient Society* Morgan presented a vast scheme of cultural evolution on several interrelated levels. He began with the general stages of savagery, barbarism, and civilization, defined—somewhat inconsistently—as stages of hunting and gathering, plant and animal domestication, and "the state." Each of these stages was divided—again somewhat inconsistently—into substages of "lower," "middle," and "upper." Morgan recognized that there were two kinship types. The **classificatory** type lumped together kinship categories that Anglo-Americans split into two or more categories, using, for example, a single term for "brother" and "brother's children." The **descriptive** type, exemplified by Anglo-Americans, maintained such split categories. Morgan believed that the classificatory type of kinship had predominated during savagery and barbarism, then evolved into the descriptive type with the advent of civilization, when property superseded kinship as the main determinant of social relations. Groups still practicing classificatory kinship were said to be carryovers from the savage or barbaric stage.

CLASSIFICATORY A type of kinship, contrasted with the descriptive type, that merges kinship categories.

DESCRIPTIVE A type of kinship system, contrasted with the classificatory type, that splits kinship categories.

Morgan divided kinship types into kinship systems, beginning with the Malayan system, where "mother" and "father" were lumped with "mother" and "mother's brother." According to Morgan, the Malayan system evolved into the Turanian-Ganowanian, or Iroquoian, system when **cross-cousins**, cousins related through parents of the opposite sex, became distinguished. Then, when social relations reckoned through descent superseded social relations based on distinctions between sex,

CROSS-COUSINS Cousins related through parents of the opposite sex.

there evolved **unilineal kinship systems** of sibs, clans, and tribes. At first, still in the stage of savagery, descent was reckoned through the female line because, owing to pregnancy, female parenthood could be determined more reliably than male parenthood. In the stage of barbarism, however, kinship reckoning through the male line commenced, changing matrisibs, matriclans, and **matrilineal** tribes into patrisibs, patriclans, and **patrilineal** tribes. Male kinship became even more important in the stage of civilization. To all these stages, kinship types, and kinship systems, Morgan added family types, beginning with the **consanguine** type, which is based on group marriage between brothers and sisters, and evolving through a series of prohibitions of marriage between relatives into the monogamous nuclear family of civilized times.

UNILINEAL KINSHIP SYSTEMS Kinship systems reckoned through one parental line, either matrilineal or patrilineal.

MATRILINEAL Unilineal kinship systems reckoned through the female line.

PATRILINEAL Unilineal kinship systems reckoned through the male line.

CONSANGUINE A family type based on group marriage between brothers and sisters.

A pivotal part of Morgan's scheme was his belief that a fundamental cultural shift occurred in the transition from the prehistoric stage of barbarism into the stage of civilization, which he characterized by writing, cities, monumental architecture, and other anthropological hallmarks of states (contrasted with bands, tribes, and chiefdoms). For Morgan, this shift occurred when, because of the demands of plant and animal domestication in cities, territorial relations became more important than kinship relations. The growth of private property at the expense of community property prompted certain privileged groups to retain private property by inheritance through the male line. This shift in turn led to the emergence of stratified social classes whose access to strategic material resources was unequal. Thus, beginning in antiquity, the stage of civilization became fundamentally different from the preceding stages of savagery and barbarism. Moreover, like other cultural evolutionists, Morgan considered present-day primitive cultures to be vestiges of the prehistoric past.

When Karl Marx and Friedrich Engels read *Ancient Society*, they were excited to find in it anthropological support for their belief that class-based inequalities were not engrained in human nature and that, under certain circumstances, a more egalitarian political system could work. They set about using Morgan's scheme to augment the theory of dialectical materialism by showing how the institution of private property had originated and how, when it was abolished, the world would return, at least figuratively, to the communism with which humanity began. When Marx died, Engels completed the task. In his book *Origin of the Family, Private Property, and the State* (1884), Engels

STATUS SOCIETIES In the schema of Henry Maine, societies that are family-oriented, hold property in common, and maintain control by social sanctions; contrasted with contract societies.

CONTRACT SOCIETIES In the schema of Henry Maine, societies that stress individualism, hold property in private, and maintain control by legal sanctions; contrasted with status societies.

FEMALE INFANTICIDE The practice of treating male children more favourably than female children, resulting in more female deaths.

POLYANDRY Mating or marriage involving one woman and more than one man.

EXOGAMY The practice of marrying or mating outside one's kinship group; contrasted with endogamy.

ARMCHAIR ANTHROPOLOGIST An anthropologist who has done little or no fieldwork.

ADHESIONS Edward Burnett Tylor's name for cultural traits that are statistically significantly associated.

SURVIVALS Edward Burnett Tylor's name for nonfunctional cultural traits that are clues to the past.

added Morgan to the select group of non-Marxists whose thoughts have been declared compatible with the Marxist cause.

Although partially dated, the body of Morgan's work has endured, and most modern anthropologists consider him to be the father of kinship studies. His nineteenth-century contemporaries disputed certain points. Differences between Morgan and minor classical cultural evolutionists centred on the sequence of cultural stages and the causes of their transformations. Morgan proposed a general evolutionary sequence of group marriage, or marriage ungoverned by complex kinship, followed by kinship determined through matrilineal and patrilineal descent. In *Ancient Law* (1861), Henry Maine disagreed, arguing that the first form of family was patrilineal. Maine also added an evolutionary distinction between **status societies**, which were family-oriented, held property in common, and maintained social control by social sanctions, and **contract societies**, which stressed individualism, held property in private, and maintained social control by legal sanctions. In *Primitive Marriage* (1865), John McLennan agreed with Morgan that group marriage had preceded patrilineal descent but disagreed with him on how the transition from one to the other had occurred. According to McLennan, group marriage was a period of great struggle in which not everybody who was born could survive. This situation led to **female infanticide**, the preferential killing of female over male children. The resulting shortage of females meant that they had to share males as mates, leading to **polyandry**. Males also captured females from other groups, leading to **exogamy**, or "mating out." In *Mother Right* (1861), Johann Bachofen made similar arguments. Judged by modern standards, all of these schemes were excessively speculative, far beyond the ability of empirical evidence to determine.

Morgan's British counterpart was Edward Burnett Tylor, the "father" of cultural anthropology in Britain and, some say, in the West. Tylor was a prototypical Victorian **armchair anthropologist**, who based his evolutionary schemes on reason as much as on ethnographic and archaeological data. In reconstructing culture, he correlated cultural components, called **adhesions**, and looked for clues to the past in cultural vestiges, called **survivals**. He argued vigorously against the Christian idea of human degeneration, arguing instead in favour of the secular Victorian idea of human progress. Tylor is credited with a number of important anthropological "firsts." He became the first academic professor of anthropology, at Oxford University in 1884; he wrote the first anthropology textbook, *Anthropology* (1881); and, in *Primitive Culture* (1871), he offered the first definition of culture by a professional anthropologist: "[that] complex whole which includes knowledge, belief, art, law, morals, custom and any other capabilities and habits acquired by man as a member of society."

Tylor's principal interest was the evolution of magico-religious beliefs and institutions, which he explained as the accumulation of rational answers to reasonable questions about the natural world. This approach was also taken by John Lubbock, who in *The Origin of Civilization* (1870) outlined a scheme for the evolution of magic and religion. Lubbock's scheme began with atheism, the belief in no deity, and ended with the belief in an omnipotent, or all-powerful, God. Evolutionary philosopher Herbert Spencer, author of *Principles of Sociology* (1876), took a similar approach to the evolution of magic and religion. A synthesis of Tylor's and Spencer's views can serve to illustrate the role of reason in this group of classical cultural evolutionists.

In the Tylor-Spencer synthesis, religion, or proto-religion, began when the earliest prehistoric people tried to solve natural puzzles. Prehistoric people might have observed, for example, that clouds appear and disappear and the sun rises and sets, while rocks fail to move. Why were some natural objects animated, and others not? The answer was that animated objects possessed **anima**, an invisible and diffuse supernatural force. Organisms were particularly animated, so their anima must have been especially powerful. Human organisms were animated in curious ways. In dreams, for example, people experienced themselves in different places, then awoke to find themselves somewhere else. People cannot be physically present in more than one place at the same time, so, the reasoning went, they must have two dimensions, a physical dimension and a non-physical, or spiritual, dimension, which "travels." This spiritual dimension became the "soul." Observations on death served to confirm the existence of souls. When people die, initially they look the same as in life, but they are no longer animated. Therefore, their invisible souls must have departed. But where do souls go? Many never return, so they must gather in another world, the "afterlife." Other souls return to haunt and possess the living as "ghosts." Therefore, these ghost-souls, some good and others bad, must be able to **transmigrate.**

ANIMA An invisible and diffuse supernatural force that can take the form of souls and ghosts.

TRANSMIGRATE To pass into another body after death, as do spirits and ghosts.

SHAMANS Magico-religious specialists who communicate with ancestral ghosts and souls.

ANCESTOR WORSHIP The veneration of departed relatives; in classical cultural evolutionism a religious phase.

POLYTHEISM The belief in multiple deities; contrasted with monotheism.

MONOTHEISM The belief in a single deity; contrasted with polytheism.

SYMPATHETIC MAGIC Magic that can affect an object through a similar object.

If souls survive after death, should they not be open to post-mortem "conversation"? In the Tylor-Spencer synthesis, contacting souls became the job of magico-religious specialists such as sorcerers and **shamans**. Furthermore, in a non-literate and kin-based culture, souls would be reckoned as ancestors and venerated for their wisdom and advice, leading to **ancestor worship**. But how was the supernatural world of ancestral ghost-souls to be imagined? According to the synthesis, it could only be imagined as a reflection of life on earth, and, when culture evolved, images of the afterlife would evolve in tandem. For this reason, in prehistoric and primitive cultures, with multiple, equally ranking lineages and clans, there would be multiple, equally ranking ghost-souls revered as deities—**polytheism**. When, in civilization, culture became class-based and stratified, deities became ranked; and when, early in civilization, authority came to rest in the hands of a single pharaoh, emperor, or priestly king, the number of deities shrank to one, for instance, the omnipotent "King of Kings" of Christianity. In this way, "advanced" **monotheism**, the prevailing form of religion in Victorian Britain, was the end product of a series of cultural transformations starting with primitive animism at the beginning of pre-historic time—the idea of "progress."

Evolution results in continuity as well as change. In biological evolution, *Homo sapiens* retains traits of ancestral species, including pre-human species with ape-like and monkey-like traits. For many people, the suggestion that humanity is even partially animalistic provokes a visceral, negative reaction. Likewise, in Victorian Britain, cultural evolutionists such as Tylor and Spencer were criticized and became controversial when they suggested that Christianity, like the beliefs of people everywhere, had "primitive" roots. Anthropology has had a somewhat radical reputation ever since.

The remaining major classical cultural evolutionist was James Frazer, whose multi-volume work *The Golden Bough* (1890) was a cross-cultural compendium of myths, folklore, and literature. Like Tylor, Frazer was interested in the evolution of the mental processes involved in magic, religion—and science. In his evolutionary scheme, magic came first and was based on the principles of contact and **sympathetic magic**. Magicians believed that they could control nature by bringing special elements together or, where direct contact was impossible, by substituting a concordant element. When magic failed, as Frazer knew it usually would, magicians turned to religion,

Sir James Frazer (1854–1941)

The distinguished late Victorian cultural evolutionist sits in his armchair.

distinguished by a sense of humility and acceptance that people cannot control nature but can only *ask* for divine intervention through prayer and other acts of supplication. Finally, as "correct" knowledge of the world increased, religion was supplanted by science, which, like magic, exerted control over nature, but control that worked. Like monotheism for Tylor, science for Frazer represented the mature stage of a cultural evolutionary sequence that retained features of ancestral stages. The present was a product of the past; thus, seemingly trivial, exotic, and irrelevant aspects of culture made sense.

Cultural evolutionism was the preeminent theory of nineteenth-century anthropology, and, because anthropology as a profession emerged in the nineteenth century, it is the earliest theory for which anthropology is widely known. Not all nineteenth-century anthropologists embraced the theory, however, notably many of the fledgling ethnographers working on the American frontier and in European colonies overseas. For these fieldworkers, experiencing rather than theorizing about Native cultures was more important. As fieldwork intensified, the penchant for grand synthesizing subsided, and anthropologists adopted new, non-evolutionary and even anti-evolutionary perspectives. Cultural evolutionism fell out of favour, reemerging only temporarily in the United States after World War II.

Evolutionism vs. Diffusionism

PSYCHIC UNITY The doctrine that all peoples have the same fundamental capacity for change.

Classical cultural evolutionists embraced the nineteenth-century doctrine of **psychic unity**, formulated by German geographer and ethnographer Adolf Bastian (1826-1905). According to this doctrine, all peoples, primitive and civilized alike, had the same basic capacity for cultural change. Primitive peoples were less advanced than civilized peoples not because their primitiveness was innate but because they had been stunted in evolutionary growth through contact with other peoples or simply because they had started evolving later. The doctrine of psychic unity represented a continuation of the eighteenth-century Enlightenment belief that all peoples could progress.

INDEPENDENT INVENTION The doctrine linked to psychic unity that cultural innovation can occur independently in more than one place; contrasted with diffusionism.

DIFFUSIONISM The doctrine that cultural innovations evolve once and are then acquired through borrowing or immigration; contrasted with independent invention.

Related to psychic unity was the doctrine of **independent invention**, an expression of faith that all peoples could be culturally creative. According to this doctrine, different peoples, given the same opportunity, could devise the same idea or artifact independently, without external stimulus or contact. Independent invention was one explanation of cultural change. The contrasting explanation was **diffusionism**, the doctrine that inventions arise only once and can be acquired by other groups only through borrowing or immigration. Diffusionism can be construed as non-egalitarian because it presupposes that some peoples are culturally creative while others can only copy. When cultural evolutionism fell out of favour in the early twentieth century, diffusionism was there to take its place.

CULTURE AREA A geographical area associated with a culture.

A simple diffusionist concept was **culture area**, introduced in 1917 by American anthropologist Clark Wissler (1870-1947). Motivated by New World pride, Wissler wanted to show European anthropologists that American Native groups were not all the same. Therefore,

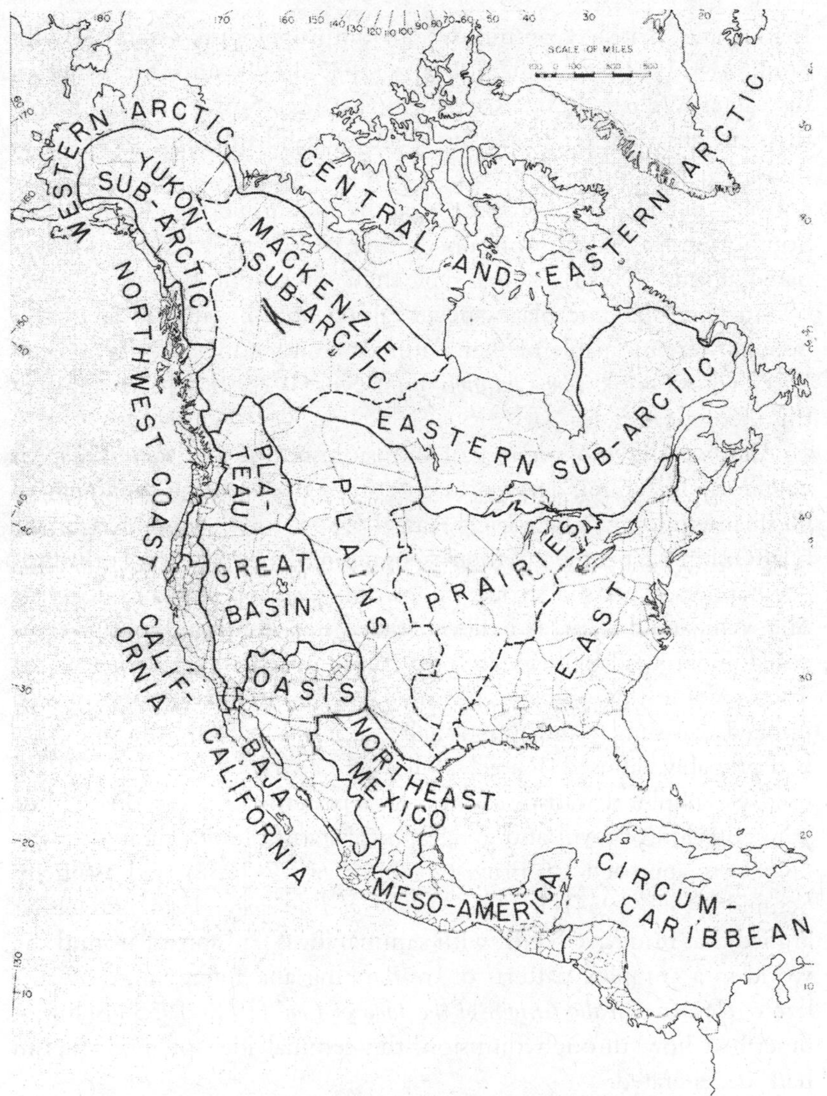

Culture Areas of North America

Each culture area is an implied centre of cultural diffusion.

he divided them into distinct culture areas, each with a centre where the most important traits of the group originated and from which they had outwardly diffused. Following Wissler's lead, other students of American Native peoples used the culture area concept to organize data, catalogue artifacts, and arrange museum displays.

European versions of diffusionism were much more theoretically extreme. One notorious version was **heliocentrism**, promulgated by

HELIOCENTRISM Literally sun-centredness, the diffusionist view that world civilizations arose from sun worship in Egypt and then spread elsewhere.

British and British Commonwealth anthropologists Grafton Elliot Smith (1871-1937), William Perry (1887-1949), and, for some of his career, William H.R. Rivers (1864-1922). Smith and his fellow theoreticians were fascinated by stone megaliths like Egyptian pyramids, which they linked to a cult of sun worship. Citing similarities between pyramids and stone megaliths in Europe and Central and South America, Smith pronounced that world civilization had originated around 4000 B.C. in Egypt, then spread out, becoming more "dilute" and in some places never taking hold because local Native peoples were incapable of assimilating it. Smith converted Rivers and Perry, whose book *The Children of the Sun* (1923) became a staple of this theoretical trade.

KULTURKREIS Translated "culture circle,"; according to certain theorists, the pattern of diffusion of cultural traits.

CULTURE CIRCLE In German *kulturkreis*, a concept used to represent the process of cultural diffusion.

ANTHROPO-GEOGRAPHY The study of relationships among geographically contiguous cultures, as practiced by Friedrich Ratzel.

CRITERION OF FORM The criterion used by anthropo-geographers to determine that similar cultural forms are the result of diffusion.

Another extreme version of diffusionism was the ***kulturkreis***, or **culture circle**, school, derived in part from the **anthropo-geography** of German ethnologist Friedrich Ratzel (1844-1904). Interested in the relationship of people to their geographical neighbours, anthropo-geographers expressed strong opposition to Adolf Bastian's doctrine of psychic unity. Ratzel believed that, after diffusion, culture traits could undergo adaptations to local conditions, masking their sources. To overcome this obstacle, he invoked the **criterion of form**, which implied that similar and functionally useless traits were the ones that had probably diffused. Ratzel's follower Leo Frobenius (1873-1938) used geographical statistics to explore patterns of diffusion further. The criterion of form and geographical statistics both figured in the *kulturkreis* approach of Fritz Graebner (1877-1934) and Wilhelm Schmidt (1868-1954). In *The Method of Ethnology* (1911), Graebner argued that primitive bands with seminal ideas had spread around the world in a complex pattern of overlapping and interacting concentric circles. In *On the Origin of the Idea of God* (1926-1955), Schmidt described how, through diffusion, the seminal idea of monotheism had "degenerated."

The appeal of heliocentrism and the *kulturkreis* approach in anthropology turned out to be relatively limited. An undercurrent of both approaches was the hereditarian belief that some human races were more capable of cultural innovation than others. Hereditarianism, or "racism," was an attitude that early twentieth-century anthropologists strongly opposed. For this reason, doctrinaire diffusionism never achieved a wide following. In the wake of the racial policies of National Socialism (i.e., Nazism), it became disreputable and faded from mainstream theoretical view. Accordingly, in recent decades, anthropologists, including archaeologists, who propose early human contact over long distances have been held accountable with the burden of proof. This is especially true in New World archaeology, where efforts to prove trans-Atlantic and trans-Pacific—and even extraterrestrial—contact have been greeted with varying degrees of skepticism. A sensational example is the effort to prove that certain Native American earthen works, glyphs, and "astronomical" structures are the legacy of contact with alien beings from Outer Space. Less sensational are claims that Viking explorers once penetrated deep into North America, leaving behind mysterious "rune stones." A more respected example is the 1947 voyage of Thor Hyerdahl (1914-2002) between South America and Polynesia on his wooden raft *Kon-Tiki*. In the 1990s, the discovery in the State of Washington of the 9,000-year-old skeleton of "Kennewick Man," with alleged Caucasian features, and the recognition of surprisingly old archaeological sites in South America softened the hard opposition of some New World archaeologists to the idea of early trans-oceanic voyages. The result is that archaeological investigation of the peopling of the Americas is more open-minded on this issue than it was a generation ago.

Archaeology Comes of Age

Archaeology, the study of past **material culture**, arose during the Renaissance when scholars began to study classical artifacts to supplement what they could learn from classical texts. During the Enlightenment, archaeology continued to be the handmaiden of history, even though in northern Europe written records of the past were much more scant. An autonomous archaeology required that artifacts be the *only* kind of evidence of the past. This requirement could be met only after acceptance of the existence of "pre"-history.

MATERIAL CULTURE Cultural meaning expressed in the products of human artifice, or artifacts.

The scientific community began to accept the existence of prehistory toward the middle of the nineteenth century. This acceptance was built on decades of preceding archaeological work. The first significant archaeological chronology independent of written records was the **Three Age System** of Christian Thomsen (1788-1865). Thomsen was a Danish museum curator who organized artifacts into the sequence of Stone, Bronze, and Iron ages, then subdivided these ages **seriationally**,

THREE AGE SYSTEM The archaeological ages of Stone, Bronze, and Iron.

SERIATIONALLY According to the archaeological principle of seriation, or relative dating by the evolution of artifact style.

according to the evolution of artifact style. He implemented his chronology in the Museum of Northern Antiquities in Copenhagen and incorporated it into his influential *Guide-book to Scandinavian Antiquity* (1836). Fellow countryman Jens J.A. Worsaae (1821-1885) continued Thomsen's work by investigating the **stratigraphy**, or systematic layering, of artifacts in Danish shell middens. In *The Primeval Antiquities of Denmark* (1843), Worsaae generalized the Three Age System to most of Europe. Daniel Wilson (1816-1892), a British archaeologist who later emigrated to Canada, employed the Three Age System in *The Archaeology and Prehistoric Annals of Scotland* (1851); it was Wilson who actually coined the term "prehistory." In the 1850s, archaeological examination of ancient dwellings on lake shores in Switzerland showed that the late **Stone Age** of Europe had seen plant and animal domestication. To designate this new phase of agriculture and animal husbandry, archaeologists added **Neolithic**, or **New Stone Age**, to their chronologies.

STRATIGRAPHY The archaeological dating of artifacts relative to their placement in systematically layered earth.

STONE AGE The Old Stone Age, or Paleolithic, and the New Stone Age, or Neolithic.

NEOLITHIC Or New Stone Age, the period of prehistory characterized by polished stone tools and the domestication of animals and plants.

NEW STONE AGE Or Neolithic, the period of prehistory characterized by polished stone tools and the domestication of animals and plants.

These early archaeological chronologies had to fit within the relatively brief time span of approximately 6,000 years, which is how long most Christian scientists believed that human beings had been living on the Earth. In order to make prehistory longer, new archaeological evidence was required. This evidence came from Stone Age caves and glacial deposits on river terraces in Britain and France. The key finds here were human skeletal remains and stone tools in geological association with skeletal remains of extinct prehistoric animals, mainly mammoth and woolly rhinoceros. These finds conflicted with fundamentalist Christianity because the fundamentalist, or literal, interpretation of the Bible was that God had created human beings *after* other forms of life. Non-fundamentalist Christians were more inclined to accept this new archaeological evidence and the longer period of prehistory it implied. In 1859, British geologist Charles Lyell (1797-1875) led a contingent of distinguished scientists to the Somme River Valley in northern France, where amateur archaeologist Jacques Boucher de Crèvecoeur de Perthes (1788-1868) had discovered a series of old Stone Age tools. The contingent pronounced the tools authentic. Their action marked the first scientific consensus about the great time depth of prehistory and is the symbolic birth of the science of prehistoric archaeology.

This action spurred more prehistoric archaeological research that was incorporated into major syntheses such as Lyell's *The Geological Evidence of the Antiquity of Man* (1863) and *Pre-Historic Times* (1865)

Grave Creek Burial Mound, West Virginia

Proponents of the nineteenth-century "Moundbuilder Myth" refused to believe that mounds such as this one, depicted here by an artist, could have been constructed by American Indians or their ancestors.

by John Lubbock, who coined the term **Paleolithic**, or **Old Stone Age**. Well before the end of the century, archaeologists had established a detailed chronology of the Paleolithic and all other major stages of European prehistory.

Like cultural evolutionists, archaeologists used the comparative method to reconstruct the prehistoric past. A prime example was Lubbock, whose 1865 book was fully titled *Pre-Historic Times, as Illustrated by Ancient Remains, and the Manner and Customs of Modern Savages*. But prehistoric archaeologists were less generous than cultural evolutionists in granting modern "savages" the ability to progress. Lubbock believed that white Europeans were the prime beneficiaries of a material progress that had been achieved through millennia of human struggle. In *A History of Archaeological Thought* (1989), Bruce Trigger represents Lubbock's attitude as **The Imperial Synthesis** and characterizes it as racist rationalization for European colonial expansion. Racism was certainly widespread because, outside Europe where the prehistoric past was not "white," the accomplishments of prehistoric races were denigrated. In North America, archaeologists were loath to accept the idea that Native peoples could have built the complex earthen mounds found along the Mississippi River Valley. Instead, they proposed the **Moundbuilder Myth**, according to which the mounds had been built by a pre-Native race that either

PALEOLITHIC Or Old Stone Age, the period of prehistory characterized by chipped and flaked stone tools and hunting and gathering.

OLD STONE AGE Or Paleolithic, the period of prehistory characterized by chipped and flaked stone tools and hunting and gathering subsistence.

THE IMPERIAL SYNTHESIS A name for the nineteenth-century synthesis of archaeology, racism, and colonialism.

MOUNDBUILDER MYTH The myth that a mysterious people other than Native Americans built impressive earthen mounds throughout the American Midwest.

had migrated to Central and South America to build the grand monuments of Aztecs and Incas or had "degenerated" into "Indians." A cornerstone publication on this controversy was *Ancient Monuments of the Mississippi Valley* (1848) by Ephraim G. Squier (1821-1888) and Edwin H. Davis (1811-1888). The same racist attitude prevailed in Africa, where archaeologists attributed mysterious stone ruins to King Solomon or other ancient Near Easterners. British colonial capitalist Cecil Rhodes (1853-1902) embraced this opinion and used it to argue that, in colonizing former Rhodesia, Europeans were really reclaiming lands that were formerly white. Colonialist archaeology came into play almost everywhere European archaeologists encountered non-white Native peoples.

In modern times, more and more archaeologists have come to recognize the political nature of their discipline and to acknowledge that racism was endemic in their nineteenth-century forerunners. A case in point is archaeologist David Hurst Thomas's book *Skull Wars: Kennewick Man, Archaeology, and the Battle for Native American Identity* (2000). In his book, Thomas recounts the troubled history of grave robbing, public display of Native peoples, and other dehumanizing practices that characterized American archaeology and physical anthropology well into the twentieth century. He concludes on an optimistic note that current generations of American archaeologists and Native Americans have begun to work together to explore the human past in mutually acceptable ways. Thomas and other influential archaeologists have helped make contemporary archaeology highly engaged politically, ethically, and theoretically. Archaeologists today embrace the full range of current anthropological theories and perspectives, including Marxism, feminism, anthropological political economy, postmodernity, and globalization.

Charles Darwin and Darwinism

DARWINISM A general label for ideas associated with Charles Darwin's theory of evolution.

The racism of nineteenth-century anthropology was linked to the smug optimism and sense of superiority of Victorian times. **Darwinism**, the name given to ideas associated with Charles Darwin's theory of biological evolution, was part cause and part effect of these Victorian attitudes. The long, complex story of Darwinism begins with the Scientific Revolution.

While dynamic, the universe envisioned by Isaac Newton was not evolving. Bodies moving according to the law of universal gravitation were not being transformed into *new* bodies or arranged in new ways. Evolution, however, was a logical next step. The first Newtonian-era scientists to explore evolution were geologists interested in the origin and development of the Earth. In medieval cosmologies, the Earth was "special" because it was the centre of the universe and the habitat of people, the most noble creation of God. In the seventeenth century, such views persisted, so geology had to be carefully reconciled with scripture. One reconciliation was attempted by Thomas Burnet (1635-1715) in *The Sacred Theory of the Earth* (1691). After Creation, the Earth had cooled, and layers of land formed above seas. The shape of the Earth was a perfect circle, created for people who then sinned and had to be punished. Punishment took the form of a deluge, or global flood, that caused almost all land to collapse under water, leaving "ugly," imperfectly shaped mountains as a reminder of this sin. Another reconciliation was attempted by William Whiston (1667-1752) in *A New Theory of the Earth* (1696). After Creation, a comet had passed Earth and distributed dust that solidified into land by the force of gravity. Later, another comet distributed drops of water that precipitated the biblical Flood. Both Whiston's and Burnet's reconciliations were theologically ominous because they implied that the Earth was very old and rendered constant divine intervention redundant.

Meanwhile, as faith in science began to supplant faith in Christianity, a pressing problem arose. Geologists discovered fossils of marine forms of life embedded in sedimentary rocks formed underwater but currently far above water on land. How did these fossils get there? Answering this question was a preoccupation of eighteenth-century geology. An initial explanation was that the rocks were products of the geological destruction, dislocation, and receding waters of the biblical Flood. It soon became apparent, however, that marine fossil-bearing strata were far more geologically complex. There were two options: either water had receded or land had risen. Geologists who preferred the first option were called **Neptunists**, named after Neptune, the Roman god of the sea; those who preferred the second option were called **Vulcanists**, named after Vulcan, the Roman god of fire. Pursuing the initial explanation, Neptunists maintained that marine fossils were deposited in sedimentary rocks

NEPTUNISTS Geologists who proposed that the principal agent of major geological change was the subsidence of water; contrasted with Vulcanists.

VULCANISTS Geologists who proposed that major geological changes were caused by the elevation of land brought about by volcanic heat; contrasted with Neptunists.

Carolus Linnaeus's Biological Classification of Humanity

In *Systema Naturae* (1735), Linnaeus (1707–1778) was one of the first naturalists to classify the genus *Homo* within the animal kingdom.

MAMMALIA.

ORDER I. PRIMATES.

Fore-teeth cutting; upper 4, parallel; teats 2 pectoral.

1. HOMO.

Sapiens. Diurnal; varying by education and situation.

2. Four-footed, mute, hairy. *Wild Man.*
3. Copper-coloured, choleric, erect. *American.*
   Hair black, straight, thick; *nostrils* wide, *face* harsh; *beard* scanty; *obstinate*, content free. *Paints* himself with fine red lines. *Regulated* by customs.
4. Fair, sanguine, brawny. *European.*
   Hair yellow, brown, flowing; *eyes* blue; *gentle*, acute, inventive. *Covered* with close vestments. *Governed* by laws.
5. Sooty, melancholy, rigid. *Asiatic.*
   Hair black; *eyes* dark; *severe*, haughty, covetous. *Covered* with loose garments. *Governed* by opinions.
6. Black, phlegmatic, relaxed. *African.*
   Hair black, frizzled; *skin* silky; *nose* flat; *lips* tumid; *crafty*, indolent, negligent. *Anoints* himself with grease. *Governed* by caprice.

Monstrosus Varying by climate or art.

1. Small, active, timid. *Mountaineer.*
2. Large, indolent. *Patagonian.*
3. Less fertile. *Hottentot.*
4. Beardless. *American.*
5. Head conic. *Chinese.*
6. Head flattened. *Canadian.*

The anatomical, physiological, natural, moral, civil and social histories of man, are best described by their respective writers.

Vol. I.—C 2. SIMIA.

formed underwater and then exposed as water receded. Vulcanists also believed that sedimentary rocks were formed underwater, but they maintained that the rocks were then thrust above water by earthquakes and volcanoes caused by pressure from a hot, molten subterranean earthly core. When Vulcanists asked Neptunists where all the water went, Neptunists had no answer. But until there was more geological evidence of the power of earthquakes and volcanoes, Vulcanists were vulnerable too.

A convincing, essentially Vulcanist geology was finally achieved by James Hutton (1726-1797) in *Theory of the Earth* (1795), later popularized by John Playfair (1748-1819) in *Illustrations of the Huttonian Theory of the Earth* (1802). In the Hutton-Playfair model, not all sedimentary rocks were formed in universal water. Some debris washed into water from land, while molten masses penetrated the ocean floor and deposited additional strata, which were then thrust above water by volcanoes. These geological processes had been operating for so long that the age of the Earth was almost beyond scientific comprehension. Hutton summarized his view of relentless geological activity as "no vestige of a beginning, no prospect of an end."

All these developments culminated in Charles Lyell's landmark multi-volume work *Principles of Geology* (1830-1833), a foundation of modern geology. To account for geological change, Lyell invoked a combination of agents, some Neptunist and others Vulcanist, that worked slowly over long periods of time. Because present-day agents of change like wind and water erosion were slow, yet the changes they had produced were dramatic, Lyell was forced to conclude that the Earth was extremely old. His geology was a brand of **uniformitarianism**, the doctrine that the same nondramatic agents of geological change have been operating throughout history. Uniformitarianism contrasts with **catastrophism**, the doctrine that agents of geological change have been more dramatic in the past than in the present. Conservative scientists of Christian background who believed that the Earth was extremely young favoured catastrophism over uniformitarianism because dramatic geological agents like global floods could produce major change quickly. A distinguished catastrophist and antagonist of Lyell, was French paleontologist Georges Cuvier (1769-1832), who interpreted change in the fossil record as evidence of a series of mass near-extinctions interspersed with survivals of a few fortunate life forms. Cuvier's catastrophism was "progressive," because it involved positive directional change. But Cuvier was not an evolutionist because change for him was essentially discontinuous, without transformation. Lyell's uniformitarianism was less progressive because, like his predecessor Hutton, he regarded constructive and destructive agents as offsetting each other, in the long run achieving equilibrium. Lyell was a geological evolutionist,

UNIFORMITARIANISM The doctrine that gradual geological agents of change have operated throughout the past; contrasted with catastrophism.

CATASTROPHISM The geological doctrine that agents of geological change have been more dramatic in the past than in the present; contrasted with uniformitarianism.

Comparison of Ape and Human Skeletons

By comparing the skeletons of apes and "man," Thomas H. Huxley (1825–1895) compiled circumstantial evidence for human evolution.

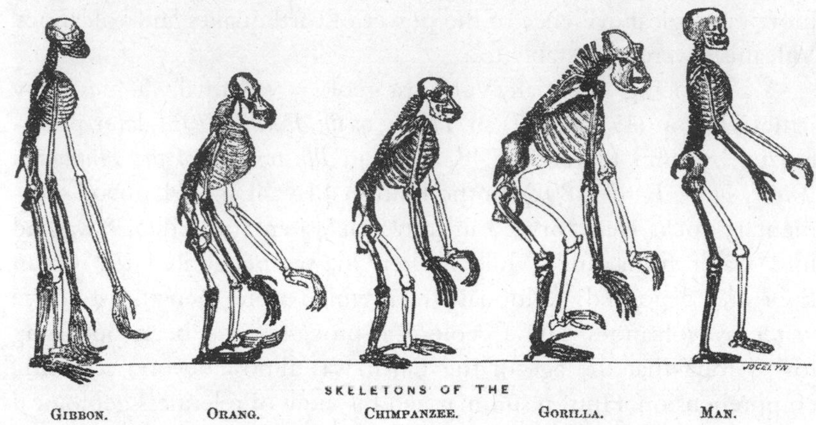

however, because his geological agents caused transformational change. And while Lyell opposed uniformitarianism in biology, the great achievement of his friend Charles Darwin was to combine the transformism of uniformitarianism with the progressivism of catastrophism into a comprehensive theory of biological evolution.

SPECIES A group of organisms whose members can reproduce only with one another.

GREAT CHAIN OF BEING A medieval philosophical schema that ranked all cosmic and earthly elements, including people, in a single ascending line of importance.

BINOMIAL NOMENCLATURE The hierarchical system of classifying living things into named scientific groups, with one name for genus and a second name for species.

In the history of the idea of biological evolution, the great debate was about the origin of species. A **species** is a group of plants or animals whose members can reproduce with one another but cannot reproduce with members of other species. Where do species come from? The traditional scientific answer, based on Judeo-Christianity, was that God created all species, which were immutable, or fixed. New species did not appear in Creation through evolution, and old species did not disappear through extinction. Moreover, species were arranged in a fixed linear hierarchy, constructed by medieval philosophers as the **Great Chain of Being**. Traditionally, species were "real," not merely names for groups of individuals. They were transcendental, Platonic essences attesting to the perfection of Creation. A prime example of traditional creationism was developed by Carolus Linnaeus (1707-1778), the Swedish biologist who classified living things into a hierarchy of taxonomic categories, using a system of **binomial nomenclature**, or two names, for the category of species. In his *System of Nature* (1735), Linnaeus introduced many of the taxonomic names (of kingdoms, phyla, genera, and so forth) that are used in evolutionary biology today. Until late in his life, however, Linnaeus denied evolution and adhered strongly to the creationist position.

Charles Darwin's Study at Down House, Kent, England

Darwin (1809–1882) wrote *Origin of Species* and other books here.

More liberal, or radical, Enlightenment biologists broke rank with traditional creationists. Their answer to the question of the origin of species was that species were created by nature and were mutable, or susceptible to change. New species appeared and disappeared through natural causes. Species were not necessarily arranged in a fixed linear hierarchy, and they were not "real" in the Platonic sense of the term. Instead, they were transient categories that altered the face of Creation. Biologists who adhered to this set of ideas were called transformists, developmentalists, or, later, evolutionists.

Before Darwin, a number of scientists proposed theories of biological evolution, among them Georges-Louis Leclerc, Comte de Buffon (1707-1778) and Darwin's own grandfather, Erasmus Darwin (1731-1802). The most influential pre-Darwinian evolutionist was Jean-Baptiste Pierre Antoine de Monet Lamarck (1744-1829), whose *Zoological Philosophy* (1809) appeared exactly 50 years before Darwin's *Origin of Species* (1859). Lamarck's approach to evolution differed from Darwin's in ways that can be illustrated by the example of the evolution of the long-necked giraffe. According to Lamarck, the ancestor of the long-necked giraffe was a giraffe with a short neck. These short-necked giraffes lived on savannah-like grasslands where desirable edible vegetation was available on trees. To reach this vegetation, the giraffes stretched their necks. As a result, their offspring were born with longer necks, that is, necks longer than they would have been if their parents had not stretched. This new generation of giraffes stretched *their* necks for the same reason, so *their* offspring were born with still longer necks. Over time, as this process continued, neck length increased, until the present-day long-necked giraffe evolved. Lamarck was unable to *prove* that ancestral and descendant giraffes belonged to different species because, with ancestral giraffes extinct, he could not demonstrate that members of the two groups were unable to reproduce. Nonetheless, by comparing the magnitude of their difference to the magnitude of differences among known species, he was able to render this judgment.

The non-Darwinian feature of Lamarckian evolution illustrated in this example will be obvious to any student of modern biology. It is the feature known as **inheritance of acquired characteristics**. In the example, the characteristic of longer necks was inherited by offspring because it was acquired by parents. Modern biologists have shown that acquired characteristics are not inherited unless their acquisition itself is hereditary, or pre-programmed in deoxyribonucleic acid, **DNA**. Except for recombination, DNA is inherited from generation to generation intact. Other non-Darwinian features of Lamarckian evolution, not illustrated in this example, are **vitalism**, the doctrine that evolution is self-motivated, or willed; **teleology**, the doctrine that evolution adheres to a long-range purpose or goal; and **orthogenesis**, the doctrine that evolution has worked in a straight line to produce *Homo sapiens*. From many moral points of view, these features make Lamarckian evolution more palatable than Darwinian evolution. In the early nineteenth century, when Darwin was growing up, the Lamarckian version of evolution was the one most commonly discussed.

INHERITANCE OF ACQUIRED CHARACTERISTICS The mechanism of biological evolution proposed by Jean Lamarck whereby traits acquired in one generation can be transmitted to subsequent generations.

DNA Deoxyribonucleic acid, the biochemical substance of heredity.

VITALISM The idea that biological evolution is self-motivated or willed.

TELEOLOGY The idea that biological evolution adheres to a long-term purpose or goal.

ORTHOGENESIS The idea that biological evolution operates in one direction, usually leading to *Homo sapiens*.

Charles Darwin (1809-1882) grew up in England at the dawn of the Victorian era. As a young man, he wanted to study medicine, but he soon learned that he could not stand the sight of blood, so he dropped out of medical school in Edinburgh and enrolled in Christ's College, Cambridge. At Cambridge, he became a budding naturalist and was encouraged by a number of faculty "mentors." One helped arrange his appointment as naturalist on the ship *H.M.S. Beagle*, which in 1831 set out on a five-year voyage around the world. The voyage of the *Beagle* was a crucible for Darwin's ideas.

Before the *Beagle* left England, Darwin had begun reading Lyell's *Principles of Geology*. During the voyage, he completed reading this work and became inspired to search for a biological process equivalent to uniformitarian processes in geology. As the *Beagle* sailed around the Atlantic and Pacific coasts of South America, Darwin observed that the geographical distribution of varieties of plants and animals correlated with the distribution of variation in useful environmental resources. When he visited the Galapagos Islands off the coast of Ecuador, he observed that varieties of finches and tortoises differed slightly from one island to another and also differed from varieties on the South American mainland. How and why did these differences develop?

When the *Beagle* arrived back in England, Darwin was already converted to the idea of evolution. He undertook years of scientific research to strengthen his reputation as a naturalist while he pondered new non-Lamarckian mechanisms that might make evolution work. Then he read *An Essay on the Principle of Population* (1798) by Thomas Robert Malthus (1766-1834). Malthus was the pessimistic political theorist who explained how the human population of the world was increasing geometrically (2, 4, 8, 16, 32, etc.) while global resources needed for human survival were increasing only arithmetically (2, 4, 6, 8, 10, etc.). The inevitable consequence of these trends was that not everyone born could possibly survive. Darwin embraced this Malthusian vision and broadened it to include all of biological nature, where organisms engage in a **struggle for existence** producing **survival of the fittest.**

STRUGGLE FOR EXISTENCE Charles Darwin's view that evolution by natural selection involves competition for limited resources and results in survival of the fittest.

SURVIVAL OF THE FITTEST In Charles Darwin's theory of evolution by natural selection, the adaptive outcome of the struggle for existence.

NATURAL SELECTION Charles Darwin's mechanism for biological evolution, involving struggle for existence and survival of the fittest.

Knowing now how evolution worked, Darwin began to draft his book on evolution. He worked on it off and on for many years until in 1858 he received a letter from fellow naturalist Alfred Russel Wallace (1823-1913). Wallace, writing from the Pacific South Seas, described a theory of evolution by **natural selection** that Darwin recognized immediately as almost exactly like his own. After consulting with friends, he decided to finish his book quickly. First, however, Darwin and Wallace presented a joint paper on evolution to a meeting of the Linnaean Society in London (neither man was actually there). The following year, in 1859, Darwin's *Origin of Species* appeared. Ever since, the theory of evolution by natural selection, independently formulated by both Darwin and Wallace, has been known as "Darwinism."

A good way to understand Darwin's theory of evolution is to contrast it with Lamarck's theory using the example of the long-necked giraffe. Darwin would have approached this example with a different premise. A group, or population, of ancestral short-necked giraffes was living on savannah-like grasslands. They needed to eat vegetation from trees to survive. Some giraffes had slightly longer necks than others. These giraffes had a slight advantage over the other giraffes in the competitive struggle for vegetation needed to survive. Beating out the competition because of this natural advantage, they ate more, became healthier, or in some other way had more offspring. Gradually, over time, as the long-necked giraffes had more offspring than the short-necked giraffes, average neck length in the population increased, until the present long-necked giraffe species evolved.

Darwin represented this sequence of events as "natural selection," meaning, metaphorically, that "nature" selects advantageous traits just like human breeders "artificially" select advantageous traits when they domesticate plants and animals. The result in both cases is that organisms become adapted to their environments. To argue his case in *Origin of Species*, Darwin adduced several kinds of evidence. Except for the results of plant and animal breeding, almost all of this evidence was circumstantial. He argued that anatomical and embryological similarities among organisms, the presence of vestigial organs, and, although incomplete, the record of fossils were all consistent with his theory. A problem for Darwinism—then and now—is that this same evidence is consistent with many versions of **creationism**. Suffice it to say that eventually the scientific community came to accept Darwin's theory. His theory represents an extension of the Scientific Revolution from astronomy and physics into biology. Darwin really went *beyond* Newton, because he showed that basic structures of the universe evolve.

CREATIONISM The view that biological species are divinely created and do not evolve.

Origin of Species provoked a barrage of moral, religious, and social criticism. Many critics failed to realize, or admit, that the book made hardly any reference to the evolution of *Homo sapiens*. Darwin ducked this controversial topic for several years. Some of his friends, however, confronted the controversy head on. The main implication for *Homo sapiens* was the evolution of human mental and moral qualities. Most Christians believed that animals lacked spirituality and were, mentally and morally, a world apart from human beings. Could evolution bridge this gap? In *The Geological Evidence of the Antiquity of Man* (1863), Charles Lyell described human evolution as a natural leap onto a new plane of life. Alfred Russel Wallace disagreed, arguing that mental and moral superiority would have conferred no real selective advantage on animals and, therefore, could not have evolved in the first place. Why, for example, would an animal *need* to be artistic, mathematical, or philosophical? According to Wallace, divine intervention must have been responsible. Other scientists were more open to the idea of Darwinian human evolution. At the time, only a few human fossils were known, and, unfortunately for human evolutionists, these fossils appeared neither particularly old nor particularly primitive. Still, in *Evidence as to Man's Place in Nature* (1863), Thomas Henry Huxley (1825-1895)—nicknamed "Darwin's Bulldog" because he defended Darwin so staunchly in public debates—classified people and apes in the same taxonomic order. Without fossils, the artifact record of prehistory became more important, so human evolutionists also cited the work of archaeologists such as John Lubbock and cultural evolutionists such as Lewis Henry Morgan and Edward Burnett Tylor.

Darwin eventually published his views on human evolution in *The Descent of Man* (1871). Much of this book, and also much of Darwin's *The Expression of the Emotions in Man and the Animals* (1872), was devoted to the argument that differences between animals and people are differences in degree rather than in kind. To explain the evolution of human physical traits, Darwin used the mechanism of **sexual selection**. With sexual selection, traits evolve not because they confer an adaptive advantage in the struggle for existence but because they make members of one sex more attractive to the other and in this way increase reproductive success. Human intelligence, Darwin said, was evolved by natural selection as a by-product of upright stature, which freed human hands for the use of tools. To explain the evolution of human morality, Darwin relied on the mechanism of **group selection**. The core of morality was **altruism**, the willingness to sacrifice oneself for the good of others. Altruism was initially selected in groups, when one member behaved altruistically and, as a result, other groups members benefited. Later, after human beings became intelligent, they extended altruism beyond the local group to all humanity in the form of abstract moral codes.

SEXUAL SELECTION Charles Darwin's evolutionary mechanism whereby members of one sex compete for the attention of members of the opposite sex.

GROUP SELECTION A form of natural selection in which individuals behave altruistically, helping their group, and thereby helping themselves; contrasted with kin selection.

ALTRUISM In sociobiology, "self-sacrificing" behaviour explained by kin selection.

Viewed from the perspective of modern science, Darwin's explanations appear to conflate, or confuse, biological and cultural evolution. In this regard, he was not much different from his Victorian scientist contemporaries. Almost all nineteenth-century human evolutionists were extremely hereditarian. Like "racism" in archaeology, racism in biological anthropology was a legacy from the nineteenth century.

Darwin and his friends did not espouse many of the religious, moral, and social attitudes now labeled "Darwinian." The main religious challenge to his theories was not based on biblical fundamentalism, because by the 1860s the Bible was no longer widely accepted as necessarily historically accurate. Instead, it was based on morality. If human beings were the product of evolution, not divine creation, would not a system of morality have to be based on the process of evolution itself? And if so, would not the easiest way to construct such a system be to treat evolution as intrinsically and ultimately purposeful? The problem was that, contrasted with Lamarckian evolution, Darwinian evolution appeared to lack ultimate purpose; instead it operated opportunistically, selecting characteristics adapted to only a circumscribed time and place. Alternatively, if Darwinian evolution were a divine instrument—God's way of creating—the mechanism of natural selection appeared excessively brutal. It involved relentlessly harsh struggle, competition, and death for individuals unable to adapt. It was always possible, of course, to argue, as many Darwinians did, that these unfortunate losses were compensated for by evolutionary "winners," who helped humanity "improve." But this position was morally precarious, and in most cases it was easier to abandon Darwinian evolution in favour of the Lamarckian mechanism of inheritance of acquired characteristics, which seemed more humane and offered hope that people might take charge of their evolutionary fate. In the late nineteenth century, **Lamarckism** became the doctrine of choice for the majority of scientists seeking to reconcile evolution with religious morality.

LAMARCKISM The evolutionary philosophy of Jean Lamarck, notably his mechanism of the inheritance of acquired characteristics.

SOCIAL DARWINISM A loosely used term referring to social philosophies based on Darwinian evolutionism, especially the mechanism of natural selection.

SYNTHETIC PHILOSOPHY The all-encompassing philosophy of Herbert Spencer based on the premise that homogeneity is evolving into heterogeneity everywhere.

In discussions of social morality, the term **Social Darwinism** is historically misleading. Most of the social attitudes denoted by this term derive not from Darwin but from Herbert Spencer, the most philosophical and sociological of the classical cultural evolutionists. Spencer promoted a grandiose **synthetic philosophy** based on the premise that homogeneity was evolving into heterogeneity in several universal domains. Referring to the domain of evolutionary biology, Spencer was Lamarckian rather than Darwinian, but referring to the domain of *social* evolution, he believed that vigorous individual enterprise had risen to the fore. According to Spencer, a system of individuals acting in their own self-interest produced the maximum social good. There were no moral absolutes. Instead, "might" made "right." Spencer believed that human evolution should be allowed to take its "natural" course, unfettered by interventions that would "artificially" bolster human weaknesses otherwise slated for defeat.

Spencer's was the most popular version of Social Darwinism and the one used most often to rationalize social inequities among races, classes, and genders. Meanwhile, Huxley, Darwin's "bulldog," advocated an opposing version. Huxley was an agnostic who actively doubted religion and believed that science should maintain moral neutrality. He opposed Spencer and anyone else who based social morality on biological evolution. To the contrary, argued Huxley, through cosmic accident *Homo sapiens* has evolved to the point where people are able to understand that evolution has *no* purpose. Why not take advantage of this opportunity and create a morality that is independent of evolution and even goes *against* the harshness of nature? In the nineteenth century, between the extremes of Huxley and Spencer, there were so many different versions of Social Darwinism that the term really needs to be redefined almost every time it is used.

Amidst all the wrangling over religious and social morality, Darwin's theory of evolution by natural selection suffered major scientific setbacks. From the beginning, there had not been much experimental proof that natural selection could produce new species, even with artificial breeding, which produced mainly subspecies, or varieties. Another problem was the fossil record. Darwin admitted that the record was imperfect and contained gaps, or **missing links**. Some scientists filled these gaps with speculative evolutionary sequences, such as those based on the **biogenetic law**. This law stated that **ontogeny**, the growth of an individual, recapitulated **phylogeny**, the evolutionary growth of a species. Proponents of the law made extreme statements about embryological and paleontological similarities and detracted from the credibility of evolution as empirical science. Yet another problem was the age of the Earth. Evolution by natural selection was a slow process that required a great deal of time to account for changes observable in the fossil record. Contemporary physicists, thinking about volcanic activity as an agent of geological change, decided that the Earth had been much hotter in the past than in the present and that volcanic activity had been much more forceful. A troubling implication was that this volcanic activity had

MISSING LINKS Perceived gaps in the evolutionary record.

BIOGENETIC LAW The principle that ontogeny, the growth of the individual, recapitulates phylogeny, the growth of the species.

ONTOGENY The biological growth of an individual.

PHYLOGENY The evolutionary growth of a species.

SWAMPING EFFECT The observation in Charles Darwin's time that small variations would always be diluted by heredity and therefore could not increase or intensify through natural selection.

wrought geological changes too quickly for Darwinian evolution to have worked. A final problem for Darwin was the **swamping effect**, the name given to the observation that small variations serving as raw material for natural selection would always be "swamped out" through heredity, preventing natural selection from ever getting started. Darwin was aware of all these scientific problems and as a result grew discouraged. He lost confidence in the complete efficacy of natural selection and, in later editions of *Origin of Species*, turned to other evolutionary mechanisms, including the Lamarckian mechanism of inheritance of acquired characteristics.

The solutions to Darwin's scientific problems were beyond his nineteenth-century grasp. What Darwin needed was the theory of biological heredity pioneered, unknown to him, by Austrian monk Gregor Mendel (1822-1884). By experimenting with pea plants, Mendel observed patterns of inheritance that showed heritable traits to be discrete rather than blended. Some traits, called recessive, disappeared temporarily in the presence of other traits, called dominant, but reappeared later when they were by themselves. Mendel knew little about the physical substance of heredity, now known to be DNA, located on genes on chromosomes in the nuclei of cells. His observations went largely unnoticed until 1900, when they were rediscovered by biologists investigating inheritance in plants. These biologists stressed heritable change by mutation, or large changes that occur within a single generation. In contrast, Darwinian natural selection involves small changes that occur over many generations. Biologists thereby separated into two camps: one, the Mendelians, promoting mutation, and the other, the Darwinians, promoting natural selection as the mechanism of evolution. In the 1930s, a group of mathematically inclined biologists showed that Mendelism and Darwinism are complementary, not antagonistic, because genes are subject to both mutation and natural selection. These biologists devised the **Synthetic Theory of Evolution**, whereby an evolving population is conceived as a "gene pool" and evolution is defined as a change in the relative frequency of genes in that gene pool. The Synthetic Theory of Evolution forms the basis of population genetics, the branch of biology with the scientific vocabulary used to study evolution today.

SYNTHETIC THEORY OF EVOLUTION The twentieth-century theoretical synthesis of Darwinian evolutionism and Mendelian genetics.

Sigmund Freud

Besides Charles Darwin and Karl Marx, the nineteenth century produced four other intellectual giants whose influence on anthropology has been profound: Sigmund Freud, Émile Durkheim, Max Weber, and Ferdinand de Saussure. Each of these theorists warrants special attention, beginning with Freud.

Sigmund Freud (1858-1939) was a clinical psychologist who tried to help his patients overcome psychological disorders. He became an anthropologist of sorts when he speculated on the origin of these disorders. Ironically, anthropologists ended up rejecting most of Freud's anthropological speculations, while accepting many of his clinical insights.

Freud was born in Vienna into a middle-class family headed by a strict father. In the 1880s, while he was a medical student, he became interested in radical medical experiments in which **hysteria**, a psychological state characterized by morbid or senseless emotionalism, appeared to be cured by hypnosis. Under hypnosis, hysterical patients recalled some experience, usually from childhood, that had been traumatic, then woke up and were no longer hysterical. For Freud, these experiments pointed to the existence of a mental **subconscious**. Patients with psychological disorders had concealed from themselves some action or thought that conflicted with the moral codes of society, Freud thought, and had then repressed the conflict in their subconscious mind, where it festered. Freud set out to determine how such patients might resolve their conflicts therapeutically. He began by studying dreams. In classical Freudian psychology, dreams are expressions of the subconscious mind. They express, in symbolic form, wishes or desires of which society disapproves. Freud probed the subconscious by deciphering dream symbols, most of which he interpreted as sexual because he believed that sex was the desire that society disapproved of most strongly and, therefore, was the desire most likely to lead to conflict and repression. In 1900, he published these views in his first major book, *The Interpretation of Dreams*.

HYSTERIA The clinical condition of calm hallucination that got Sigmund Freud interested in psychology.

SUBCONSCIOUS According to Sigmund Freud, the part of the mind that is the seat of the psyche, of which people are aware only unconsciously.

Freud proceeded to analyze art, literature, religion, and even politics in the same manner he analyzed dreams. These were ideologies and institutions that expressed, in symbolic form, feelings that could not be expressed in reality. They, too, held clues to repressed desires. Eventually, Freud's distinction between psychologically "sick" and

PSYCHE According to Sigmund Freud, the subconscious, comprising the id, ego, and superego.

ID Or libido, according to Sigmund Freud, the part of the human psyche that expresses natural desires.

EGO Translated "I," according to Sigmund Freud, the part of the psyche that interacts with the outside world.

SUPEREGO According to Sigmund Freud, the part of the psyche, sometimes called conscience, that monitors the id and mediates between the ego and the outside world.

RACIAL MEMORY According to Sigmund Freud, the subconscious awareness of the history of the human psyche.

PLEASURE PRINCIPLE According to Sigmund Freud, living libidinously, as directed by the id; contrasted with reality principle.

SUBLIMATE According to Sigmund Freud, to rechannel libidinous desires into culturally acceptable thoughts and behaviours.

REALITY PRINCIPLE According to Sigmund Freud, the principle of realizing that acting on the pleasure principle is dangerous and immature.

healthy people blurred, and he decided that the subconscious mind was universal. He divided the subconscious, sometimes called the **psyche**, into three levels: the **id**, or libido, the source of desire; the **ego**, or "I," which experienced the outside world; and the **superego**, or conscience, which monitored the id and mediated between the ego and social norms. According to Freud, the ego and superego could be molded by culture, which restrained the id, the animalistic part of human nature with instinctive appetites and drives. The thrust of Freudian psychotherapy was to probe the subconscious to find the source of repressed conflict, make the patient consciously aware of the conflict, and thereby open the door to curing the patient with therapeutic devices.

The Freudian depiction of human nature was pessimistic: everyone was born into a psychological minefield of potential conflict. Some people negotiated this minefield better than others, avoided conflict, and grew up psychologically healthy. Others, less fortunate, succumbed to conflict, developed psychological disorders, and ended up in therapy.

After Freud had finished creating his clinical framework, he wondered why this troubled state of human affairs had come into existence. His answer to this question was anthropological, with a twist. He presented his version of anthropology in a trilogy of three books: *Totem and Taboo* (1918), *The Future of an Illusion* (1928), and *Civilization and its Discontents* (1930). His central insight was that people in the present experience conflict because humanity in the past experienced conflict. Each person relives, or recapitulates, this past as **racial memory**. Freud's account begins with the **pleasure principle**, his name for the natural libidinous tendency of people to seek psychosexual pleasure and avoid psychosexual pain. Culture opposes the pleasure principle because the consequence of everybody seeking pleasure would be chaos. Most people come to accept that they cannot seek pleasure directly, even though their desire to do so remains a source of tension. Instead, they rechannel, or **sublimate**, their desires into fantasies and institutions, which, according to Freud, represent an escape from libidinous reality. These people are acting on the **reality principle** because they are psychologically mature and realize that acting on the pleasure principle will get them into trouble. Psychologically immature people are inclined to act on libidinous impulse, experience conflict, undergo repression, and become neurotic or psychotic. For Freud, the least "civilized" cultures were the least repressive, so "primitive" adults were like civilized children.

For Freud, civilization was opposed to human biological nature because it tried to tame the animal instincts of people. In fact, civilization was built on sublimated desire. How did this happen? He answered this question with a story about human evolution. The story began with the **primeval family**, which, for Freud, was monogamous, nuclear, patriarchal, and characterized by unrestricted sex. This family was fraught with problems and could not continue in its original form for very long. In the primeval family, sons desired their mother sexually, but their authoritarian father had priority of sexual access. Therefore, the sons resented their father, even though they respected and loved him at the same time. These ambivalent feelings were a source of major conflict. Eventually, resentment built up to the point where the sons got together and killed their father in the **primal patricide**, an act of profound consequence.

Patricide was a libidinous act that the larger social group recognized as too disruptive to be allowed to recur. Moreover, the sons felt crippling remorse and guilt as a result of what they had done. To prevent a repeat performance, the group created cultural prohibitions—**taboos**—against unsanctioned killing and, equally important, against **incest** that might allow disruptive sexual feelings to come to the fore. The group also invented **totems**, objects of collective veneration, in the form of **father figures**, toward which sons could sublimate their ambivalent feelings. For Freud, these actions ushered in the totemic phase of human history. This phase, characterized by the superego, insured that the expression of libidinous drives was repressed by guilt.

For men, the psychological legacy of all this was the **Oedipus complex**, named after the legendary Greek son of Laius who unwittingly slew his father and went on to marry his mother. This complex was characterized by unresolved guilt-inducing desire of men for sexual gratification through their mothers. The corresponding legacy for women was the **Electra complex**, named after the legendary Greek daughter of Agamemnon who sought to kill her mother to avenge her father's murder. The Oedipus and Electra complexes were not equivalent, because Freud believed that male and female sexuality fundamentally differed.

From the perspective of twenty-first century anthropology, Freudian theory certainly appears "sexist." From the perspective of early

PRIMEVAL FAMILY In Sigmund Freud's reconstruction of human history, the first family form—monogamous, nuclear, and patriarchal.

PRIMAL PATRICIDE In Sigmund Freud's hypothetical primeval family, the killing of the father by his sons.

TABOOS Culturally sanctioned prohibitions.

INCEST Culturally proscribed inbreeding that, according to Sigmund Freud, is an act that led to the primal patricide.

TOTEMS Objects of collective cultural veneration, according to several anthropological theorists, that are central to the maintenance of social stability.

FATHER FIGURES In the psychology of Sigmund Freud, totems that represent culturally ambivalent attitudes toward adult men.

OEDIPUS COMPLEX According to Sigmund Freud, the troublesome psychological state of boys induced by their sexual desire for their mothers; contrasted with the Electra complex.

ELECTRA COMPLEX According to Sigmund Freud, a troublesome psychological state of girls induced by their sexual desire for their fathers; contrasted with the Oedipus complex.

twentieth-century anthropology, his account of how each person relives the psychic development of humanity appeared to be a caricature of classical cultural evolutionism. If they were to incorporate some of Freud's themes, early twentieth-century anthropologists had to jettison a hefty amount of his theoretical apparatus. This was accomplished by the school known as American psychological anthropology.

Émile Durkheim

Émile Durkheim (1858-1917) was a distinguished nineteenth-century French sociologist. The theoretical foundation of twentieth-century French anthropology can be found in his work on social structure. Durkheim was also a major influence on key twentieth-century British anthropologists, in particular Alfred Reginald Radcliffe-Brown and his theory of structuralism and functionalism. For these reasons, he can be considered a forerunner of the two European schools known as **French structural anthropology** and **British social anthropology**.

FRENCH STRUCTURAL ANTHROPOLOGY The theoretical orientation of Claude Lévi-Strauss and his followers invoking elementary mental structures, reciprocity, and binary oppositions.

BRITISH SOCIAL ANTHROPOLOGY The school of structuralism and functionalism led by Alfred Reginald Radcliffe-Brown and Bronislaw Malinowski.

Durkheim's familial legacy was Jewish. While young, he had a mystical experience that led him temporarily to Catholicism, but he ended up agnostic, albeit with a passionate interest in the cultural dimensions of religion. In 1879, he entered the elite École Normal Supérieure, where his philosophical bent set him apart from other students. At the time, following the Franco-Prussian War, France was experiencing a resurgence of nationalism and Catholicism, and Durkheim, a socialist as well as a Jew, found himself in the minority. In 1887, he moved to Bordeaux, site of the first teacher training centre in France, where he worked to reform the French school system, introducing social science into the curriculum. His theories then developed in progression with the publication of four books: *Division of Labour in Society* (1893), *The Rules of Sociological Method* (1895), *Suicide* (1897), and *The Elementary Forms of the Religious Life* (1912).

In *Division of Labour in Society*, Durkheim explored the diversification and integration of culture, identifying two integrative patterns. Older, more "primitive" cultures were less diversified and had little division of labour. More homogeneous, they cohered because individuals were *similar*. Durkheim called this pattern of integration **mechanical solidarity**. Recent, more "civilized" cultures were more diversified and had considerable division of labour. More heteroge-

MECHANICAL SOLIDARITY According to Émile Durkheim, social cohesion maintained by similarities among individuals; contrasted with organic solidarity.

neous, they cohered because individuals were *different*. His vision was of individuals functioning independently but in harmony—much as the various organs of the body do to maintain an organism's life. Because this metaphor seemed so apt, he called this second pattern of integration **organic solidarity**. Durkheim's central insight was that social solidarity could be achieved in two different, organizationally opposite ways. His focus on social coherence, rather than change, represented a preference for what Auguste Comte called social statics rather than social dynamics. The Durkheimian vision of society was very different from that of Karl Marx, who saw solidarity as ephemeral and society riven with class conflict. For Marx, the state would eventually "wither away" and give rise to communism. For Durkheim, the more organic solidarity increased, the more government was necessary to regulate socially interdependent parts. Increased organic solidarity submerged the individual in an expanded social reality, where social interactions superseded individual interactions as determinants of social life. The academic discipline that would study social interactions was sociology.

ORGANIC SOLIDARITY According to Émile Durkheim, social cohesion maintained by differences and interdependence among individuals; contrasted with mechanical solidarity.

Durkheim established the theoretical framework for sociology in *The Rules of Sociological Method*. Social interactions were to be considered **social facts** and explained in terms of other social facts, not in terms of biology or psychology. Behind this pronouncement was Durkheim's understanding that society was a realm unto itself, *sui generis*. He gave his conception of the social realm a special French twist. For Durkheim, social facts were **collective representations** of the **collective consciousness**, or **group mind**. This conception was Cartesian, following the rationalist French philosopher René Descartes, rather than Lockean, following the empiricist British philosopher John Locke. Rationalism was a fundamental part of the Durkheimian legacy to French structural anthropology.

SOCIAL FACTS Émile Durkheim's name for social phenomena, his units of sociological analysis.

COLLECTIVE REPRESENTATIONS According to Émile Durkheim, manifestations of the collective consciousness, or group mind.

COLLECTIVE CONSCIOUSNESS According to Émile Durkheim, the source of collective representations of social facts, sometimes called the group mind.

GROUP MIND According to Émile Durkheim, the source of collective representations of social facts, sometimes called collective consciousness.

In *Suicide*, Durkheim demonstrated how to use his sociological rules to explain a particular social fact. He chose the fact of suicide because it was an act that seemed so individualistic yet, explained sociologically, could be shown to have a strong social dimension. Durkheim correlated types of suicide with patterns of social integration. With mechanical solidarity there was "altruistic" suicide, whereby individuals dissolved themselves into the homogeneous group, while with organic solidarity there was "egoistic" suicide, whereby individuals engaged in a dramatic form of self-expression.

When social solidarity was in flux—that is, neither mechanical nor organic—individuals could commit a third type of suicide, which was brought about by ***anomie***, Durkheim's name for the feeling of alienation caused by the absence of familiar social norms.

ANOMIE According to Émile Durkheim, the sense of personal alienation caused by the absence of familiar social norms.

The purpose of Durkheim's fourth book, *The Elementary Forms of the Religious Life*, was to expose the social origins of religion. To Durkheim, "origins" meant something very different than it meant to cultural evolutionists and other kinds of anthropologists whose orientation was diachronic and who considered the origin of something to be its source in the past. For Durkheim, the origin of something was its source in the group mind. Accordingly, the **elementary forms** of religion were collective representations of the collective consciousness of people who attached sacred meaning to moral principles and then gave those moral principles a social reality in order to make them persuasive. Some empiricists have found Durkheim's logic circular: collective representations demonstrate the existence of the collective consciousness, which is posited to demonstrate the existence of collective representations. But Durkheim was not a consistent empiricist. He was a rationalist who believed that knowledge could exist independent of observation. Rationalism was imparted to French structural anthropology when Durkheim's elementary forms of religion became Claude Lévi-Strauss's **elementary structures** of kinship.

ELEMENTARY FORMS For Émile Durkheim, the equivalent of collective representations, similar to elementary structures.

ELEMENTARY STRUCTURES In French structural anthropology, universal mental logics and their cultural manifestations.

For Durkheim, the origin of religion, and ultimately of society itself, lay in the impact of social ritual on individuals. His thesis was that "primitive man" (exemplified in particular by Aboriginal societies in Australia) experiences a sense of "effervescence" when interacting with his fellows that can only be accounted for by reference to a greater power existing outside the individual. Once the ritual has ended, and large clans have broken into smaller bands and dispersed to resume the mundane activities associated with "making a living," individuals long for the cascade of sentiment that they had encountered during these periods of togetherness. Durkheim enshrined this distinction between the ritual and the everyday in his oppositional concepts of the **sacred** and the **profane**. These terms are appropriate, because they convey the forms of activity and emotion that surround the pure and powerful occasions of ritual togetherness as opposed to those that indicate the routine, the mundane, and the "polluted." In particular, Durkheim took great pains to show how the effervescent

SACRED According to Émile Durkheim, that which is pure, powerful, and supernatural; contrasted with the profane.

PROFANE According to Émile Durkheim, that which is routine, mundane, impure, and "of the world"; contrasted with the sacred.

sensations born in ritual are embodied in totems. These objects are, for Durkheim, powerful representations, or elementary forms, which bring these powerful sentiments to the surface of consciousness, even in the absence of ritual. Thus, they are icons *par excellence* of group integration and solidarity. Perhaps more importantly, they serve to remind primitive societies of the greater reality existing just outside themselves, a reality that only fully makes itself felt during social ritual. It is with some justification, therefore, that anthropologists have equated some people's understanding of God with Durkheim's vision of society, for in *The Elementary Forms of the Religious Life* the concepts of God and society seem interchangeable.

In 1902, Durkheim was rewarded with the prestigious academic appointment as Chair of Education at the Sorbonne in Paris, where he came to exert considerable academic influence. A few years earlier he had founded the journal *Année Sociologique* to publish his work and the work of the growing number of his students. It is significant ly through this journal that his theories became known to French and British anthropologists. Tragically, during World War I, many of Durkheim's students died, as did his son, a death that affected him deeply. In 1917, before the war ended, he died while recovering from a stroke.

Max Weber

In the nineteenth century, Durkheim employed an organismic analogy to understand how social groups cohere, and Marx understood control of the material conditions of life to be the engine driving human history. Both theorists, therefore, believed that forces existing outside the individual (psychosocial on the one hand, dialectical on the other) act to condition cultural meaning and structure social relations. In neither formulation is much room left for the creative **agency** of individuals, and, in fact, both Durkheim and Marx are often criticized for treating the subjects of their theories as homogenous drones, mindlessly obeying the relentless forces that shape and control every facet of their existence. In contrast, the late nineteenth- and early twentieth-century German theorist Max Weber (1864–1920) is credited with viewing the holistic individual—acting, thinking, feeling—as central to the creation, maintenance, and innovation of social and cultural forms. For this reason, his work is often

AGENCY In recent anthropological theory, creative acts of intentioned individuals that generate social form and meaning.

IDEALISTIC Pertaining to idealism, a perspective that looks to ideas and meanings, rather than material conditions, as the wellspring of culture.

thought of as **idealistic**, or "ideational," and is frequently contrasted with the materialism of Marx. Such a characterization is misleading because the creative agency that Weber attributes to individuals is grounded nevertheless in the relations of production and reproduction in any given society. In part because his work so effectively synthesized the supposedly antithetical forces of idealism and materialism, Weber became deeply influential in anthropological writing of the later twentieth century.

Weber was the son of a prominent German politician and civil servant and grew up in a stimulating intellectual environment. In 1882, he enrolled as a law student at the University of Heidelberg, where he embellished his studies with economics, history, and theology. In 1894, he became a Professor of Economics at Freiburg University, the first of several academic appointments he held interspersed with other occupations. Early on, Weber developed an interest in social policy, and at the conclusion of World War I, he served as a consultant to committees drafting the Treaty of Versailles and the Weimar Constitution for postwar Germany. After the war, he resumed teaching but suffered opposition from right-wing students, dying shortly thereafter of pneumonia.

In two of his most important works, *The Protestant Ethic and the Spirit of Capitalism* (1920) and (posthumously) *The Sociology of Religion* (1922), Weber presented his strategy for understanding how societies develop through time. Although his ideas were essentially evolutionist, they bore little resemblance to the unilineal theories of his nineteenth-century contemporaries Edward Burnett Tylor or Lewis Henry Morgan. Rather than reducing the great variety of social forms in the world to a single unidirectional model that charts social evolutionary change from the "primitive" through the "civilized," Weber sought a theory that placed existing beliefs and structures in particular historical contexts. For this reason, he is often thought of as a multilineal evolutionist whose theory accounts for the great diversity of human life but resists the temptation to rank this diversity according to a rigid **Eurocentric** scale of norms and values.

EUROCENTRIC The rating of non-European cultures according to a generalized European scale of norms and values.

The principal elements of Weber's schema may be outlined as follows. Complex societies arise from a progressive differentiation and intensification of labour, which in turn gives rise to a stratified hierarchy of social and economic classes. As a given social and historical environment grows in complexity, so too do the material inequities between these classes. These inequities, notably between the ruling elite and military classes and what Weber calls the **relatively non-privileged** classes of urban artisans and merchants, lead the latter to experience both a profound sense of alienation from sociopolitical power and a growing awareness of economic marginalization. This discrepancy between the world of their experience and that of their expectation (what *is*, as opposed to what *should be*—the problem of evil, or **theodicy**) is embodied in and expressed through an explicitly religious framework.

This point is crucial to Weber's model because, in his view, **religion** is the engine that drives social transformation through time. The merchant-class's despair and alienation from power foster deep anxieties about the apparent senselessness of the world: if one lives in accordance with a good and powerful deity's wishes, fulfilling all **ritual** observances and prescribed ritual behaviour, why does the world continue to be so problematic? This dilemma cries out, Weber maintains, for resolution. There is a need, using his terminology, for **salvation** from the world. Coming to the heart of his formulation of social change, Weber believes that this salvation is accomplished through the radical restructuring of beliefs about the world, which in turn prescribes **ethical** behaviours to bring people into accord with this ethical new vision.

Inner-worldly asceticism is the central disposition involved in this process because it entails "removing" oneself from corrupt worldly indulgences while (paradoxically) remaining within the world of human activity. For Weber, inner-worldly asceticism opposes the "outer-worldly" ascetics—monks, hermits, etc.—who seek literally to escape the social world and its influences by retreating to special spaces (e.g., monasteries, deserts) where worldly things have no power or authority. By refraining from indulgence in specific corruptions that inhere in the world, the inner-worldly ascetic remains virtuous (by Judeo-Christian standards) even while participating in a world that is inherently corrupt. Crucially for Western society, material prosperity is not only excluded from this catalogue of iniquity but becomes a hallmark of one's standing *vis-à-vis* divine will. The stimulus for such reformulation and renewal is understood to come from especially creative individuals, **charismatic prophets**, who generally claim to receive a new revelation of divine Truth that will reintegrate belief and action and in so doing restore psychosocial harmony to humanity.

RELATIVELY NON-PRIVILEGED A phrase coined by Max Weber to describe those socioeconomic classes in complex societies most prone to the creation of new social forms.

THEODICY A Christian term used by Max Weber to describe the explanation of evil in the world despite the existence of an omnipotent, just, and loving God.

RELIGION An integrated system of meanings and practices that seeks to connect humankind with a divine or metaphysical order.

RITUAL Any form of prescribed behaviour that is periodically repeated and links the actions of the individual or group to a metaphysical order of existence.

SALVATION According to Max Weber, escape from worldly capriciousness and evil through social arrangements rationalized in accordance with a divine plan, typically revealed by charismatic prophets.

ETHICAL Pertaining to prescriptions for correct behaviour that put the individual in accordance with a metaphysical order.

INNER-WORLDLY ASCETICISM According to Max Weber, the ethical demand of Calvinist Protestantism that Christians not retreat from the world in order to live piously.

CHARISMATIC PROPHETS As identified by Max Weber, individuals who experience a revelation that mandates the establishment of a new social order based on new ethical ideals.

CALVINIST PROTESTANTISM The Christian doctrines and practices traced to John Calvin that oppose Roman Catholicism on the basis of scripture and justification by faith.

RATIONALIZED According to Max Weber, evolved through the systematization of ideas, corresponding norms of behaviours, and motivational commitment to those norms.

COSMOLOGICAL ORDER A religious phrase describing the nature of otherworldly deities or powers and their relationships to human beings.

POLITICAL ECONOMY An anthropological perspective viewing sociocultural form at the local level as penetrated and influenced by global capitalism.

POSTMODERNISM A movement within the social sciences and humanities that questions the possibility of impartiality, objectivity, or authoritative knowledge.

For Weber, the most significant example of an embodiment of this process occurred in the form of **Calvinist Protestantism**, an urban merchant's religion that **rationalized** a new relationship between human beings and God. In this way, John Calvin (1509-1564), the French theologian, is to be considered a prophet, bearing a new vision of human life. Under this new covenant "revealed" to Calvin, individuals are directed to recreate heaven on Earth through hard work, as prescribed by God in Scripture, and obedience to the divine will. In this model, middle-class professionals—namely, merchants and artisans—are elevated to a position of ethical superiority; no longer are they to be ideologically dominated by ruling elites. Rather, urban merchants and artisans come to view themselves as a community of believers united by certain ethical tenets, adherence to which will certainly lead to a more materially rewarding and emotionally satisfying life. Therefore, a merchant might look to his material prosperity as a sign of God's grace, or lack thereof. The burgeoning culture of sixteenth-century Renaissance commerce, once linked in this way to a **cosmological order**, became an increasingly compelling blueprint for action in the world. If people behaved in a certain way, in accordance with God's will, they could expect to be materially rewarded in the here and now, and spiritually justified in the hereafter. Small wonder, then, that this new system of meaning and action ultimately resulted in the global triumph of industrial capitalism.

Weber's ideas about social evolution have been especially useful to anthropologists of recent generations because there has been an increasing reluctance to view societies and cultures as the static pristine organisms of Durkheimian theory. Moreover, in recent years the discipline has become more concerned with issues pertaining to the creative agency of individuals, the cultural worlds they construct and inhabit, and the various permutations of consensus and conflict that exist within and between societies. Weber's ideas really resurfaced in the 1970s and 1980s with the schools known as **political economy** and **postmodernism**. Until then, they were eclipsed by the more fashionable ideas of Durkheim and, to a lesser extent, Marx.

Ferdinand de Saussure

Ferdinand de Saussure (1857-1913) is among the most important precursors to twentieth-century linguistic and cultural anthropology.

He is also one of the least celebrated figures in these disciplines and among the least read. In part, this is doubtless due to the fact that he rarely published during his lifetime and the bulk of his legacy is vested in a posthumous collection of lectures compiled and published by a number of his students. Another reason for his relative obscurity outside linguistic circles probably relates to his low-key, generally conventional (even uneventful) academic career. As Jonathan Culler has put it, he seems to have had "no great intellectual crises, decisive moments of insight or conversion, or momentous personal adventures." Nevertheless, Saussure remains one of, if not *the* founding father of the modern discipline of linguistics as well as diverse streams of cultural and linguistic anthropology, influencing in different ways such important figures as Edward Sapir, Claude Lévi-Strauss, and Pierre Bourdieu.

A contemporary of Marx, Freud, Durkheim, and Weber, Saussure was born in Geneva, Switzerland in 1857. A precocious student and fluent in several languages, his early writings on the system of language, composed when he was only 15, drew the interest of older scholars who saw in the adolescent an emerging new talent. Despite this evident talent for the study of language, Saussure's family had strong ties to the natural sciences, and he first studied physics and chemistry at the University of Geneva before reverting to his early passion for language in completing his bachelor's degree. After two years study of **historical linguistics** in Leipzig and another two in Berlin, in 1880 Saussure was awarded a doctorate and moved to Paris where he entered the École Pratiques des Hautes Études as "Maître de conférences" (lecturer in historical linguistics). In 1891, he was named "Chevalier of the Legion of Honor"—a token of the deep esteem in which his Parisian colleagues held him—and accepted a professorship in Geneva, where he taught at his alma mater.

HISTORICAL LINGUISTICS
The study of language consisting in the reconstruction and descriptive tracking of language genealogies over time.

The work for which Saussure is best known was produced between 1907 and 1911 in the form of three consecutive lecture series on "general linguistics." Seminal though these lectures were, his insights into linguistic analysis remained unpublished at the time of his death in 1913. It remained to a number of his most devoted colleagues and students, especially linguists Charles Bally and Albert Sechehaye, to redact and publish a series of notes taken over the course of Saussure's lectures together with a number of his own lecture notes. These were published in 1916 under the title *Cours de linguistique générale*. While this work was an immediate sensation in continental linguistic circles, Saussure's influence among anglophile linguists and anthropologists was understandably inhibited by the late translation of the *Cours* into English in 1974.

Much of Saussure's innovation stems from his deep misgivings about the adequacy of linguistic theory in the late nineteenth century. In particular, language scholars of this era were more interested in tracking the genealogical lineages of discrete language forms (especially of the Indo-European language family) over time in order to "reconstruct" them and discover their temporal interrelatedness within a grand "tree" of many branches. Never, in his estimation, did his peers stop to ask the most pertinent question of all: what *is* language? Saussure's answer is at face value deceptive in its simplicity. A language, he proposes, is a system of "signs" in which speech communicates ideas. The **sign**, as Saussure understands it, is made up of two distinct elements: the ***signifier*** (that which communicates meaning) and the ***signified*** (the concept communicated by the signifier). Without the capacity for communicating meanings as understood by a community of speakers, a sign cannot be linguistically relevant. This insight, obvious though it might appear, was little short of revolutionary for its focus on the *systematic* quality of language. By necessity, the sign is arbitrary, meaning there is no "natural" connection between the signifier and signified. If one uses the English signifier "tree" to denote the object that one recognizes to be a tree, this is obviously a different signifier than its French cognate, "*arbre*." Different though they are, both convey the same meaning. In other words, there is nothing intrinsic about the sequence of sounds, "tree," that connects to its referent. Its meaning varies from one sign system, or language, to the next. For Saussure, a few exceptions to this principle *do* exist—most famously onomatopoeia, in which the signifying sound seems to imitate or mimic the signified (for instance, the English word-sound "meow" signifying the sound made by a cat).

SIGN In Ferdinand de Saussure's linguistics, the pair formed in the relation of a signifier to a signified, the essence of relations among meaningful units in a language.

SIGNIFIER In Ferdinand de Saussure's linguistics, one of two units making up the sign, the word or image that represents a concept, the signified.

SIGNIFIED In Ferdinand de Saussure's linguistics, one of two units making up the sign, the concept generated in our minds when represented by a sound or image, the signifier.

A number of important consequences stem from these observations, which in and of themselves suggest little of the true complexity behind language. Discrete languages are not, of course, simple collections of signs. Rather, each language exists in the *system of relations* among its many signs. It is not the fact that each language encompasses different groups of signs that matters but that each organizes the relations among signs differently. It is for this reason that each language presents a basically different vision of the world. An old adage of anthropological lore (originating with Franz Boas) has it that the Inuit possess many different words for which anglophone Euro-Americans have one—"snow"—because there is a more complex relationship between the Inuit language community and the natural circumstances of their environment that requires a variegated knowledge of what is signified. In other words, whether snow is known primarily through its aridity, weight, shape, texture, position in relation to the ground, and so on, actually *makes* a different world for the Inuit than what anglophone Euro-Americans might be expected to experience. Technically, this analogy may be inaccurate because linguists have demonstrated that the allegedly "many" Inuit words for snow actually reflect fundamental differences in grammar between English and Inuit, in particular in terms of what constitutes a "word." Nevertheless, the general point Saussure makes about the system or structure of language influencing experience had an important legacy in French and British social anthropology and among early American linguistic anthropologists in the work of Edward Sapir and Benjamin Lee Whorf. Note too, that the meaning of "snow" (or any other concept) can only be fully grasped *in relation* to other features of weather—rain, hail, sunshine, and so on. In the absence of these, snow cannot signify what we understand it as signifying because there is no way of distinguishing "it" from other objects in the world.

Another important and related point Saussure makes about signs is that they are not fixed or stable. Instead, they are endlessly shifting, creating new meanings and new social contexts. In English, there are many examples that spring readily to mind. Until several decades ago, the word "gay" invoked the concept of happiness or joviality. In contemporary usage, the term is seldom employed except in reference to homosexuality. The signifier has stayed the same, but that which is signified has been transformed. Muddying these waters still further, if one says "I'm planning on buying new shoes today," a reasonable reply might be to ask "what type of shoes?" The signifier, "shoe," references not just a particular kind of footwear but a genre of footwear; boots, stilettos, sneakers, and loafers all qualify depending on contextual factors. Signifiers are thus **polysemous** in character—they generate meanings that are utterly different from one another depending on such factors as speakers, listeners, and social and cultural context. It is possible to hear anglophones of an older generation still using the word "gay" to denote its earlier significance, whereas few

POLYSEMOUS Having more than one meaning or significance.

under the age of 50 could now use the term without being aware of its plural significance.

This quality by which the signifier and signified "mutate" according to usage leads to another important contribution of Saussure to linguistic theory—one that continued to be debated several generations after his death. This is the difference between a language system as a theoretical object (that is, each language consists of a system that is intangible) and a language as it is actually used—with all its incoherences, exceptions, and short-cuts. However "objective" a linguistic structure of relations might appear on paper, it obviously cannot account for language as spoken in its concrete manifestations. One might learn the "rules" of the language system but choose to ignore them in use. The results would not necessarily be incoherence but simply the imperfect outward expression of a coherent system. Saussure refers to this important distinction with the terms "**langue**," the system of a language, and "**parole**," objective instances of speech. When individuals are socialized in the conventions of a language, they learn the langue—the network of interrelated signs that permits both the understanding and reproduction of language. In contrast, parole involves the creative combination by individual speakers of signs within this system to express particular kinds of meanings. Of this difference, he says that "we are separating what is social from what is individual and what is essential from what is ancillary or accidental." For Saussure, it is the langue that must occupy the attention of linguists, rather than parole, which tends to distract from this all-important goal of grasping the essential rules whereby signs are related to each other.

LANGUE In Ferdinand de Saussure's linguistics, reference to language as an abstract system that can be studied independently of actual speech, or parole.

PAROLE In Ferdinand de Saussure's linguistics, reference to language as actually used in speech, often deviating from the abstract structural system of language, or langue.

Like his contemporary Émile Durkheim, Saussure was also a key figure in distinguishing the **synchronic** from the **diachronic**. Whereas linguists of previous generations had been more concerned with tracking the historical development of languages and language families (diachrony), Saussure recognized that however contingent and evolving language forms might be, their study could only be done through the mapping of relations among meaningful units in an integrated, idealized, and unchanging structure (synchrony). Like Durkheim's perspective, Saussure's concern with linguistic statics was in later generations overemphasized at the expense of interest in language transformation—a development that process-oriented anthropological linguistics only began to redress in the second half of the twentieth century. The

SYNCHRONIC Concerned with the present more than the past; contrasted with diachronic.

DIACHRONIC Historically oriented, or concerned with the past; contrasted with synchronic.

tendency to reify language *and* culture as structures of interrelated signs can be deduced from the perspective of many anthropologists working in the middle 1900s who produced an influential body of theory that includes the **Sapir-Whorf hypothesis**, French structural anthropology, and different branches of **ethnoscience**. While later theorists, especially Pierre Bourdieu, have attempted to do away with what they rightly regard as a false dichotomy between social statics and change, or structure and agency, the very fact that history and diachrony are perceived as absent from the study of language says much about the enduring influence of Ferdinand de Saussure.

SAPIR-WHORF HYPOTHESIS The proposition of Edward Sapir and Benjamin Whorf that the structure of language conditions the nature of cultural meaning.

ETHNOSCIENCE A term for the collection of methods used in cognitive anthropology.

SPEAKING ABOUT ANTHROPOLOGICAL THEORY

Janice Boddy

As an undergraduate student at McGill University I was caught up in the wave of interest in myth and ritual, structuralism, and cultural symbolism that swept anthropology in the early 1970s. That focus continued through my Master's thesis on popular culture—advertising—into my doctoral program at the University of British Columbia, where Claude Lévi-Strauss had visited (the year before I arrived) to study myths of the North West Coast. In a film by the National Film Board I saw his masterful account of symbolic transformation between two North West Coast ritual masks ("*Behind the Masks*," 1973), and I was smitten. Apart from Lévi-Strauss, my main inspirations at the time were Victor Turner, Mary Douglas, Gregory Bateson, Edmund Leach, E.E. Evans-Pritchard, and James Fernandez. The feminist turn in anthropology was just getting underway, and though I was familiar with early feminist scholarship, I resisted identification as someone interested in "the anthropology of women."

In 1976 I began doctoral fieldwork in Hofriyat, a contemporary village near the site of ancient Meroe in northern Sudan. I went planning to study the *zar*, a set of spirit possession beliefs and practices found throughout the Nile Valley and Horn of Africa that is typically the domain of women. The experience challenged all my presuppositions. As I learned local Arabic and gradually became familiar with Hofriyati women's world, I realized that my theoretical toolkit was inadequate to the task of understanding what was going on. Instead, following villagers' lead, I began to trace how and in what contexts they used certain words, specifically adjectives describing states of value. I learned that, for Hofriyati, meaning was immanent in qualities shared by persons and things, and could not be described independently of them. Thus, rather than resting on dualistic relations, as when a symbol stands for something else that constitutes its meaning, Hofriyati cultural logic was constructed through metonymy: everything was part of something else, each fragment of meaning led to another, and then another, in a recursive chain of significance that did not resolve to an underlying explanation but stood as its own truth. My analyses of the symbolic context of pharaonic circumcision in Hofriyat (1982) and of *zar* (1988, 1989) were informed by this realization. I have found the works of Roy Wagner and Marilyn Strathern to be valuable for fathoming cultural logics, and also the practice theory of Pierre Bourdieu. But above all I have been inspired by Clifford Geertz's (1973) example of imaginative ethnographic interpretation. Selves are formed and bodies shaped in dynamic interaction between people and their humanly constructed environment of objects, spaces, others—through practical engagement with the world that they themselves make and that indeed makes them.

Zar is in part a comment on local power relations, and as such Antonio Gramsci's appreciation of hegemony and the complexities of political subordination has been helpful for understanding its dynamics, as has the ethnographically nuanced feminist anthropology of the 1980s and beyond (e.g., Ortner and Whitehead 1981; Collier and Yanagisako 1987). My later work on British interventions into women's health and education in colonial Sudan (1998, 2007) is also indebted to Michel Foucault's discussion of biopower. Perhaps my theoretical approach could best be described as "grounded eclecticism": while drawing on scholarship of several theoretical stripes, I remain convinced that the greatest ethnographic insights come from careful listening and writing, assembling the ethnographic data so as to reveal the analysis they contain.

Janice Boddy is a Fellow of the Royal Society of Canada and Professor and Chair of the Department of Anthropology, University of Toronto. Among her many publications are *Wombs and Alien Spirits: Women, Men, and the Zar Cult in Northern Sudan* (Madison, WI: University of Wisconsin Press, 1989) and *Civilizing Women: British Crusades in Colonial Sudan* (Princeton, NJ: Princeton University Press, 2007).
For other works cited in this essay, see Speaking About Anthropological Theory in the Sources and Suggested Reading at the end of this book.

PART TWO
The Early Twentieth Century

To varying degrees, twentieth-century anthropological theories represent a departure from those of the nineteenth century as new theorists sought to distance themselves from the unilineal evolutionary and hereditarian doctrines of their predecessors. In so doing, they drew for inspiration upon the theories of, among others, Sigmund Freud, Émile Durkheim, Max Weber, and Ferdinand de Saussure. Under the influence of strong anthropological personalities, modern American, French, and British national traditions emerged. These traditions are known as American cultural anthropology, French structural anthropology, and British social anthropology.

American Cultural Anthropology

Under the leadership of Franz Boas and the first generations of his students, the professionalization of academic anthropology in the United States involved the cultivation of a distinctively **holistic**, "four-field" approach to the study of human life, which generally stressed the significance of historical change and the relativistic character of Euro-American and non-Western cultural norms and practices. Together with its pre-eminent geographical focus on Native American peoples, these were the epistemological foundations upon which theory in American anthropology was erected in generations after Boas, helping to set the burgeoning field apart from its British and French counterparts as a distinctive expression of anthropological knowledge.

HOLISTIC Pertaining to an overarching or integrated outlook, often associated with the broad scope of anthropological inquiry.

Franz Boas

Almost singlehandedly, Franz Boas (1858-1942) launched American anthropology on the course it maintained throughout much of the twentieth century. At the outset of the twenty-first century, his influence continues to be felt in the curricula of most North American anthropology departments, which as a group continue to adhere to the four-field approach he pioneered.

Boas was born and educated in Germany, where he earned a doctoral degree in physics based on research into the optical properties of colour. He took a field trip to northern Canada to study Native peoples' perception of colour and while there converted to geography and then anthropology. Boas next visited the United States, where he spent time in New York City before becoming a curator at the new Field Museum of Natural History in Chicago. There, he built up an impressive collection of artifacts from the Pacific Northwest Coast, where he did ethnographic and linguistic field research among the Kwakiutl and related Native groups. In the aftermath of a dispute with museum administrators, Boas left Chicago and joined the faculty of Clark University in Worcester, Massachusetts. A short time later, he moved back to New York and joined the faculty of Columbia University, where he remained for almost half a century.

Boas was principally a cultural anthropologist, but he also did important work in linguistic anthropology, physical anthropology, and, to a limited extent, archaeological anthropology. He was an extraordinarily self-disciplined and prolific scholar, publishing more than 700 articles and books. He also had a strong hand in establishing and strengthening professional organizations such as the American Anthropological Association and its flagship professional journal, *American Anthropologist*. The list of anthropologists trained by Boas really does read like a *Who's Who*. For example, in general anthropology and ethnography, there were Melville Herskovits, E. Adamson Hoebel, Alfred Louis Kroeber, and Robert Lowie; in psychological anthropology, Ruth Benedict and Margaret Mead; in American Indian studies, Alexander Goldenweiser, Paul Radin, and Clark Wissler; and in anthropological linguistics, Edward Sapir. When these students established other anthropology departments—Herskovits at Northwestern University, Sapir at the University of Chicago, and Kroeber and Lowie at the University of California at Berkeley—the Boasian approach to anthropology spread across the United States.

In spite of all this personal influence, it is sometimes said that Boas established no anthropological "school." This is because he did not make formulating new theory a high priority; rather, he spent much time criticizing old theory from the nineteenth century. Nevertheless, his approach to anthropology had pronounced characteristics. First

Franz Boas (1858–1942)

Almost singlehandedly, Boas launched American anthropology on the path it followed throughout the early twentieth century.

and foremost, Boas was an ardent empiricist, much more rigorous than his late nineteenth-century American predecessors. He was motivated to record as much information as possible about Native North American cultures before they were "lost" through assimilation to expanding Euro-American cultures. This missionary-like zeal for **salvage ethnography** inspired students and attracted them to anthropology, especially students who, like Boas, were prone to social activism.

SALVAGE ETHNOGRAPHY Ethnography motivated by the need to obtain information about cultures threatened with extinction or assimilation.

Furthermore, Boas was an arch-inductivist, urging anthropologists to "let the facts speak for themselves," reject deductive schemes, and avoid premature generalizations. He was particularly critical of the comparative method of classical cultural evolutionists, who made unwarranted use of present-day ethnographic information in reconstructions of the past. Nobody, Boas protested, was "living in the Stone Age." Because he considered evolutionary explanations "one-sided," he urged anthropologists to consider diffusion as another cause of culture change. Overall, Boas wanted detailed, well-rounded stories of cultural development. In *The Rise of Anthropological Theory* (1968), anthropologist Marvin Harris labels Boas's approach to anthropology **historical particularism**—"historical" because Boas described the present in terms of the past and "particular" because he considered the history of each culture to be unique. Other anthropologists disagree with this label, focusing instead on Boas's overarching commitment to both natural and human science.

HISTORICAL PARTICULARISM The theoretical orientation of Franz Boas and many of his students who focused on the particular histories of particular cultures.

Boas was heir to the tradition of Enlightenment egalitarianism, eclipsed during the nineteenth century by a surge of national chauvinism, hereditarianism, and racist views. Racism was particularly strong in nineteenth-century American anthropology, where Samuel George Morton (1799-1851), Josiah Clark Nott (1804-1873), and other members of the "American School" espoused racial polygenism, the doctrine that races are immutable, separately created species. The American School linked polygenism to the defence of black slavery in the antebellum American South. Rejecting the legacy of the American school, Boas insisted that environment dominates heredity in the determination of cultural differences. Having suffered prejudice as a Jew growing up in Christian surroundings, he was determined to shape anthropology into an academic discipline that would demonstrate to the world how race, language, and culture are causally unlinked. He did this creatively with a physical anthropological study of head shape. In nineteenth-century anthropology, head shape—in particular, **cephalic index**, the ratio of head width to head breadth—was considered "fixed" and, because the head contains the brain, a fixed measure of intelligence. Using sophisticated statistical techniques and a large body of data, Boas documented how head shape had changed in only one generation, as the American-born children of immigrants benefited from improved health and nutrition and other culturally conditioned inputs. Although some anthropologists have questioned the magnitude of this documented change, Boas's landmark study remains an important beginning of the attempt to end racism in modern anthropology.

CEPHALIC INDEX The measured ratio of head breadth to head length, used in nineteenth-century racial classifications.

Having come to cultural anthropology from physics, the rigorous Boas might have been expected to model cultural anthropology on natural science. This was not the case. In Germany, he had been influenced by Wilhelm Dilthey (1833-1911) and members of the Neo-Kantian **Southwest School** of German philosophy. This group derived their ideas from philosopher Immanuel Kant (1724-1804), who taught that experience is filtered through innate categories of the mind. Neo-Kantians reformulated Kant's teachings into the proposition that there are two kinds of sciences: ***naturwissenschaften***, or natural sciences, and ***geisteswissenschaften***, or human sciences of mental phenomena. The natural sciences could aim to be **nomothetic**, or seek explanatory generalizations and laws. The human sciences, however, had to concern themselves with mental phenomena, the core of human existence, and, according to Neo-Kantians, could aim to be only **idiographic**, or seek descriptions of particular events. When Boas converted from physics to anthropology, he had this distinction between generalizing and particularizing sciences in mind. As a result, he stressed culture as a mental construct, paving the way for psychological anthropology and later brands of American anthropology that represented culture as something carried around in people's heads.

Boas was a social activist. In commenting on world affairs, he was an internationalist, opposing narrow-minded nationalism and overzealous patriotism. During World War I, he published a letter in *The Nation* denouncing four unnamed anthropologists for serving as American spies. For this action, the American Anthropological Association censured him, a censure not rescinded until 2004. In the late 1930s, Boas undertook a study of American high school textbooks and found that the majority of them misrepresented the concept of race, one-fifth of them promoting what might be called white supremacy. To counter this attitude, he asked his student Ruth Benedict to translate his ideas on race into a popular pamphlet, published later as *The Races of Mankind* (1943). At this time, during World War II, Nazism was denouncing "Jewish science." Boas replied that there was only one science, the universal science of humankind. For speaking out like this, he is regarded by subsequent generations of activist anthropologists as a towering pioneer. In 1942, while Boas was having lunch at Columbia University, he suddenly slumped over and died. Anthropologist Claude Lévi-Strauss, who was sitting next to him, recalled later that he had witnessed the death of an intellectual giant and the end of an anthropology era.

SOUTHWEST SCHOOL A group of German philosophers who differentiated human sciences, or *geisteswissenschaften*, and natural sciences, or *naturwissenschaften*.

NATURWISSENSCHAFTEN Translated "natural sciences"; contrasted with *geisteswissenschaften*.

GEISTESWISSENSCHAFTEN Translated "human sciences," including anthropology; contrasted with *naturwissenschaften*.

NOMOTHETIC Generalizing; contrasted with idiographic.

IDIOGRAPHIC Pertaining to a particularizing approach to description and explanation; contrasted with nomothetic.

Robert Lowie and Alfred Louis Kroeber

The first two anthropologists to earn doctoral degrees under Boas at Columbia were Robert Lowie and Alfred Louis Kroeber.

Robert Lowie (1883-1957) started out with an interest in language and science but, after meeting Boas in New York, switched his interest to anthropology, earning a doctoral degree in 1907 on the basis of fieldwork among American Native peoples. In 1917, he joined the faculty of the University of California at Berkeley, remaining there until his retirement in 1950. Lowie's first important book was *Primitive Society* (1920) in which he criticized the cultural evolutionary approach, especially that of Lewis Henry Morgan. Following Boas, Lowie rejected the "one-sided" explanations of cultural evolutionists, although he also rejected extreme versions of diffusionism. There was, he insisted, no *one* determinant of culture. In *History of Ethnological Theory* (1937), he pursued this same theme, cautioning anthropologists against theoretical extremism of any kind. Behind his position were intellectual influences shared with Boas, namely, the Southwest School of German philosophy and an uncompromising empiricism, in Lowie's case derived from philosopher Ernst Mach (1838-1916). The Lowie program for anthropology consisted of undoing the ethnographic analyses of cultural evolutionists and redoing them in the framework of Boasian historical particularism. In *Skull Wars*, David Hurst Thomas casts Lowie's arch-empiricist agenda in an unflattering light, showing how it led Lowie to deny credence to Native Americans' oral history of their past. This denial raises the larger issue of who "owns" the prehistoric past: archaeologists and anthropologists or Native Americans themselves? Answering this question became a preoccupation of later anthropological theorists.

A long-time California colleague of Lowie was Alfred Louis Kroeber (1876-1960). Kroeber's first love was literature, but this changed when he met Boas and decided to take his doctorate in anthropology. Reflecting his literary background, Kroeber's dissertation was a study of patterns, or configurations, of American Native style. In 1901, Kroeber moved to California to become curator of the Academy of Sciences Museum. He soon joined the University of California at Berkeley, where he stayed until his retirement in 1946. Kroeber is well known for his textbook *Anthropology* (1923), his ethnographic compendium *Handbook of the Indians of California* (1925),

Robert Lowie (1883–1957)

Lowie pursued the theoretical agenda of Franz Boas while criticizing nineteenth-century cultural evolutionists.

and his theoretical treatise *Configurations of Culture Growth* (1944). While Lowie remained true to Boasian anthropology, Kroeber departed from Boas in an unexpected way. This happened when he promoted the concept of the **superorganic**.

SUPERORGANIC The idea that culture is distinct from and "above" biology.

The concept of the superorganic goes back to Herbert Spencer and Émile Durkheim and, after Kroeber, was "revisited" by anthropologist Leslie White. It represents an emphatic statement of the importance of environment over heredity, "nurture" over "nature," or culture over biology. It also represents an effort to give social scientific disciplines such as anthropology a particular identity by showing that they have something special to study—culture, a realm *sui generis*, or unto itself, separate from psychology and "above" biology. Kroeber first published his ideas about the superorganic in 1917 in an article in *American Anthropologist*. In the article, he stressed the power

GREAT MAN THEORY OF HISTORY The theory that individuals affect the course of history more than do historical circumstances.

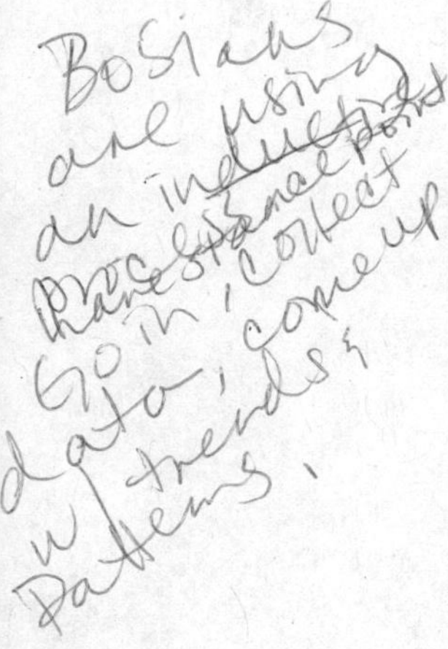

of culture to shape human behaviour, arguing against the **great man theory of history**, which stressed the power of individuals. Using historical examples, he sought to show that great men were only great because they happened to be in the right place at the right time.

Instead of proposing cultural laws that determine behaviour, Kroeber proposed cultural patterns, or trends. To illustrate the power of trends, he chose fashion, commonly considered to be subject to artistic whim and the caprice of the fashion industry. Instead, he countered, fashion features seemingly as capricious as hem length, lapel shape, and the number and placement of buttons all change cyclically, precisely enough to be plotted on graphs. The implication was that while people might *think* they are creative geniuses or manipulators, in fact they are creatures of culture, implementing changes for which the cultural time is ripe. The superorganic is one example—some say a caricature—of a scientific contrasted with a humanistic orientation for anthropology. It was an unexpected orientation for Kroeber, a student of literature, especially since he was a student of Boas, who opposed one-sided explanations.

Throughout his career, Kroeber vacillated back and forth between the superorganic and traditional Boasian approaches. In 1944, he published *Configurations of Culture Growth*, a book on which he had been working almost day and night for years. This book was a survey of major world civilizations, in which Kroeber tried to determine whether there were any overall trends, or trajectories, of civilized development. His finding was largely negative: each civilization appeared to have its own unique trajectory—a historical twist to the Boasian doctrine of cultural relativism. After *Configurations*, Kroeber gradually retreated from the concept of the superorganic and returned to the Boasian fold.

A famous, or infamous, anthropological episode reveals Kroeber's own psychological configuration. In 1911, a disoriented man speaking an undecipherable tongue appeared in the wilderness in northern California. Kroeber took a keen interest in the man and arranged for him to visit San Francisco, deciding that he was the sole survivor of a little-known Native American group, the Yana. Kroeber named the man Ishi, for "man," and declared him to be the last pristine Native American alive. Ishi moved into the San Francisco Museum of Anthropology, where he greeted the public and consulted with anthropologists, in the process learning to speak limited English. Through

Alfred Louis Kroeber (1876–1960)

Kroeber was mainly a "configurationalist," but he also pursued the idea of the "superorganic."

interacting with Ishi for five years, Kroeber learned about the culture of his vanished ancestors. Sadly, Ishi developed tuberculosis and died in 1916.

At the time of Ishi's death, Kroeber was living temporarily in New York and Europe and had become engaged by the psychoanalytic psychology of Sigmund Freud. Troubled at the news, he sent a letter to his colleagues in California instructing them to respect the traditions of Ishi's ancestors by cremating his body and burying it in an urn. There was to be no autopsy. Unfortunately, Kroeber's letter arrived after an autopsy had already been performed and Ishi's brain removed for preservation and study. Kroeber was distraught and entered a period of professional self-doubt. He remained in New York to undergo psychoanalysis and when he returned to California temporarily practiced psychoanalysis himself. For the rest of his life he rarely spoke or wrote about the Ishi affair. After his death, his wife Theodora Kroeber published a book about it, *Ishi in Two Worlds: A Biography of the Last Wild Indian in North America* (1961). Her book kept the memory of Ishi alive.

Many years later, it came to light that Ishi's brain had been sent to the Smithsonian Institution in Washington, DC, where it remained in storage and largely forgotten for decades. In 1999, a coalition of interested parties, including the Butte County Native American Cultural Committee, located the brain. In anthropology circles a heated discussion ensued about what to do and, in retrospect, what to think about the events surrounding Ishi's death. In 2000, leaders of the Redding Rancheria and Pit River groups, which claim descent from the Yana, took possession of the brain to return it to California and rebury it with Ishi's exhumed ashes in a secret location. The whole Ishi episode, spanning nine decades, attests to the dramatic shift in attitudes toward stewardship of the Native American past that has taken place since Kroeber's time.

Margaret Mead and Ruth Benedict

As American cultural anthropology developed, the search for cultural patterns launched by Kroeber, sometimes called **configurationalism**, took a turn into **psychological anthropology**, a uniquely American contribution to anthropological theory. This school was rooted in the Boasian teaching that culture is a mental phenomenon; was popularized by his most famous students, Margaret Mead and Ruth Benedict; and was taken in new directions by anthropologists reacting to the psychology of Sigmund Freud.

CONFIGURATIONALISM The search for cultural patterns, often in the idiom of psychology.

PSYCHOLOGICAL ANTHROPOLOGY Anthropology concerned with the relationship between cultures and personalities.

ENCULTURATION The process of an individual acquiring culture, usually while growing up.

Early psychological anthropologists were curious about the relationship between culture and personality, namely, how individuals contribute to culture and how, through **enculturation**, culture contributes to, or shapes, individuals. Psychological anthropologists understood that this relationship would differ from culture to culture. Under the influence of Boas, they began to incorporate observations of human feelings, attitudes, and other psychological states into their fieldwork and publications. Anthropology became livelier and more engaging as it put on a human face.

The anthropologist primarily responsible for this transformation was Margaret Mead (1901-1978). The precocious daughter of academically

Margaret Mead (1901–1978)

An outspoken advocate of "cultural relativism," Mead was the most famous American anthropologist of the mid-twentieth century.

oriented parents, Mead grew up in and around Philadelphia, attended college for one year in the American Midwest, and then headed east for what she expected would be a more cosmopolitan education at Barnard College, which was affiliated with Columbia University. An aspiring poet and writer, she gave up literature when she decided that she lacked the talent for commercial success and gravitated instead to Boas and his colleague Ruth Benedict, who convinced her that anthropology "mattered." Boas was deeply involved with his effort to use anthropology to counteract hereditarian doctrines, one of which was Freudian psychology, then growing in academic popularity. Freud had pronounced that certain phases of human psychological development were fixed by nature and were universal. Boas disagreed, believing that Freud's doctrine was culture-bound, or ethnocentric. He directed Mead to select a psychological phase of individual development, study it in a non-Western culture, and hopefully demonstrate that its manifestation there was different than in the West. Mead selected (or ended up with) female adolescence in Samoa, a group of islands in the South Pacific. She lived there for several months with the family of a missionary, venturing out into villages to interview a select number of adolescent Samoan girls. The result of this pioneering fieldwork was the first of her many books, *Coming of Age in Samoa* (1928), an all-time anthropology "classic."

The message of *Coming of Age in Samoa* was that female adolescence in the islands was a psychologically untroubled transition from girlhood to womanhood, during which time Samoan adolescents were spared the "normal" trials and tribulations of sexual awakening because they, unlike their North American counterparts, had been sexually permissive as girls. The conclusion was that adolescence was not troubled by hereditary nature, and the inference was that American adolescents would be less troubled if Americans adopted a more permissive attitude toward sex. Mead's book was an immediate commercial success, garnering public attention because of its bold and controversial pronouncements. The book launched her life-long career as spokesperson for liberal causes, preaching tolerance and understanding and how learning about exotic behaviour in faraway places provided an opportunity to reflect on "normal" behaviour back home. In this capacity, she became the most famous anthropologist of the twentieth century and the anthropologist primarily responsible for giving anthropology its reputation for cultural relativism.

Mead's other groundbreaking books were *Growing Up in New Guinea* (1930) and *Sex and Temperament in Three Primitive Societies* (1935), which featured ethnographic examples of how sex roles are enculturated and, like adolescence, not programmed by nature. In some of her early work, Mead collaborated with her second husband, Australian anthropologist Reo Fortune, and later she collaborated further with her third husband, British anthropologist and psychological researcher Gregory Bateson (her first husband was minister-turned-archaeologist Luther Cressman). Mead also maintained a close relationship with Ruth Benedict, who encouraged her to persevere and provided counsel in times of distress. In 1982, four years after Mead's death, Australian ethnographer Derek Freeman (1916-2001) published a critical account of her Samoan research in his book *Margaret Mead*

Ruth Benedict (1887–1948)

Benedict, a "configurationalist," was a leading theoretician of the American culture-and-personality school.

and Samoa: The Making and Unmaking of an Anthropological Myth, following it up in 1999 with *The Fateful Hoaxing of Margaret Mead: A Historical Analysis of her Samoan Research*. Freeman took Mead to task (posthumously) for being methodologically superficial and for failing to study Samoan history, which, according to Freeman, involved sexual violence and turmoil that belie Mead's ethnographic portrait of Samoa as a peaceable, sexual paradise. In Freeman's account, Mead was a naïve product of Boas, who pushed her too hard to do research that would turn out the way he wanted. Freeman's books sparked a vigorous and protracted debate among his, and Mead's, defenders and detractors, creating a small cottage industry of polemical scholarship.

When Mead arrived at Columbia, Ruth Benedict (1887-1948) was already there. Benedict had studied literature at Vassar College, taught high school, and, like Mead, reluctantly abandoned aspirations to be a commercial poet and writer. Seeking to fill her life with new meaning, she enrolled in an anthropology course at the New School for Social Research in New York City, where she met Franz Boas. Finding anthropology to be an outlet for her creativity and an intellectual vehicle to explore the underpinnings of her own sense of cultural alienation, she chose anthropology as her career. She did fieldwork under Kroeber, who introduced her to configurationalism, and then returned to Columbia to teach with Boas, helping to train Mead and other distinguished students.

Like Mead, Benedict was interested in the relationship between culture and personality. But while Mead described the culturally conditioned personalities of individuals, Benedict described the personalities of whole cultures. According to her, each culture had its own personality configuration, or **gestalt**. Compelling illustrations of this approach were the focus of her book *Patterns of Culture* (1934), for decades a venerated best-seller. In it, Benedict contrasted the personalities of three cultures: the Kwakiutl of the Pacific Northwest, the Zuñi of the American Southwest, and the Dobuans of the South Pacific. Borrowing names from German philosopher Friedrich Nietzsche (1844-1900), she characterized the Kwakiutl as "Dionysian" because they appeared megalomaniacal and prone to excess, staging vision quests involving self-torture and potlatch ceremonies with conspicuous consumption and destruction of material goods. In contrast, the Zuñi were "Apollonian" because they appeared peaceable and restrained by moderation, with low-key ceremonies that reined in sexual licence. On the basis of ethnographic research conducted by Reo Fortune, Benedict characterized the Dobuans as "paranoid" because they appeared preoccupied with sorcery and suspicious of one another for stealing sweet potatoes. Benedict explained how these three cases illustrated the power of culture to shape divergent normative personalities, resulting in divergent definitions of "deviance." In typical Boasian fashion, she concluded that, because what was deviant in one culture could be normative in another, deviance was not determined by nature.

GESTALT A psychological configuration, attributed by some psychological anthropologists to an entire culture.

After *Patterns of Culture*, Benedict continued to implement the Boasian mandate for anthropology by promoting cultural relativism and combating ethnocentrism and racism both intellectually and politically. To show that the concept of race was scientifically weak and politically destructive, she wrote *Race: Science and Politics* (1945), and during World War II she joined other anthropologists in helping to defeat Nazism and the Axis powers by working for the American federal government in Washington, DC. A result of this morally patriotic effort was her book *The Chrysanthemum and the Sword* (1946), a study of Japanese **national character**. During the World War II era, other national character studies—sometimes called **culture-at-a-distance** because they had to be done without the benefit of fieldwork—lost credibility when anthropologists made grandiose generalizations about the ability of childhood personality to shape the cultural behaviour of adults. An infamous case in point was Geoffrey Gorer, who attributed the "obsessive-compulsive" culture of Japan to premature toilet-training and the "manic-depressive" culture of Russia to prolonged infant swaddling. These theoretical debasements of the psychological approach were caused, in part, by reckless application of the psychology of Sigmund Freud.

NATIONAL CHARACTER According to certain psychological anthropologists, the dominant personality of a nation.

CULTURE-AT-A-DISTANCE The study of cultures without the benefit of fieldwork, practiced by American psychological anthropologists in the era of World War II.

Mead and Benedict were the two most famous female anthropologists of the early twentieth century. The rise of feminist anthropology in the late twentieth century sparked a renewed interest in their lives, times, and friendship. This interest then spread to lesser-known female students of Boas, such as African-American folklorist and author Zora Neale Hurston (1891-1960). Mead, Benedict, and Hurston, along with other anthropologists, are now subjects of numerous biographies (more than 10 biographies of Mead alone) that explore how individuals who feel culturally alienated may gravitate to anthropology, "find themselves" in anthropology, and even, if unconsciously, fashion anthropology according to their own psychological needs.

The Development of Psychological Anthropology

Psychological anthropologists like Margaret Mead and Ruth Benedict knew about Freudian psychology but were unwilling to use it as the basis of their work. Nevertheless, Boasian-era anthropologists found elements of Freudian theory appealing. Psychological anthropology entered a new phase when anthropologists critiqued Freudian theory, rejected much of it, and then incorporated some of it into a revised theoretical perspective.

In many ways Freudian theory represented the very kind of anthropology that Franz Boas and his students were trying to overcome. Freud's ideas were highly speculative, overly generalized, evolutionary, hereditarian, sexist, and, in equating non-Western adults with Western children, racist and ethnocentric. Boas used Mead to try to disprove Freud's pronouncement that adolescent psychosexual turmoil was universal. British social anthropologist Bronislaw Malinowski had a similar goal in mind when he demonstrated that the Oedipus complex was irrelevant for the matrilineal South Pacific Trobriand Islanders because, in their kinship system, "mother's brother," not "father," was the source of authority over sons. This kind of research showed that if any parts of Freudian theory were to be salvaged for anthropology, the whole theoretical edifice would have to be reconstructed with cross-cultural **variables**.

While finding Freudian theory objectionable and anachronistic, Boasian anthropologists at the same time found it stimulating and engaging. Like anthropology, Freudian psychology was iconoclastic, forcing people to analyze thoughts and behaviour they usually accepted as "normal." And it was a body of thought about personality, a subject in which anthropology could claim no special expertise. Psychological anthropologists were drawn to Freudian psychology in the 1930s, and, when this happened, they had to change it in major ways. They abandoned Freud's explanation of psychic evolution, downplayed his emphasis on sex, recast his formulations in terms of cultural relativism, and focused on the development of normal, as opposed to pathological, personality. The result was a new Freudian phase in psychological anthropology, characterized by the study of the development of personality cross-culturally, with a strong emphasis on the importance of early childhood experiences.

The chief theoretical architect of **Freudian anthropology** was Abram Kardiner (1891-1981), a psychoanalyst who studied with Freud but who realized that Freud's ideas were culture-bound—a partial product of Freud's own childhood—and had to be overhauled. To accomplish this task, he convened a seminar of anthropologists in New York City in the late 1930s. Major participants included Boasians Ruth Benedict, Ruth Bunzel, Edward Sapir, and Cora Du Bois. Their objective was to develop a theoretical framework for investigating how different cultural experiences nurtured different personality types. With input from the seminar, Kardiner devised a research model with three major components: **primary cultural institutions**, **secondary cultural institutions**, and **basic personality structure**. Primary institutions were institutions that affected childrearing practices, for example, arrangements for the feeding, weaning, and daily care of infants.

VARIABLES Carefully defined units of analysis that can be manipulated statistically and yield correlations.

FREUDIAN ANTHROPOLOGY The school of psychological anthropology incorporating certain elements of the psychology of Sigmund Freud, also called psychodynamic anthropology.

PRIMARY CULTURAL INSTITUTIONS In psychodynamic anthropology, institutions that affect how children are raised and that shape basic personality structure.

SECONDARY CULTURAL INSTITUTIONS In psychodynamic anthropology, social institutions that are projections of basic personality structure and help people cope with the world.

BASIC PERSONALITY STRUCTURE In psychodynamic anthropology, core personality, shaped by primary cultural institutions and projected onto secondary cultural institutions.

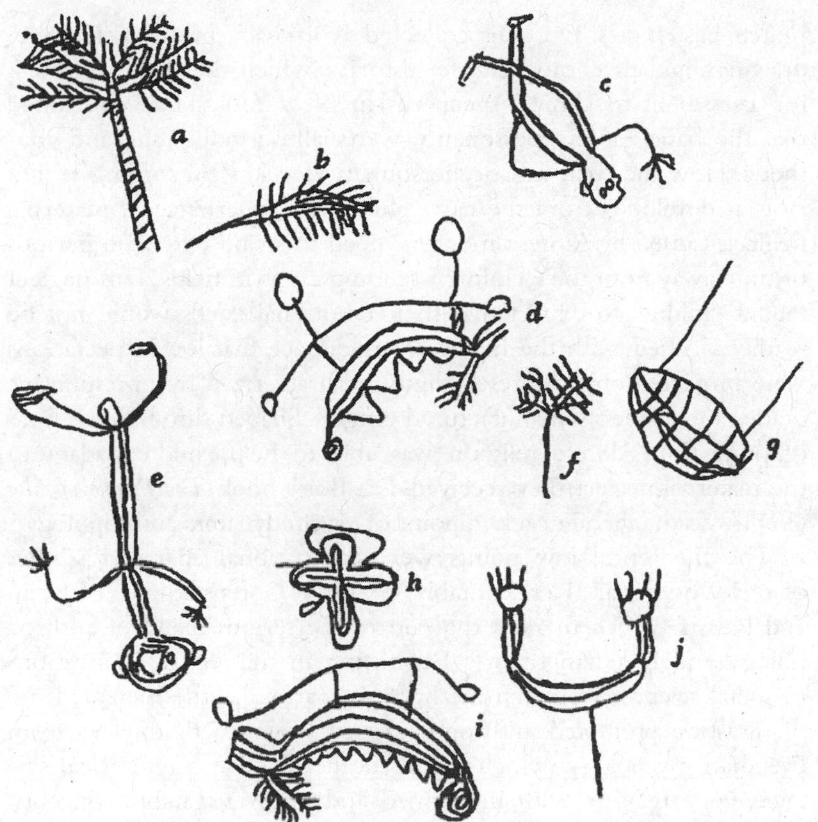

Alorese Youth Drawings
Cora Du Bois (1903–1991) used these drawings by 14-year-old male Atamau Maugliki to interpret Alorese "basic personality": a) coconut tree; b) fern: c) evil spirit; d) village guardian spirit carving; e) seer's evil familiar spirit; f) fern; g) spirit altar; h) hawk (flower); i) village guardian spirit carving; j) spirit boat carving.

Secondary institutions were the major institutions of society, politics, and religion. In Kardiner's model, basic personality structure was shaped by primary institutions and then "projected" onto secondary institutions, which functioned to help people cope with the world by depicting the world in familiar culturally adaptive terms. Kardiner called this approach **psychodynamic**.

PSYCHODYNAMIC Pertaining to the school of psychological anthropology that adopted certain elements of the psychology of Sigmund Freud; often called Freudian anthropology.

The task of psychodynamic research was to assess primary institutions, secondary institutions, and basic personality structure independently, and then to correlate them in terms of Kardiner's model. To assess basic personality structure, psychodynamic anthropologists used clinical tests like the Thematic Apperception Test, or TAT, and the Rorschach, or "ink blot," test to get informants to "project" their personalities on paper. The first systematic research of this kind was done by Cora Du Bois (1903-1991) on the island of Alor in the

Dutch East Indies. Du Bois collected Rorschach profiles, children's drawings, and psychological life histories, which she then sent back for assessment to clinical specialists in New York. They concluded that the basic Alorese personality was shallow, indifferent, and apathetic. How did such a basic personality develop? According to Du Bois, it developed from the early childhood experience of maternal neglect, caused by Alorese mothers' need to spend extended periods of time away from their children tending crops in fields. This neglect taught children to expect that their emotional needs would not be readily satisfied, with the further consequence that low expectations were projected onto Alorese religion, characterized by unresponsive deities and carelessly manufactured effigies. Shaped through this kind of projection, Alorese religion was able to help children adapt to the maternal neglect they received. Du Bois's book *The People of Alor* (1944) was the theoretical highpoint of psychodynamic anthropology.

The theoretical low points were the national character studies of the World War II era, notably Geoffrey Gorer's studies of Japan and Russia, which marked the end of the serious blend of anthropology and Freudian theory. Beginning in the 1950s, innovations in social scientific research methods, in particular the increased use of statistics, prompted anthropologists to distance themselves from Freudian psychology, which, from the perspective of empirical science, appeared rife with ill-defined and uninvestigatable concepts. A new generation of psychological anthropologists began to purge anthropology of these concepts and to use statistics to make cross-cultural generalizations precise. The pioneering effort in this new direction was John Whiting and Irvin Child's *Child Training and Personality: A Cross-Cultural Study* (1953). Whiting and Child generated cross-cultural data from, among other sources, the new Human Relations Area Files at Yale University and manipulated these data statistically to reveal significant cross-cultural associations. One of these, described by Marvin Harris in *The Rise of Anthropological Theory*, involved the following traits: prolonged periods of nursing at mother's breast; prolonged post-partum prohibitions of sexual intercourse; polygyny, or the practice of a man having more than one wife; infants sleeping exclusively with their mothers; patrilineality and patrilocality, or determination of genealogical descent and post-marital residence through the male line; and strict, often severe, male puberty rites.

In statistics, association does not necessarily *prove* cause, but it can *suggest* cause and help narrow the search for cause-and-effect relationships. Anthropologists have been able to link Whiting and Child's traits in a cause-and-effect chain of events beginning with the need for prolonged periods of nursing to supplement dietary protein and ending with the need for strong male puberty rites to sever the close attachment of son to mother in cultures with male domination. Whiting and Child modified Kardiner's psychodynamic model and renamed its major components. Thus, primary institutions became **maintenance systems**, especially as they affected child training practices; secondary institutions became **projective systems**; and basic personality structure became **personality variables**.

MAINTENANCE SYSTEMS In the psychological anthropological model of John Whiting and Irvin Child, the equivalent of Abram Kardiner's primary cultural institutions without Freudian components.

PROJECTIVE SYSTEMS In the psychological anthropological model of John Whiting and Irvin Child, the equivalent of Abram Kardiner's secondary cultural institutions without Freudian components.

PERSONALITY VARIABLES In the psychological anthropological model of John Whiting and Irvin Child, the equivalent of Abram Kardiner's basic personality structure without Freudian components.

In the 25 years between *Coming of Age in Samoa* and *Child-Training and Personality: A Cross-Cultural Study*, American psychological anthropology evolved through pre-Freudian, Freudian, and post-Freudian phases. A brand of anthropology that began as a humanistic, almost literary attempt to make Americans more tolerant of different kinds of cultures and personalities ended up, in the middle of the twentieth century, modeled after psychologically "detached" social science. Throughout all these transformations, the investigation of culture and personality remained a uniquely American contribution to anthropological theory.

French Structural Anthropology

While Franz Boas and his students were promulgating their brands of anthropology in North America, other theoretical influences were at work in France and Britain. In France, classical cultural evolutionism never really took hold. In its place, the seminal and pervasive influence of Émile Durkheim ensured that, when French anthropology assumed its twentieth-century identity, it did so in a way that was more continuous with, rather than a radical departure from, its nineteenth-century legacy. Durkheim, a rationalist as much as an empiricist, had understood thought to precede observation and the origins of social phenomena to be in the group mind. In his theoretical terms, the elementary forms of social phenomena were collective representations of the collective consciousness of people. This outlook became the basis for French structural anthropology when Claude Lévi-Strauss converted the concept of elementary forms into that of elementary structures.

Marcel Mauss

The intellectual transition from Durkheim to Lévi-Strauss and French structural anthropology was accomplished by Durkheim's student and nephew Marcel Mauss (1872-1950). A decorated veteran of World War I, Mauss enjoyed a productive career that included a professional collaboration with his uncle at the helm of *Année Sociologique*. This was succeeded by lectureships in ethnology and religious studies at two French universities—first, the Institute of Ethnology, and later, the Collège de France.

Contrasting the careers of many of his peers in the British and American schools, Mauss's influence in the field of anthropology did not derive from his ethnographic monographs or fieldwork but rather from a meticulous attention to theoretical issues that lay at the heart of many published essays and lecture notes published posthumously. A life-long Durkheimian, Mauss's overriding concern was to understand the structured nature of social cohesion, which he took to be embodied in a series of general mental principles that constituted "total social facts." His most well-known elaboration of the idea of the total social fact was expressed in his essay *The Gift* (1924), in which the apparently spontaneous act of gift exchange was shown to be regulated according to integrated mental rules of reciprocity that were binding on all parties to the exchange. These elementary principles or structures were understood to be the logic, or "glue," that unified different kinds of social institutions (kinship, religion, aesthetics, economics, etc.). Hence, the phenomenon of the gift was to be sociologically interpreted as an embodiment of a basic principle of social life, situated at the intersection of different "domains" of social life and containing within it many types of meaning.

RECIPROCITY According to Marcel Mauss, the elementary principle of exchanging gifts; according to Claude Lévi-Strauss, the elementary principle of exchanging women.

One of Mauss's most important contributions was to shift focus from Durkheim's "mind" of the group to the minds of individuals. In Mauss's scheme, elementary structures of individual minds precede elementary structures of the group mind, which in turn precede elementary structures of the outside world. Mauss was particularly interested in elementary structures of the practice of giving gifts. For him, gift-giving was exchange, or **reciprocity**, which operated according to the elementary reciprocity principle: "to give, to receive, and to repay." Reciprocity was an inherent mental structure, a logic shared by everyone. Unlike economic anthropologists, who considered reciprocity to be restricted to non-market economic transactions, Mauss considered it to be a universal principle of exchange governing, besides economics, social organization and kinship—an idea elaborated by Lévi-Strauss through much of his writing.

Claude Lévi-Strauss

Claude Lévi-Strauss (b.1908) was the guru of French structural anthropology and one of the most celebrated, even if not always understood, anthropologists of the twentieth century. Lévi-Strauss studied at the University of Paris before leaving France in the 1930s to become a professor at the University of Sao Paulo in Brazil. In Brazil, he conducted himself as a kind of expatriate, doing fieldwork published later as the ethnographic travelogue *Tristes Tropiques* (1955). In the 1940s, he spent several years as a professor at the New School for Social Research in New York, where he interacted with Franz Boas. In 1950, Lévi-Strauss became director of studies at the École Practique des Haute Études, followed in 1959 by an appointment as chair of social anthropology at the Collège de France.

During his years as a student, Lévi-Strauss flirted with politics while immersing himself in the traditions of French ethnography and the ideas of Marcel Mauss. Following his Brazilian fieldwork, he turned his attention to anthropological theory, publishing *The Elementary Structures of Kinship* (1949) and *Structural Anthropology* (1958). These books present a complex analysis of kinship based on one aspect of reciprocity: the reciprocal exchange of women.

Working in the tradition of Durkheim, whose concern was solidarity, Lévi-Strauss began with the proposition that reciprocal exchange among social groups promotes alliances, which facilitate social interaction and make society cohere. These alliances are achieved through the reciprocal exchange of women as "gifts." The propensity, or structure, for gift-giving is innate in the human mind, which operates with a universal logic of dualities, called **binary oppositions**, something he learned from the **Prague School** of structural linguists, led by linguist Roman Jakobson (1896-1982), who helped formulate the concept of **phonemes**. In structural linguistics, phonemes are minimally contrasting pairs of sounds that create linguistic meaning. In structural anthropology, binary oppositions are contrasting pairs of mental constructs that create social meaning. Some of the binary oppositions Lévi-Strauss

BINARY OPPOSITIONS In French structural anthropology, the universal logic of dualities.

PRAGUE SCHOOL A school of linguists based in Prague that pioneered the analysis of phonemes.

PHONEMES Minimally contrasting pairs of sounds that create linguistic meaning.

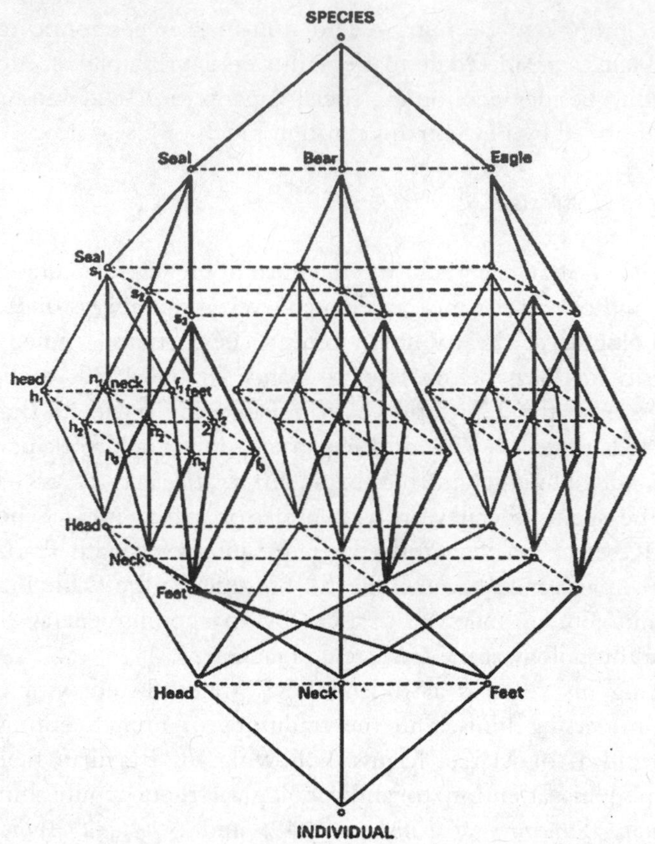

The Totemic Operator

This is a model of totemic "structure" in the theoretical schema of Claude Lévi-Strauss.

discussed at great length are life versus death, culture versus nature, and self versus other. With binary oppositions, the *relationship* between elements is as important as the elements themselves. This relationship is "mediated." For example, the binary opposition between kinship groups, a transformation of the binary opposition of self versus other, is mediated by the exchange of women. In structuralism, binary oppositions are part of an integrated system of logically connected categories of meaning that structure social activity and the way that activity is conceptualized.

Because Lévi-Strauss analyzed social organization in the way that structural linguists analyze language, form was as important as content. In the case of the elementary structures of kinship, Lévi-Strauss observed that kinship groups who exchange women create a form, or relationship, among themselves, as well as relationships among exchanged women. This relationship helps to mediate the groups, that is, it brings them closer together. Implicated in exchanges of women are four basic relationships: brother and sister; husband and wife; father and son; and mother's brother, or "uncle," and sister's son, or "nephew." Each of these relationships is either "positive," promoting harmony and happiness, or "negative," promoting hostility and antagonism. According to Lévi-Strauss, the mind balances positives and negatives, so in a given exchange system, two of the relationships must be positive and two must be negative. From culture to culture, the content of the relationships can change, but their form, logic, or structure remains the same.

In Lévi-Strauss's scheme, the reciprocal exchange of women can assume either of two forms. **Restricted exchange** creates a relationship between two kinship groups through "symmetrical" cross-cousin marriage, whereby brothers and sisters in one group marry cross-cousins—cousins related through parents of the opposite sex—in the other group. **Generalized exchange** creates a relationship between more than two kinship groups through "asymmetrical" cross-cousin marriage, whereby brothers and sisters are not exchanged between two groups directly but return to their groups after having been circulated through other groups. According to Lévi-Strauss, generalized exchange promotes more solidarity than restricted exchange because it creates alliances involving more kinship groups. Beyond this, he identified two forms of generalized exchange, one of which he thought promotes more social solidarity than the other. **Matrilateral cross-cousin marriage**, or marriage to mother's brother's children, leads to a "long cycle" of generalized exchange, while **patrilateral cross-cousin marriage**, or marriage to father's sister's children, leads to only a "short cycle." The long cycle promotes more solidarity than the short cycle because it creates alliances involving more kinship groups. This difference, Lévi-Strauss thought, explains why matrilateral cross-cousin marriage is more prevalent than patrilateral cross-cousin marriage in the ethnographic record.

RESTRICTED EXCHANGE According to Claude Lévi-Strauss, the exchange of women between two kinship groups.

GENERALIZED EXCHANGE According to Claude Lévi-Strauss, the exchange of women among more than two kinship groups, promoting greater social solidarity than restricted exchange.

MATRILATERAL CROSS-COUSIN MARRIAGE Marriage to a child of one's mother's brother; contrasted with patrilateral cross-cousin marriage.

PATRILATERAL CROSS-COUSIN MARRIAGE Marriage to a child of one's father's sister; contrasted with matrilateral cross-cousin marriage.

Besides kinship, where Lévi-Strauss made substantial theoretical contributions to anthropology, structural anthropologists have analyzed a wide range of cultural domains, including, notably, food preferences and myths. In an analysis of the North American Native myth of the "tricky coyote" (re-analyzed by Marvin Harris in *Cultural Materialism* [1979]), Lévi-Strauss set up two pairs of analogous binary oppositions—agriculture is to warfare as life is to death—and claimed that hunting mediates agriculture and warfare because hunting preserves human life while leading to the death of animals. Scavenging animals like the coyote mediate yet another pair of binary oppositions—herbivore to carnivore, also analogous to life and death—so coyotes must be tricky. In *The Raw and the Cooked* (1969), a book devoted to the structure of cuisine, Lévi-Strauss contrasted raw, cooked, and rotted foods. For cooked foods, boiling is to roasting as culture is to nature. Boiled foods are served to kinspeople while roasted foods are served to strangers because kinspeople are associated with culture while foreigners are associated with nature.

Many have noted that, perhaps more than any other anthropologist of the twentieth century, and regardless of which side of the Atlantic Ocean one hails from, Claude Lévi-Strauss was responsible for the single most original body of theory and writing to emerge in the discipline. Indeed, it often seemed as though much of the theoretical agenda of late twentieth-century anthropology was set by Lévi-Strauss—both by those who explicitly and implicitly championed his ideas and by others who argued against them. It was certainly not long before the structuralist thesis he proposed caught the interest of anglophone anthropologists, who began to expand upon his work in earnest during the 1960s.

Edmund Leach and Mary Douglas

While structural theory flourished in the francophone world, it required translation for most Anglo-American anthropologists, both in the literal and figurative senses, because the British and Americans were not accustomed to Durkheimian analysis that was mentalistic and synchronic. Those anthropologists responsible for communicating and championing the work of their French colleagues in the anglophone world were accordingly looked to as "filters" and interpreters of structuralist analysis. Two of the most articulate exponents of Lévi-Strauss's structuralism during the 1950s and 1960s were Edmund Leach and Mary Douglas.

Edmund R. Leach (1910-1988) figures among the most important of British social anthropologists, in particular for his highly original analysis of social structure and conflict in Burma in which he challenged many tenets of the perspective of his mentors, Bronislaw Malinowski and Raymond Firth. He did this by developing a distinctive approach to structural-functionalism, modeled on the theory of Lévi-Strauss, with which he became acquainted in the early 1950s. In *Political Systems of Highland Burma* (1954), written while Leach was a professor at the London School of Economics, he emphasized the shifting nature of cultural meaning and political power among the diverse Kachin of the Burmese highlands, among whom he had lived while serving as a British officer during World War II.

In *Political Systems of Highland Burma*, Leach argued that the language of myth served as a window onto the Burmese social order, and anthropological interpretation of that language would reveal the underlying structures of the Kachin social order. Wary of the structural-functional tendency to impose rigid grids of behaviour on what he viewed as the fluid and highly changeable character of social life, he proposed that instead of viewing as immutable their own theoretical constructs, anthropologists might instead consider their method of analysis—structural-functionalism—as a "necessary evil": an explanatory framework that enabled social scientists to artificially "capture" the workings of a society that was, in reality, always in a state of flux, or, to employ Leach's term, **oscillating equilibrium**. Among the Kachin, he argued, there existed a single social system that was nevertheless internally differentiated along an axis running between two social "poles": the hierarchically ranked *gumsa* Kachin at one extreme and the egalitarian *gumlao* Kachin at the other.

OSCILLATING EQUILIBRIUM Edmund Leach's term for the continuing existence of social structure, even against the backdrop of constant social change.

In his later years at Cambridge University, Leach became an ardent and eloquent exponent of French structuralism, largely from the proverbial "armchair," with his own coterie of students interested in structural analysis. Among his areas of study in the 1970s was mythology in the Judeo-Christian tradition, within which, he posited, religious mythmaking generally involved attempts by exegetes, or interpreters, to bridge a structural opposition between life and death with the concept of "another world."

While having generally less stature in British anthropology than Leach, Mary Douglas (1921-2007) is likewise recognized as one of the most important interpreters of French structuralism for an anglophone readership. A student under Meyer Fortes and Max Gluckman, Douglas, an Africanist, was also deeply influenced by the work of Evans-Pritchard and, subsequently, Lévi-Strauss.

A professor at the University of London and Oxford University before taking a position at Northwestern University, Douglas has been influential for her groundbreaking study of the mental rules of classification governing the universal concepts of **purity** and **pollution**. In particular, her cross-cultural study of ritual prohibitions against things that are "dirty"—regardless of how this concept is locally constructed—has been of lasting value to anthropologists seeking to understand how social boundaries are created, sustained, or transgressed. In her best-known work, *Purity and Danger: An Analysis of Concepts of Pollution and Taboo* (1966), she argued that Durkheimian principles of social order were expressed in culturally generated formulations of the pure and the impure: purity is structurally connected to ideas concerning social harmony, coherence, logic, and boundaries, while impurity is associated with "dirty things" that are morally "dangerous" insofar as they suggest ambiguity and uncertainty about social rules and meaning. Famous examples from the work include analyses of Old Testament temple rituals and food prohibitions in a chapter entitled "The Abominations of Leviticus."

PURITY According to Mary Douglas, the ideal of a seamless social order symbolically excluding that which threatens a society's basic categories of understanding; contrasted with pollution.

POLLUTION According to Mary Douglas, aspects of the world unexplained by a society's basic categories of understanding, thereby threatening the social order; contrasted with purity.

The Legacy of French Structural Anthropology

French structuralism has continued to exert considerable influence across the social sciences, even though its impact has in recent years been largely indirect. At the very least, the notion of "structure," whether cognitive (as Lévi-Strauss has emphasized) or social (as early generations of British social anthropologists proposed) has been a resilient "straw man" in contrast to which more recent generations of anthropologists have developed more "process"-centred theories and epistemologies. Still, it seems clear that the Durkheimian tradition in anthropology, which stresses the integrated aspects of social and cultural life, is still a fundamental orientation for those seeking to break new theoretical ground. Accordingly, others have refused to throw the proverbial baby out with the bathwater and have instead attempted to infuse French structuralism with a concern for social class and power dynamics.

Early on, one of the most theoretically abstract offshoots of French structuralism was so-called "structural Marxism." This body of theory grew out of an anthropological debate that began during the 1960s between economic **formalists** and economic **substantivists**. Formalists like Scott Cook maintained that the traditional Western definition of economics, the allocation of scarce resources among unlimited wants,

FORMALISTS Economic anthropologists who maintained that Western economic concepts apply to non-Western economies; contrasted with substantivists.

SUBSTANTIVISTS Economic anthropologists who maintained that Western economic concepts do not apply to non-Western economies; contrasted with formalists.

also applies to non-Western economies. Substantivists like George Dalton, Karl Polanyi, and Marshall Sahlins disagreed, maintaining that formalists were ethnocentric and that capitalist conceptions do not apply to economies lacking markets and the political apparatus of states. According to substantivists, people in cultures governed by kinship do not *think* like economic materialists and strategize to maximize their material advantages because the primary significance of their economic transactions is social. Some substantivists even argued that economic exploitation does not exist if people do not think of themselves as exploited. Structural Marxists aimed to resolve the tensions arising from these debates. In some ways, their idea was to apply Hegelian dialectics to social theory itself—the formalist "thesis" and substantivist "antithesis" being resolved in a new synthesis that linked materialism and idealism.

This marriage of materialism and idealism would not, it seems, be unappealing to Lévi-Strauss himself. In his autobiographical *Tristes Tropiques*, he describes Marxism as one of "three mistresses" guiding the development of structuralism from its inchoate beginnings to coherent maturity. This being said, it is difficult to divine Marxist leanings in Lévi-Strauss's sprawling corpus of ethnography. Although hints of a Marxist position emerge in *The Savage Mind* (1962), in which he claims as one of his goals the development of a theory of superstructures "scarcely touched upon by Marx," this line of reasoning has been generally underdeveloped in his writing. There is, however, some idea of what he had in mind. In his analysis of Native American mythology, Lévi-Strauss argues that contradictions in the place of women as both commodities and social beings are reflected in myths that specify conflict between different species of animals.

As pioneered by Maurice Godelier and Jonathan Friedman in the 1970s, the central ambition of structural Marxism was to relate the theory of dialectical materialism to a theory of dialectical idealism by demonstrating that the structure of economic transactions derives from the structure of thought. As discussed by Marvin Harris in *Cultural Materialism* (1979), under the influence of Lévi-Strauss, structural Marxism was little short of an effort to "dematerialize" Marxism—that is, the theory of dialectical materialism—and refocus it on the structure of dialectical thought. Thought, as opposed to behaviour, is implicated by the Marxist concepts of "class consciousness" and "social relations" of the means of economic production.

Pursuing these ideas, structural Marxists like Friedman began searching for hidden "dialectical" structures that make economies tick. Friedman found that the structure of capitalist economies is a fetish for money, while the structures of non-capitalist economies are rooted in social and religious values.

The apogee of structural Marxism within anthropology came in the late 1970s, as another Marx-inspired perspective, political economy, and post-structural analyses inspired by such theorists as Michel Foucault, Jacques Lacan, and Antonio Gramsci began to grow in influence. On the other hand, perhaps the most famous post-Lévi-Strauss exponent of structuralism within anthropology is Marshall Sahlins (b.1930), who, as a convert from cultural neo-evolutionism, published his most evocative and controversial theses on the subject in the 1980s—well into a period of introspective malaise and uncertainty in the discipline. Best known among these is Sahlins's application of structuralist concern for symbolic patterning to his interest in colonial encounters in the Pacific. In *Islands of History* (1985), Sahlins offers an ingenious resolution to the tension between cultural structure and historical change by way of analyzing the colonial encounter between European eighteenth-century explorer-colonists and Native Melanesians. In particular, he explores English-Hawaiian relations that culminated in the fabled death of British Royal Navy officer and explorer Captain James Cook at the hands of Native Hawaiians in 1779. The problem lies in how to explain the reception of Europeans by Native Hawaiians possessed of their own cultural structure of symbols and meanings. From Sahlins's vantage, this dark episode proves an ideal case study in which to explore the relations between culture and history. He argues that the cultural structure of any community is not static but open to transformation depending on context. When circumstances warranted, pre-contact Hawaiian culture adapted to the new situation—framing their encounter with Europeans within an indigenous logic of social relations. In this way, the presence of Englishman Cook and his crew not only provoked but required explanation. Sahlins argues that contact, or "conjuncture," between two distinct cultural structures—that of the Hawaiian and that of the European—precipitated change to both, in effect creating a hybrid structure at the point of encounter. It is this "**structure of the conjuncture**" that must be explored in order to understand both why Cook was killed and, more relevant for anthropology, how apparently static cultural structures change through time.

STRUCTURE OF THE CONJUNCTURE Marshall Sahlins's phrase describing the space of intersection between different cultural structures, where contingency produces historical change.

In essence, Sahlins's argument is that Native Hawaiians in the late eighteenth century understood Cook to be a fertility god because he acted in accordance with Hawaiian mythical expectations of divinity. He "became" **Lono**, whose annual return and ritual sacrifice was crucial to the smooth functioning of Hawaiian society—a people dependent on Lono's divine power (*mana*) to ensure health, fecundity (of women, animals, and the earth), and prosperity from one agricultural cycle to the next. When Cook, after a period of tension and miscommunication with Hawaiians, was killed by a sharp blow to the head (provoked by the attempted kidnapping of a Hawaiian king), his crew saw the event as nothing short of murder. Sahlins makes the case that, to the contrary, for the Hawaiians, the killing of Cook was a symbolically powerful act within the indigenous cultural structure. Given their belief in Cook's divinity, it was entirely predictable, as was the idea that he would appear postmortem during the following year's rites of fertility renewal. In this structure of the conjuncture, Cook is recreated in the image of Hawaiian mythology, both in terms of his quality as a being and his relationship to Hawaii and Hawaiians.

LONO In pre-colonial Hawaii, a god responsible for fertility and fecundity.

This perspective has been taken to task by anthropologist Gananath Obeyesekere, in what may be described as one of the livelier, engaging, and protracted debates (spanning at least three books) in contemporary social and cultural anthropology. In brief, Obeyesekere argues for a reading of Cook's encounter with the Hawaiians that places awareness of the depredatory intentions of European colonials at the forefront of Hawaiian consciousness. Far from lack of awareness of Cook's colonial ambitions, it was precisely the conflict created by these that resulted in the captain's killing. The idea that Cook was made a god is, in this wise, itself a myth of European auto-aggrandizement. To this, Sahlins has responded by hoisting Obeyesekere by his own petard: if the perception of eighteenth-century Hawaiians was more complex than permitted by deterministic cultural structures, then so too was European self-imagining. And so the debate goes—more enlightening, perhaps, of recent debates in anthropology than of structuralism per se.

Lévi-Strauss's perspective on linguistic and cognitive structure, which (via linguist Roman Jakobson [1896-1982]) draws heavily on Saussure's theory of signs, has been the central target of criticism on several fronts. Some, such as materialist Marvin Harris, have derided structuralism for assuming, as Lévi-Strauss appears to in places, that cultural structures *are* the empirical "reality" of any given society—an assumption that would seem to set aside the possibility of scientific understanding not to mention common sense. If this is the case, then relativism is privileged as more than just a research principle: it becomes a precondition of anthropological understanding and comparison. Even Sahlins, eloquent expounder of structuralism though he is, has not been able to resolve this inconsistency, which has significant implications for his work on the colonial encounter in Hawaii. Among Hawaiians, the historical moment of encounter with the English is informed by and fused with cosmology. If this can be the case, he argues, the notion of historical objectivity, too, must be investigated for its mythical properties. Taken seriously, this reduction of anthropological analysis to poetics would seem to rob the field of its power to explain cultural process.

Others, ranging from post-structural guru Michel Foucault to the preponderance of social and cultural theorists today, are less polemical. Their view is that Lévi-Strauss's focus on cognition *tends* to ignore the practical, emotive, and diachronic aspects of culture. In denying, at least tacitly, the somatic, social, and historical, structuralism is exposed to the criticism that it leaves the door open for obscurantism, **solipsism**, and extreme relativism—all of which stand in stark contrast to structuralism's universalist pretensions. Still, the idea that patterned sequences of symbolic meaning stand in observable, "decipherable" relation to other such sequences is of enduring appeal, and many anthropologists have made efforts to adapt this aspect of French structuralism to more contextually—and historically—sensitive ethnography.

SOLIPSISM The idea that the individual self is the only reality and that the external world exists only in one's imagination.

One might consequently ask how valid these critiques are and to what extent they have been accepted by anthropological theorists. As Joel Robbins has noted in a recent essay, such critiques amount to "willfully simple-minded interpretations of the hot/cold distinction" that ignore Lévi-Strauss's more subtle arguments concerning social and historical change. In Robbins's view, Lévi-Strauss's supposedly ahistorical perspective must be considered a meditation on "the danger of universalizing a Western cultural model of the nature and value of change as a theoretical construct." For this reason his legacy, and that of French structuralism, must be seen as contributing to a growing disciplinary awareness of the need for caution in exporting Western models of society and culture: a contribution that would be of great significance in later decades.

British Social Anthropology

In Britain, the leading early twentieth-century anthropologists were Alfred Reginald Radcliffe-Brown and Bronislaw Malinowski. By force of personality and intellect, these two figures infused British anthropology with a theoretical agenda far different from that which had consumed the efforts of their nineteenth-century forebears. Working separately and, in the case of Radcliffe-Brown, under the influence of Émile Durkheim, they founded the school known as British social anthropology. The pivotal "isms" of British social anthropology were **structuralism**, **functionalism**, and, sometimes, **structural-functionalism**. These "isms," especially as incorporated in the work of Radcliffe-Brown and his students, were based on Durkheim's **organismic analogy**, the conceptualization that society is like an organism.

Analogies between social and biological phenomena were rooted in the Scientific Revolution, which inspired social scientists to model their enterprise on natural science, and flourished after Darwinism, which drew attention to both biological and social evolution. Biological organisms have both structures and functions. The scientific study of organic structure is morphology, while the scientific study of organic function is physiology. According to the organismic analogy, the scientific study of societies should include **social morphology** and **social physiology**. A further inference is that the scientific study of society should include social *evolution*, but British social anthropologists associated evolutionism with nineteenth-century anthropology and did not wish to elaborate this part of the organismic analogy. Their orientation was synchronic, meaning ahistorical, rather than diachronic, or concerned with change through time.

The British understanding of "society" was significantly different from the American understanding of "culture." American anthropologists understood culture to comprise economic, social, political, and religious thoughts and behaviour, with both synchronic and diachronic dimensions. In contrast, British anthropologists focused more narrowly on the synchronic study of society. **Social structure** was the matrix, or enclosing form, of society, while **social function** was the role that individual parts of society played in maintaining the structural whole. The result of proper social functioning was a social structure maintained in equilibrium, or, in terms of the organismic analogy, structural "health." Derived from Durkheimian thought, the

STRUCTURALISM In British social anthropology, the synchronic concern with social structure, sometimes called social morphology, and in French structural anthropology, the concern with the elementary forms of minds and cultures.

FUNCTIONALISM In British social anthropology, either Alfred Reginald Radcliffe-Brown's theory of how parts of a society contribute to the whole of society or Bronislaw Malinowski's theory of how culture responds to biological needs in a hierarchically organized way.

STRUCTURAL-FUNCTIONALISM In British social anthropology, the synchronic concern with social structure and social function.

ORGANISMIC ANALOGY Likening society to an organism.

SOCIAL MORPHOLOGY In British social anthropology, according to the organismic analogy, the study of social structure.

SOCIAL PHYSIOLOGY In British social anthropology, according to the organismic analogy, the study of social function.

SOCIAL STRUCTURE In British social anthropology, the social matrix of behaviour; sometimes called social morphology.

SOCIAL FUNCTION In British social anthropology, the contribution of a part of society to the whole of society; sometimes called social physiology.

twinned theories of structuralism and functionalism inclined British anthropologists to see society as harmonious and stable, unlike evolutionists, who saw culture as prone to change, or Marxists, who saw it as conflicted. British social anthropologists also differed from American historical particularists in their synchronic orientation and their relative lack of involvement with material culture, which American anthropologists maintained through closer affiliations with archaeologists.

A.R. Radcliffe-Brown

The prototypical British social anthropologist, Alfred Reginald Radcliffe-Brown (1881-1955) embodied, more than any other figure of his generation, the emerging aspirations of an increasingly professionalized group of scholars seeking ways to move beyond the evolutionist principles bequeathed to them by the armchair-bound speculation of Tylor, Morgan, and others.

Trained in natural science and introduced to anthropology at Cambridge University, Radcliffe-Brown was initially influenced by members of the 1898-1899 Cambridge Anthropological Expedition to the Torres Straits, a body of water separating Australia and New Guinea. This expedition was a groundbreaking deployment of a multidisciplinary team of researchers to gather information about Native peoples in the Straits area. Members of the team included anthropologist Alfred Cort Haddon (1855-1940), physician Charles Seligman (1873-1940), psychologist William H.R. Rivers (1864-1922), psychology student William McDougall (1871-1938), and several linguists and photographers. The expedition set new standards for excellence in fieldwork, yielded numerous publications, and helped launch or solidify the careers of key members. Rivers, for instance, went on to found the **genealogical method** of anthropology, a method based on the insights that the nub of non-Western social organization is kinship and that kinship can best be understood through the study of cultural history and psychology. Early in his career, and under the tutelage of Rivers, Radcliffe-Brown conducted genealogical research in the Andaman Islands in the Bay of Bengal and made a name for himself with his now classic monograph, *The Andaman Islanders* (1922). Subsequently, he held teaching appointments in England, Australia, South Africa, and the United States, where in the early

GENEALOGICAL METHOD
The method of focusing ethnographic fieldwork on kinship, pioneered by British social anthropologists, notably William H. R. Rivers.

1930s he taught and was chair of the Anthropology Department at the University of Chicago. There, he interacted with Boasian anthropologists such as Robert Lowie and Fred Eggan (1906-1991) and by most accounts, perhaps aided by his sometimes flamboyant personality, exercised a great deal of personal and professional influence, widening the appeal of what he conceived of as a natural science of primitive society beyond the confines of British anthropology. Besides *The Andaman Islanders*, his major publications include *The Social Organization of Australian Tribes* (1930-1931); *A Natural Science of Society* (1948); *African Systems of Kinship and Marriage* (1950), edited with C. Daryll Forde (1902-1973); and *Structure and Function in Primitive Society* (1952).

In spite of his early exposure to Rivers's ethnology, in his own work Radcliffe-Brown balked at the non-comparative work of his mentor and sought a more "scientific" basis for anthropology. Accordingly, among British anthropologists he is frequently credited with employing Durkheim's ideas about mechanical and organic solidarity as the theoretical basis of his original ethnographic fieldwork in Australia and Africa. Ultimately, his original insights transformed Durkheimian theory into a more empirically grounded variant in which mechanical and, especially, organic solidarity served as a framework within which a comparative, synchronic sociology of non-Western social systems might be carried out. The primary question that Radcliffe-Brown attempted to answer in his research was how ritual activity and different social institutions, especially kinship, contributed to the maintenance of social structure in and across "primitive" societies. Among his best-known contributions to structural-functionalist theory were delineations of the structural principles that informed the solidarity of sibling groups and **lineages**, and the various social practices associated with them, whose primitiveness made them invisible to the Western eye.

LINEAGES Multi-generational kinship groups with membership determined by ties to common ancestors.

Generally speaking, Radcliffe-Brown is better represented in the work and thought of the many students he influenced within the British tradition and beyond than he is by his own corpus of research and writing, which was not vast. With the exception of Malinowski, who developed his own distinctive perspective on functionalism, most anthropologists working in the British tradition in the first half of the twentieth century followed in the mendicant footsteps of Radcliffe-Brown, who introduced many in the profession to the work of Durkheim.

Bronislaw Malinowski

Second only to Radcliffe-Brown, the most influential British anthropologist of the first half of the twentieth century was Bronislaw Malinowski (1884-1942). Malinowski was born and raised in Poland and studied anthropology at the London School of Economics, where he entered the British scene. In 1914, he set out to do fieldwork in New Guinea and had stopped at the Trobriand Islands when World War I broke out. The British government allowed him to stay in the Trobriands, where he spent several years doing ethnographic research that led to his ethnography *Argonauts of the Western Pacific* (1922), widely regarded as the best of the early classics. Eventually, Malinowski returned to the London School of Economics, where during the 1920s and 1930s he helped train the second generation of British social anthropologists. In the twilight of his career, he also taught briefly at Yale University, although his influence there in no way rivaled that of Radcliffe-Brown among American anthropologists in Chicago. The titles of some of Malinowski's books were titillating and "juicy": for example, *Sex and Repression in Savage Society* (1927) and *The Sexual Life of Savages* (1929). He also wrote *Freedom and Civilization* (1944), *A Scientific Theory of Culture* (1944), and *A Diary in the Strict Sense of the Term* (1967). The diary was published 25 years after Malinowski's death and is noteworthy for its intensely personal, often brooding and melancholy account of his years as a Trobriand fieldworker.

PARTICIPANT-OBSERVATION The style of anthropological fieldwork requiring the fieldworker to see things from both the "native" and the fieldworker's points of view.

Anthropologists acknowledge Malinowski to be the first and foremost early practitioner of the ethnographic method of **participant-observation**, by which fieldworkers attempt to achieve ethnographic understanding through an artful synthesis of "insider," "subjective" participation and "outsider," "objective" observation. In *Argonauts of the Western Pacific*, Malinowski also rendered a classic analysis of the Trobriand *kula* ring of economic exchange and explored Freudian psychology in the context of a non-Western matrilineal culture. At the level of theory, however, Malinowski's claim to anthropological fame rests primarily on his theory of functionalism.

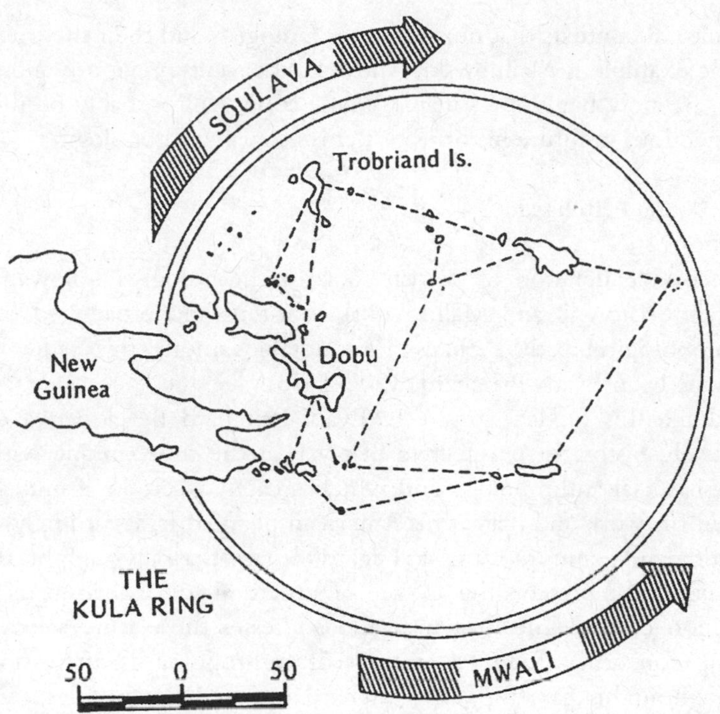

The Kula Ring

As analyzed by Bronislaw Malinowski (1884–1942), in the "ring," necklaces (soulava) are exchanged clockwise, armshells (mwali) counter-clockwise.

Malinowski's formulation of functionalism differed from Radcliffe-Brown's by being rooted in biology *actually* rather than analogously. Like Freud, Malinowski acknowledged that people have basic biological needs, including a basic need for sex. Culture functions to satisfy these basic needs with basic responses. In so doing, it creates a second level of cultural needs, or instrumental needs, which are satisfied with instrumental cultural responses. Instrumental responses create integrative cultural needs, which, in turn, are satisfied by integrative cultural responses. This whole theoretical hierarchy of needs and responses that themselves become needs was inspired by Malinowski's fieldwork in the Trobriands, where, according to his own diary, he suffered because his basic biological needs were not being satisfied in a "foreign" culture.

In recent years, historians of anthropology have set their sights beyond the mainstream national anthropological traditions of Britain, France, and the United States. Increasingly, they have recognized not only the international character of anthropology but also the diversity of cultural contexts that nurture anthropologists and their theories. A prime example is Malinowski, whose Polish roots, previously glossed over, are now being investigated. These roots will probably be more conspicuous in future histories of British social anthropology.

E.E. Evans-Pritchard

A second generation of British social anthropologists followed in Radcliffe-Brown's and Malinowski's footsteps and broadened their anthropological path. Perhaps most notable among this cadre was Edward Evan Evans-Pritchard (1902-1973).

Unlike his predecessors, E.E. Evans-Pritchard developed a distinctively historicist perspective that was at the time unique within British social anthropology and which created a certain affinity between his work and that of his American peers. It is, accordingly, the paradox and genius of Evans-Pritchard's legacy that, although his theory perhaps represents the apogee of structural-functionalism in the tradition of Radcliffe-Brown, it also addresses those issues of overriding concern to later generations of anthropologists. Increasingly throughout his career, Evans-Pritchard opposed the positioning of anthropology as an experimental or natural science. Instead, he preferred to regard it as one of the humanities and saw the proper role of the ethnographer as an interpreter of history and cultural meaning. For this reason, many have felt that he might justifiably be cited as the father of interpretive or **symbolic anthropology**. More than any other figure of his generation, working within the structural-functionalism established by Radcliffe-Brown, Evans-Pritchard moved Radcliffe-Brown's science-oriented British social anthropology in a more "cultural" direction by proposing that the best approach to investigating social structure was to frame it as a series of flexible, logical, cognitive "maps" giving form and meaning to social behaviour.

SYMBOLIC ANTHROPOLOGY The anthropological school, associated with Victor Turner, espousing the view that social solidarity is a function of the systems of symbolic logic that connect people.

Between the 1920s and 1940s, Evans-Pritchard established a reputation as an East Africanist, composing a number of elegant ethnographic studies based on his fieldwork among the Azande and Nuer societies of the southern Sudan; best known among them are *Witchcraft, Oracles, and Magic Among the Azande* (1937), *The Nuer* (1940), *African Political Systems* (1940, with Meyer Fortes), *Kinship and Marriage Among the Nuer* (1951), and *Nuer Religion* (1956). Particularly in his work among the Nuer, he revisited Radcliffe-Brown's notion

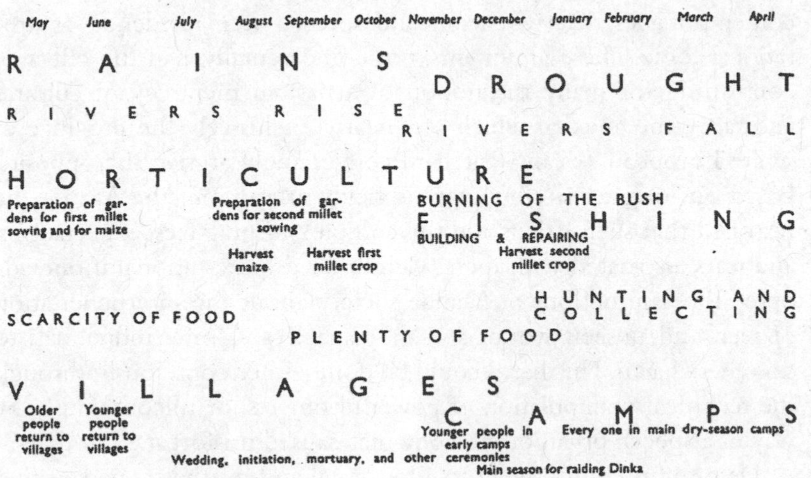

Nuer Seasonality

This is how British social anthropologist E.E. Evans-Pritchard summarized the seasonality of the Nuer of eastern Africa in 1940.

of social structure and rejected the idea that societies are best understood through the machine-like organismic analogy. In a manner that prefigured the work of Lévi-Strauss and Clifford Geertz, Evans-Pritchard chose instead to seek interpretations of cultural structures that provided meaning for members of a society by weaving together various aspects of life experience. For example, the Nuer are possessed of a unified cultural structure, or system of abstract logic, that informs *both* the ideas that individuals have about ecology, space, time, and kinship, *and* the social relations and practices that are generated by these ideas.

In addition to his reputation as a prolific fieldworker, Evans-Pritchard is also legendary for having been an early champion of the cause of cultural relativism. Unlike his American peer, Boas, for whom a relativistic perspective derived from his conviction that different societies have fundamentally incommensurable historical experiences, Evans-Pritchard was primarily concerned to prove the coherence and logic of what many anthropologists and philosophers (notably the French scholar, Lucien Lévy-Bruhl [1857-1939]) took to be "primitive" thought, in order to show that the capacity for order and rationality was not limited to the Western world but was, rather, a *sine qua non* of all human social life. Famously, he set out to affirm the logic of the primitive world view in his ethnographic masterpiece *Witchcraft, Oracles and Magic Among the Azande* (1937). Evans-Pritchard rejected arguments set out by some of his contemporaries that witchcraft and sorcery were evidence of pre-rational logic. These arguments, not coincidentally, had the effect of confirming for many the notion of a natural hierarchy of cultures and races, the apex of which was nearly exclusively the province of white Europeans. Evans-Pritchard convincingly argued the opposite. Based on long-term ethnographic fieldwork among the Azande, he reasoned that such beliefs and the complex of practices, expectations, and fears associated with them, were indeed quite rational if one adopted the assumptions of Azande society about the interpenetration of seen and unseen worlds and the capacity of some individuals to do others harm. This harm could be done either consciously, through the technical manipulation of powerful objects, or unconsciously, by way of a special organ of the body that caused misfortune in others.

Despite his commitment to a historical and relativistic perspective, it is of some irony that Evans-Pritchard's work is frequently cited as an excellent example of research conducted under the shadow of European colonialism in Africa. While recognizing his contributions, latter-day political-economic and postmodern critics of the "**colonial encounter**" have also viewed his research, and that of others of his generation, as being both morally tainted and theoretically suspect. Nevertheless, even his harshest critics recognize the careful thought, eloquent prose, and eye for detail that informed Evans-Pritchard's ethnographic writing.

COLONIAL ENCOUNTER The historical encounter between European colonizers and the Indigenous peoples of the world, who were then often marginalized or oppressed by colonialism.

Max Gluckman and the "Manchester School"

Max Gluckman (1911-1975) is recognized by many within the British anthropological tradition as the figure most responsible, perhaps even more so than Edmund Leach, for infusing Radcliffe-Brown's formulation of social structure with an intensive focus on the mechanisms of social control and change. Ethnographically he helped to train a generation of anthropologists through his association with the **Rhodes-Livingstone Institute** (later, the Zambian National Research Institute) in the late 1930s and early 1940s; under his tutelage, such important figures as Victor Turner helped shift the focus in British social anthropology away from largely static and atemporal social structure towards a concern for dynamic **social process**.

RHODES-LIVINGSTONE INSTITUTE A research institute in Zambia that conducted much ethnographic research in the final years of British colonialism, later called the Zambian National Research Institute.

SOCIAL PROCESS According to late structural-functionalism, social change as the ongoing creation of a fluid, dynamic social structure.

A South African who had received his doctoral training in social anthropology at Oxford University, Gluckman was especially concerned to identify and explain the dynamics of social equilibrium and change in southern Africa. In 1949, following his association with the Rhodes-Livingstone Institute and after several years at Oxford University, Gluckman founded the department of social anthropology at the University of Manchester, where he established a coterie of students committed to his distinctive approach to processual and political theoretical exposition. This fabled **Manchester School** of social anthropology was responsible for producing a number of the key texts in anthropology of the 1950s and 1960s, all of which bore the mark of Gluckman's influence. His own body of work included a number of classics in the subgenres of political and legal anthropology (which he created), including *Rituals of Rebellion in Southeast Africa* (1954), *Custom and Conflict in Africa* (1955), *Order and Rebellion in Tribal Africa* (1963), and *Politics, Law and Ritual in Tribal Society* (1965).

MANCHESTER SCHOOL A coterie of anthropologists trained under Max Gluckman at Manchester University in the 1950s and 1960s.

The distinctive character of Gluckman's research and theory derived from its overarching concern with the nature of social stability and its inverse, social change, interests that led him and his students to develop an original body of research in urban areas as well as the traditionally rural environments studied by anthropologists. In particular, the urbanizing and industrializing **Copperbelt** of central Africa, a region that straddles Zambia and the Democratic Republic of Congo, was an important site of research for a number of anthropologists working out of the Rhodes-Livingstone Institute, who sought to better understand processes of rural-urban migration.

COPPERBELT A region of central Zambia and the Democratic Republic of Congo that served as a research site for Max Gluckman and other associates of the Rhodes-Livingstone Institute.

With respect to anthropological theory, Gluckman is especially well known for developing the notion that all societies incorporate what he termed **rituals of rebellion**. These, he argued, were important "release valves" for any social order, because of their potential to minimize real conflict by sublimating it within ritual performance. Such performances were powerful because of their capacity to draw attention both to conflict itself and to the need for legitimate authority to contain disruptions of the social order. In this way, social stability was maintained through the incorporation of tension and hostility into conventional and socially legitimate ritual. Local ideas about law and legality played a large role in this approach, because of the influence that Gluckman believed these had on the adjudication of disputes and conflict.

RITUALS OF REBELLION A phrase coined by Max Gluckman to describe the socially constructive role of ritual in helping to avoid real conflict.

The Legacy of British Social Anthropology

From the remainder of an exceptionally large and diverse corpus of British research, theoretical insight, and biography, a few additional contributors to the first decades of social anthropology merit attention. In the main, as Evans-Pritchard had done, the most significant ethnographic monographs from the 1930s through the 1960s expanded upon and gave cultural, historical, and/or political "teeth" to the structural-functionalist admonitions of Radcliffe-Brown.

Prominent among these additional contributors was Raymond Firth (1901-2002), whose 600-plus page monograph, *We the Tikopia* (1936), helped transform prevailing notions of what structural-functionalist ethnography could be by adding considerable historical and economic depth to his analysis of society in the Solomon Islands. Also, Edmund Leach's lauded work *Political Systems of Highland Burma* (1954) infused Durkheimian structural-functional analysis, to that point predicated on the notion of a pre-reflective social solidarity, with a structuralism inspired by his celebrated "conversion" to the work of Lévi-Strauss, which led to the idea that common social conventions and institutions might be shared by otherwise very diverse linguistic and cultural groups. Likewise, Meyer Fortes (1906-1983) wrote prolifically concerning the complexity of social relations in Ghana (see, for instance, *The Web of Kinship Among the Tallensi* [1949]) and drew sharp distinctions between the kind of social mechanisms responsible for creating solidarity in the domestic familial sphere (psychological and moral) and those responsible for maintaining solidarity within the larger jural and political **descent group**.

DESCENT GROUP Individuals who perceive themselves to be descended in a lineage from a real or hypothetical common ancestor.

In addition to these, Victor Turner (1920-1983), a student of Gluckman's, cultivated an extremely influential body of process-oriented research on social organization among the Ndembu of Zambia, before going on to be the pre-eminent figure in British symbolic anthropology. At an early stage in his career, the monograph *Schism and Continuity in an African Society* (1957) proved to be, perhaps, the most politically sophisticated structural-functional monograph of the period.

Lastly, the influence of British research, especially in the personage of Radcliffe-Brown, was such that it also had a sustained impact in Boasian America, where Fred Eggan, who partially converted to structural-functionalism as a result of his interaction with Radcliffe-

Brown in Chicago, infused the epistemology with his own diachronic and historical perspective.

The colonial encounter spoken of by later generations of anthropologists loomed large in the research of British social anthropologists in the first half of the twentieth century. This was primarily because the British Empire, a colonial power of global influence, occupied many territories, especially in Africa, perceived by all as ripe for ethnographic fieldwork—all, that is, except their Native inhabitants. Accordingly, many anthropologists, including Evans-Pritchard, Fortes, and Gluckman, set about conducting intensive fieldwork among people who had little choice but to bear the presence of these intrusive strangers for what were often long periods of time.

In 1940, Fortes and Evans-Pritchard published *African Political Systems*, a controversial book of essays on African ethnography. Some of these essays aimed to counter the contention of evolutionary anthropologists that the evolution of pristine political organization, contrasted with kinship organization, was linked to high population density. The authors cited African examples to show that, contrary to this linkage, some groups with low population density had political organization, while other groups with high population density lacked political organization. Anthropologists critical of British social anthropology have used *African Political Systems* to illustrate the shortcomings of this approach, which, they argue, paid insufficient attention to African history and, therefore, failed to recognize that these ethnographic exceptions were evolutionary distortions caused by colonialism and slavery. British social anthropologists have also been criticized for implicitly and explicitly supporting the British foreign policy of **indirect rule**, which relied on ethnographic knowledge to manipulate, co-opt, and cooperate with Native leaders, thus avoiding the need to govern by deployment of brute force.

INDIRECT RULE The British colonial policy of co-opting Native leaders in order to avoid having to govern by force.

Malinowski and Radcliffe-Brown were antagonists who sparred over theoretical details and never managed to agree on who the *real* functionalist was. Given the eventual rejection of functionalism as an epistemology in anthropology, this turned out to be a moot point, and the melodrama and rhetoric that characterized these early debates today seem somehow quaint. Nevertheless, it should not be forgotten that together, like Franz Boas, their counterpart in the United States, Malinowski and Radcliffe-Brown gave British anthropology distinction and a twentieth-century identity that was grounded in empirical research and rigorous theory rather than the arm-chair speculation and hypothesizing of unilineal evolutionists like Tylor and Morgan.

While Malinowski's variety of biocultural functionalism was the first to be discredited and discarded (together with his conclusions and personal biases) by his disciplinary progeny, his painstaking, long-term ethnographic fieldwork among the Trobriand Islanders continues to be the paradigmatic model for all graduate students heading "into the field." Likewise, the detail and quality of his numerous monographs established a seminal style of data analysis as literary genre that has yet to be displaced as a vehicle for the exposition of research within sociocultural anthropology. Just as importantly, the structural-functionalism pioneered by Radcliffe-Brown served as a bridge between the seminal work of Émile Durkheim and the interests of a second and then a third generation of British social anthropologists peopled by scholars of such high calibre and diverse abilities as Evans-Pritchard, Fortes, Leach, Gluckman, Firth, Douglas, and Turner. These anthropologists were able to combine notions of structure with a political and cultural nuance and sophistication that still stands up to scrutiny in the twenty-first century.

SPEAKING ABOUT ANTHROPOLOGICAL THEORY

Lee D. Baker

Anthropology as a social science has always articulated an authoritative discourse regarding race, racism, and culture; as well, politicians, philanthropists, and activists have always called upon anthropology to help support particular projects. Sometimes anthropology has been used to advance equality and achieve justice, while other times it has been called to defend segregation and maintain oppression. Anthropology is always in dialogue and within a dialectal relationship with race, language, and culture. As both discourse and discipline, it has shaped the subject with which it holds authority; at the same time, it has achieved authority because it resonated with people's world view within powerful institutions. Of equal import, however, the science of race and culture itself has been shaped by changes in race relations and shifting ideas regarding culture. The production of anthropological knowledge is always tethered to the society in which that knowledge is produced, and like all social sciences, it has neither been an objective nor a disinterested science.

Anthropological theory is never produced in a context-less sterile laboratory, ivy-covered college, or granite-blocked museum. For the most part, anthropological theory has been produced by affluent white men who were studying black and brown people who were often viewed as out of the way and remote. Often, these scientists had personal stakes in the subjects whom they were studying and partisan-like perspectives on the way their research should be read and interpreted.

I study the history of anthropology in the United States, and I pay particular attention to the way anthropology is appropriated within public policy, popular culture, and the law. Anthropology is part of history and history is part of anthropology. Although understanding the history of ideas is important, understanding how and why those ideas shaped history is even more exciting because this enables us to understand both the limits of anthropology as well as the opportunities anthropology can provide to make a better, more just world.

By evaluating anthropological theory and the role anthropology has played in history, we can also understand the role it can and does play today. Anthropology today is an important but somewhat marginal social science when compared to psychology, economics, and sociology. An important question is, why? In the late nineteenth and early twentieth centuries, anthropology was one of the most powerful and important social sciences, but after World War II, it became an unreliable narrator in the story of white supremacy, imperial desires, and colonial exploits; at the same time, as it became less scientific and more literary, anthropology became a more reliable partner in the quest for civil and human rights. The legacy and history of anthropological theory is much more than a collection of abstruse writings by a bunch of dead white guys; it is the foundation of anthropology today. One of the more popular Adinkra symbols of the Akan of Ghana is the image of the Sankofa bird, which looks backwards with an egg in her bill. It is used to inform people that in order to move forward wisely in the future, one must understand the past. The same holds true about the history of anthropological theory.

Lee D. Baker is an Associate Professor of Cultural Anthropology and African and African American Studies at Duke University. He is author of *From Savage to Negro: Anthropology and the Construction of Race, 1896-1954* (Berkeley, CA: University of California Press, 1998), editor of *Life in America: Identity and Everyday Experience* (Oxford, UK: Blackwell, 2003), and editor of the journal *Transforming Anthropology*. He has also written many articles and essays on the history of anthropology. He is currently working on a book entitled *Performers, Reformers, and Racists; or a History of Anthropology*.

PART THREE

The Later Twentieth and Early Twenty-First Centuries

Early in the twentieth century, both the British and French schools of social research fell heavily under the sway of Émile Durkheim and his intellectual progeny, especially Mauss, Lévi-Strauss, and Radcliffe-Brown. In North America, meanwhile, an altogether different configuration of anthropological knowledge was taking shape under the careful tutelage of Franz Boas. Unlike the structuralist and functionalist perspectives espoused by the Europeans, American anthropologists cultivated an avowedly historical approach that emphasized the radical diversity of cultural form, rather than its psychosocial solidarity. Despite its emphases on change through time and empiricism, this epistemology of culture historicism often sacrificed breadth of analysis for the sake of precision. As a result, even those innovations made by Mead and Kroeber, and later by cognitive anthropologists, have been seen by subsequent generations as theoretically impoverished. The perceived central weakness of historical particularism was precisely its inability to grasp broader cross-cultural historical patterns and processes.

In the later decades of the twentieth century, this tension between the particular and the general was to emerge as a central problem on both sides of the Atlantic for the rapidly expanding discipline of anthropology. While the nineteenth-century evolutionist schemes developed by Morgan and Tylor no longer seemed tenable to the increasingly sophisticated student of culture, the largely descriptive approach championed by Boas also seemed inadequate, in that it suffered from a dearth of explanatory theory. By midway through the twentieth century, many anthropologists felt the need for approaches that charted a middle course between these extremes—for approaches that united historical change and variation with social structure and integration, all within an analytically powerful body of theory.

In filling this lacuna, the work of several anthropologists, including Leslie White, Julian Steward, and Marvin Harris, has been very influential. One of the most enduring and influential twentieth-century perspectives for anthropology, particularly in its most recent schools and epistemologies, is that of Max Weber. As well, other theoreticians have broken new ground in the study of human social and cultural life.

Cognitive Anthropology

COGNITIVE ANTHROPOLOGY The school concerned with folk taxonomies and semantic domains as practised in ethnolinguistics and by ethnoscientists in the New Ethnography.

EMIC In the theory of cultural materialism, the epistemological perspective of the investigated, or "the insider point of view"; contrasted with etic.

ETIC According to Marvin Harris, the epistemological perspective of the investigator, or "the outsider point of view"; contrasted with emic.

PHONEMICS The study of linguistic meaning created by sounds.

PHONETICS The study of linguistic sounds that create meaning.

Cognitive anthropology was rooted in Boasian cultural relativism with input from anthropological linguistics. Its theoretical orientation was **emic**, contrasted with **etic**. This contrast originated in the 1950s with linguist Kenneth Pike (1912-2000), who made an analogy with the contrast between **phonemics** and **phonetics** in linguistics. Phonemics is the study of linguistic *meaning*, while phonetics is the study of linguistic *sounds*. Linguistics can study the sound systems of languages by themselves, with language speakers supplying raw data. To discover which sounds are meaningful, however, they must rely on language speakers as authorities. Phonetics represents the point of view of the "outsider," the linguist investigator, while phonemics represents the point of view of the "insider," the speaker being investigated. Relating this distinction to the anthropological fieldwork technique of participant-observation, Pike decided that participation was "emic" because, in principle, its goal was to enable anthropologists to think and behave like Native peoples, while observation was "etic" because its goal was to have anthropologists remain detached. The emic approach was "seeing things from the Native's point of view," which, according to Pike, would promote cross-cultural understanding and combat ethnocentrism in accordance with the doctrine of cultural relativism. Pike advocated both emic and etic approaches to anthropology, but he preferred the emic.

Edward Sapir

Another precursor to cognitive anthropology was the Sapir-Whorf hypothesis, named after anthropological linguist Edward Sapir and his associate Benjamin Lee Whorf. Sapir (1884-1939) was a student of Boas and close friend of Benedict and Mead. Like them, he wrote

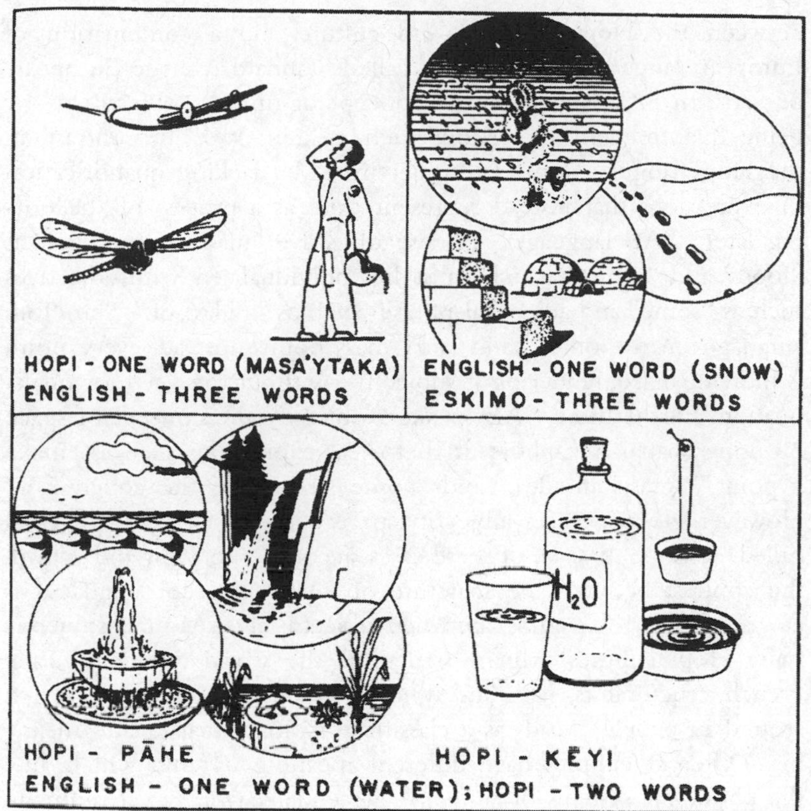

The Sapir-Whorf Hypothesis

The hypothesis of Edward Sapir and Benjamin Lee Whorf states that languages, in this case Hopi and English, classify experiences differently.

poetry and explored the relationship between personality and culture. Talented both artistically and mathematically, Sapir devoted most of his career to the study of language, first in Canada, then at the University of Chicago, and finally at Yale University, where he co-founded the anthropology department. Whorf (1897-1941) worked for an insurance company in Hartford, Connecticut, not too far from Yale in New Haven, where he met Sapir. Under Sapir's influence, Whorf disciplined his penchant for philosophizing about the relationship between language and culture and in the 1930s collaborated with Sapir in the formulation of their hypothesis.

The Sapir-Whorf hypothesis expresses the view that the mental structures of languages and cultures are correlated—the one influences the other, and vice versa. Sapir and Whorf were especially interested in the influence of language on culture, which Whorf in particular held to be significant. Their chief example was a contrast between the Hopi language and culture and a combination of European languages and cultures called Standard Average European, or SAE. In SAE languages, the concept of time is "objectified" by being quantified in expressions such as "ten days." In contrast, in the Hopi language, time is "subjectified" by lacking quantification in expressions that instead represent time as a process of "becoming later." SAE languages also use objective "mass" nouns such as "food" and "water," which must be individualized with adjectives such as "some" and adjectival phrases such as "a glass of." The Hopi language on the other hand lacks mass nouns; instead, every noun is individualized, rendering it subjective without the need for qualification. Furthermore, SAE speakers objectify the concept of space by using spatial metaphors in rhetorical expressions such as "make a point," "grasp an idea," and "come straight to the conclusion." However, Hopi speakers subjectify space with special parts of speech called "tensors." In each of these cases, according to Sapir and Whorf, the contrast between the structure of SAE and Hopi languages is correlated with a contrast between objectifying SAE and subjectifying Hopi cultures, which "structure" the world differently. Like French structuralists, Sapir and Whorf believed that culture is carried around in people's heads as a classificatory logic that creates meaning. Different cultures have different meaning systems, which, like the phonemic systems of language, are equally worthy yet mutually incomprehensible in the absence of a means of cross-cultural communication.

ETHNOLINGUISTICS The name for linguistically oriented research methods of cognitive anthropology.

NEW ETHNOGRAPHY A name for cognitive anthropology focusing on the methodologies of ethnoscience and ethnolinguistics.

SEMANTIC DOMAIN A mental domain of cultural meaning that is the focus of inquiry in cognitive anthropology.

COMPONENTIAL ANALYSIS A research technique of cognitive anthropologists used to generate folk taxonomies of semantic domains.

Ethnoscience and the "New Ethnography"

Cognitive anthropology emerged during the 1960s when a faction of American anthropologists, growing out of the tradition of Boas, sought to make their emic orientation explicit and, inspired by linguistics, improve their methodological rigour. The school, sometimes called ethnoscience, **ethnolinguistics**, or the **New Ethnography**, is best known for its investigative techniques, devised mainly by practitioners Harold Conklin (b.1926), Charles Frake (b.1930), and Ward Goodenough (b.1919). The object of these techniques was to describe Native cognition, or perception, as a **semantic domain**, or domain of meaning, with a cognitive "code" that could be "cracked." The most compelling technique of this sort was **componential analysis**, which generated **folk taxonomies** of meaning resembling the Linnaean taxonomy of Western biology. Just as the Linnaean taxonomy classifies living things using a hierarchy of categories defined by biological criteria, folk taxonomies classify cultural realms using hierarchies of categories defined by cultural criteria. The goal of componential analysis was to uncover these criteria. By interviewing Native informants in the manner of anthropological linguists, who utter contrasting sounds and then ask informants whether the contrasts are meaningful, componential analysts produced "cultural grammars," or "maps" of semantic domains, ranging from Subanum boils and Zeltal firewood to "ethnobotanical" classifications of Amazonian pharmaceutical plants. Cognitive anthropologists shared the view that culture is a formal system of rules for thought and behaviour. Unlike in Western biology, however, where the Linnaean classification has traditionally been held to be "right" and folk classifications of living things "wrong," in cognitive anthropology all classifications were treated as culturally context-dependent.

FOLK TAXONOMIES
According to cognitive anthropologists, culturally conditioned maps of semantic domains.

The popularity of cognitive anthropology peaked in the 1960s and then declined, but not before the school had attracted criticism from anthropologists of opposing theoretical orientations, conspicuous among them new cultural evolutionists and materialists.

Cultural Neo-Evolutionism

By the time Franz Boas died, his grip on American anthropology had loosened. In the post-Boasian era, historical particularism faded into the background of an increasingly crowded picture of anthropological theories. One new element in this picture was a revival of a nomothetic anthropology, which had been eclipsed by Boas's preference for idiographic approaches. The search for cross-cultural generalizations was aided by the Human Relations Area Files, established in the 1940s by George Peter Murdock (1897-1985) at Yale University and used in the 1950s to do research for Whiting and Child's *Child Training and Personality*. The outstanding new nomothetic theory was **cultural neo-evolutionism**, a reformulation of nineteenth-century classical cultural evolutionism that in some ways was *anti*-Boasian.

CULTURAL NEO-EVOLUTIONISM
Twentieth-century cultural evolutionism, a revival and reformulation of classical cultural evolutionism.

The new cultural evolutionism was thc brainchild of four American anthropologists: Leslie White (1900-1975), Julian Steward (1902-1972), Marshall Sahlins (before his conversion to French structuralism), and Elman Service (1915-1996), with input from British archaeologist V. Gordon Childe (1892-1957). All played significant roles in the development of neo-evolutionist theory, and their perspectives are worth discussing in some detail. In addition to Childe's contribution, cultural evolutionism also had a significant impact in the subdiscipline of archaeology, where it informed a body of new theory called the **New Archaeology.**

NEW ARCHAEOLOGY The nomothetic archaeology advocated by Lewis Binford; also called processual archaeology.

Leslie White

Leslie White was an anthropologist trained in the Boasian tradition but who broke rank with Boas radically during his long career at the University of Michigan. His Marxist, or Marxist-like, orientation made him a controversial figure both on campus and in the anthropology profession, so much so that he was investigated by the FBI. White's views are summarized in two books: *The Science of Culture* (1949), a collection of essays, and *The Evolution of Culture* (1959), an exposition of the course and process of evolution.

CULTUROLOGY Leslie White's name for the nomothetic study of culture.

THERMODYNAMICS The study of conversion of energy in the universe, a fundamental part of culturology as expressed in the second law of thermodynamics.

SECOND LAW OF THERMODYNAMICS The scientific proposition that the universe is running down, thereby increasing disorder, or entropy.

ENTROPY Disorder in the universe, increasing according to the second law of thermodynamics.

THERMODYNAMIC LAW E × T > P, or energy times technology yields cultural product, the nomothetic basis of Leslie White's culturology.

White considered culture to be a system of its own kind, *sui generis*, akin to Kroeber's concept of the superorganic. Cultural "laws" would constitute the science of **culturology**. The linchpin of the system was **thermodynamics**, the study of the conversion of forms of energy in the universe. White was impressed with the **second law of thermodynamics**, which stated that the universe is running down structurally and dynamically, resulting in increased **entropy**, or disorder. According to White, biological evolution works in the opposite direction, taking "negative entropy" from the universe and increasing order in the production of complex forms of life. Cultural evolution, which supplants biological evolution in the case of *Homo sapiens* and ancestral species, enhances this trend. To explain the evolution of culture, White proposed a **thermodynamic law**: culture evolves as the amount of energy harnessed per capita per year is increased or as the efficiency of the means of putting this energy to work is increased. The law was symbolized E × T > P—energy times technology yields cultural product. White defined four major stages of cultural evolution, each of which began with an energy "revolution." The first revolution was the invention of tools, which increased the ability of the human body to obtain food calories. The second was the "Neolithic Revolution," a term coined by archaeologist Childe

Leslie White (1900–1975)

White was the leading exponent of mid-twentieth century cultural neo-evolutionism.

to describe the increased control over food energy achieved by the domestication of plants and animals. The third and fourth revolutions were the harnessing of fossil fuels in the eighteenth century and atomic energy in the twentieth century. In between these revolutions, culture evolved as the technology for using these new energy sources improved.

An integral part of White's thermodynamic system was his **layer-cake model of culture**, a depiction of culture comprising a layer of technology and economy at the bottom, a layer of ideology at the top, and a layer of social and political organization in between. In the "determination" of cultural evolution, the bottom layer predominated, because innovations in technology and energy took place there. In assigning priority to technology and economy over ideology as the impetus for cultural change, White was an avowed

LAYER-CAKE MODEL OF CULTURE Leslie White's model of culture, with technology and economy at the bottom, ideology at the top, and social and political organization in between.

cultural materialist. Some of his materialism came from Marxism, which he is alleged to have "discovered" on a trip to the Soviet Union in the 1920s. Connected to Marxism was the work of Lewis Henry Morgan, whose views on the importance of private property impressed Friedrich Engels. White also "discovered" Morgan and became determined to rehabilitate Morgan's reputation as a cultural evolutionist while criticizing Franz Boas for bringing that reputation into disrepute. White's criticism of Boas (posthumously) was even stronger than Derek Freeman's criticism of Margaret Mead.

Julian Steward

While White was promulgating evolutionism in Michigan, an antagonist was gathering strength in Illinois: Julian Steward, the "father" of modern **cultural ecology**. Steward, another Boasian by intellectual upbringing, was a long-time professor at the University of Illinois, who influenced a host of distinguished political and economic anthropologists, including Morton Fried, Andrew Vayda, Eric Wolf, and Elman Service. Cultural ecology nurtured a nomothetic approach to anthropology because it focused on the articulation between culture and nature, linking anthropology to nomothetic natural sciences such as biology, demography, and chemistry. Steward's work grew out of the "culture area" concept used by Boasians Alfred Louis Kroeber and Clark Wissler to demarcate American Native groups. Each group inhabited a geographical area to which, through culture, it adapted. **Adaptation** became the rubric of cultural ecology. In 1936, Steward published a seminal essay on the economic and social basis of bands. In this essay he defined **band** as distinguished from what Service later called "tribe," "chiefdom," and "state." He also defined three types of bands—patrilineal, matrilineal, and "composite"—and linked each type to particular ecological circumstances. Steward's approach prompted some Boasians to rethink their eclectic approach to anthropological explanation and concentrate instead on cultural ecology. The result was a reinterpretation of some famous ethnographically reported events, notably the Northwest Coast ceremony of the **potlatch**, which Ruth Benedict had depicted as a conspicuously wasteful drive for social status but which Helen Codere and Wayne Suttles later explained as an ecologically adaptive redistributive feast.

CULTURAL ECOLOGY The examination of interactions between cultural and environmental variables.

ADAPTATION In cultural ecology, the result of cultures adjusting to environments, or in Darwinian evolution, the result of natural selection.

BAND The simplest form of human social organization, placed in evolutionary sequence before the tribe, chiefdom, and state.

POTLATCH A Pacific Northwest Native ceremony characterized by conspicuous exchange and consumption of goods.

As a cultural ecologist, Steward was not primarily a cultural evolutionist. Nevertheless, he took enough interest in evolutionism to find White's pronouncements extreme. He distanced himself from White by calling the latter's brand of evolutionism **universal** and his own brand **multilineal**. He called the nineteenth-century brand **unilineal**. Implied by these labels was Steward's view that he was a specialist while White was a generalist. The labels "unilineal" and "multilineal" meant that classical cultural evolutionists believed that evolution proceeds in only one direction and cannot skip stages, whereas Steward believed that evolution can branch off in numerous directions as cultures adapt to varied circumstances. For years, Steward and White sparred over points of cultural evolutionary theory, with Steward accusing White of being so general that he could not explain anything in particular and White accusing Steward of being so particular that he could scarcely be called an evolutionist. It took two of their colleagues, Sahlins and Service, to resolve this dispute in 1960.

UNIVERSAL Pertaining to a single schema for global cultural evolution; contrasted with unilineal and multilineal evolution.

MULTILINEAL According to Max Weber, culture change occurring in fits and starts in different historical contexts; according to Julian Steward, "branching" cultural evolution; contrasted with universal and unilineal cultural evolution.

UNILINEAL Pertaining to the view that cultural evolution proceeds along the same lines everywhere, as in classical cultural evolution; contrasted with multilineal and universal evolution.

Marshall Sahlins and Elman Service

For many years, Marshall Sahlins and Elman Service were colleagues at the University of Michigan, where they worked in close association with Leslie White. A onetime student of Julian Steward, Service maintained an interest in the ecological basis of social groupings, the theoretical framework for his popular text *Primitive Social Organization* (1962). Sahlins began his work in economic anthropology and was a strong proponent of cultural evolutionism and materialism before he began to combine French structural and historical analyses in the late 1960s. In 1960, Sahlins and Service co-authored *Evolution and Culture* in which they sought to reconcile the views of Steward and White. In the time-honoured anthropological tradition of treating biology and culture as analogues, they argued that, like biological evolution, cultural evolution has two different dimensions. The dimension of general evolution was being pursued by White, who was concerned with long-range evolutionary progress and trends, while the dimension of specific evolution was being pursued by Steward, whose explanation of local adaptation was analogous to Darwin's mechanism of natural selection. Having demonstrated that White and Steward were really complementary rather than antagonistic, Sahlins and Service settled down to a decade of work together at Michigan, where, with White, they formed a powerful evolutionary triumvirate. The "Michigan school" influenced a number of other cultural evolutionists and ecologists, for example, Alexander Alland Jr. (b.1931), Robert Carneiro (b.1927), and Yehudi Cohen (1928-1998), who kept the nomothetic approach to cultural anthropology alive. Later, Sahlins moved to the University of Chicago, and Service moved to the University of California at Santa Barbara, Sahlins largely abandoning and Service maintaining their cultural evolutionary orientation.

The New Archaeology

The new cultural evolutionism had a major impact on prehistoric archaeology, mainly through White. Since its establishment in the mid-nineteenth century, prehistoric archaeology had progressed through several stages linked to stages in the development of cultural anthropology. There was **functionalist archaeology**, **Marxist archaeology**, and, under the influence of Boas, **culture-historical archaeology**, represented in the United States by the **Midwestern Taxonomic Method**. Archaeologist Betty Meggers (b.1921), a student of White, was inspired by his thermodynamic formula for cultural evolution, $E \times T > P$. Finding the culture-historical approach unproductive, she decided to apply the formula to archaeology, believing that if archaeologists *knew* technology (T) and environment (E), they could *reconstruct* cultural product (P). This idea was developed further by another student of White's, Lewis Binford (b.1930), who became the leader of the New Archaeology of the 1960s.

FUNCTIONALIST ARCHAEOLOGY Archaeology practiced in accordance with the theory of functionalism.

MARXIST ARCHAEOLOGY Archaeology conducted in accordance with the principles of Marxism.

CULTURE-HISTORICAL ARCHAEOLOGY Archaeology as practiced in the era of Franz Boas's historical particularism.

MIDWESTERN TAXONOMIC METHOD The archaeological classification used in culture-historical archaeology.

Binford grew up with the "old" culture-historical archaeology but changed under the influence of White. He decided that archaeology ought to be an integral part of anthropology because archaeologists and anthropologists share the same goal: to explain similarities and differences among cultures. To "explain" meant to offer generalizations about cultural systems and cultural evolution. Binford acknowledged that cultures change in response to both the natural environment and other cultures, but he maintained that, in explaining change, some parts of culture are more important than others. He rejected the conception of culture as "shared values," a concept promulgated by psychologically oriented students of Boas, such as Benedict and, later, Clyde Kluckhohn (1905-1960), for whom culture was **ethos**, or spiritual character. Instead, Binford adopted White's layer-cake model of culture and argued that, in archaeology, artifacts, as objects of material culture, can reflect all three layers, yielding a well-balanced picture of cultures in the past. To realize this potential, archaeologists need to be trained as ethnologists so they can learn how artifacts function in the present and then "read" these functions back in time. Under Binford's influence, the New Archaeology revived the nineteenth-century "comparative method."

ETHOS A term meaning spiritual character, used by some anthropologists to characterize a whole culture.

Aiming to make archaeology scientific, Binford adopted a number of nomothetic devices. One was the **hypothetico-deductive model** for scientific explanation, developed by philosopher of science Carl G. Hempel. This model directed scientists to hypothesize "covering laws" from which specific circumstances could be deduced—predicted or retrodicted—and then compared with empirical reality. Another was **general systems theory**, a cybernetic model for culture that involved "feedback loops" and "positive," or system-maintaining, and "negative," or system-changing, cause-and-effect chains. Binford argued vigorously against psychological explanations of culture. Like White and Kroeber (when he promoted the concept of the superorganic), Binford opposed the great man theory of history, believing instead that human behaviour is determined by forces—laws—of which individuals are largely unaware and over which they can exert little control.

HYPOTHETICO-DEDUCTIVE MODEL A philosophical model for scientific explanation used in the New Archaeology.

GENERAL SYSTEMS THEORY A cybernetic model for culture used in the New Archaeology.

This hyper-scientific, anti-humanistic, and "positivist" attitude made the new cultural evolutionism and the New Archaeology pills too bitter for many anthropologists to swallow. Because of its preoccupation with cultural process, the New Archaeology came to be called **processual archaeology**. Beginning in the 1980s, it attracted severe criticism from **post-processualists**, who saw in it almost everything that was wrong with modern science. At the same time, in cultural anthropology, "postmodernists" severely criticized modern science for many of the same reasons.

PROCESSUAL ARCHAEOLOGY A name post-processual archaeologists use for the nomothetic New Archaeology.

POST-PROCESSUALISTS Archaeologists critical of the New Archaeology; also called contextual archaeologists.

Cultural Materialism

An important part of the resurgence of nomothetic anthropology in the post-Boasian era was **cultural materialism**, an unabashedly scientific perspective developed by iconoclastic anthropologist Marvin Harris (1927-2001). Harris spent most of his career at Columbia University

CULTURAL MATERIALISM The theory of Marvin Harris that distinguishes emic from etic perspectives and mental from behavioural domains, and that advocates infrastructural determinism.

before moving to the University of Florida. The tenets of cultural materialism can be found in four of his many books: *The Nature of Cultural Things* (1964), *The Rise of Anthropological Theory* (1968), *Cultural Materialism* (1979), and *Theories of Culture in Postmodern Times* (1999). *Cultural Materialism* was his theoretical manifesto.

Marvin Harris

Harris began to develop cultural materialism in an effort to purge modern anthropology of some of the legacy of Boas and continued to develop it in an effort to combat the spread of new nonscientific and antiscientific attitudes in the profession.

Cultural materialism addresses a central problem for scientific anthropology: people can be both subjects and objects of scientific investigation. They can think and say things about themselves, just as scientists think and say things about them. Where, then, does true knowledge reside? The answer, according to Harris, can be found by maintaining two pairs of cross-cutting epistemological criteria: mental versus behavioural domains and emic versus etic domains. The mental domain is what people *think*; the behavioural domain, what people *do*. The emic domain belongs to the participant, the etic domain to the observer. Combined, these two pairs of distinctions yield four epistemological perspectives: the emic behavioural perspective is what people think about their own behaviour; the emic mental perspective is what people think about their own thoughts; the etic behavioural perspective is what the observer observes about other people's behaviour; and the etic mental perspective is what the observer observes about other people's thoughts. While all four perspectives are *possible*, two are *problematic* and ought to be approached with caution. The emic behavioural perspective is problematic because, according to Harris, people can develop **false consciousness** and misrepresent the meaning of their own behaviour to themselves and to others. The etic mental perspective is problematic because it is difficult to find out what is going on inside someone else's head. According to Harris, the etic behavioural and emic mental perspectives lack these drawbacks and are more likely to yield useful information.

FALSE CONSCIOUSNESS In the theories of Marxism and cultural materialism, the capability of people to misrepresent the meaning of their behaviour to themselves and others.

In Harris's understanding of scientific anthropology, there is room for both emic and etic perspectives, but they must be kept separate and maintain their own operational definitions and data languages. In the end, the etic perspective predominates. In emics, the Native informant is the ultimate judge of validity; in etics, it is the scientific observer. Both Natives and scientists can be "objective," but when Natives are objective, they themselves become scientists. For Harris, objectivity is not mere intersubjectivity, or mutual understanding and the ability to participate in one another's cultures; there is only one objective truth—the etic truth of science.

Like White, Harris divided culture into several levels, which form a **universal pattern**. Harris's levels are mode of production, mode of reproduction, domestic economy, political economy, and behavioural superstructure. Each has an etic behavioural dimension and an emic mental dimension. Favouring the etic behavioural dimension, Harris combines the modes of production and reproduction into the component *etic behavioural infrastructure*, combines domestic and political economies into the component *etic behavioural structure*, and relabels behavioural superstructure the component *etic behavioural superstructure*. A fourth component, *mental and emic superstructure*, applied to all levels of the universal pattern. The core of cultural materialism is the principle of **infrastructural determinism**, the name Harris gave to his presupposition that, more often than not, culture changes first in the etic infrastructure and then reverberates through etic structure and superstructure to affect emic superstructure last. In Harris's vocabulary, cultural **idealists** explain culture change as occurring in the opposite direction, while cultural **eclectics** explain culture change inconsistently.

UNIVERSAL PATTERN In cultural materialism, the levels of culture-infrastructure, structure, and superstructure—with emic and etic and mental and behavioural dimensions.

INFRASTRUCTURAL DETERMINISM In Marvin Harris's theory of cultural materialism, the name for the belief that culture change usually begins in the etic infrastructure.

IDEALISTS According to Marvin Harris, followers of cultural idealism, the misguided belief that culture change usually begins in the emic superstructure.

ECLECTICS According to Marvin Harris, anthropologists who are sometimes cultural materialists and other times cultural idealists.

The "materialism" in cultural materialism derives from Marxism, which Harris acknowledged as the source of this part of his theory. But, according to Harris, Marx and Engels omitted mode of reproduction from their formulation; confused mental and behavioural and emic and etic realms; and were saddled with the Hegelian dialectic, a metaphysical rather than scientific principle. Once Harris rid dialectical materialism of these "mistakes," the name cultural materialism seemed more appropriate.

Why infrastructural determinism? According to Harris, it is because infrastructure is the primary interface between culture and nature and the place where people are obliged to start using culture to cope with nature in orderly ways. Scientists, looking for order, are probably going to find it there.

As a theoretical agenda for anthropology, cultural materialism had much in common with neo-evolutionism and the New Archaeology. All three of these approaches are, or were, staunchly pro-science. All have been espoused by forceful anthropology personalities, notably Harris, who spent much of the latter part of his career defending scientific anthropology against inroads by structuralist, symbolic, interpretive, and postmodern approaches. In several high-profile cases, Harris excoriated Lévi-Strauss and other structuralists for their symbolic analyses of myth, hygiene, and cuisine, and he sided with Michael Harner in his debate with structuralist Marshall Sahlins over whether Aztecs practiced cannibalism for calories or religion. In these efforts, he was criticized for theoretical intolerance, "one-sidedness," and a lack of appreciation for alternative "culturally sensitive" ways of doing anthropology. Although the number of Harris's "disciples" remained small, he is widely credited with stimulating polemical discussions that enriched anthropology overall. He also brought anthropology to a wide readership with popular best-selling books such as *Cows, Pigs, Wars, and Witches* (1974), *Cannibals and Kings* (1977), and *America Now* (1981).

Biologized Anthropology

Another, very different intellectual current in late twentieth-century anthropology was the move in some quarters to biologize cultural anthropology. All the earlier Boasian and post-Boasian anthropological "isms" had shared an opposition to such hereditarian interpretations of human cultural variation. "Nurture," not "nature," was a hallmark of early twentieth-century anthropology in Britain, France, and the United States, where anthropologists sought to put much of Darwin's century, the nineteenth century, behind them.

In the decades following World War II, from the late 1940s through the early 1970s, anthropology expanded in universities, especially in North America, where the discipline was organized into the four subdisciplines of cultural, physical (now often called biological), archaeological, and linguistic anthropology. As universities prospered, these subdisciplines grew and became highly specialized, but cultural anthropology dominated, attracting by far the largest number of practitioners and setting the intellectual tone for the profession. Meanwhile, in biological anthropology, specialists such as osteologists, primatologists, and geneticists practiced their trades and were largely ignored by their more academically influential colleagues. But in the 1960s, this relationship changed.

Biology of Behaviour

The impetus for change was the emergence in biological anthropology of an interest in the biology of human *behaviour*. Preliminary explorations of this topic were several "popular" accounts of human aggression, territoriality, and sexuality as "genetic." Two examples were *African Genesis* (1961) and *The Territorial Imperative* (1966) by Chicago playwright and anthropology aficionado Robert Ardrey (1908–1980). Ardrey was captivated by the earlier discovery of South African fossil **australopiths**, an extinct group of ape-like human ancestors. In *African Genesis*, he argued that one species of australopith, *Australopithecus africanus*, killed off another species, *Australopithecus robustus*, and that all modern people are descended from this "killer ape." In other words, violence was "in our genes." In *The Territorial Imperative*, he pursued a similar hereditarian argument, that a primitive human propensity to seek and defend private property made socialist programs of communal property "contrary to human nature." A third, and more notorious, example was *The Naked Ape* (1967) by primate zoologist Desmond Morris (b.1928). Morris attributed all kinds of human characteristics to evolved bipedal locomotion, including pendulous female breasts, which, according to him, evolved as substitutes for female buttocks when males needed a sexual symbol appropriate for "face-to-face" sexual intercourse. Generally, cultural anthropologists and mainstream biological anthropologists disputed the claims of these authors as unsupported by science, and, in disrespect, some dubbed their approach **naked apery.** Nevertheless, in criticizing naked apery as extreme, some anthropologists began to wonder what *might* be true about a biological basis for human nature.

AUSTRALOPITHS Primitive ape-like human ancestors known from fossils found in Africa.

NAKED APERY A disparaging term used to describe unfounded assertions about the inheritance of human behaviour.

Two other anthropologically noteworthy controversies of the 1960s concerned the biological basis of race. The first took place in the early part of the decade following publication of biological anthropologist Carleton Coon's book *The Origin of Races* (1963). Coon (1904–1981) proposed that five major geographical races of the species *Homo sapiens* had originated in the species *Homo erectus* and evolved into *Homo sapiens* separately, the Caucasoid race achieving *sapiens* status first, the Negroid race last. For these views, Coon

SCIENTIFIC RACISM Improper or incorrect science that actively or passively supports racism.

was accused of **scientific racism**. The second controversy took place in the late 1960s when educational psychologist Arthur Jensen (b.1923) proposed that variation in intelligence quotient, or IQ, was predominantly genetic and that the measured 15-point difference in IQ between American blacks and whites could never be entirely eliminated by education. Anthropologists' objections to this proposition were so strong that the term "Jensenism" became synonymous with "racism" in subsequent debates about genes and behaviour. One such subsequent debate was precipitated by Richard Herrnstein and Charles Murray's book *The Bell Curve: Intelligence and Class Structure in American Life* (1994). Herrnstein and Murray argued that variation in intelligence is highly heritable and correlated with variation in social success, making the upper class a kind of "genetic meritocracy." Anthropologists' reactions to *The Bell Curve* were just as negative as they had been to the work of Arthur Jensen. Still, in some quarters, the feeling lurked that Jensen had been treated unfairly, that his research had been rejected for ideological rather than scientific reasons, and that the biological basis of human behavioural differences was a legitimate subject for scientific investigation.

The New Physical Anthropology

In the wake of the scientific and political controversies created by Ardrey, Morris, Coon, and Jensen, other developments brought cultural and biological anthropologists closer together. One such development was promulgation of the **New Physical Anthropology**, launched in the 1950s by biological anthropologist Sherwood L. Washburn (1911-2000).

NEW PHYSICAL ANTHROPOLOGY The name for physical anthropology committed to the synthetic theory of evolution.

The New Physical Anthropology had little to do with the new cultural evolutionism and the New Archaeology launched at approximately the same time. Washburn simply urged biological anthropologists to embrace the Synthetic Theory of Evolution, the synthesis of Darwinism and Mendelian genetics that biologists had achieved in the 1930s. Extended to biological anthropology, this synthesis directed anthropologists to study biological process more than form and to abandon **typological thinking**, or thinking in terms of fixed "pure" races. This change in scientific attitude made biological anthropology more acceptable to cultural anthropologists. Meanwhile, biological anthropologists worked out cultural explanations for the geographical

TYPOLOGICAL THINKING Thinking of biological groups as homogeneous or pure when in fact they are heterogeneous and mixed.

distribution of sickle-cell anemia and intolerance of lactose, or milk sugar. These explanatory successes led to the emergence of the new field of **biocultural anthropology**, aimed at exploring interactions between human biology and culture in accordance with the principles of evolutionary ecology. The resulting cooperation between biological and cultural anthropologists primed some anthropologists to be more receptive to the next wave of biological explanations of human behaviour.

The 1970s saw the emergence, or ascendance, of three such bio-behavioural explanatory approaches, which affected anthropology in varying degrees: human ethology, behavioural genetics, and sociobiology.

Ethology and Behavioural Genetics

The first bio-behavioural approach to come of age in the 1970s, **human ethology**, grew out of animal psychology and zoology and involved a commitment to hereditarian concepts such as **fixed action pattern**, **innate releasing mechanism**, and **key stimulus**. Human ethologists examined both the ontogeny, or individual growth, and phylogeny, or evolutionary growth, of biologically linked behaviours that, in the language of ethology, constitute the **human biogram**. According to ethologists, cultural "universals," like some facial expressions and gestures, are potentially genetic. A diluted form of ethology found its way into the anthropological study of non-verbal communication, or **body language**, in the sciences of **kinesics** and **proxemics**, the studies of body motion and body position. Anthropologists Lionel Tiger (b.1937) and Robin Fox (b.1934) also promoted a diluted form of ethology in books such as *Men in Groups* (1970) and *The Imperial Animal* (1971), where they expounded their views on "natural" human tendencies. While human ethology could trace its lineage back to Charles Darwin's treatise *The Expression of the Emotions in Man and the Animals* (1872), and while it had popular appeal, the approach failed to earn widespread scientific respect. Many critics ended up using the adjective "ethological" to describe *any* proposition that attributed human behaviour to heredity recklessly.

The second bio-behavioural approach to be developed in the period was **behavioural genetics**: the extension of genetic analysis from anatomy and physiology to behaviour, which behavioural geneticists

BIOCULTURAL ANTHROPOLOGY Anthropology aimed at exploring interactions between human biology and culture, usually according to ecology.

HUMAN ETHOLOGY A hereditarian approach to the study of human behaviour, derived in part from Darwinism and employing the analytical constructs of fixed action pattern, innate releasing mechanism, and key stimulus.

FIXED ACTION PATTERN As conceived by human ethologists, an innate sequence of behaviour released by a key stimulus of an innate releasing mechanism.

INNATE RELEASING MECHANISM As conceived by human ethologists, the mechanism that, when triggered by a key stimulus, releases a fixed action pattern.

KEY STIMULUS As conceived by human ethologists, the device that triggers an innate releasing mechanism, thus releasing a fixed action pattern.

HUMAN BIOGRAM A term used in human ethology to describe the alleged suite of inherited predispositions of *Homo sapiens*.

BODY LANGUAGE A colloquial term for non-verbal communication.

KINESICS The scientific study of human body motion.

PROXEMICS The scientific study of posture as a form of non-verbal communication, which is sometimes called "body language."

BEHAVIOURAL GENETICS The branch of genetics that investigates inherited contributions to behavioural differences.

PHENOTYPE The product of gene action, often affected by environment.

POLYGENIC Variation in phenotype affected by the action of many genes.

treat as a **phenotype**, or product of gene action. Behavioural geneticists study both "normal" and "abnormal" behavioural phenotypes in order to determine whether they might have either a simple Mendelian or a more complex **polygenic** component. Some human behavioural geneticists rely on contrasts of behaviours of twins reared together and apart to help them assign the sources of behavioural differences to nature and nurture. Arthur Jensen's investigation of race, genes, and IQ employed some of these techniques, as did *The Bell Curve*. Because behavioural genetics is a highly specialized science published in journals read by few anthropologists, it has proved challenging to mount effective scientific, contrasted with ideological, counter arguments from the anthropological perspective. One set of stimulating counter arguments can be found in Jonathan Marks's book *What It Means to Be 98% Chimpanzee: Apes, People, and their Genes* (2002). Marks urges caution in accepting at face value geneticists' claims to have discovered individual genes that govern human behaviour.

Sociobiology

SOCIOBIOLOGY An investigation of the biological basis of social behaviour using the evolutionary principles of kin selection and inclusive fitness.

The bio-behavioural approach that made the greatest inroads in late twentieth-century anthropology was **sociobiology**. This approach became controversial almost immediately after the publication of Edward O. Wilson's landmark book *Sociobiology: The New Synthesis* (1975).

Wilson (b.1929) was a Harvard University entomologist who had been working on the evolutionary problem of altruism, or self-sacrificing behaviours, such as sterile worker ants devoting themselves to helping a queen ant reproduce. The problem with altruism was how to explain it in terms of Darwinian evolution by natural selection. If altruistic behaviour is genetic, it should be subject to the action of natural selection, but the result of such action should be the *reduction* or elimination of the genes responsible. Still, altruism persisted. How? Earlier zoologists had proposed the mechanism of group selection, whereby individuals sacrifice themselves for the good of groups and then, as group members, benefit indirectly. This mechanism was never entirely convincing, however, so in the early 1970s a number of geneticists proposed the alternative mechanism of **kin selection**. This mechanism became the scientific cornerstone of Wilson's book.

KIN SELECTION In sociobiology, reproductive success via genes shared with relatives; sometimes called the biology of nepotism.

Wilson solved the problem of altruism essentially by defining it out of existence. Altruism is not really altruistic; instead, it is "selfish," as he explained with his new concept of **inclusive fitness**. According to Wilson, the genetic basis of most behaviours is polygenic, meaning the result of the action of multiple genes. Genetic relatives share these genes, so individuals who sacrifice themselves can still transmit their sacrificing genes to future generations, as long as they sacrifice themselves for *relatives*. Sociobiology has been called the **biology of nepotism**, an apt nickname, because sociobiologists predicted that genes incline individuals to behave more favourably to relatives than to non-relatives and more favourably to close relatives than to distant ones. In this way, individuals maximize their inclusive Darwinian fitness and reproductive success. Evolutionary biologist Richard Dawkins (b.1941) captured many of these ideas in the title of his provocative book *The Selfish Gene* (1976).

INCLUSIVE FITNESS
In sociobiology, the measure, or result, of kin selection.

BIOLOGY OF NEPOTISM
A colloquial label for sociobiology focusing on the preferential treatment of kin.

For sociobiology, life is a series of strategic choices in which individuals unconsciously assess the personal costs and benefits of alternative behaviours and end up choosing the alternative with the greatest inclusive yield. Because sociobiologists argued that overall degrees of genetic relatedness can be quantified—parents and children share 50 per cent of their genes, half-siblings 25 per cent, "first" cousins 12.5 per cent, and so forth—they were able to make precise predictions about behaviour and then compare them with empirical reality. To explain altruism among non-relatives, sociobiologist Robert Trivers introduced the supplementary evolutionary mechanism of **reciprocal altruism**. According to reciprocal altruism, individuals behave altruistically toward non-relatives in the understanding that non-relatives will behave altruistically toward them, a kind of Biological Golden Rule.

RECIPROCAL ALTRUISM
In sociobiology, the "Biological Golden Rule," said to account for altruistic behaviour among non-relatives.

Some of the most controversial pronouncements of sociobiology concerned differences between males and females. Both males and females are motivated to maximize their inclusive fitness but, according to sociobiologists, in fundamentally different ways. In species with two distinct sexes, males produce a large number of mobile sperm and do not themselves bear children, while females produce a small number of non-mobile eggs and do bear children. These biological differences imply the evolution of behavioural differences. Males are selected to compete for females because females are a reproductively relevant resource. The reproductive potential of males depends on the number of females they can inseminate. On the other hand, females are selected to resist male advances because, once inseminated, they cannot become pregnant again until after giving birth. The reproductive potential of females depends on the "quality," not quantity, of male suitors. By depicting males as sexually indiscriminate and females as "choosey," sociobiologists exposed themselves to the criticism that they were affirming Western sex-role stereotypes. By proposing that both males and females prefer their "own kind" over "foreigners," sociobiologists exposed themselves to the further charges that they are racist and **xenophobic**.

XENOPHOBIC Pertaining to xenophobia, the fear and dislike of foreigners.

The bulk of Wilson's book focused on insects and other nonhuman animal species. In the final chapter, however, he speculated on how sociobiology might account for at least some of the behaviour of *Homo sapiens*. Later, he and other sociobiologists refined these speculations and developed a scaled-down modified version of "human sociobiology." Human sociobiology, featured in Wilson's book *On Human Nature* (1994), provoked a storm of opposition in anthropology, where culture was held to be vastly more important than biology as the determinant of behavioural differences. Cultural anthropologists as otherwise divergent as cultural materialist Marvin Harris, in *Cultural Materialism*, and structuralist Marshall Sahlins, in *The Use and Abuse of Biology* (1976), united to criticize human sociobiology as erroneous and irrelevant and to condemn it as an ideology of disguised Social Darwinism. This staunch judgement was the opinion of the majority of cultural anthropologists. At the same time, a small minority came to adopt the sociobiological perspective, notably ethnographer Napoleon Chagnon (b.1938), who used it to explain the outcome of matings among South American Yanomamo Indians. In primatology, sociobiology, in one form or another, became a dominant research strategy. A milestone in this regard was *The Langurs of Abu* (1977), a book in which primatologist Sarah Blaffer Hrdy explained how new langur monkey "alpha males" killed the infants of displaced alpha males in order to make the infants' mothers sexually receptive, then impregnated the mothers in order to propagate their own genes. Sociobiology still pervades primatology, often identifiable under the more recent rubric **evolutionary psychology**.

EVOLUTIONARY PSYCHOLOGY An outgrowth of sociobiology that uses Charles Darwin's theory of evolution to explain aspects of human mentality and behaviour as adaptations from the past.

Symbolic and Interpretive Anthropology

Paralleling developments in self-consciously materialist, ecological, and bio-behavioural anthropology in the latter half of the twentieth century was a new concern: understanding the systematic character of cultural meaning. In Britain, the ascendancy of social analysis rooted in Durkheimian structuralism and structural-functionalism had long since begun to show signs of strain. For many anthropologists, including Leach, Gluckman, and their students, the static nature of structural analysis seemed increasingly a fatal flaw, as did an overall lack of focus on the flexible character of social and cultural meaning and its central role in social and political change cross-culturally. One influential answer derived from a new body of research that came to be called symbolic anthropology.

Meanwhile, for a new generation of American anthropologists coming of age in the 1960s in particular, the Boasian-inspired frameworks bequeathed to them by the culture and personality and cognitive schools were inadequate for at least two pivotal reasons. First, they were perceived as being ethnocentrically biased on a number of levels, especially with respect to the supposedly universal importance of the individual psyche; and second, because both bodies of theory were in fact quite schematically rigid, neither was sufficiently able to address the increasingly important theoretical problem of social and cultural change. In the United States, this concern surfaced with, among other influences, the rediscovery of the theories of Max Weber, particularly by the theoretical school that would be known as **interpretive anthropology**.

INTERPRETIVE ANTHROPOLOGY The anthropological school, associated with Clifford Geertz, espousing the view that culture is lived experience integrated into a coherent, public system of symbols that renders the world intelligible.

The rediscovery of Max Weber both reflected and stimulated a new concern for the importance of meaning and the human potential to act creatively in the world. While this had arguably been a concern of cultural anthropologists all along, the essential premise of structuralist theory (in its various guises) was that culture constrained, or controlled, people more than it served, or enabled, them. It was as if people were simply the vehicles for social and psychological structures and not the other way around. This dominion of structures was unacceptable to a growing number of anthropologists, and yet, in the United States, the "obvious" second option—historical particularism in the Boasian tradition—remained equally unpalatable, mainly for its narrowness of focus and its relative lack of theory. An emerging consensus was that ways had to be found to explain society and culture without appealing to minutely controlling social structures or to inaccessible psychological ones. In the 1960s and 1970s, this fresh interest in exploring meaning was expressed in the language of symbols and interpretation.

One of the earliest to adapt Weber's thought to explicitly anthropological analysis was Anthony F.C. Wallace (b.1923). In his influential historical ethnography about the Iroquois, *The Death and Rebirth of the Seneca* (1972), Wallace applied his concept of the **revitalization movement**, which was more fully formulated in his theoretical revitalization work *Religion: An Anthropological View* (1966). In both, the author drew heavily on Weber's idea that during periods of cultural dissonance or crisis, it is the charismatic prophet who rationalizes a new and more satisfying religious world view for the members of a society. A second now-classic Weberian study was Peter Worsley's *The Trumpet Shall Sound* (1968), which describes how many Native peoples of Indonesia and New Guinea are led by a variety of charismatic prophets in a series of millennial "cargo cults." Worsley's and Wallace's studies were strikingly similar in that both sociocultural contexts examined were ones in which colonial powers placed severe economic, political, and cultural stress on the colonized, generating a "breakdown" in the indigenous social order. In both settings, the revitalizing social movements rationalized the impact of colonialism into world views that stipulated the omnipotence of a supernatural power or agent who would ultimately restore harmony and happiness if specific ethical and behavioural criteria were adhered to.

REVITALIZATION MOVEMENT A term coined by Anthony F.C. Wallace to describe the spontaneous evolution of culture that occurs when communities experience conditions of extreme social and economic duress or marginalization.

Wallace's and Worsley's analyses highlighted the socially transformative potential of human agency. They incorporated Weber's synthesis of materialism and idealism, which to some anthropologists seemed more useful than Marx's theory, often viewed as reducing culture to a reflex of material conditions. This particular Weberian theme became conspicuous in the writings of later postmodern anthropologists, for whom cultural **hermeneutics** and relations of political and economic power loomed large.

HERMENEUTICS The study of meaning, especially in literary texts, applied by interpretive and postmodern anthropologists to the study of culture.

In addition, the roots of what came to be called symbolic anthropology in Great Britain and interpretive anthropology in the United States can be traced back, at least indirectly, to the neo-Kantian philosophy of Wilhelm Dilthey (1833-1911) and others, who helped formulate the distinction between the natural sciences, or *naturwissenschaften*, and social sciences, or *geisteswissenschaften*. According to this distinction, promulgated by Franz Boas, the natural sciences deal with entities amenable to generalizations, while the social sciences deal with "mental" entities unique to individuals and groups. To this distinction phenomenologist-philosopher Edmund Husserl (1854-1938) added the observation that natural science is unsuitable for the study of cultural life because cultural life has meaning, which is best understood subjectively as "lived experience."

Husserl's assertions notwithstanding, it would, finally, be difficult to argue that symbolic and interpretive anthropologists were inspired by anything less than a desire to do sound empirical research in the best anthropological tradition. What differentiated symbolic and interpretive anthropologists from their colleagues working in explicitly materialist or ecological traditions was their relentless insistence that human societies are distinctive because of their capacity for culture and that social and cultural life is held together by interpenetrating networks of symbols, each of which is a carrier of cultural meaning. This much, at least, the symbolists and interpretivists had in common. In spite of this underlying similarity, it must be kept in mind that even from the outset, clear differences existed between the two schools and that these differences both derived from, and had a deep impact on, the respective characters of British and American research.

Victor Turner and Symbolic Anthropology

In Britain, the most influential and academically respected symbolic anthropologist was Victor Turner (1920-1983). A student of Max Gluckman, Turner was, like most British anthropologists of his generation, heavily influenced by Émile Durkheim's dictum that social cohesion was achieved "organically" through the interpenetration of a given society's component parts. Like Gluckman, Turner was concerned to expose the political character of social relations, with the general goal of accounting for social coherence, even in contexts where many interpersonal conflicts seemingly threatened to tear a community apart. Fieldwork among the Ndembu of Rhodesia (now Zambia) convinced him of the centrality of ritual, in particular, to the maintenance of social order. This insight garnered the young anthropologist much respect when his findings were published in one of the most important monographs of late structural-functionalism, *Schism and Continuity in an African Society* (1957).

Turner's early perspective on the importance of ritual informed much of his later work and shaped the direction of his theoretical interests. Throughout the 1960s, he continued to move still further afield of the previous generation of structural-functionalists, for many members of which the essence of organic solidarity lay in the concrete institutions and formalized relations of society. Instead, Turner focused on the Durkheimian idea that social solidarity is a function of the systems of symbolic logic that connect people. In this way, his symbolic anthropology had much in common with Lévi-Strauss's structuralism, similarly inspired by Durkheim. Unlike his French peers (indeed, unlike Durkheim himself), for whom symbolic contrasts and correspondences were seen as a universal mental template on which all culture is built, Turner's main innovations in anthropology derived from his view that social unity is basically *problematic* and should not be taken for granted. Whereas Durkheim believed that primitive humankind came together out of some primordial psychological need for togetherness, Turner argued that people are essentially forced to repeatedly construct social life against those forces in the natural world that constantly threaten to destroy it. Because symbols are the primary vehicles whereby this solidarity is organized, they are instruments, or "tools," employed by people to achieve a particular end—the reproduction of social order.

Again drawing on his work among the Ndembu, Turner explored ways in which various objects and actions of ritual are deployed as complex "**instrumental**" **symbols** that are the "means to the ends" of any given ritual, such as rootlets from fruit-bearing trees wielded in the context of ritual with the explicit purpose of enhancing female fertility. At a broader level, another set of symbols, which Turner dubbed "dominant," possessed a role that he considered to be both **multivocal** and ubiquitous, being present in any number of ritual events and being used for a variety of meanings, some of which might represent conflicting interests in the Ndembu community.

Among the many examples Turner explored ethnographically, one that is frequently cited concerns the Ndembu *mudyi* tree. A **dominant symbol** *par excellence*, Turner viewed the *mudyi* tree, which contains a white latex, as the equivalent of a national flag among the Ndembu—a symbol that might, depending on the ritual context,

INSTRUMENTAL SYMBOLS Victor Turner's term for those symbols that can be consciously wielded in ritual as a form of technology in order to achieve particular ends.

MULTIVOCAL The quality of having more than one possible meaning or interpretation.

DOMINANT SYMBOL Victor Turner's term for a symbol with multiple, and sometimes contradictory, meanings.

evoke milk, the kin bonds between mothers and children, and the continuity of Ndembu kinship from one generation to the next. Less harmoniously, Turner deciphered the *Nkang'a*, or girl's puberty ritual, to be an occasion in which Ndembu women's mobilization about the *mudyi* tree symbolized the opposition of females to males, thus revealing the conflicted, rather than consensual, character of the Ndembu social order. For Turner, this was evidence that Ndembu social integration and coherence had to be *forcibly* maintained in light of these and other self-destructive tendencies. He argued that symbolism was the key to understanding this process, because of the dominant symbol's capacity to "stand for unity and continuity in the widest Ndembu society, embracing its contradictions." Much of Turner's theoretical exposition of symbols and symbolic performance was published in a widely read collection of ethnographic essays, *The Forest of Symbols* (1967).

Beyond this extension of Durkheimian theory, Turner is also credited with breathing fresh life into the ideas of Arnold van Gennep (1873-1957), who, much earlier in the twentieth century, had speculated about the "**ritual process**." In his work *The Rites of Passage* (1959), van Gennep argued that ritual involves the passage of individuals from one social state to another and that this entailed three stages: "separation" from the group, "transition" to a new state, and "incorporation" (more properly thought of as "re-incorporation") within the social order.

RITUAL PROCESS Arnold van Gennep's term for the tripartite nature of ritual, involving separation from society, transition to a new social status, and a new incorporation into society.

Intrigued by his predecessor's insights, Turner elaborated his still largely Durkheimian concept of ritual, in which the coming together of individuals involves the performance of solidarity, to include a theory of process largely modeled on van Gennep's concept of "liminality." Turner believed that rituals generate a **liminal** period in which all notions of social "structure" are undone through the physical and symbolic separation of certain individuals from society. In being marked, or set apart, as special, these individuals cease for a period of time to occupy a certain position within the social order and, in effect, are for that period considered both "outside" society and in some cases even a danger to it.

LIMINAL An ephemeral psychosocial space in which social arrangements are subject to transformation, inversion, and affirmation.

This temporary negation of social structure Turner named "**anti-structure**." In many instances, anti-structure and liminality might be observed with respect to particular individuals undergoing transitional "rites" in which they pass from one life stage to another. Examples

ANTI-STRUCTURE According to Victor Turner, the side of culture expressed through ritual "chaos," as during liminal states.

of such events might include coronation ceremonies, death rituals, or the ubiquitous rites of transition from boyhood to manhood and girlhood to womanhood. On a larger scale, anti-structure is more familiar to many in, for instance, the guise of carnival: an event at which the ritualized chaos of anti-structure involves inverting "normal" identities and roles, so that men are ritually transformed into women and women into men, kings into servants and servants into kings, old into young and young into old, and so on.

Anti-structure is possible, Turner argued, because the liminal state is one in which all the limitations of everyday structure are dispensed with and new creative possibilities opened up. A central aspect of this theory is that, throughout all inversion and liminal transformation of norms and identities, members of a society ultimately come to recognize and reaffirm the basic structural cohesion that they had known all along in their routine existence outside of ritual. It is by way of this new-found solidarity, or reintegration, that society avoids the truly revolutionary implications of liminality and is instead fused by what Turner called **communitas**—an increased awareness of the social order, reminiscent of Durkheim's idea that rituals are emotionally effervescent events.

COMMUNITAS A term employed by Victor Turner to refer to the ritual fusion of individuals into a collective identity.

Clifford Geertz and Interpretive Anthropology

In the United States, meanwhile, a new generation of avowedly cultural anthropologists was busily developing its own **semiotic**, or cognition-focused, perspective, which also depended on the social circulation and ritual performance of symbols. The two central players in this evolving Americanist approach were David Schneider (1918-1995) and, especially, the founder of "interpretive anthropology," Clifford Geertz (1926-2006).

SEMIOTIC Pertaining to the relationship between symbols and what they represent.

Whereas Turner derived his core insights from Durkheim, Geertz's intellectual lineage originates with Max Weber, whose emphasis on meaning, as opposed to structure, gave Geertz's work a very different orientation from that of his British counterpart. Taking his cue from Boasian anthropologist Clyde Kluckhohn, Geertz's theory incorporated the idea that at the core of culture is a set of integrated moral values that preserve the correspondence of the world "as it is" with the world "as it should be." More specifically, this prototypical interpretive anthropologist set out to show how lived experience is integrated in a coherent public system of symbols that both renders the world intelligible and seems uniquely suited to do so. For Geertz, this epistemology was deeply grounded in the assumption that "man is an animal suspended in webs of significance that he himself has spun" and that the study of culture is not, therefore, an "experimental science in search of law" but rather "an interpretive one in search of meaning." The meaning Geertz set about describing in his prolific career is not locked inside the discrete psychologies of individuals, however, but in a network of significations that are on public display.

In his enormously influential book, *The Interpretation of Cultures* (1973), Geertz set out his own vision of the ethnographic method, the centrepiece of which was a research technique called "**thick description**." Geertz prescribed this method as the most effective tool in the ethnographer's toolkit for teasing out the "**text**" of culture, that is, the fine details of human life that make behaviour intelligible. "Doing ethnography," he wrote, was like "trying to read ... a manuscript." Geertz held this method to be particularly effective in unraveling the various layers, or "webs," of meaning performed by participants in ritual.

THICK DESCRIPTION In the interpretive anthropology of Clifford Geertz, the process of interpreting culture as text.

TEXT In the interpretive anthropology of Clifford Geertz, the equivalent of culture, interpreted through a process of thick description.

In a famous example that formed the focus of one of the best-known essays in *The Interpretation of Cultures*, Geertz analyzed the "Balinese cockfight" from an interpretive perspective. The significance of the event, he argued, was in its power to convey multiple messages about the cultural "ethos" in which participants lived—a social environment characterized by status competition between individuals sorted into hierarchical, gendered rankings. Tongue deeply in cheek, Geertz offered that men of locally high rank competed with one another by proxy through their "cocks" (i.e., roosters), which fought to the death in primal blood-sport. He hypothesized that when such rivalry occurred between individuals of near or equal ranking, the performative force of the ritual could be said to be emotionally "deep" for onlookers; that is, such rituals were of great social force in imparting a sense of the meaning of social relations. For Geertz, such relations constituted an important theme of the Balinese social order, which, because they lurked just below the level of awareness, had to be symbolically performed in order to have public force. In sum, the cockfight was a symbolic microcosm, or text, of Balinese society, collectively shared by all witnesses to the event. The ritual was, in short, a "story they [the Balinese] tell themselves about themselves."

In the twenty-first century, following the rise of postmodernism, interpretive anthropology seems increasingly anachronistic. Nevertheless, Geertz remains iconic among American anthropologists and is still revered by many for infusing the discipline with a heavy dose of much-needed Weberian corrective to earlier ethnocentric approaches. A prolific writer, Geertz also remains highly respected for his extensive fieldwork in, and ethnographic portraits of, Java, Bali, and Morocco.

Post-processual Archaeology

In the subdiscipline of anthropological archaeology, the interpretive perspective was to find favour as well, especially among those disenchanted with the "excesses" of Lewis Binford's avowedly scientific approach to archaeology. Many archaeologists had been uncomfortable with the so-called New Archaeology and its adherence to key canons of Cartesian rationalism and objectivity. For them, archaeology was allied to history more closely than to science, and, because history was a humanity, the holistic explanations of Boasian particularism seemed more appropriate than the covering-law model and "economic determinism" of Binford. Some of these archaeologists embraced the viewpoint of **critical anthropologists** that science is elitist and those of French structuralists and structural Marxists that material culture has a symbolic dimension, consciousness causes change, and artifacts reflect social relations as well as adaptation to environments.

CRITICAL ANTHROPOLOGISTS Anthropologists who self-reflect and share criticisms of positivism.

In the 1980s, British archaeologist Ian Hodder (b.1948) codified these views into what he called contextual, or "post-processual," archaeology. This new perspective spread with the publication of Hodder's several influential books, notably *Symbolism in Action: Ethnoarchaeological Studies of Material Culture* (1982) and *Reading the Past: Current Approaches to Interpretation in Archaeology* (1986). Echoing the influential French historian Michel Foucault, "**contextual**" refers to Hodder's view that artifacts are embedded in a web of cultural "discourse" that affirms social relations and enhances the power of privileged groups. "Post-processual" referred to his view that the quest to discover law-like processes of culture change, characteristic of the New Archaeology, should be abandoned. A latter-day version of post-processual archaeology is **landscape archaeology**, in which the spatial distribution of artifacts and features is rendered a cultural

CONTEXTUAL Pertaining to post-processual archaeologists critical of the nomothetic New Archaeology.

LANDSCAPE ARCHAEOLOGY Archaeology that considers artifacts and features to be expressions of culture, both incorporating and modifying elements of the natural world.

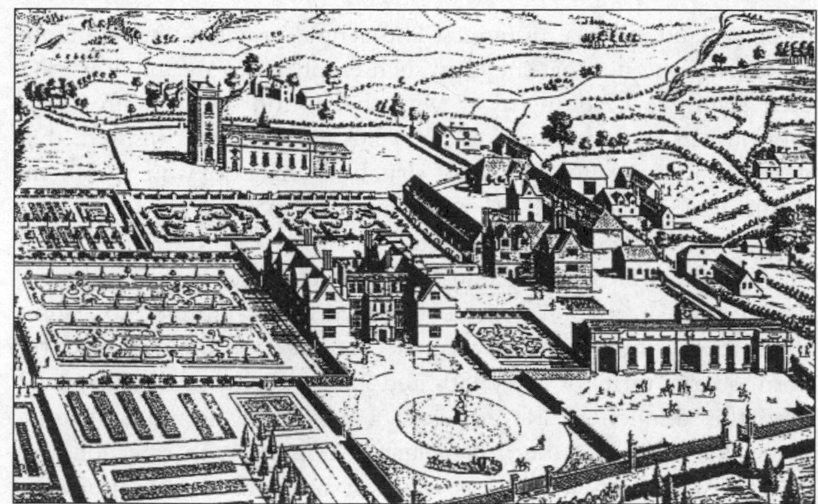

Formal Gardens at Castle Bromwich Hall, West Midlands, England

A "contextual" interpretation of this eighteenth-century archaeological site is that formal gardens make "statements" about socially accessible and inaccessible space.

landscape that both incorporates and modifies meaningful elements of nature. Like symbolists and postmodernists in anthropology, post-processualists in archaeology largely abandoned pure positivist scientific objectivity as an unattainable and undesirable theoretical goal. In so doing, they unsettled the profession and helped pave the way for a new wave of culturally sensitive critiques.

The Influence of Symbolic and Interpretive Approaches

From the 1960s into the 1980s, symbolic and interpretive approaches both expressed and nurtured a growing apprehension within the discipline, namely, that those claims to authoritative knowledge that anthropologists had previously taken for granted were at best tenuous—at least in the cynical environment of the late twentieth-century academy. It is, therefore, ironic that the same cynicism that cultivated the particularistic, neo-Kantian tendencies in that period also gave rise in the mid-1970s to political economy, a perspective that opposes symbolic and interpretive anthropology in its renewed emphasis on history and objectivity. This was not to be the "old" structuralism of classical British and French approaches but a new body of thought heavily inspired by the historicism of Marx and Engels. Cultures, the new anthropological political economists argued, were not local and internally undifferentiated. Rather, they were translocal phenomena, shaped and directed by unequal access to power and material resources. The central problem with symbolic approaches was not that they laid such emphasis on meaning but that their claims to be doing away with the notion of "structure" were spurious. In fact, anthropological political economists insisted, they were busily constructing a new structural orthodoxy in which individual agency still had no real place and in which social change could not really be accommodated.

Whereas both symbolic and interpretive perspectives were essentially Cartesian, at least to the extent that they continued to assume a theoretical distinction between the observer and the observed, the postmodern "turn" of the 1980s and 1990s sought to do away even with this distinction. Nevertheless, a reasonable argument can be made that the postmodern **paradigm** so popular with a recent generation of anthropologists has its most immediate anthropological antecedent in those analyses of symbols and meaning pioneered by Turner, Geertz, and archaeologist Hodder.

PARADIGM According to Thomas Kuhn, an intellectual framework for "normal" science, which is superseded by another paradigm in a scientific "revolution."

Transactionalism

The transactionalist perspective within anthropology represented an attempt to overcome the limitations of traditional structural-functionalism by revisiting the notion of the individual as the basic unit of social life, a notion that had featured prominently in the work of Malinowski but which was largely eclipsed by Radcliffe-Brown's vision of Durkheimian social structure. Also frequently referred to as "methodological individualism" and sharing much common ground with symbolic interactionism, a counterpart school in sociology, transactionalism was characterized by a sharp focus on the decision-making strategies adopted by individuals living in particular political "arenas." The perspective enjoyed a degree of success between the late 1950s and 1970s, largely as a result of the influence of Norwegian anthropologist Fredrik Barth (b.1928). Other important figures within the transactionalist school included British anthropologist George Bailey (b.1924) and British-Canadian anthropologist Robert Paine (b.1926).

Fredrik Barth

A one-time student of Raymond Firth and Edmund Leach, Fredrik Barth was widely respected for his fieldwork conducted in Pakistan, which produced the influential ethnography *Political Leadership among Swat Pathans* (1959). Barth's best-known theoretical exposition, and the one in which the key tenets of transactionalism are discussed in the greatest detail, is *Models of Social Organization* (1966).

Reflecting the thought of philosopher Karl Popper (1902-1994), who considered the individual social agent or actor the "linchpin" in the creation and maintenance of social relationships, a Barthian perspective holds that social life is, at base, a complex series of economic transactions between individual social actors, all of whom share the same goal of maximizing their interests or gain through the strategic choices they make. In this view, structured systems of norms and values are created and sustained through the economic interests of individuals. For this reason, social structure should be considered for its emergent rather than fixed nature. Social relationships are "generated," sustained, and changed as a result of the economic choices made by individuals, each of whom has learned to play and manipulate the "rules" of a social "game." Perhaps the most important implication of this line of reasoning is that individuals, rather than social systems or cultures, should be looked to as the engines of social continuity and change. Among the Swat Pathans, for instance, Barth argued that the social structure was subject to manipulation by leaders and clients, each of whom worked to realize their own self-interest.

Like those political-, conflict-, and urban-oriented approaches championed by Gluckman and, later, by anthropological political economists, transactional theory proved especially appealing for its apparent transcendence of a key dilemma posed by structural-functional analysis: that individuals are caught in and defined by the social and cultural structures in which they are, in a sense, "imprisoned." Where, in this form of analysis, was room to be found for social and cultural change? Certainly by the 1950s, many British social anthropologists were searching for ways to move beyond what were increasingly seen as, at best, the partial truths of classical Radcliffe-Brownian structural-functionalism. While transactionalism seemed for a time to hold out the promise of a new paradigm for social relations, practitioners of this form of analysis have also been taken to task for assuming, rather than providing evidence for, the rational, economically driven character of human social activity. Several questions were frequently raised. First, was the nature of social and cultural structure really determined by the calculating, voluntary, decision-making processes of individuals; and, second, were these notions about the rational and the cognitive not themselves Western in origin? Furthermore, in light of the historical conditions and regimes in and under which different peoples have lived and died, were individuals really always "free" to make choices that maximized their social or economic gain?

Calling these latent assumptions of transactionalism into doubt meant that, in spite of its laudable attempts to draw concern for the individual into orthodox British structural-functionalism, Barthian theory was ironically subject to much of the same criticism as other forms of structural anthropology, namely, that the individuals of transactional analysis were hardly more creative than those of structural-functionalism because the theory depended on a particularly narrow, prepolitical, overly rational, unhistorical perspective of how individuals act *vis-à-vis* one another. Nevertheless, the preoccupation of the transactionalist approach with the individual cultural agent deepened the concern for understanding social and cultural change within anthropology and in so doing hastened an emerging crisis over the nature of social integration and structure.

Feminism and Anthropology

The rise of a self-consciously "feminist anthropology," or, for some, "anthropological feminism," can be attributed to the advent of new, progressive, or "radicalized" political and social agendas in the 1960s and 1970s, both in and outside academia, and to the disciplinary introspection that had begun to plague (or liberate, depending on one's point of view) anthropology entering the final decades of the twentieth century. As the conditioning adjective suggests, *feminist* anthropologists have argued that a more powerful and inclusive understanding of society and culture can only be achieved by studying the cultural representations and experiences of, and practices associated with, women.

From the outset, this emerging body of theory and research was intended to bear little resemblance to previous generations of struc-

Louise Lamphere, President of the American Anthropological Association 1999–2001

Since 1980, more than half of the presidents of the American Anthropological Association have been women.

turalism and structural-functionalism, for two reasons. First, the goals of an effloresciing "anthropology of women" were to be emancipatory: feminist anthropology was unabashedly partisan, in that practitioners actively sought redress for imbalances created and sustained by an unjust social order—at home and abroad—that accorded men and women different status and privilege. Second, a distinctive feature of early feminist scholarship in anthropology was that it attempted to expose the sins of a discipline scarred by a legacy of **androcentrism** with respect to both the identity and the interests of its core of practitioners. At issue was a troubling fact of much ethnographic research: notwithstanding important contributions made by Margaret Mead, Ruth Benedict, and others to advancing a women-oriented perspective, it was clear that most fieldwork and writing in American, French, and British anthropology had to that point been conducted by Western men, who undoubtedly brought with them to their various fieldsites all the gender biases and assumptions inherent in their

ANDROCENTRISM The deeply held cultural bias to view the male as intellectually, spiritually, and physically superior to the female.

own societies. In practical terms, one consequence was that these male ethnographers were far more likely to have access to male-dominated institutions and practices than they were to those associated with women, a fact that almost inevitably skewed their research focus and emphasis in favour of such cultural institutions as war, politics, economics, and religion. This focus and emphasis, feminist anthropologists argued, had formed a nucleus of research priorities to the exclusion of child-rearing, domestic life, and other spheres of social and cultural life dominated by women in many non-Western societies. In such oeuvres as Michelle Rosaldo and Louise Lamphere's *Women, Culture, and Society* (1974) and Rayna Reiter's *Toward an Anthropology of Women* (1975), feminist anthropologists wondered aloud how a holistic and inclusive anthropological perspective could be hoped for under these conditions.

The most widespread solution advanced during the 1960s and 1970s bore a resemblance to the salvage ethnography of decades past, in that a new generation of feminist researchers (the overwhelming majority of whom were female) was encouraged to investigate those women-centred practices and institutions that had until that time been neglected by their male counterparts. In so doing, it was hoped that these efforts would redress what they considered to be a gross imbalance in research foci. However sanguine, this ambition to "level the playing field" between the anthropological study of men and women, so eagerly embraced by a first generation of feminist thinkers, seems in hindsight rather awkward or even naïve. One effect of the postmodern turn of the 1980s was to cast doubt on the possibility of objective renderings of all social categories—including those implied by the terms "men" and "women." As the field developed, a universal application of the thesis that women were everywhere subordinate to men was coming under increasing criticism from feminists in the non-Euro-American world, for whom such assumptions both side-stepped the issue of very real differences between women of different ethnic and socioeconomic background and obscured the fact that relations between men and women in the non-Western world could be (and often were) very different from those assumed by Western feminists, with their largely unquestioned ideas about global **patriarchy** and the subordination of women to men.

PATRIARCHY A social group governed exclusively by males or groups of males.

At a broader level, another important product of the disciplinary introspection that took anthropology by storm in the 1980s was a willingness, even eagerness, to examine with new eyes the guiding premises of anthropology. Although this was universally hailed as a significant development within the discipline, at least some were uncomfortable with the easy, **Thomas Kuhn**-like assimilation of a new branch of scholarship within the accepted canon. Marilyn Strathern, for instance, has written of her dismay at recognizing feminism as subject to a tendency within sociocultural anthropology to fetishize eclecticism while simultaneously rejecting it. That is, while by the 1980s the normative state of anthropological science involved trumpeting diversity and relativism as key virtues of anthropology, a significant irony of this truism was that this same concern for diversity was subject to an underlying drive towards *integration*. As new perspectives emerged, those deemed to be of enduring value by some segment of the scholarly community were grafted to the existing corpus of theory, igniting it like so many neglected campfires, individually insignificant but merging under the right conditions in conflagration. Indeed, this assumption continues to prevail in introductory texts that wed, however imperfectly, four internally diverse subfields into a "functioning" machine or organism. For Strathern, it has been important to draw a sharp distinction between what feminism can contribute and has contributed to the anthropological body—a splinter field that has been dubbed "feminist anthropology"—and a critical and provocative area of scholarship she refers to as "anthropological feminism." Contrasting a watered-down feminism/anthropology hybrid, anthropological feminism preserves its autonomy and refusal to be obscured through absorption. That this has occurred constitutes nothing less, in her view, than violence done to the integrity of feminism's core ethic: a commitment to viewing social life as riven with hierarchical relations of domination and inequity. In this way, the vision of smooth integration and holism, although doubtless comforting and encouraging for the many champions of a unified anthropology, seems almost utopian.

Strathern's perspective has to varying degrees been shared by many anthropologists working within a feminist perspective. Oyèrónkẹ́ Oyewùmí, for instance, examines sex and gender in **Yoruban** society from the vantage of **deconstructionism**, refusing to accept the "ground rules" of Western scholarship in which the social world reflects underlying biological realities. In her analysis, this form of determinism, "**bio-logic**" or "**body-reasoning**" as she calls it (an elaboration of ideas

KUHN, THOMAS The American historian and philosopher of science who represented science as paradigmatic.

YORUBAN Pertaining to the Yoruba, an ethnolinguistic African society whose historic homeland is in southwest Nigeria and eastern Benin.

DECONSTRUCTIONISM A term describing the ambition of postmodernism to understand the political and cultural contexts "hidden" behind the writing, or "construction," of narratives.

BIO-LOGIC A term used by anthropologist Oyèrónkẹ́ Oyewùmí to describe the basic assumption of biological determinism that underlines Western scientific knowledge of sex and gender.

BODY-REASONING A term used by anthropologist Oyèrónkẹ́ Oyewùmí to describe Western science's assumption that the human body is a universal foundation for objective knowledge of identity.

explored by Michel Foucault), distorts the capacity of Native Africans to produce and manage categories of knowledge that diverge from what is taken for granted in colonially imposed and, by definition, universalizing scientific discourse. This privileging of biology impairs the development of a more sophisticated, nuanced feminist anthropology insofar as the physical body and the social meanings accruing to it have been collapsed. By way of example, she points to the non-existence of gender as a category of social distinction in pre-colonial Yoruban society. Instead of social rank tied to anatomical features, she argues that Yoruban hierarchy is based on "a different kind of map": seniority as a function of relative age. Even more problematic for bio-centric science is the fluidity with which hierarchy appears to have been managed in pre-colonial Africa. Social statuses are not fixed or immutable, as is assumed in bio-logic, but flexible and situational, permitting those constructed as fundamentally "different" to be fundamentally "the same" if warranted by a given situation or context. In this case, there is no need for conditional identification, such as that made in Anglo-American society when occupational categories are qualified according to gender, as in "female soldier" and "male nurse."

Oyewùmí's study, published in the 1990s, points to another critical insight of 1980s anthropology—one that has enduring value for postmodern and **poststructural** theorists: that **gender** identities are not natural phenomena to be assumed *a priori* but rather are highly variable and fluid social processes to be observed in use and context. For the purposes of cross-cultural analysis, in the 1980s it was argued persuasively that anthropologists should be careful to draw a distinction between sex and gender. Sex, it was observed, refers solely to empirically verifiable, universal, biological differences between males and females. In contrast, and as ethnographic research continued to confirm, gender is always and everywhere the product of distinctive cultural and historical contexts. Although these terms have frequently been conflated in the history of Western society (and elsewhere), resulting in the development of many unquestioned assumptions about the "natural" characters and propensities of men and women, a point of consensus among postmodern feminists (and among the majority of anthropologists who accept their insights) has been that the vast majority of allegedly fundamental differences between males and females—and all that such differences mean for engendered

POSTSTRUCTURAL An adjective that expresses disenchantment with static, mechanistic, and controlling models of culture, with a consequent interest in social process and agency.

GENDER The various social roles and identities attributed to individuals and groups on the basis of their biological sex.

identity, behaviour, division of labour, and ideas about nature—are in fact cultural constructs that are highly variable among societies.

Reflecting this general agreement that there is no universally binding set of characteristics, roles, or practices that set human males apart from human females, a comparative and historical anthropology continues to be seen by the broader feminist movement as an important vehicle for the study of the many cultural processes informing the social organization of ideas and practices related to gender and sexuality. While any shortlist of leading figures in this diffuse stream of scholarship that resists labeling must, perforce, seem rather arbitrary, a few names do stand out. Besides Marilyn Strathern, among the most widely read are Lila Abu-Lughod, Judith Butler, Louise Lamphere, Micaela di Leonardo, Henrietta Moore, Sherry Ortner, Rayna Reiter, and Michelle Rosaldo (d.1981).

Political Economy

For many anthropologists working in the 1960s and 1970s, among the most influential of the new perspectives to emerge in social theory were two related schools of analysis: **development and underdevelopment theory** and **world-system theory**. Within sociocultural anthropology, these, together with a fresh reflection on the key tenets of Marxist analysis, became the foundation for a critical perspective generally called political economy, or, more precisely, anthropological political economy.

DEVELOPMENT AND UNDERDEVELOPMENT THEORY André Gunder Frank's theory about the systematic exploitation of underdeveloped nation-states and regions by developed nation-states and regions.

WORLD-SYSTEM THEORY Immanuel Wallerstein's theory that core nation-states are engaged in the systematic exploitation of peripheral nation-states for labour and natural resources.

Marx and the World System

The first incarnation of "political economy" *per se* dates to the eighteenth century and was originally devised by Enlightenment-era social theorists in their investigation of the origin and nature of, and relationships between, nation-states and their colonial holdings around the world. By way of definition, in his work *A Discourse on Political Economy* (1755), Jean Jacques Rousseau (1712-1778) distinguished between the terms "particular economy," which signified "the wise and legitimate government of the house for the common good of the whole family," and "general" or "political" economy, which extended the particular meaning to "that great family, the State."

Early theorists such as Rousseau deemed general economic institutions "political" in character because they were manipulated by national governments seeking to maximize gain through capitalist appropriation and exchange. While the governmental and narrowly economic aspects of this first generation of "classical" political economics were soon segmented into distinctive academic disciplines (political science and economics, respectively), this original emphasis on the political character of capitalist exchange persisted in the nineteenth century, when Marx and Engels sought to understand the morally exploitative dimensions of wealth distribution.

In the twentieth century, the political and economic disparities between the "developed" and "underdeveloped" worlds, growing apace since the breakup of colonialism following World War II, nevertheless remained largely unexamined by social science until the 1960s, when the influential economist André Gunder Frank (1929-2005) began to criticize **modernization**. Frank believed the global capitalist agenda to be more sinister than benign, making dependent satellites of those "developing" nation-states with which the Western world came into contact and systematically extracting surplus goods and labour in exchange for much less. Underdevelopment was not, in Frank's estimation, a product of local conditions but the result of progressive capitalist exploitation.

MODERNIZATION The Western practice of transforming non-capitalist, preindustrial economies into capitalist, industrial economies.

CORE In world-system theory, Western nations and regions that expropriate and control resources of non-Western nations and regions; contrasted with the periphery.

PERIPHERY In world-system theory, non-Western regions dominated economically and politically by Western regions; contrasted with core.

WORLD SYSTEM According to political economists, the global expansion of Western capitalism creating a world system of unequal commodity exchange.

The most detailed exposition of this kind emerged in the work of Immanuel Wallerstein (b.1930), whose best-known writings on the globalizing character of capitalist economies are found in the three volumes of *The Modern World-System* (1980). In them, he identified the historical emergence of a Euro-American "world-economy" in which bourgeois capitalists in the "**core**" nations of Europe and America appropriate the profits generated by proletarians in the "**periphery**," or the rest of the world. Like Frank, Wallerstein understood the proletariat to be trapped in a **world-system** of unequal exchange in which Euro-American society penetrated, politically subjugated, and economically exploited external populations and their produce.

Like the theory of Marx and Engels before them, the work of Wallerstein, Frank, and others did not spring into existence *ex nihilo* but was, rather, emblematic of broader trends in and outside of academia. By the early 1960s, radical emancipatory social agendas—such as those associated with the countercultural, anti-war, anti-colonial, gay and lesbian rights, and feminist movements—began to emerge on a large scale in Western society. In the main, the philosophical foundations on which such liberation movements were based originated within the academic world itself and had a marked impact on the development of intellectual discourse from the 1960s through the 1990s.

For sociocultural anthropology, especially, these trends heralded an upheaval in how the discipline was to regard itself—an intense period of reflection and introspection that has, to this day, not abated. During the 1960s and 1970s, it was becoming increasingly clear to many anthropologists that their discipline had not only failed to problematize the impact of Western colonial and economic imperialism around the world, it had also neglected to recognize the essential links between the rise of anthropological knowledge and colonialism. They began to realize that a large majority of the ethnographic texts composed in the first half of the twentieth century had been written by white Euro-American men, whose work was often made possible by the political and military subjugation of the peoples they studied. In short, many of the remote and exotic communities of the classic ethnographic gaze were captive to, and dependent on, a global system of capitalism and militarism. Many anthropologists came to believe, with horror, that their discipline had been the unwitting accomplice of the colonial endeavour and that it had profited from the oppression of the very peoples whom many well-intentioned ethnographers sought to frame in a sympathetic manner.

Sins of the Fathers

Arguably, the epistemological challenge posed by Frank and Wallerstein, together with the revolutionary political climate of the 1960s intellectual world, represented the culmination of a number of theoretical and moral crises that had been troubling anthropologists for a generation, primarily in relation to the growing disaffection with structural analysis in its various forms. Therefore, disaffection and disillusionment among the anthropological rank-and-file were not, strictly speaking, new developments, even occurring as they did in the tumultuous 1960s.

In the British tradition, Gluckman and Leach, among others, had been steadily working since the 1940s to correct the "sins" of their disciplinary fathers by advocating sweeping revisions to structural-functionalism in order to make it more politically and historically

Robert Redfield (1897–1958)

Redfield developed a theoretical distinction between "great" and "little" traditions, foreshadowing some of the insights of anthropological political economy.

GREAT TRADITION Robert Redfield's term for cultures characterized by literacy, industrialization, and rational religions; contrasted with little tradition.

LITTLE TRADITION According to Robert Redfield, cultures characterized by illiteracy, preindustrial economies, and "irrational" supernatural beliefs; contrasted with great tradition.

relevant. Moreover, as early as the 1950s, American anthropologists had also been feeling less and less comfortable with the idea that the discipline must study timeless, self-contained, and largely rural communities. Notably, in an effort to cultivate a more historically aware anthropology, Robert Redfield (1897-1958) developed a theoretical distinction between the **great tradition** of the literate, religious, and urban to contrast with the **little tradition** of the oral, magical, and rural. Formulations heavily grounded in a Durkheimian concept of structure or organismic analogy, as were those of British and French anthropologists, were subject to particular scrutiny.

Still, the theoretical insights that were to revolutionize anthropological theory merely simmered until the 1960s. It was during this decade that many basic assumptions about the character and truth-value of anthropological knowledge came under serious attack from various quarters both within the field and without. Among the most strident of anthropological criticisms was that the pristine, timeless, and self-contained organic community of anthropological invention was, in reality, just that—a figment of the ethnographic imagination. A more powerful understanding of human societies, it was argued, would seek to circumvent Cartesian assumptions of Western bourgeois culture: that there existed an untamed and unchanging primitive "Other" that would undoubtedly benefit from contact with the materially wealthy, the literate, the industrial, and the otherwise "civilized." Similarly, a much-cherished notion of the empirical researcher was also called into question. No longer was it taken for granted that the world was easily or dispassionately observed or that the authors of ethnography were themselves utterly impartial or objective. Seeking to displace these anachronistic perspectives, a number of scholars began to display, rather than conceal or mystify, the various conflicts, class-interests, and arrangements of power and dependency embedded in the history of global capitalism—a history in which anthropology itself had played a role. It was out of this "post-" structural concern for social process, power, conflict, and the origin of **authoritative knowledge** that anthropological political economy was born.

AUTHORITATIVE KNOWLEDGE
The idea that one body of knowledge is privileged over other bodies in that it has greater access to ultimate reality or the "Truth."

Ideology, Culture, and Power

Anthropological political economy was, then, a product of its times. Distinguishing these anthropologists from their colleagues working in one or another materialist or symbolic subdiscipline was their desire to understand the nature of encounters between large-scale regional, national, and international capitalist forces and local, non-Western societies and cultural traditions. To this extent, the new perspective shared the general goals of economic historians like Frank and Wallerstein.

In contrast to world-system theory, however, anthropologists working within this perspective remained resolute in their commitment to understanding the autonomy and integrity of local societies and cultures, especially in the non-Western world. These, it was argued, were not culturally fragile communities that could (or should) be simply dissolved by the imperialist policies and agendas of global capitalism, no matter how well-intentioned the ambitions of international development or patronizing Western powers. Rather, a more enlightened moral and theoretical stance demanded study of the *mutually* significant encounters between capitalist economies and local societies around the world, arguing, in effect, that there did not exist a single world-system, but many. Explicit in this research objective was the idea that the effects of capitalism did not constitute a "one-way street" and that local peoples and cultures exercised a degree of agency in accepting, transforming, or even rejecting the expansion of market economies. If such subtle and multifarious processes were taking place, these anthropologists wanted to know, how did they do so and in what ways?

In sum, as a group, anthropological political economists remained anthropologists in the best traditions of sociocultural analysis dating back to Malinowski and Boas.

At this point, an important question arises about the nature of political economic theory in anthropology. It is well and good to advocate a study of the encounter between radically different systems of cultural and economic behaviour, but *how*, precisely, do these worlds of experience interpenetrate and affect one another?

The political economic tradition within anthropology has viewed culture as being shaped in the context of unequal access to wealth and power. This perspective, drawing as it does on Marxist assumptions about conflict between social and economic groups, may be thought of as materialist because the material conditions of human existence are understood to condition the character of social relations. However, unlike cultural materialism, which viewed infrastructure (modes of production and reproduction) as a primary determinant of culture, political economy, like structural Marxism, has considered the material conditions giving rise to these as being grounded in **ideology**. Because ideologies are constructed systems of ideas, they reflect and perpetuate the specific interests of their authors. For political economy, following Marx, such interests are inscribed in the ways a society differentiates itself according to socio-economic class, gender, and ethnicity, to name but a few prominent criteria. Whoever controls the means of producing wealth and power, it is argued, also controls conditions for the production of knowledge itself. When knowledge about the world is taken for granted, or unquestioned, it loses its arbitrary character and comes to be seen as "natural." Ideology at this stage ceases merely to embody the interests of one group within society and becomes a dominant perspective of the society; it is taken for granted by the powerful and power-

IDEOLOGY A term used by Karl Marx and Marxist scholars denoting a system of beliefs that influences the outlooks of individuals and groups.

less alike. Unchallenged dominant ideologies, such as that cluster of heterogeneous meanings and activities that make up global capitalism, assert the economic and political interests of some while simultaneously "mystifying" this essential inequality in power-relations for others. Political economists refer to this mystification as **hegemony**.

HEGEMONY A term for the capacity of one social group to impose particular beliefs or political and economic conditions upon another group.

As this suggests, the anthropological concept of culture had the potential to be reformulated when set within a political economic context. Positioning themselves in the idealist-materialist "breach" between the cognitive, symbolic, and interpretive camps on the one hand and various manifestations of materialism on the other, political economists redefined culture as a system of objective and concrete forces, or ideologies, the effects of which might be investigated ethnographically. Accordingly, a recent generation of theorists has proposed that the unity, objectivity, and even the existence of culture ought not to be assumed. Rather, the matter-of-fact, taken-for-granted quality of culture should be recast as problematic because a political economic perspective on the relationships between nation-states raises significant (and troubling) theoretical and moral questions about the historical conditions in which particular "cultures" and social groups come to exist, become powerful or, as the case may be, become dependent or subjugated.

Abstract though this theoretical edifice undoubtedly is, the main tenets of political economy are grounded and given practical depth in much of the detailed ethnographic research that has characterized publishing in this subfield. For example, in his influential ethnography *The Devil and Commodity Fetishism in South America* (1980), Michael Taussig (b.1940) argues that the inequities of capitalism are the subject of critical evaluation by poor labourers, who employ the Judeo-Christian Devil as a moral commentary on a system of economic relations over which they have little or no control. In Taussig's scheme, it is the local culture, rather than the doctrines of industrial capitalism, that creates meaning out of an encounter between radically different societies. More recently, the two-volume series entitled *Of Revelation and Revolution* (1991, 1997), by John Comaroff and Jean Comaroff, has similarly analyzed the impact of colonialism in South Africa by applying many of the same concepts.

Other prominent examples of anthropological texts that incorporate an explicitly political economic framework are *Europe and the People Without History* (1982) by Eric Wolf (1923-1999); *Sweetness and*

Power: The Place of Sugar in Modern History (1985) by Sidney Mintz (b.1922); *Anthropologies and Histories: Essays in Culture, History, and Political Economy* (1989) by William Roseberry (1950-2000); and *Anthropology and the Colonial Encounter* (1973), edited by Talal Asad.

The effort within anthropological political economy to understand the complex character and interdependency of global and local processes certainly illuminated the changing and malleable character of culture, but for many anthropologists such issues raised more questions than they answered. Among the most troublesome was this: if past ethnographic representations of the "exotic" peoples did not so much reflect objective reality as further the norms, values, and assumptions of Western society (i.e., that there were indeed primitive and timeless cultures in dire need of civilizing), how was a new generation of cultural anthropologists to liberate itself from ethnocentrism and still construct accurate and meaningful accounts of cultures which, in the final analysis, were still very different from those of Euro-American scholars? Grounded as it was in Marx's political philosophy, even political economy could ultimately be read as ethnocentric, because it insisted that culture is the product of materialist power struggles—a uniquely Western form of analysis. Anthropologists began to question whether it was even desirable, let alone ethical, to continue to seek any one cause or configuration of causes that determine culture, given the historical connections between industrial capitalism, colonialism, and the post-Enlightenment ideal of scientific progress. These questions are significant because they cut to the very heart of what anthropology attempts to do: devise powerful and streamlined models that explain how people interact with each other and the world. As most cultural anthropologists came to realize, however, extracting anthropology from its "modernist" heritage—a heritage that divides the world into the Cartesian oppositions of subject and object, male and female, self and other, rational and irrational, and culture and nature, among others—would prove extraordinarily difficult.

Postmodernity

While transactionalism, feminist anthropology, and political economy hastened the demise of the traditional structural anthropological picture of society and culture, the advent of the postmodern perspective, or postmodernity, is often credited with "exploding" the culture concept once and for all. While this is an exaggeration, it is certain that the theoretical concerns that ethnographers began to express during the 1960s and 1970s—concerns that feminist anthropologists and anthropological political economists, in particular, sought to address—were not easily resolved. While not forming a movement properly labeled as homogeneous, postmodernists working within a variety of disciplines have certainly shared a perspective that emphasizes the subjectivity of experience and, consequently, the impossibility of any one form of authoritative knowledge. In anthropology, the so-called "postmodern turn" had the effect of advancing and refining debate over the theoretical and ethical issues first raised by political economists and others.

Unfortunately, the precise meanings of the terms "postmodern" and "postmodernity" are still further obscured by their all-too-frequent conflation with another weighty adjective: "poststructural." Strictly speaking, the terms poststructural and the noun derived from it, poststructuralism, refer, straightforwardly enough, to the growing malaise and increasing uneasiness with structuralism that erupted in the 1970s, particularly from within the academic field of literary criticism. Especially in France, where Lévi Strauss's work and person had achieved a lofty interdisciplinary stature and influence during the 1960s and 1970s, fickle dissatisfaction with what came to be seen as an overly cognitive, insufficiently political, socially uncontexted body of theory fueled a wave of "post" Lévi-Straussian zeal among such philosophical and literary luminaries as Jacques Derrida (1930-2004) and Jacques Lacan (1901-1983).

This initial flood of interest in deconstructing mental, cultural, and social structures as manifested in literary and philosophical discourse has had a deep impact on the shape and focus of anthropological theory, notably in the work of Michel Foucault and Pierre Bourdieu, and has understandably become identified with a broader philosophical and political-economic critique of Enlightenment objectivity within anthropology and other human sciences. Therefore, while a contemporary generation of anthropologists tends to employ the terms postmodern and poststructural interchangeably, it is worth noting that postmodernity embraces a much wider range of interdisciplinary dispositions in which the "modernist" acquisition of scientific and objective knowledge is critiqued as a Western, Enlightenment-inspired project. This discussion will henceforth concern itself primarily with the notion of the postmodern, although where postmodernity illumines (or stalks, depending on one's point of view), poststructuralism is seldom far behind.

Postmodernists have been accused of seeking to transcend and supplant modernity and even to do away with scientific anthropology, narrowly conceived, altogether. There are two major objections to this rather hyperbolic rush to judgement. First, even the most zealous champions of postmodernism acknowledge that the logic of modernity is not easily dispensed with because it is embodied in key Western assumptions about an objective world that can and should be subdued and controlled—politically, economically, and ideologically—by orderly, dispassionate, and rational Europeans and Euro-Americans. More important is a misunderstanding that many have about the purposes of cultural deconstruction and **reflexivity**. There is a significant distinction to be made between the brands of **nihilism** and solipsism many postmodernists are accused of embracing and the pursuit of more penetrating insights into social and cultural processes. Most anthropological theorists who are dismissed with the epithet "postmodernist" reject the idea that they are not engaged in developing new knowledge that more accurately reflects the experienced world. The difference is that these scholars—a majority of contemporary social and cultural anthropologists—accept that scientific accounts are like any other, the products of social negotiation and construction, not the mere description of objective self-evident facts. Because so-called postmodernists push the definition of what it means to do science, a serious claim can be made that they are *more* scientific than their positivistically inclined colleagues.

REFLEXIVITY A popular postmodern analytical strategy of reflecting on the biases and assumptions that inform one's own theories and perspectives.

NIHILISM The perspective that traditional values and beliefs are fundamentally uncertain, and that existence is at base nonsensical.

This, however, is a debate best reserved for the professional journals and classrooms. For the moment, some roots of the postmodernist perspective can be explored in the works of three seminal theorists: Paul Feyerabend, Michel Foucault, and Pierre Bourdieu. Though not necessarily "postmodern" per se, each has influenced the emergence of a distinctive perspective that underscores much contemporary anthropological theory. These are followed with discussions of current approaches that unite critical cultural analysis with interpretive anthropology. Most conspicuous among such approaches has been **medical anthropology**, a diverse body of research devoted to the cross-cultural investigation of health and healing systems and practices.

MEDICAL ANTHROPOLOGY The cross-cultural, pan-historical study of sickness and health.

Paul Feyerabend

A genealogy of postmodernity might begin with the **philosophical anarchist** Paul Feyerabend (1924-1994), who argued that there is no logical way to choose between conventional scholarly models, or paradigms. The concept of paradigms came from historian and philosopher of science Thomas Kuhn (1922-1996), who in his highly influential book *The Structure of Scientific Revolutions* (1962) argued that science is largely conventional, consisting of answers to questions that scientists agree are appropriate to ask at a particular time and place. For a while, according to Kuhn, this period of "normal" science yields results, but, eventually, nonconforming observations instigate scientific "revolutions" whereby old questions are superseded by new ones to which the observations conform. A new period of normal science ensues, until other nonconforming observations instigate another scientific revolution. Kuhn called the intellectual framework for normal science a "paradigm" and the process of scientific revolution a "paradigm shift." His prime example was the shift from Aristotelian to Newtonian science in the Scientific Revolution of the seventeenth century. Although he acknowledged that the history of science is progressive, his most influential point was that scientific paradigms fundamentally differ.

PHILOSOPHICAL ANARCHIST Following Paul Feyerabend, someone who believes that all scientific paradigms are logically equivalent, with no logical way to choose among them.

Extending Kuhn's perspective, Feyerabend argued that there is no logical way to choose between paradigms because all such explanations are inevitably *interpretations*. Scientific thought and institutions, like any others, are the products of lived experience, as are their assumptions about the "truth," or authoritative nature, of their special knowledge. The truth-claims of scientists, Feyerabend insisted, cannot therefore be understood as superior to other manners of explanation for social phenomena; rather, *all* explanations are basically incommensurable. Likewise, an important insight of anthropologists in recent years has been that modernity has carried forward these truth-claims since at least the sixteenth century. The recognition has been that this project is *itself* an historical event. The modernist perspective itself constitutes an **invented tradition**—the product of creative social action through time and *not* a "revelation" or awakening to the true understanding of an external objective reality.

INVENTED TRADITION A phrase describing the modern invention of historical events and personages, often with the goal of legitimizing contemporary political or religious ideologies by linking them directly to Antiquity.

This revolution in perspective has caused both great excitement and upheaval in the humanities and social sciences. While a number of scholars stand out for their extensive contributions to developing a postmodern perspective—Antonio Gramsci (1892-1937), Anthony Giddens (b.1938), and Raymond Williams (1921-1988), for instance—two in particular have directly influenced the course of anthropological theory and deserve special consideration: the French social theorists Michel Foucault and Pierre Bourdieu. At the outset of this discussion, it is only fair to point out that neither theorist has identified his own work with that of "radical" postmodernists within cultural anthropology. In fact, Foucault's work has been dismissed by some as an overly structural approach that does little to account for the agency and creativity of individuals, while Bourdieu went to some pains to distance his work from that of those he considered to be nihilistically minded cultural interpretivists and deconstructionists who deny outright the possibility of objectivity in social science. Rejecting this proposition, Bourdieu felicitously, if cynically, dubbed this philosophy within anthropology the "**diary disease**." Foucault and Bourdieu should not, therefore, be thought of as "postmodern" in narrow terms. Rather, their contribution has been to theorize such concepts as power, resistance, and agency in ways that have importantly influenced a recent generation of cultural anthropologists.

DIARY DISEASE Pierre Bourdieu's tongue-in-cheek label for the radical deconstruction of some postmodern theorists, particularly those preoccupied with second-guessing their own analyses.

Michel Foucault

Writing in the 1970s, Michel Foucault (1926-1984), a philosopher and historian of culture, viewed social institutions and relationships as being intimately grounded in a pervasive economy of **discourses of power** that shape relations between people at all levels in a society. In his formulation, "power" ceased to be solely a function of formal political institutions and became something inscribed in everyday life. The many different roles played by individuals (employers, employees, doctors, patients, men, women, priests, faithful, teachers, students, etc.) all bear the stamp of certain kinds of relations between people in which some dominate and others are subjugated. Whoever dominates these relationships, Foucault argued, also controls the economic and ideological conditions under which "knowledge" or "truth" (and therefore "reality") are defined. Dominating classes inscribe their power, in Foucault's scenario, in and through a series of tactics and strategies that instruct people to "be" a certain way in the world. In this way, beginning with the Enlightenment and the rise of the

DISCOURSES OF POWER Michel Foucault's phrase for the spectrum of institutions, rhetorics, and strategies employed by one group to dominate another group.

nation-state in the eighteenth century, discourses of science, sexuality, and humanism became dominant in European society, preserving their power through mechanisms of control such as prisons, hospitals, asylums, and museums. Foucault's central contribution to postmodern social theory has been to show how power determines different social forms through history. Because modernity is viewed, alongside other configurations of knowledge, as the product of power, the objective character of scientific knowledge is shown to be an historical construct.

An influential example of the Foucauldian perspective can be found in his work *Madness and Civilization* (1973) in which he charted the development of the concept of insanity in Western society. While often subtle and complex, a simplified synopsis of his argument runs as follows. Until the late eighteenth century, what Western society currently calls "insanity," or "madness," was viewed by educated Europeans and Americans as being of supernatural origin. This reflected the European medieval and post-medieval assumption that the world and the universe were understood with recourse to the inscrutable and purposeful Will of God.

In this context, there was a social tendency to accommodate "mad" people because such individuals were often viewed as being "touched" by, or "fools" for, God—a belief often accompanied by the idea that they were spiritually powerful, or wise, people, capable of better expressing divine will than those around them. Interestingly, anthropologists have observed this phenomenon in small-scale, non-Western societies in which "shamans" and "witch-doctors" are often people who are perceived to be gifted with spiritual authority or power. Likewise, a good example of this social role being expressed in Western literature is the importance of the "fool" in Shakespeare's play *King Lear* (*c.*1605).

Foucault argued that during the European Renaissance of the late fifteenth and early sixteenth centuries, scholarly knowledge was characterized by a rediscovery of classical antiquity and an interest in the Platonic ideal of rationality and the power of the human intellect—a process that anticipated the rise of humanism. Under this new epistemological regime, the beginnings of a fabled "Age of Reason," the world ceased to be God-centred, and those conditions which had to that point been thought of as tinged with divine power came to be revisited under the sharp gaze of humanism and rationality. One effect of this process was that those considered to be mad were re-evaluated and found wanting within the new human-centred scale of norms and values. Far from being chosen by God, henceforth these individuals were no longer even fully considered people as such. Having lost or been denied the faculty of reason—a defining characteristic, in the early humanistic perspective, of what it means to be human—they came to be seen as almost certainly defective.

In the seventeenth through nineteenth centuries, with the rise of science and the philosophy of positivism (i.e., the possibility of acquiring objective knowledge), the role of the divine in human affairs was reduced still further, and "insanity" came to be seen as a disease in which the intellect was no longer under the control of those afflicted. With the insane no longer perceived as being fit to live in society, the asylum was founded to enforce and institutionalize a separation between rational society and that which was considered pathologically irrational.

What becomes of those considered to be insane under these new conditions? Because their new status precluded consideration as complete human beings, such individuals began to be considered a part of the natural world. Like other aspects of the natural world subject to the scrutiny, penetration, and investigation of science, their bodies, too, became the objects of scientific fascination and investigation. One goal of this work was to find new ways to contain and investigate the insane—a process that inaugurated the disciplines of psychiatry, psychology, and, indeed, the medical professions as a whole.

For a late twentieth-century readership, such a description of events could not help but be disturbing from an ethical point of view, given its assumptions about the essentially inhumane nature of science and medicine. Still, Foucault's central objective in this history of madness was not to moralize but to shore up his theoretical position on the power of authoritative discourses to shape and define what people accept as objective truth. Hence, none of the changes that took place between the medieval era and the Enlightenment occurred because there was a truly objective transformation in the condition of people designated as mad. Whereas the modern world considers scientific discovery and knowledge to be the result of a gradual accumulation of objective information, Foucault argued that what in any time or place are considered truth and objective knowledge are themselves contingent on a dialectical relationship between the vagaries of history and shifting power relations between social classes. In short, what counts as "real" knowledge about the natural world—in this example, the mental condition of those designated as insane—is determined by those classes of people that possess authority to shape and control knowledge itself.

In this way, Foucauldian theory redefines the concept of "knowledge" itself. No longer a reference to real or objective understanding, knowledge is primarily a way of naming and ordering the world that favours the powerful and seeks to maintain the status quo. Moreover, the quality of knowledgeable "expertise" in a given field is bestowed upon accredited individuals who participate in institutions that help to maintain this status quo. Specialists such as judges, lawyers, doctors, teachers, and scientists are experts only because they are designated to be experts by the socially powerful. In the case of the transition from the medieval to Enlightenment eras, Foucault identifies a "changing of the guard": the epistemological authorities and assumptions of the medieval world (the Church and its earthly representatives) are replaced by a new set of authorities whose authority derives from their insight into the newly emergent epistemologies of humanism and science.

Pierre Bourdieu

Addressing similar issues relating to power and domination, but coming at the problem from another angle, Pierre Bourdieu (1930-2002) worked during the 1970s and 1980s to develop a theory that places the social actor at the centre of social process. Unlike Foucault, whose theory viewed individuals and their interrelationships as being determined by discourses of power, Bourdieu held that these same persons and social arrangements are created by human agents who assemble their cultures through **practice**, or **praxis**. What people "do" in practice is create, reproduce, and change a variety of "taxonomies" that are understood to be the basis of social relations. These taxonomies are made up of symbolic representations that do not merely reflect ideas about the world but actually *make the world* what it is for the people who live in it. Individuals are powerful to the extent that they can *impose* on others taxonomies that reproduce their own power and authority; they are powerless to the extent that they are unable to escape their social positioning in relation to the

PRACTICE Or praxis; according to Pierre Bourdieu, the concept that society is constructed by purposeful, creative agents who bring society to life through talk and action.

PRAXIS Or practice; according to Pierre Bourdieu, the concept that society is constructed by purposeful, creative agents who bring society to life through talk and action.

taxonomies created by others. Either way, the taxonomies wielded by the powerful in relation to the powerless are only relevant insofar as they are lodged within a configuration of social relations.

The notion of the "relational" is so significant in Bourdieu's thought because it helps to move social science away from those various formulations of social structure as conceived by an earlier generation of Durkheimian thinkers. For Bourdieu, social structures and cultures were not to be compared to machines or organisms, because culture and society are ultimately not things but systems of relationships, or **fields**. He defined fields as fluid, open-ended "networks" of "objective relations between positions." Complex societies, he argued, were comprised of any number of fields (i.e., artistic, intellectual, economic, religious, etc.) that, although coexisting spatially and temporally, were nevertheless discrete and integrated according to their own internal "logics." Within fields, the total imposition of one group's set of taxonomies upon another's results in the production of a "natural" order, or **doxa**, in which the essentially arbitrary character of the powerful taxonomies is obscured. What emerges, for the powerful and powerless alike, is a sense that certain thoughts, feelings, and actions are part of the outer objective world, while others (those of the dominated) are "unnatural."

In short, social relations that come to be taken for granted are actually the result of one interest group's **symbolic domination** of others within a society. What is seen to be "real" in any society, from this perspective, inevitably reflects the point of view of whoever's interests are served *by* that reality. Unlike Foucault's model, in which individuals are simply dominated by a powerful system that exists independently of their own actions, Bourdieu's model stipulates that this system of meaning-in-conflict is characterized by individual social actors participating in a pervasive economy of symbols in which autonomous individuals and groups attempt to accrue and distribute **symbolic capital**, or symbols of prosperity and prestige, with differing degrees of success. A critical feature of this system, and one that distinguishes Bourdieuian from Foucauldian thought, is that even individual members of the dominated classes within this economic system are sometimes able to transform the nature of what counts as the socially prestigious or valuable by creating alternative taxonomies that resist those imposed by the powerful. Bourdieu referred to the wellspring of this individual agency as the **habitus**, or the ways in

FIELDS According to Pierre Bourdieu, the dynamic configuration, or network, of objective relationships among social agents and positions.

DOXA Pierre Bourdieu's term for a psychological state in which all members of a community consider relations natural, including relations of social, economic, and political inequality.

SYMBOLIC DOMINATION According to Pierre Bourdieu, the tendency of dominant social groups to create and sustain a world view in which all members of a society, including subjugated members, participate.

SYMBOLIC CAPITAL According to Pierre Bourdieu, the body of meanings, representations, and objects held to be prestigious or valuable to a social group.

HABITUS Pierre Bourdieu's term for the capacity of individuals to innovate cultural forms based on their personal histories and positions within the community.

which personal history and social positioning allow individuals to improvise or innovate.

Anthropology as Text

Throughout the 1980s and 1990s, Foucault's and Bourdieu's ideas had a dramatic impact on anthropological theory. Depending on one's sympathies, their work has been highly illuminating or deeply mystifying. In either case, it is clear that for many anthropologists, suddenly there seemed no centre, no firm ground from which students of human life could gaze objectively at their subject matter. Henceforth, no "truth" would be taken for granted and no perspective left unchallenged. Deconstruction became a new watchword for anthropologists, because the sanguine ambition of positivism to explain the world was no longer seen as a possibility. On the contrary, to be a "vulgar" positivist was to be misguided or naïve because it was not the culture itself that needed explaining so much as the anthropologist's explanation of that culture. It was the representation or account of a people, in other words, that required understanding, or deconstruction, because discrete cultures as "objects" are only apprehended at all through such accounts, which are themselves enshrined in the ethnographic *text*. Some years before, Clifford Geertz and the interpretive school had also employed the metaphor of text in an effort to show that, like the written page, cultures might also be read and deciphered for meaning. Unlike Geertz's approach, which has been considered rather naïve and inconsistent by postmodernity for its perceived willingness to turn the ethnographic gaze on everyone's cultural meanings but the ethnographer's own, postmodernist authors claim to probe greater depths of social reality by self-consciously reflecting on the contingent cultural factors embedded in their own representations.

Over the years, some critics have mistakenly understood this to mean that postmodernity denies outright the existence of objective reality and, thus, have accused postmodernist researchers of solipsism. These claims notwithstanding, it is ironic that the postmodern perspective in effect recapitulates an idea that has been prominent in anthropology since Boas and his students first championed the cause of cultural relativism in the first decades of the twentieth century: that culture mediates and conditions all knowledge of the world, like a lens. In this way, while it is clear that a world truly does exist independently of how we know it, it is equally clear that there is no perspective, scientific or otherwise, that is not in the last instance rooted in particular histories and biases—an integral feature, seemingly, of our common humanity.

In anthropology, the postmodern perspective has been most influential in the writing of ethnography. Anthropologists working in the final decades of the twentieth century became extremely conscious of the subjective nature of the documents they produced. James Clifford and George Marcus's edited volume *Writing Culture: The Poetics and Politics of Ethnography* (1986) has been particularly influential in advancing the ideas that cultural accounts are constructed "texts" and that the relations between the writer, reader, and subject matter of ethnography are complex and problematic. Whereas standard interpretive approaches would view subjects as creative actors busily constructing their social worlds out of symbols, postmodernists have noted with deep irony that these same ethnographers privilege their own status as external observers. Accordingly, while everybody else was evidently forced to build culture, anthropologists were exempt from this process: it was for them to observe, rather than to be observed. In contrast, postmodern writers argue that ethnography, no less than any other form of creative writing, privileges the authorial perspective. This insight has had deep implications for anthropological theory. Because the account being produced always comes from a particular viewpoint—most often that of the white, middle-class, educated Euro-American male—it reflects and asserts (albeit implicitly) the concerns and interests of its author. True objectivity is hardly possible, because even if researchers deliberately adopted a non-stereotypical object of study, they would still have little choice but to employ the analytical categories and concerns explicitly and implicitly fashioned by the academy and (more broadly) the society in which the knowledge they "possess" has been formed. What goes unquestioned—the division of the ethnographic project into subject and object—betrays the subtle yet powerful influence of modernity on anthropological theory.

Recognizing the impossibility of pure objectivity, a recent generation of ethnographers has attempted to circumnavigate the ethical and methodological dilemmas raised by postmodern theory. They have done so by looking for ways in which to describe different cultures and societies *without* denying the subjectivity of the people being analyzed and *without* laying claim to absolute, or authoritative, knowledge about them. Needless to say, given that anthropology has been suffused with and directed by modernist concerns, this lofty ambition is easier proclaimed than accomplished. Heavily influenced by the writings of Foucault and Bourdieu, one popular strategy has been to show how the subjects of ethnography themselves set about creating and negotiating the categories of meaning that inform their social worlds. Often labeled **social constructionism**, after a phrase popularized by sociologists Peter Berger and Thomas Luckmann in the 1960s, this methodology attempted to highlight the essentially contingent nature of culture by demonstrating how ethnographic subjects employ language and patterned activity to create, sustain, and change meaning. This approach has been highly influential in anthropological writing. For instance, *The Invention of Tradition* (1992), edited by Eric Hobsbawm and Terence Ranger, is a collection of historical essays that points to the recent "invented" origins of traditions and practices that are often portrayed as being ancient markers of ethnic identity. In this vein, much attention has been focused by a recent generation of anthropologists on how different forms of human community, such as those identified according to social positioning (i.e., according to such criteria as socioeconomic class, race, ethnicity, and gender), are constructed in and inscribed on a wide variety of historical contexts.

SOCIAL CONSTRUCTIONISM The theory that sociocultural phenomena are products of historically-situated interpersonal negotiation accomplished through patterned language and activity.

Medical Anthropology

While the origins of medical anthropology predate the ascendancy of postmodernity within sociocultural anthropology by a number of years, it has been with the emergence of the postmodern perspective in particular that the subfield has come to prominence.

Especially within American anthropology, the term "medical anthropology" has incorporated a range of approaches that variously study the objective role of biology and ecology and interpret the cultural foundations of "folk" medical institutions and practices around the world. While the literature is voluminous across the various branches of medical anthropology, a short-list of widely used texts includes David Landy's edited volume *Culture, Disease, and Healing: Studies in Medical Anthropology* (1977), Thomas Johnson and Carolyn Sargent's edited volume *Medical Anthropology: A Handbook of Theory and Method* (1990), Nancy Scheper-Hughes's influential ethnography *Death Without Weeping: The Violence of Everyday Life in Brazil* (1992), and Andrea Sankar's *Dying at Home* (1999).

In its broadest aspect, medical anthropology may be defined as the study of the social and cultural dimensions of health and illness, together with indigenous theories of cause and treatment. In contrast with many other subfields of academic anthropology, however, many medical anthropologists have successfully created a professional niche for themselves outside the university system, primarily by turning their knowledge of theory to practical advantage by offering "actionable" insights into clinical practice and public policy formation.

ETHNOMEDICAL Pertaining to ethnomedicine, the anthropological study of non-Western medical systems.

Classical ethnographers have long concerned themselves with the investigation of non-Western practices related to medical knowledge and treatment, or **ethnomedical** systems. One example is Evans-Pritchard's study of witchcraft as a folk-illness. Generally speaking, ideas about health, illness, misfortune, and supernatural power were viewed by earlier generations of sociocultural anthropologists as part of an integrated social and cultural structure. More recently, the influence of postmodernity, feminist anthropology, and political economy has been felt by ethnomedical researchers, who have come to emphasize the ideological or conflicted nature of indigenous practice. Rather than being elements in an integrated social "whole," folk medical practices have come to be seen in recent years as one site of contest between conflicting local and translocal ideologies that variously square off against one another or mingle to create new forms of practice, belief, and power relations.

ALLOPATHIC The treatment of illness and disease using the knowledge and techniques of Western biomedicine.

BIOMEDICINE The science-based form of ethnomedical knowledge and practice dominant in Western societies.

In recent years, Western, or **allopathic**, **biomedicine** has itself been subject to this level of analytical scrutiny. For instance, building on the work of Foucault, "critical" medical anthropologists such as Nancy Scheper-Hughes, Mark Nichter, and Margaret Lock view medicine as having an ideological component. More than a set of insights about how to diagnose and treat illness, biomedicine is treated as but one aspect of Euro-American ideological expansion into the non-Western world. For this reason, many medical anthropologists working from this perspective have advocated a radical de-centring of medical knowledge and practice from the Western medical establishment, itself treated as the product of Enlightenment-era struggles to define the "real." Thus, biomedical practice cannot be extracted from the political economy of capitalism in which social behaviours and institutions are inevitably shaped and controlled by the experience of Western hegemony.

Other medical anthropologists have been involved in investigating the often complex dynamics that obtain between distinctive medical systems that come to compete with one another in socioeconomically stratified and heterogeneous societies, such as those one finds in modern Western nation-states. This concern for understanding medical pluralism has been at the heart of an efflorescence of "applied" research undertaken by such anthropologists as Andrea Sankar and Sandra Lane, which, in recent years, has become a prominent feature of debates regarding the formation of public health policy and clinical and psychiatric practice. In contrast to critical medical anthropology, a defining feature of this perspective is that practitioners seek to contribute to the amelioration of health care by introducing local, or indigenous, knowledge into biomedical practice, thus making Western medicine of greater utility, especially in non-Western settings. For instance, many applied practitioners are employed by hospitals or international development organizations to assist biomedical professionals in better understanding the cultural factors at work in influencing particular health practices that may, or may not, be perceived as problematic from the position of Western medicine.

Though diverse in its approaches, the mainstream within medical anthropology has in these ways focused squarely on the sociocultural nature of health and illness. Contrasting with both of these, another branch of practice within the subfield has struck a distinctly more "etic" position that also lays claim, in the best Boasian tradition, to being a truly holistic approach to studying human phenomena. Those with an ecological orientation within medical anthropology have looked for patterns in the interrelationships between environmentally conditioned, health-relevant variables (for instance, the prevalence of particular diseases or the availability of food) and sundry human social and economic practices (for instance, those relating to agriculture or migration). All claims to holism notwithstanding, however, ecologically oriented medical anthropology has drawn withering fire from other quarters within the subfield, and from sociocultural anthropology more generally, for its allegedly "reductionist" position *vis-à-vis* social and cultural behaviour. According to critics, ecologically oriented medical anthropologists consider culture to be a mere reflex, or **epiphenomenon**, of ecological processes. For this reason, they

EPIPHENOMENON A phenomenon resulting from another phenomenon.

are accused of too seldom considering cultural practice and institutions to be central to shaping human ecology.

Globalization

GLOBALIZATION The expansion of Western institutions and lifeways into non-Western cultures and the emergence of new forms of cultural practice that are global in scope.

A latter-day heir to world-system theory and anthropological political economy, the study of **globalization**, or "globalization theory," has been one of the most conspicuous bodies of work to derive from the mingling of these perspectives with postmodernity in the 1980s and 1990s. Because the perspective does not so much prescribe a single method or research agenda as it advocates a general outlook, its supporters have been many and diverse. Among the better known anthropological texts that have been included in this corpus are *Modernity at Large: The Cultural Dimensions of Globalization* (1996), by Arjun Appadurai; *Global Culture: Nationalism, Globalization, and Modernity* (1990), edited by Mike Featherstone; and *Globalization: Social Theory and Global Culture* (1992) by Roland Robertson.

GLOBAL VILLAGE Marshall McLuhan's term for an increasingly interconnected global society.

In the 1960s, Canadian communications theorist Marshall McLuhan (1911-1980) famously foreshadowed attention to globalization within the social sciences when he speculated that the world was increasingly being homogenized into a "**global village**" in which the diversity of local cultures was being radically reshaped (and, ultimately, limited) through increasingly advanced and universal systems of communications and travel technology. The "message" conveyed by such technology, he speculated, was in fact identical with the "medium" of its transmission. Hence, societies the world over would inevitably and inexorably become less heterogeneous, forever conditioned by a new global orientation and sensibility.

While the most ominous implications of this prediction have yet to be realized, McLuhan's insight continues to be valuable for anthropologists working in the 1990s and the early twenty-first century. As one of the perspective's most eloquent exponents, Roland Robertson, has defined it, the phenomenon of globalization describes both an etic "compression of the world" through processes of increased technological, economic, and cultural interdependence, and an emic awareness of the transformations stimulated by this interdependence—what he calls an "intensification of consciousness of the world as a whole." Another way of putting this is that globalization-oriented anthropologists ask what are perhaps the next obvious questions to follow from the ideas pioneered by Frank, Wallerstein, and the anthropological political economists: namely, *beyond* the imbalances in political and economic power generated by a capitalist world-system, what *other* sociocultural phenomena do we observe to be consequences of the interpenetration of Western and non-Western cultural worlds, and how are we to characterize and account for these? Infusing these questions with the postmodern concern for individual agency and creativity, students of globalization further inquire how new forms of subjective understanding and reflexivity are produced as a result of these new global forms of interdependence.

This "collision" between the objective forces of the world-system and the capacity of individuals and communities to construct their own worlds socially and subjectively is not easily described, let alone explained. Following its coining by economists, Robertson uses the term "**glocalization**" to denote the coexistence or co-presence of the universal and the particular in any society. Other terms, such as "**creolization**," have been borrowed by anthropologists from linguists to articulate much the same concept. How can anthropologists account, precisely, for this hybridizing tendency?

GLOCALIZATION A term popularized by Roland Robertson to describe the coexistence of globalizing and particularizing tendencies in a society.

CREOLIZATION An anthropological term borrowed from linguistics suggesting the fusion of divergent cultural concepts and practices, particularly in the context of postcolonial and globalization studies.

World-system theorists assert that global capitalist expansion involved the progressive interpenetration, mingling, and outright domination of some social and cultural institutions and practices (those of the so-called developing world) by others (those of the so-called developed world). Adding much-needed nuance to this view, anthropological political economy went on to insist that, while such imbalances in power and authority are certainly created by this encounter of the West with the Rest, they are hardly "totalizing," or wholly determinative, of cultural form and meaning. Through the subjective understanding and activity of local cultural agents, the hegemony of global capitalism is both changed and resisted. The globalization perspective represents a further refinement of these political-economic ideas, one that is leavened by what we might call a cautionary tale of postmodernity: that society and culture cannot simply be reduced to, or "written off," as mere effects of a capitalist world-system, no matter how powerful and all-embracing this system might appear from the standpoint of Western eyes. In particular, one insight grounded in this postmodern dictum has been instrumental in shaping globalization theory into a distinctive branch of research in the 1990s and early twenty-first century. This concerns a recognition by many anthropologists that, far from there being a simple reaction to or against the world-system, the "core" of the system is *itself* transformed through contact with its own "periphery," so much so, in fact, that it becomes difficult to speak of a single world-system at all. A more exact description would identify a multitude of overlapping, interpenetrating world-system*s* that shape and condition one another.

This "brave new world" sketched by globalization-oriented theorists certainly defies easy description. One useful analogy might be that the world's societies are now "woven" together culturally, economically, and politically. Like any tapestry or quilt, the threads that comprise this global society are stronger in some places and weaker in others. They merge and intertwine to form patterns, colours, and textures that are quite distinct from those of each thread considered independently. It is these overarching patterns and colours, rather than their local variants, that are the new substance of cultural form in a globalizing age.

To the extent of focusing on the character and influence of the linkages that bind localities together across geographical regions, the globalization perspective has shared a concern with anthropological political economy. However, a new insight introduced by globalization theory is that the linkages do not describe merely a set of *objective* social, economic, or political relationships between people who are geographically distant from one another. Instead, drawing on postmodern concerns with understanding subjectivity and agency, globalization theorists look to the *subjective* dimensions of this process: how does a growing local awareness of global connections and identity both inspire and lay the foundation for new forms of consciousness, cultural meaning, and social practice?

To cite but one prominent example, in his pioneering work *Imagined Communities* (1983), Benedict Anderson reconstructs the concept of the nation-state from the ground up, effectively arguing that the original European nation-states were "imagined" into being as a result of the post-medieval influence on vernacular languages of what was in the sixteenth century a radically new technology: the print media. Once invented, the exponential dissemination of knowledge, ideas, and language permitted by this new technology empowered local cultural actors both to reflect on the larger political, economic, and cultural processes around them and to develop new perspectives and meanings rooted in the experience of common language and homeland.

It is this emphasis on the production of wholly new social and cultural forms and "systems" that distinguishes globalization-oriented anthropologists from their predecessors in world-system theory. The globalization perspective insists that local cultures are not passively overwritten by or dissolved within that unidirectional, apparently unstoppable, global steamroller known as Western industrial capitalism. More often than not, globalization theory holds, the world's allegedly peripheral cultures and societies "hegemonize the hegemonizers" by generating new forms of global cultural practice whose roots are neither Western nor easily explained by the logic of political-economic expansion. To the contrary, such formerly "peripheral" cultural phenomena as reggae music, Buddhism, Japanese Sushi cuisine, Scots-Irish folk dancing, and Native American artwork and sculpture, to cite but a few examples, would all seem to be non-Western cultural exports that are themselves becoming the bases for global cultural practices. This same phenomenon takes place within the "West" as well. Consider, for instance, the replacement in France of the McDonald's character, Ronald McDonald, with Asterix the Gaul, a popular French character more appealing to the French public, or the decision to serve alcoholic beverages to teenagers in restaurants at Disneyland Paris ("Euro-Disney"), breaking with its American counterparts, Walt Disney World and Disneyland.

Such processes have been facilitated in no small measure by the advent of sophisticated electronic media, communication, and travel technologies. These have created a transnational environment in which many different forms of cultural innovation are possible. No longer limited by geopolitical "places" or "homelands," social movements as different in their goals as Amnesty International and al-Qaeda may both flourish in the "non-place" space of the Internet. Moreover, the expanding possibilities for the movement of people around the world have intensified global phenomena such as tourism and migration. Although a bewildering number of human futures seem possible as a result of these developments, one thing does seem all but certain: such transformations are unlikely to slow down at any point in the near future. The same might therefore be said of globalization-oriented anthropology. Conceptually unfettered from assumptions about the effects of colonialism, with its tacit opposition of the Western to the non-Western world, and from the regional or national bias of earlier generations of anthropologists, the globalization perspective seems on track to expand the horizon of anthropological research well into the twenty-first century.

Public Anthropology

Finally, the twenty-first century has witnessed a new (or *re*newed) approach to doing anthropology that is often set apart from its academic cousins on the grounds that it is applied, atheoretical, and constrained by "real world" considerations. While these characterizations are understandable, given the generally cloistered history of academic disciplines, they are also misleading. Contrasting themselves with ***applied* anthropology**, in which a sharp distinction is often drawn between "pure" scholarship and how it is used outside the **Ivory Tower**, a recent generation of anthropologists concerned with expanding the breadth of theory has written of *public* anthropology as a means of making their discipline relevant in the world beyond universities. The word "beyond" rather than "outside" is used deliberately. For the self-declared public anthropologist, scholars *both* within and without the university system are part of a larger project to, as Trevor Purcell says, "directly and indirectly [contribute] to the general good—not just to the academic or career good." Anthropologists conduct their daily lives "as the embodiment of socio-political participation." They are, in this view, direct heirs to the postmodern controversy of the 1980s and 1990s during which, in Ben Feinberg's enigmatic characterization, "debates within the discipline involved tearing at our own flesh and flaunting the sackcloth of self-doubt" while "we sparred with each other and devoured our elders in the hidden corners and footnotes of obscure journals."

APPLIED ANTHROPOLOGY Anthropology conducted by anthropologists working outside traditional academic settings such as universities.

IVORY TOWER A euphemistic and usually pejorative term for the Academy, or universities.

This call to action is not simply a new trend in how anthropologists manage their professional lives. If it were, discussion of public anthropology would not be justified in a volume about theory. The goal of scholars advocating a public orientation is more subtle than this, and it has deep implications for social and cultural epistemology. The question of who constitutes this "public" is central. The adjective does not refer simply to the wider world outside the hallowed halls of academia. Rather, the notion of what counts as public is set within the context of "anthropology" as a distinctive historical product and event within Western scholarship and anthropologists as distinctive agents in the formation and propagation of knowledge about human beings. Anthropologists have now recognized and "owned up to" the discipline's role in (among others) supporting colonialism, justifying ethnocentrism, and reifying differences between the sexes.

It seems clear that, at the very least, twenty-first century anthropologists will no longer be uncritical of their own biases and assumptions. Instead, the globalizing world of free markets, homogenizing popular culture, and techno-rationalizing industry to which *all* are rapidly, if differently, becoming witness places anthropologists and anthropology squarely within a network of global movements, debates, and conversations. They are, in other words, part of the public—not elevated above it as lofty observers. It is in their capacity as members of the public that they participate, bringing the professional skills and critical insights of anthropology to the wider world. Rather than submit to professional imperatives that buy "respectability" and "esteem" by acceding to careerism (for example, by jumping the many hoops of the tenure system) and unspoken assumptions about the authoritative status of doctorates and the professoriate, anthropologists, those promoting a public orientation assert, must come down from Olympus to wallow in the lived and eminently political struggles of their erstwhile subjects—now peers and the mere objects of their scrutiny no longer. Consequently, to the holy grail of positivist science Robert Borofsky extends the following olive branch: objectivity, he writes, is to be found "less in the pronouncement of authorities than in the conversation among concerned parties."

So, what does this mean, exactly, for the work of anthropologists seeking to cultivate a "public" orientation? It means, first of all, that the work of the anthropologist must disdain all notion of objectivity and distance, putting into practice those principles advanced in the canons of postmodern, feminist, and globalization theory. In practical terms, realizing this ideal involves recognizing that anthropologists are neither unbiased nor dispassionate observers, *nor should they be.* Public anthropology proposes that anthropologists, like any other sector of society, are morally and ethically accountable for the subjects of their study, a responsibility that cannot simply be wished away by laying claim to the old chestnuts of objectivity and relativism. To the contrary, anthropologists must by definition be activists and interventionists—seeking, as Karl Marx once observed in a critique of philosophy, to change rather than merely interpret the world. They must bring their expertise and skill to the public and political arenas of popular (that is, accessible) writing, community action, and policy formation, as well as to the "traditional" areas of applied research: the medical, corporate, **museological**, and **cultural resource management (CRM)** sectors. While anthropologists have of course "doubled" as activists for generations (within American anthropology, Franz Boas and Margaret Mead are conspicuous examples), anthropological theory itself has seldom if ever been scrutinized in this way, save in the wishful musings of prescient scholars such as Sherry Ortner, who in her (now) classic 1984 essay on the history of anthropology advocates for a practice-oriented approach in which such binaries as theory and action are reconsidered. The public anthropologist is not the "opposite" of the academic anthropologist but a public intellectual engaged in important debates and controversies of concrete significance for the world in which he or she lives.

MUSEOLOGICAL Pertaining to museology, the academic discipline focusing on museum organization, management, and cultural representation.

CULTURAL RESOURCE MANAGEMENT (CRM) Activities that share the practical goal of protecting and preserving objects and places deemed to be of cultural significance.

One main difference, then, between applied and public anthropology is that the latter in a sense calls upon a far greater commitment on the part of researchers. Ironically, this focus has sometimes put public anthropologists at odds with other applied or "practicing" anthropologists. Many of these, especially those trained in the more positivistic or quantitatively oriented branches of the discipline, retain a sense that anthropologists are scientists in search of objective knowledge. Precisely because it insists that moral and ethical accountability is part of the anthropological enterprise by definition, public anthropology calls into question venerable canons of method. While many sociocultural anthropologists have long been accustomed to interrogating the interpretive and subjective aspects of their practice, many biological and archaeological anthropologists have not, paving the way for a fresh rift between the subfields over questions of method, epistemology, and purpose. It is important to note that while these trends exist and persist, many positivist anthropologists do acknowledge responsibility to their subjects in many official and unofficial ways, even while stopping short of embracing the revolution in theoretical perspective called for by public anthropology.

While there are many instances of public engagement within contemporary anthropology, a recent volume edited by Catherine Bestemen and Hugh Gusterson serves as a powerful exemplar. In *Why America's Top Pundits are Wrong: Anthropologists Talk Back* (2005), Bestemen and Gusterson invite readers to reconsider the role of the "**pundit**" in American society. The authors show that popular and

PUNDIT A person deemed to be authoritative who renders opinions publically, frequently by way of the mass and electronic media.

populist writers, journalists, and on-air personalities do not so much engage in meaningful examination of controversial issues as reproduce simplistic and long-cherished notions about social and cultural evolution, biological determinism, the timelessness of traditional society, and the intractable character of ethnic and religious animosities. That such ideas have long since been refuted in anthropological writing is in itself evidence, they argue, that the scholarly community has to date involved itself far too little in cultivating a more nuanced perspective among the wider public. In what amounts to a continuation of colonial practice, the world's powers treat developing and war-torn states as so many unruly children who will only "mature" through the firm and benevolent hand of Western-style democracy, **neoliberal economics**, and military coercion. Seemingly outside this process, well-known pundits and public intellectuals are myth-makers who persuade by providing their positions with the veneer of scientism—an elite discourse in which readers are invited to participate and which offers sure cognitive "satisfaction" by virtue of its paint-by-numbers explanations. Certain kinds of experts who have marshaled particular bodies of "facts" receive copious funding from politically and socially conservative organizations while, in the absence of such support, dissenting viewpoints recede into the horizon. By way of example, Besteman and Gusterson cite the well-known 1994 study, *The Bell Curve* by Richard J. Herrnstein and Charles Murray, in which intelligence among the American public is treated as the outcome of differential gene distribution. Left unsaid, much of the funding for **hereditarian** studies such as this is supplied from the coffers of formerly **eugenicist** organizations such as New York's **Pioneer Fund**. Objectivity, empirical validation, and truth thus become the products of ideological jostling and the politics of knowledge. According to faux pundit Stephen Colbert's withering satire, the "knowledge" deriving from such studies is not so much truth as "**truthy**." Public anthropologists, the authors maintain, can play an important role in distinguishing the truth from the truthy, the inclusively scientific from the exclusively mythological. Indeed, if anthropologists are to descend from their Ivory Towers to inhabit the conflicted world of subjects and objects, they have an obligation to do so.

NEOLIBERAL ECONOMICS A form of political-economic ideology in which governments promote competition among businesses within a capitalist market theoretically free of state oversight.

HEREDITARIAN Pertaining to the idea that differences among human beings can be accounted for primarily in terms of differential gene distribution.

EUGENICIST Pertaining to eugenics, the now-discredited science that endeavoured to "improve" humanity through selective breeding.

PIONEER FUND A philanthropic organization dedicated to advancing the "scientific study of heredity and human differences," said by its detractors to be tinged with biological determinism and racism.

TRUTHY A satirical phrase coined by television personality Stephen Colbert to describe the implicit acceptance of a proposition where logic dictates otherwise or where there is a seeming lack of supporting evidence.

SPEAKING ABOUT ANTHROPOLOGICAL THEORY

Lila Abu-Lughod

Lila Abu-Lughod Interviewing Bedouin Women in West Egypt

The history of anthropological theory is a history of debate. What has most fascinated me about the debates is that they reveal how our thinking develops both as a process of argument within a discipline that has its own terms, methods, and parameters, and as a process fundamentally shaped by and participating in the larger sociopolitical contexts within which intellectual work is done. Because anthropology's purview is the world, to study the history of anthropological theory is also to study the wider world of which it is a part.

It is often only in retrospect that one can see outlines of the relationship between theorizing and politics. I was struck forcefully by this when I read Pierre Bourdieu's objections to the easy critiques, after the fact, of anthropology as colonial. In the preface to *The Logic of Practice* he asks what prevented lucid and well-intentioned scholars like himself from understanding things that are now self-evident, even to the least of these. He wonders at what he calls the "misplaced" *libido sciendi* that drove him, in the late 1950s in war-torn Algeria when he photographed symbols on covered stone storage jars, not to appreciate that the reason he was able to pursue this passion for ritual and symbol was that the French army had destroyed the roof of the house and expelled its inhabitants (1990: 3). The problems, he argued, were both ethical and epistemological.

One of the most contentious debates in the recent history of anthropological theorizing occurred between Gananath Obeyesekere and Marshall Sahlins, two giants of the anthropological world in the last quarter of the twentieth century. At one level, the debate was about theory—about whether mythic structures determine historical action or whether all human action must be understood in terms of complex motivated pragmatic agency; it was also about cultural difference versus human similarity. At another level, however, the debate was about what the literary theorist Edward Said had captured in the catch phrase "Orientalism"—about the way knowledge and power have worked together in the "West's" domination of the "East," and, by extension, the non-West. Obeyesekere argues that Sahlins's interpretation of the Hawaiians' interpretation of Captain Cook as a god is itself another chapter in the self-serving Western myth—found earlier in Christian, evangelical, and even Shakespearean narratives—that savages see white men as gods. As himself "a native" from Sri Lanka, this anthropologist was skeptical.

Feminist anthropology has offered us a different kind of example of theorizing as worldly debate. Beginning in the 1970s, and closely tied to the political rebirth of a women's movement in the United States and Britain, women anthropologists began asking hard questions about how the anthropological canon was formed and what was missing from the ethnographic record. Women's lives had been invisible, occluding important issues about domination, relations between production and reproduction, and even about the critical role of sexuality in colonial relations. And why were women's voices excluded from anthropological theorizing, including, in the 1980s, about "writing culture"? As in other phases, as anthropologists they faced inward and outward. Efforts were directed both at critiquing a discipline that had ignored gender despite its claim that humanity was its subject matter and at answering urgent questions posed to them by feminists and activists about what anthropologists could illuminate for them about universals, cross-cultural differences, the determinants of gender equality and inequality, or the nature and culture of gender. Feminist anthropologists straddled more or less comfortably what Marilyn Strathern called the "awkward relationship" between anthropology and feminism. Since the late 1990s, as feminist anthropologists have gained prominence within the discipline—though often not for their work on gender—they have begun to be marginalized by what has become known as transnational feminism, a field of theorizing and activism that covers what conventionally was thought of as anthropological terrain: the world. In response, we now are doing ethnography on and developing theories about feminisms as social practices in the world. Surely this will engender new debates.

Lila Abu-Lughod is Professor of Anthropology and Women's Studies at Columbia University. She has written three ethnographies based on fieldwork in Egypt: *Veiled Sentiments: Honor and Poetry in a Bedouin Society* (Berkeley, CA: University of California Press, 1986); *Writing Women's Worlds: Bedouin Stories* (Berkeley, CA: University of California Press, 1993); and *Dramas of Nationhood: The Politics of Television in Egypt* (Chicago, IL: University of Chicago Press, 2005). Her contributions to anthropological theorizing are crystallized in articles such as "The Romance of Resistance" (1990); "Writing Against Culture" (1991); "The Interpretation of Culture(s) After Television" (1997); and "Do Muslim Women Really Need Saving?: Anthropological Reflections on Cultural Relativism and Its Others" (2002). For works cited in this essay, see Speaking About Anthropological Theory in the Sources and Suggested Reading at the end of this book.

Conclusion

In a 2002 letter to a Toronto newspaper, Wade Davis—a Harvard-trained anthropologist, **ethnobotanist**, and prolific writer who works mainly outside the academic anthropological mainstream—reflected on the pervasive and, from his perspective, pernicious impact of Western economic and political expansion on the world's impoverished nations. Subsequently reprinted in Roberto Gonzãlez's 2004 edited volume *Anthropologists in the Public Sphere*, Davis's letter cautions that unless the currently unbridled steamroller of capitalist expansion is curbed, the al-Qaeda attacks on the United States of September 11, 2001, might likely prove the tip of an abysmal iceberg and "the chaotic conditions of disintegration and disenfranchisement," so characteristic of the developing world, might be expected to continue breeding hatred of Western peoples and lifeways.

ETHNOBOTANIST A practitioner of ethnobotany, the sociocultural anthropological subfield that investigates the cross-cultural use of plants.

In some ways, Davis is iconic of the new interest in promoting anthropology in the public sphere as a socially relevant field of knowledge. That is, he brings anthropological insight to the critical issues of our times—among them, the structural conditions giving rise to international terrorism, the flawed and often ethnocentric reasoning of many policy-makers and pundits, and the troubling contradictions of state surveillance and the mechanisms of power in allegedly "open" societies. The events of September 2001, together with the subsequent wars in Afghanistan and Iraq, do raise important and troubling questions of direct relevance to the work that anthropologists do. What, indeed, are we to make of violent encounters that seem to pit Western "secularism" and "humanism" against what many take to be anachronistic strains of Islamic "fundamentalism"? The powerful insight of anthropology is not that such questions are easily resolved but that even to pose them assumes much that should not perhaps be assumed. For instance, **secularization theory** has been justifiably critiqued on the grounds that "secular" is surely not the best adjective to apply when considering American society (or even European societies, for that matter, despite an increasing tendency to

SECULARIZATION THEORY A body of research and theory within sociology and political science that assumes the demise of religion in a modernizing world.

be "de-churched"). Likewise, media portrayal of radical Islam often obscures the vast diversity of this world religion, alluding only in passing to the major cultural and theological differences between Sunni and Shi'ia; neglecting to examine the creolization of religion within radically heterogeneous cultural and linguistic contexts (for instance, Saudi Arabia, Turkey, and Indonesia); and reducing a rich history of science, art, engineering, architecture, and scholarship to the actions of what amounts to a very small percentage of the heterogeneous **Umma**, or global Islamic community. In this general failure to effectively grasp the conditions and causes underlying intersocietal enmity, the stakes are enormous. especially at a time of military proliferation and a frightening prospect that **weapons of mass destruction** will indeed play a part in future conflicts.

UMMA An Arabic word for "community," often used to designate the global diasporic Islamic "nation," a community of the faithful.

WEAPONS OF MASS DESTRUCTION Or WMDs, the euphemistic term for weapon technologies with the potential to cause casualties on a massive scale, for example, biological, chemical, and nuclear weapons.

Can anthropological theory, in spite of all its internal diversity, shed sufficient light on both cultural differences and similarity to ferret out the root causes of mistrust and hatred that provoke deadly action on such an enormous scale? If this question was at one time merely academic, it is no longer so. As numerous al-Qaeda attacks and their aftermath have proved, failure to understand the sources of intercultural enmity can have lethal consequences, an undeniable fact that begs the question: how does our understanding of the *history* of anthropological theory contribute to a more powerful focus on what we assume to be true, real, or taken-for-granted in current anthropological reasoning? Before attempting to tentatively answer this question, let us briefly review the current state of the field as described in the latter sections of this book.

Postmodern Predicaments

At the dawn of the twenty-first century, proponents of anthropology as an "interpretive science" seeking to understand the global interconnections among power, identity, and practice arise from a camp of humanistically oriented scholars whose proverbial tents (not to mention departmental offices) are pitched alongside those who would defend a biocultural, ecological, or materialist vision of their discipline. Generally speaking, the distinction between "public" and "applied" anthropology mirrors this rift, at least to the extent that many applied practitioners tend to embrace positivism as traditionally received within the academy at large. Self-described public anthropologists may or may not be "applied" scholars in this sense, but in all cases their chief desire is to bring to light the cultural biases, misapprehensions, and distortions in power that shape events in the world.

That undergraduate and graduate students encounter this diversity of perspective up close—in lecture halls, university corridors, and at departmental receptions—is incontrovertible. Unfortunately, although an important experience for young anthropologists, student encounters with the sharply divergent opinions of their professors can also be somewhat misleading about both the durability of the discipline and the commitment of its practitioners. One possible implication of the postmodern critique has therefore been that the field is so theoretically divided as to spell the end of academic anthropology as we know it.

As if this were not enough cause for concern, in a 1999 essay Herbert Lewis claims that, much as we might have hoped otherwise, and for all their purported insight, those fanning the flames of disciplinary critique in anthropology have failed to substantially advance the field or even to suggest new ways to address those issues that had, until disciplinary critique became the vogue, been the focus for "modernist" anthropology. Adding to this bleak evaluation, Lewis subsequently argues that an even bigger problem for the next generation of anthropologists might derive from a growing failure to adequately "dialogue with the ancestors." Thus, contemporary undergraduates, and even graduate students, are seldom required to *really* confront the work of their disciplinary forebears in other than a cursory fashion. Instead, it is largely assumed (in no small measure as a result of reading postmodern critiques) that the substance and method of earlier generations is both theoretically and morally bankrupt and that, consequently, there is little need to become acquainted with—let alone embrace—the work of "unenlightened" ancestors. Indeed, the harshest among these critics have treated anthropology in much the same manner as they claim anthropology has treated non-Western peoples: as monolithic, single-minded, internally undifferentiated, and, to state the matter baldly, primitive.

According to Lewis, a serious consequence of this state of affairs has been that student anthropologists are frequently dissuaded from immersing themselves in many of the key texts of the anthropological canon. These texts are frequently referred to in graduate seminars but are rarely explored in any sustained depth these days, and, even when they are discussed in detail, it is often for the purpose of displaying the "misrepresentation" of older schools and personalities—these are our ancestors, and here is how they got it wrong. A paradox of postmodernity, at least in its radical (and frequently misunderstood) incarnations, is that it presents itself as the final answer to a "crisis in representation"—the only legitimate perspective to take on the construction of anthropological knowledge, in comparison with which all others are naïve both in their "objective" representation of the Other and in their failure to recognize the social processes involved in their own construction.

For this reason, Lewis fears that "the basic questions that our predecessors struggled with years ago are still with us, but the hard-won lessons they taught us are being forgotten." The time is coming, he cautions, and, indeed, may already have arrived, when anthropologists will again turn away from fashionable critique in search of the "objectivity" of bygone generations. When the hour for a new paradigm shift arrives, to whom will the new generation turn? To those long-since discredited ancestors? Or will anthropologists begin again by reinventing wheels that, unbeknownst to them, have been turning (albeit creakily) for generations?

Agreeing to Disagree

All of which suggests, at the very least, that the continuing relevance of anthropology as a progressive and critical discipline is in some doubt. Might a premature demise, or fragmentation, of anthropology be just around the corner?

From this gloomy forecast, there is good reason to dissent, based on the belief that reports of the discipline's "death" have been, as someone once asserted, "greatly exaggerated." While it *is* the case that postmodern deconstructionism, lamented by Lewis, has inspired persistent rumours in recent years concerning the sealed fate of anthropology as a unified academic discipline, the apocalyptic fears of some have clearly not been realized some 20 years after the postmodern turn confronted anthropology. We need not see the world through rose-coloured glasses in order to understand this; it could be that, far from disciplinary idealism, the structural constraints and exigencies of academic colleges and departments have had as much or more to do with the persistence of anthropology as with a desire for unity. However it has come about, it seems obvious that there continues to exist at least some general agreement about the collective vision and relevance (if not unity) of anthropological theory and that this vision, expressed through a fabled anthropological canon and general trends in anthropological scholarship, remains largely intact in spite of the apprehension that epistemic malcontents might eventually dislodge it.

Evidence abounds to support this claim. For one thing, Boas, Malinowski, Radcliffe-Brown, Mead, Geertz, and Lévi-Strauss—central players in a select group of quasi-mythical "founders" of one school or another—remain firmly enshrined within an anthropological pantheon that most professional sociocultural anthropologists continue to accept as more-or-less valid. Some might view this as derailing the postmodern critique—that (at least in its more extreme guises) postmodern epistemology only really succeeds at throwing the historical baby out with the theoretical bathwater by questioning the work of ancestral generations but offering little of substance to replace them. It seems more likely, however, that the sense of foreboding cultivated through the 1970s, 1980s, and early 1990s was always somewhat overblown, infighting and hyperbole being as much stock-in-trade among anthropologists as within other professional communities. Critical medical anthropology, globalization, and feminist approaches are certainly non-positivist, but are they post*modern* in the sense of denying the value or authority of critical analysis within anthropology? The answer, clearly, is no.

Also, at the very least anthropologists consider themselves to be united by their own history, even if it *is* a history plagued with squabbling, rancour, and occasional professional jealousy. In the end, they simply agree to disagree for the sake of getting on with the business at hand. Even the most naïve would concede these days that there exists no universally valid reading of the anthropological past, at least from the point of view of theory, binding on all practitioners. This being said, there is reason to believe, as argued in this book, that, far from spinning round and round in circles, the expanded scope of anthropological work *has* led to substantially new discoveries that might be called "scientific progress" were that phrase not already sullied as naïve or clichéd. There has been progress in the sense that the diverse interests of anthropologists have led them to study all manner of groups and subgroups within and across societies, paying careful attention to relations of power and knowledge—all of which spells a widening and deepening of the discipline. In terms of the anthropological *subdisciplines* (a term that designates any of the many strands of research and perspective within four-field anthropology), insights from the burgeoning fields of medical anthropology and globalization theory have moved social science forward in its collective effort to understand social and cultural life with greater rigour and detail. With respect to anthropological theory at a more general level, a hallmark of the past quarter century has been greater attention to the fluidity of social structure and the capacity of individuals to comprehend and change the conditions of their existence. These "breakthroughs" can indeed be regarded as a substantive expansion of the field, at least in comparison to their relatively unreflective ethnocentric predecessors of the eighteenth and nineteenth centuries.

Beyond the personalities and specific theories involved, therefore, most anthropologists would also concur with the rather bland assertion that the fabled theoretical dichotomies signified by the contrasting of culture with society, synchrony with diachrony, structure with agency, and idealism with materialism, among others, do not necessarily reveal a discipline teetering on the edge of dissolution. Neither does the increasing division of what was, in North America at least, a four-field profession into a bewildering variety of subdisciplines imply the "death" of anthropology. To the contrary, most anthropologists today would affirm that the discipline's ongoing intellectual vigour is not undermined, but revealed, both by the proliferation of interests, perspectives, and methods and by the eagerness with which practitioners engage one another in hashing out what (if anything) such dichotomies make known about human social life. For these reasons, arguments over theory are perhaps better thought of as means of integrating diverse kinds of practitioners into a single, flexible, yet enduring whole.

Failure to see disputes over theory in this light tends to result in attributing far more import to them than they actually deserve: they very quickly become "red herrings" that distract anthropologists from developing new insights, instead obliging them to defend their positions both in print and in the heated salons of professional conferences. All things considered, it hardly seems controversial to maintain that it is the strength of debate, rather than the narrowness of opinion, that is the hallmark of any strong academic discipline. If such were not the case, there would likely be little or no interest in books such as this one.

"-Isms" in Schism

Even if there existed no firmly established pantheon or cumulative aspect to the work of anthropologists, the absence of *theoretical* consensus hardly makes professional disunity inevitable. Nor, it must be said, does it rule fragmentation out. In the United States and Canada, many anthropologists continue to regard as critical to the intellectual vitality of anthropology the work of biological anthropologists, archaeological anthropologists, linguistic anthropologists, and an especially outspoken and diverse subfield of cultural anthropologists, together with their numerous special interest groups. On the other hand, many North American anthropologists, and in growing numbers, no longer accept the four-field premise. It would therefore not do to adopt a smug posture on the issue, content in our comfortable certainties about the future of anthropology. As in other fields of knowledge, it makes little sense to be dogmatic on such issues. If it is true, as Eric Wolf proposed in the early 1980s, that a unified anthropology springs more from political-economic developments in the modern academy than it does from consensus about social and cultural theory, there is no reason to suppose that anthropology *needs* to be unified across four fields in order to retain its analytical value or power. The European academy provides a strong precedent, given that social anthropology, biological anthropology, linguistics, and archaeology are seldom, if ever, housed within the same departments and colleges. It is also true that schism within North American university anthropology departments has taken place and seemingly without apocalyptic consequences; witness successful (if painful) ruptures at Stanford, Duke, Calgary, and possibly Harvard, among others.

A 2006 debate on the issue in *Anthropology News* is diagnostic of an enduring fascination with the theme of unity, especially across the "sacred bundle" (as Daniel Segal and Sylvia Yanagisako have called it) of four fields. In debating the state of four-field anthropology, anthropologists, both pro- and anti-schism, are given equal time to air their differences. Some, such as R. Brooke Thomas, stand firm in a "traditional" position, arguing that "Our strength as a discipline seems to lie in the multiple perspectives we can bring to a problem." His sanguine expectation is that pressing environmental needs confronting the globe will inevitably bring together biological and cultural approaches in the coming generations. Notwithstanding the accidental origins of four fields in the United States and Canada, it is evident that generations of forebears have devoted their careers to preserving the "grandiose perspective" that different approaches bring. Can we now afford to set aside these efforts in the tenuous hope that anthropology will continue to be relevant (and anthropologists continue to be employed) into the twenty-first century?

On the other side of this issue, Fran Mascia-Lees suggests that rumours of peaceful coexistence—theoretically and practically—among the subfields have been greatly exaggerated. Despite her personal commitment to anthropological holism, the stark facts suggest that while much is made of disciplinary unity, with relatively few exceptions most professionals blithely pursue research agendas that focus squarely on one of the subfields. It is vital, therefore, that we ask ourselves the very serious question of whether there exist "compelling intellectual connections" among us, or whether assumptions to this effect are little more than an artifact of our professional past. While many have been quick to lay the blame for this at the feet of postmodernism, perhaps expecting the ***American Anthropologist*** to substitute poetry for scientific reportage and analysis, it seems beyond doubt that the moment of introspection that characterized the 1980s has now given way to other foci: globalization, **postcolonialism**, and the extent to which anthropologists are and should be responsible, ethically bound players in the public sphere. In fact, Mascia-Lees proposes, no one is to blame for this "crisis" of fragmentation; it has been a largely organic and even predictable development within a vibrant, efflorescing discipline. While some predict the death of a discipline, the very same factors leading to dysfunction and schism can be read as diagnostic of healthy, timely academic debate. On the other hand, if rapprochement is ever to be attained, especially between biological and cultural anthropologists, then new questions must be asked and new paradigms for collaboration developed. As of now, however, these "very different conversational interactions" are few and far between.

AMERICAN ANTHROPOLOGIST
The flagship professional journal of the American Anthropological Association.

POSTCOLONIALISM
A distinctive body of research and theory within anthropology that seeks to better understand the historical and cultural interconnections between colonizers and the colonized.

CONCLUSION

History of the Future

In 2002, the American Anthropological Association celebrated its centennial year, a distinguished commemoration that coincided with a chorus of voices, from all quarters of the discipline, clamouring for increased introspection and attention to the future of the field. Although it is difficult to read the tea leaves of anthropologies to come, it is possible to speculate to a limited extent about trends of the future.

To begin, one implication of the diversity encountered in this book is that, although many who fear for the future of academic anthropology will continue to consider consensus regarding the best theories and methods the "holy grail" of our discipline, this longing might well prove utopian. Short of this, at an institutional level, students of anthropology will continue to be exposed to the canon and the range of possibilities available from a discipline whose holistic character has always differentiated the field from its sister disciplines in the humanities and social sciences.

Perhaps more interestingly, there is the question posed at the outset of this conclusion: what does the historical diversity discussed in this book (especially with respect to anthropology's most recent schools of thought) suggest about future directions in the development of anthropological theory? Regna Darnell and Frederic W. Gleach, in their introduction to the centennial edition of *American Anthropologist*, wrote that we are living in and passing through a "Janus-faced" moment, in which we are "looking both to the past and to the future for inspiration." Wade Davis's admonition to cross-cultural understanding in the wake of unimaginable violence is but one example of how anthropologists are increasingly looking inward for resolutions to global misunderstanding, tension, and violence. This is not the dispassionate anthropology prized in the heydays of evolutionism and structural-functionalism. Rather, it is a perspective that suggests that the future relevance of anthropology lies in its ability to contribute to essentially moral debates about social relations. Following the lead of public anthropology, future theory may well turn on the moral implications of human diversity—a phenomenon that anthropologists and proto-anthropologists have been unveiling, arguably since classical antiquity. The sites of such theorizing may be university departments, professional journals, and conferences. Or, as Davis and others have chosen, these discussions might take place in the more public arenas that comprise today's mass media: newspapers, magazines, television, Internet, and other forms of electronic media.

If this is indeed to be the discipline's path, anthropologists must be prepared to continue divesting themselves of illusions concerning the history of their field as a "pure" science. As a consequence of a variety of political and social events and movements, especially following the end of World War II, few would now deny that the history of anthropological theory is a story firmly embedded in *Western* experience. Hence, adopting the Western analytical distinctions among religion, science, and humanism has allowed construction of a historical pedigree for academic anthropology in which the various ancient and medieval schools leading up to Christianity had a profound and lasting influence, as did the revival of humanism in the Renaissance and the origin of modern science in the seventeenth century. Arguably, the most momentous historical episodes of all in this epistemological lineage have been the voyages of geographical discovery, which brought Westerners into contact with non-Westerners and launched the period of cross-cultural encounter that, in one way or another, has been a centripetal focus for anthropology ever since.

But equally important here is what remains unstated in this "anthropology of anthropology": that *the* history of anthropological theory is really *a* history of anthropological theory. Anyone truly committed to the universalizing of anthropology as a perspective must allow for other anthropologies, other tales of discovery and cross-cultural encounter, and other methods and contexts in which knowledge is formed. Paradoxically, the more powerful anthropology becomes as an epistemology, the more fragmented and decentred it appears to be.

This recasting of anthropological knowledge is perhaps the most welcome, and perhaps inevitable, consequence of late twentieth- and early twenty-first-century theory: feminist anthropology, political economy, postmodernity, and the study of globalization by anthropologists. After all, as Darnell and Gleach observe, "there is a certain satisfaction in casting our nets so broadly that almost anything can be encompassed by the term *anthropology*, as long as it is thought about anthropologically." This sentiment warrants hearty endorsement.

CONCLUSION

Beyond "One Dead Guy A Week"

In closing, it is fitting to return to what is perhaps the most important site of anthropological practice for most university-based anthropologists: the classroom. From the perspective of teaching anthropology it bears noting that sometimes courses in the history of anthropological theory—especially those dubbed "one dead guy a week"—are taught by the "trapeze method," meaning that theories are connected by "swinging" from older to more recent orientations as the academic semester or quarter progresses. Connections among theories taught according to this method often remain implicit and are, therefore, at best superficial and at worst conducive to the false impression that theories float above real people like acrobats who never touch ground.

Notwithstanding such an often unavoidable impression, this book shows that the history of theory is defined not so much by "facts" as by the proclivities of different anthropological historians and historians of theory and by the vagaries and extent of consensus that develop around one or another perspective. Only the most novice readers will conclude, after reading the book, that theory is "out there," ready to be plucked from the air by a particularly ingenious or fortuitous "discoverer." Far from being unsullied by human hands, students of the diversity of opinion within anthropology will benefit from what is perhaps the most enduring insight of twentieth-century anthropology: that the making of knowledge about human life is a labour-intensive, contentious, and thoroughly human activity. After modernity, anthropological theory too—unlike the acrobat—has its feet planted on *terra firma*.

Review Questions

Introduction

1. What are the four traditional subdisciplines of anthropology, and what happened to these subdisciplines in the late twentieth century?
2. Why can there be no *one* history of anthropological theory?
3. What are the differences among scientific, humanistic, and religious systems of thought?

Part One: The Early History of Anthropological Theory

Anthropology in Antiquity

4. What did the pre-Socratic philosophers contribute to anthropological theory?
5. What are the differences between the Platonic and Aristotelian legacies to anthropology?
6. How did Stoicism bridge Greek and Roman thought?
7. What were the tenets of Augustinian Christianity, and how did they affect anthropology in the Middle Ages?

The Middle Ages

8. In the period of the Middle Ages, what did Islam contribute to anthropology?
9. How did the theologies of Saint Augustine and Saint Thomas Aquinas differ, and how did these differences affect the history of anthropological theory?

The Renaissance

10. What *was* the Renaissance?
11. What was the Renaissance legacy to anthropological theory?

Voyages of Geographical Discovery

12. Why were the voyages of geographical discovery so important in the history of anthropological theory?
13. What is the significance of the difference between the portrayals of Native peoples as natural slaves and as natural children?
14. What are the differences between monogenesis and polygenesis?

The Scientific Revolution

15. What is the difference between deduction, associated with French rationalism, and induction, associated with British empiricism?
16. What roles did Nicholaus Copernicus, Tycho Brahe, Johann Kepler, and Galileo Galilei play in the Scientific Revolution?
17. How did medieval cosmology differ from the cosmology of Isaac Newton?
18. How did the Scientific Revolution affect the history of anthropological theory?

The Enlightenment

19. What are the differences between deists and theists?
20. What is the anthropological significance of John Locke's concept of *tabula rasa*?
21. Who were the universal historians, and how were they anthropological?

The Rise of Positivism

22. In the early nineteenth century, what were the intellectual reactions to the French Revolution?

REVIEW QUESTIONS

23. What was Auguste Comte's philosophy of Positivism, and how did it integrate social dynamics and statics?
24. What is the significance of positivism for the history of anthropological theory?

Marxism

25. In dialectical materialism, how did Karl Marx and Friedrich Engels change the philosophy of Friedrich Hegel?
26. What is the labour theory of value?
27. On what basis did Marx and Engels predict the inevitable future collapse of capitalism?
28. What does it mean to be a Marxist anthropologist?

Classical Cultural Evolutionism

29. How did the formulations of nineteenth-century cultural evolutionists differ from the formulations of eighteenth-century universal historians?
30. How did Lewis Henry Morgan explain the evolution of marriage, family, and sociopolitical organization, and how did other evolutionists disagree with his explanation?
31. According to a synthesis of the views of Edward Burnett Tylor and Herbert Spencer, how did magico-religious beliefs and institutions evolve?
32. How did James Frazer differentiate magic, religion, and science?

Evolutionism vs. Diffusionism

33. How do diffusionism and evolutionism differ as explanations of culture change?
34. What were the differences between the heliocentric and *kulturkreis* versions of diffusionism?
35. What does the doctrine of psychic unity have to do with the difference between evolutionism and diffusionism?

Archaeology Comes of Age

36. In the nineteenth century, what developments led to scientific acceptance of the idea of prehistory?
37. In the nineteenth century, how was archaeology linked to racism and colonialism?

Charles Darwin and Darwinism

38. What was the basis of the debate between Neptunist and Vulcanist geologists?
39. What was the basis of the debate between uniformitarian and catastrophist geologists?
40. What were the major influences on Charles Darwin's theory of evolution?
41. How did Darwin's mechanism of natural selection differ from Jean Lamarck's mechanism of the inheritance of acquired characteristics?
42. Why is the term Social Darwinism historically misleading?
43. What kinds of moral systems have been based on Darwinian biology?

Sigmund Freud

44. How did Sigmund Freud come to the realization that people have a subconscious, and how did he differentiate the id, ego, and superego?
45. How did Freud explain the origin of the psychic conflict that, according to him, plagues humankind?
46. How did Freud characterize human nature?

Émile Durkheim

47. According to Émile Durkheim, what is the distinction between mechanical and organic solidarity?
48. What did Durkheim mean by social facts, the collective consciousness, and collective representations?

REVIEW QUESTIONS

49. How do the concepts of sacred and profane relate to Durkheim's theory of religion, and what is the role of the totem?
50. How did Durkheim's vision of society differ from the vision of Karl Marx?

Max Weber

51. How was the analysis of Max Weber different from the analyses of his contemporaries, especially Marx and Durkheim, and what was its central contribution to understanding the nature of culture?
52. What role did religion play in Weber's analysis? Which particular religion represents the theory he developed, and why?
53. How does Weber elaborate a theory of human agency?
54. According to Weber, what is rationalization, and why is the charismatic prophet central to his thinking?

Ferdinand de Saussure

55. How is Saussure's linguistics different from that of his predecessors?
56. In terms of its writing, what makes Saussure's *Course in General Linguistics* unusual as a text?
57. How does Saussure define the sign, what are its constituent elements, and how are these seen as changing over time?
58. According to Saussure, what is the distinction between langue and parole, and why is this distinction important?
59. Why must Saussure's theory be considered largely synchronic?

Part Two: The Early Twentieth Century

American Cultural Anthropology

60. How did Franz Boas's intellectual background shape his anthropology?
61. What is historical particularism?
62. What kind of influence did Boas exert in anthropology?

63. In what ways did Robert Lowie remain true to Boasian anthropology?
64. How did Alfred Louis Kroeber depart from Boasian anthropology?
65. Why did Margaret Mead undertake anthropological research in Samoa, what were her research findings, and what did Derek Freeman think about them?
66. What did Ruth Benedict write about in *Patterns of Culture*?
67. How did Mead and Benedict change the intellectual orientation of Boasian anthropology?
68. In what ways was Freudian psychology in theoretical conflict with Boasian anthropology?
69. In psychodynamic anthropology, how were culture and personality related?
70. How did Cora Du Bois study the Alorese psychodynamically?
71. How did John Whiting and Irvin Child attempt to make psychological anthropology rigorous?

French Structural Anthropology

72. What role do total social facts play in the work of Marcel Mauss?
73. What does the principle of reciprocity refer to?
74. How do the concepts of binary opposition and exchange figure in Lévi-Strauss's structural analysis of kinship?
75. What social function is fulfilled by the exchange of women in "primitive" societies?
76. What is the relationship among the theories of Émile Durkheim, Marcel Mauss, and Claude Lévi-Strauss?
77. In what ways, and by whom, has French structural anthropology been interpreted for an Anglophone audience?
78. What is structural Marxism?
79. What was the basis of the disagreement between economic formalists and substantivists?
80. What has Lévi-Strauss's perspective on Marxism been, and how has it affected other scholars?
81. What does Marshall Sahlins mean by the "structure of the conjunction," and how is it relevant to his study of the colonial encounter in Hawaii?

REVIEW QUESTIONS

82. What is the basis for disagreement between Sahlins and Gananath Obeyesekere?

British Social Anthropology

83. What is the organismic analogy, and what is its significance for anthropology?
84. What did Alfred Reginald Radcliffe-Brown mean by structural-functionalism?
85. What was Radcliffe-Brown's influence on American anthropology?
86. What was Bronislaw Malinowski's theory of functionalism, and how did his theory differ from that of Radcliffe-Brown?
87. How did Africa figure in British social anthropology?
88. What role did history and meaning play in the work of E.E. Evans-Pritchard?
89. What arguments did Evans-Pritchard develop to oppose the idea of prelogical thought?
90. How did Max Gluckman help to transform the notion of social structure in British anthropology?
91. What were the research interests of members of the Manchester School?
92. Besides Radcliffe-Brown, Malinowski, Evans-Pritchard, and Gluckman, who else made contributions to British social anthropology, and what were their contributions?

Part Three: The Later Twentieth and Early Twenty-First Centuries

Cognitive Anthropology

93. What is the difference between emics and etics, and how does the difference derive from the study of language?
94. What is the Sapir-Whorf hypothesis?
95. In Sapir and Whorf 's theory, how did the Hopi language contrast with Standard Average European (SAE)?
96. What methods and concepts are employed in cognitive anthropology?

97. What is componential analysis, and who was the central architect of this approach?

Cultural Neo-Evolutionism

98. How does thermodynamics figure in Leslie White's science of culturology?
99. How did Julian Steward differentiate multilineal, unilineal, and universal versions of cultural evolutionism?
100. How did Marshall Sahlins and Elman Service reconcile the evolutionary views of White and Steward?
101. What do cultural neo-evolutionism and the New Archaeology have in common?

Cultural Materialism

102. How do the distinctions between emics and etics and between mental and behavioural perspectives figure in cultural materialism?
103. What is the principle of infrastructural determinism, and why does Marvin Harris recommend it over other principles?

Biologized Anthropology

104. What developments led to the emergence of biological approaches to human behaviour in the 1970s?
105. What was the New Physical Anthropology?
106. What are the assumptions and goals of human behavioural genetics?
107. What is the sociobiological solution to the problem of the evolution of altruism?
108. How does sociobiology explain differences between females and males?
109. What are some opinions about the applicability of sociobiology to anthropology?

REVIEW QUESTIONS

Symbolic and Interpretive Anthropology

110. What difficulties did meaning-oriented anthropologists have with previous approaches, especially in the United States, and against which perspectives were these anthropologists reacting?
111. What impact did Max Weber have on subsequent generations of anthropologists, especially anthropologists A.F. C. Wallace and Jean and John Comaroff?
112. What influence have Wilhelm Dilthey and Edmund Husserl had on symbolic and interpretive anthropology?
113. Out of which intellectual traditions did the symbolic approach emerge?
114. What were the similarities and differences between Victor Turner's application of Durkheim's ideas and the applications of structural-functionalists?
115. What are instrumental symbols, and how do they contrast with dominant symbols? Which term is better applied to the Ndembu *mudyi* tree, and why?
116. According to Victor Turner, what are liminality and anti-structure, and what role do these concepts play in ritual?
117. What made Clifford Geertz's interpretive anthropology distinct from Victor Turner's symbolic anthropology? What does each of these anthropologists mean by the terms symbol and symbolic?
118. What does Geertz mean by the term "thick description"?
119. According to Geertz, how does the cockfight reveal aspects of Balinese culture?
120. How did Ian Hodder's contextual approach to archaeology differ from the New Archaeology of Lewis Binford? Are there any thematic similarities between contextual archaeology and parallel developments in sociocultural anthropology?

Transactionalism

121. How does the transactionalist approach differ from other anthropological approaches, particularly those devised by British social anthropologists?
122. What role does the individual play in the theory of Fredrik Barth?

Feminism and Anthropology

123. Within feminist anthropology, what is meant by "the anthropology of women"? To what perspectives in sociocultural anthropology were feminists who introduced this phrase reacting?
124. What differences do feminist theorists perceive to exist between sex and gender?
125. Why does Marilyn Strathern think "anthropological feminism" a more fitting term than "feminist anthropology"?
126. How might scientific anthropology be viewed as simultaneously emphasizing and subverting social differences, from the feminist perspective?
127. What is "bio-logic," and what have its effects been in the study of Yoruban society, according to Oyèrónkẹ́ Oyewùmí?

Political Economy

128. What are the historical origins of political economy?
129. In what intellectual, social, and political climate did anthropological political economy first take hold, and what impact did this climate have on anthropological theory?
130. What impact has the distinction between the developed and underdeveloped world had on the shaping of anthropological political economy?
131. According to political economy, what is the world system, and how does it relate to the colonial encounter?
132. What objections did political economists have to Cartesian forms of analysis?
133. What is the relationship between the ideas of Karl Marx and those of anthropological political economists?
134. In political economic terms, what are material forces, and how do they create hegemony? How are these forces addressed by local cultures and societies?

REVIEW QUESTIONS

Postmodernity

135. Why is the concept of subjectivity so important in postmodern thought? Why do anthropologists in this tradition reject the project of modernity?
136. What is the difference between the postmodern and the poststructural?
137. What was Paul Feyerabend's perspective on scholarly paradigms?
138. In the formulation of Michel Foucault, what are the roles of discourses of power and knowledge in generating different forms of social relationships?
139. How does Foucault show madness to be a historical product of differential power relationships?
140. What, according to Pierre Bourdieu, are practice and habitus, and what roles do these concepts play in his theory?
141. What does Bourdieu mean by the term "symbolic capital"?
142. What is social constructionism, and what importance do many of its advocates attach to the concept of the invented tradition?
143. What is medical anthropology, and how is it *professionally* distinguished from other perspectives in modern anthropological theory?
144. What is biomedicine, and how do medical anthropologists perceive it to be different from other forms of medicine?

Globalization

145. How does the anthropological perspective on globalization differ from anthropological political economy?
146. What kinds of social phenomena do anthropological students of globalization investigate?

Public Anthropology

147. How may public anthropology be distinguished from applied anthropology?
148. How do self-identified public anthropologists view the role of theory in relation to the social good?
149. In what ways does public anthropology challenge the traditions of positivist science?

150. Who is the pundit, and what role does he or she play in American society, according to Catherine Besteman and Hugh Gusterson?
151. Why might studies such as *The Bell Curve* be considered misguided from the perspective of public anthropology?
152. Why might contemporary anthropologists across the subfields consider eugenics repugnant?

Conclusion

153. According to Herbert Lewis, how have postmodern trends in anthropological theory distorted and misrepresented the value of anthropological ancestors?
154. What does the term "sacred bundle" refer to?
155. In reference to which issues have anthropologists debated the pros and cons of a four-field schism?

Glossary

This glossary provides definitions of boldfaced terms.

adaptation In cultural ecology, the result of cultures adjusting to environments, or in Darwinian evolution, the result of natural selection.

adhesions Edward Burnett Tylor's name for cultural traits that are statistically significantly associated.

agency In recent anthropological theory, creative acts of intentioned individuals that generate social form and meaning.

allopathic The treatment of illness and disease using the knowledge and techniques of Western biomedicine.

altruism In sociobiology, "self-sacrificing" behaviour explained by kin selection.

American Anthropologist The flagship professional journal of the American Anthropological Association.

ancestor worship The veneration of departed relatives; in classical cultural evolutionism a religious phase.

androcentrism The deeply held cultural bias to view the male as intellectually, spiritually, and physically superior to the female.

anima An invisible and diffuse supernatural force that can take the form of souls and ghosts.

anomie According to Émile Durkheim, the sense of personal alienation caused by the absence of familiar social norms.

anthropo-geography The study of relationships among geographically contiguous cultures, as practiced by Friedrich Ratzel.

antipodes Opposites, or peoples on opposite sides of the world.

anti-structure According to Victor Turner, the side of culture expressed through ritual "chaos," as during liminal states.

applied anthropology Anthropology conducted by anthropologists working outside traditional academic settings such as universities.

armchair anthropologist An anthropologist who has done little or no fieldwork.

australopiths Primitive ape-like human ancestors known from fossils found in Africa.

authoritative knowledge The idea that one body of knowledge is privileged over other bodies in that it has greater access to ultimate reality or the "Truth."

band The simplest form of human social organization, placed in evolutionary sequence before the tribe, chiefdom, and state.

basic personality structure In psychodynamic anthropology, core personality, shaped by primary cultural institutions and projected onto secondary cultural institutions.

behavioural genetics The branch of genetics that investigates inherited contributions to behavioural differences.

binary oppositions In French structural anthropology, the universal logic of dualities.

binomial nomenclature The hierarchical system of classifying living things into named scientific groups, with one name for genus and a second name for species.

biocultural anthropology Anthropology aimed at exploring interactions between human biology and culture, usually according to ecology.

biogenetic law The principle that ontogeny, the growth of the individual, recapitulates phylogeny, the growth of the species.

bio-logic A term used by anthropologist Oyèrónké Oyewùmí to describe the basic assumption of biological determinism that underlines Western scientific knowledge of sex and gender.

biology of nepotism A colloquial label for sociobiology focusing on the preferential treatment of kin.

biomedicine The science-based form of ethnomedical knowledge and practice dominant in Western societies.

body language A colloquial term for nonverbal communication.

body-reasoning A term used by anthropologist Oyèrónké Oyewùmí to describe Western science's assumption that the human body is a universal foundation for objective knowledge of identity.

bourgeoisie In Marxism, the middle class.

British empiricism The scientific epistemology of induction fashioned by philosophers Francis Bacon and John Locke.

British social anthropology The school of structuralism and functionalism led by Alfred Reginald Radcliffe-Brown and Bronislaw Malinowski.

Calvinist Protestantism The Christian doctrines and practices traced to John Calvin that oppose Roman Catholicism on the basis of scripture and justification by faith.

Cartesian The adjective derived from the name of philosopher René Descartes labeling a radical dualism between mind and matter, body and soul, and subject and object.

catastrophism The geological doctrine that agents of geological change have been more dramatic in the past than in the present; contrasted with uniformitarianism.

cephalic index The measured ratio of head breadth to head length, used in nineteenth-century racial classifications.

charismatic prophets As identified by Max Weber, individuals who experience a revelation that mandates the establishment of a new social order based on new ethical ideals.

classical cultural evolutionism The theoretical orientation of nineteenth-century cultural evolutionists who used the comparative method.

classificatory A type of kinship, contrasted with the descriptive type, that merges kinship categories.

cognitive anthropology The school concerned with folk taxonomies and semantic domains as practised in ethnolinguistics and by ethnoscientists in the New Ethnography.

collective consciousness According to Émile Durkheim, the source of collective representations of social facts, sometimes called the group mind.

collective representations According to Émile Durkheim, manifestations of the collective consciousness, or group mind.

colonial encounter The historical encounter between European colonizers and the Indigenous peoples of the world, who were then often marginalized or oppressed by colonialism.

communitas A term employed by Victor Turner to refer to the ritual fusion of individuals into a collective identity.

comparative method The use of extant primitive peoples to represent extinct primitive peoples, as in classical cultural evolutionism.

componential analysis A research technique of cognitive anthropologists used to generate folk taxonomies of semantic domains.

configurationalism The search for cultural patterns, often in the idiom of psychology.

consanguine A family type based on group marriage between brothers and sisters.

contextual Pertaining to post-processual archaeologists critical of the nomothetic New Archaeology.

contract societies In the schema of Henry Maine, societies that stress individualism, hold property in private, and maintain control by legal sanctions; contrasted with status societies.

Copperbelt A region of central Zambia and the Democratic Republic of Congo that served as a research site for Max Gluckman and other associates of the Rhodes-Livingstone Institute.

core In world-system theory, Western nations and regions that expropriate and control resources of non-Western nations and regions; contrasted with the periphery.

cosmological order A religious phrase describing the nature of otherworldly deities or powers and their relationships to human beings.

cosmology The branch of philosophy concerned with the origin and structure of the universe.

creationism The view that biological species are divinely created and do not evolve.

creolization An anthropological term borrowed from linguistics suggesting the fusion of divergent cultural concepts and practices, particularly in the context of postcolonial and globalization studies.

criterion of form The criterion used by anthropo-geographers to determine that similar cultural forms are the result of diffusion.

critical anthropologists Anthropologists who self-reflect and share criticisms of positivism.

cross-cousins Cousins related through parents of the opposite sex.

cross-cultural analysis Analysis of cultural similarities and differences.

cultural ecology The examination of interactions between cultural and environmental variables.

cultural materialism The theory of Marvin Harris that distinguishes emic from etic perspectives and mental from behavioural domains, and that advocates infrastructural determinism.

cultural neo-evolutionism Twentieth-century cultural evolutionism, a revival and reformulation of classical cultural evolutionism.

cultural relativism The proposition that cultural differences should not be judged by absolute standards.

cultural resource management (CRM) Activities that share the practical goal of protecting and preserving objects and places deemed to be of cultural significance.

culture area A geographical area associated with a culture.

culture-at-a-distance The study of cultures without the benefit of fieldwork, practiced by American psychological anthropologists in the era of World War II.

culture circle In German *kulturkreis*, a concept used to represent the process of cultural diffusion.

culture-historical archaeology Archaeology as practiced in the era of Franz Boas's historical particularism.

culturology Leslie White's name for the nomothetic study of culture.

Darwinism A general label for ideas associated with Charles Darwin's theory of evolution.

deconstructionism A term describing the ambition of postmodernism to understand the political and cultural contexts "hidden" behind the writing, or "construction," of narratives.

deduction In scientific epistemology, the use of logic to reason from general to particular statements; contrasted with induction.

deistic Pertaining to deism, the view that God created the universe but remains relatively uninvolved in its day-to-day operations; contrasted with theistic.

descent group Individuals who perceive themselves to be descended in a lineage from a real or hypothetical common ancestor.

descriptive A type of kinship system, contrasted with the classificatory type, that splits kinship categories.

development and underdevelopment theory André Gunder Frank's theory about the systematic exploitation of underdeveloped nation-states and regions by developed nation-states and regions.

diachronic Historically oriented, or concerned with the past; contrasted with synchronic.

dialectical In the Marxist theory of dialectical materialism, philosopher Friedrich Hegel's formulation of historical change as proceeding in the form of thesis-antithesis-synthesis.

dialectical materialism The philosophy of Karl Marx and Friedrich Engels, commonly called Marxism.

diary disease Pierre Bourdieu's tongue-in-cheek label for the radical deconstruction of some postmodern theorists, particularly those preoccupied with second-guessing their own analyses.

dictatorship of the proletariat In the theory of dialectical materialism, the temporary phase of political organization leading to permanent communism.

diffusionism The doctrine that cultural innovations evolve once and are then acquired through borrowing or immigration; contrasted with independent invention.

discourses of power Michel Foucault's phrase for the spectrum of institutions, rhetorics, and strategies employed by one group to dominate another group.

DNA Deoxyribonucleic acid, the biochemical substance of heredity.

GLOSSARY

dominant symbol Victor Turner's term for a symbol with multiple, and sometimes contradictory, meanings.

doxa Pierre Bourdieu's term for a psychological state in which all members of a community consider relations natural, including relations of social, economic, and political inequality.

eclectics According to Marvin Harris, anthropologists who are sometimes cultural materialists and other times cultural idealists.

ego Translated "I," according to Sigmund Freud, the part of the psyche that interacts with the outside world.

Electra complex According to Sigmund Freud, a troublesome psychological state of girls induced by their sexual desire for their fathers; contrasted with the Oedipus complex.

elementary forms For Émile Durkheim, the equivalent of collective representations, similar to elementary structures.

elementary structures In French structural anthropology, universal mental logics and their cultural manifestations.

emic In the theory of cultural materialism, the epistemological perspective of the investigated, or "the insider point of view"; contrasted with etic.

enculturation The process of an individual acquiring culture, usually while growing up.

Enlightenment The period of eighteenth-century intellectual history preceding the French Revolution.

entropy Disorder in the universe, increasing according to the second law of thermodynamics.

epiphenomenon A phenomenon resulting from another phenomenon.

epistemology The branch of philosophy that explores the nature of knowledge.

ethical Pertaining to prescriptions for correct behaviour that put the individual in accordance with a metaphysical order.

ethnobotanist A practitioner of ethnobotany, the sociocultural anthropological subfield that investigates the cross-cultural use of plants.

ethnocentric Pertaining to ethnocentrism, or cultural bias.

ethnolinguistics The name for linguistically oriented research methods of cognitive anthropology.

ethnomedical Pertaining to ethnomedicine, the anthropological study of non-Western medical systems.

ethnoscience A term for the collection of methods used in cognitive anthropology.

ethos A term meaning spiritual character, used by some anthropologists to characterize a whole culture.

etic According to Marvin Harris, the epistemological perspective of the investigator, or "the outsider point of view"; contrasted with emic.

eugenicist Pertaining to eugenics, the now-discredited science that endeavoured to "improve" humanity through selective breeding.

Eurocentric The rating of non-European cultures according to a generalized European scale of norms and values.

evolutionary psychology An outgrowth of sociobiology that uses Charles Darwin's theory of evolution to explain aspects of human mentality and behaviour as adaptations from the past.

exogamy The practice of marrying or mating outside one's kinship group; contrasted with endogamy.

false consciousness In the theories of Marxism and cultural materialism, the capability of people to misrepresent the meaning of their behaviour to themselves and others.

father figures In the psychology of Sigmund Freud, totems that represent culturally ambivalent attitudes toward adult men.

female infanticide The practice of treating male children more favourably than female children, resulting in more female deaths.

fields According to Pierre Bourdieu, the dynamic configuration, or network, of objective relationships among social agents and positions.

fixed action pattern As conceived by human ethologists, an innate sequence of behaviour released by a key stimulus of an innate releasing mechanism.

folk taxonomies According to cognitive anthropologists, culturally conditioned maps of semantic domains.

formalists Economic anthropologists who maintained that Western economic concepts apply to non-Western economies; contrasted with substantivists.

French rationalism The intellectual tradition associated with René Descartes and the scientific epistemology of deduction.

French structural anthropology The theoretical orientation of Claude Lévi-Strauss and his followers invoking elementary mental structures, reciprocity, and binary oppositions.

Freudian anthropology The school of psychological anthropology incorporating certain elements of the psychology of Sigmund Freud, also called psychodynamic anthropology.

functionalism In British social anthropology, either Alfred Reginald Radcliffe-Brown's theory of how parts of a society contribute to the whole of society or Bronislaw Malinowski's theory of how culture responds to biological needs in a hierarchically organized way.

functionalist archaeology Archaeology practiced in accordance with the theory of functionalism.

geisteswissenschaften Translated "human sciences," including anthropology; contrasted with *naturwissenschaften*.

gender The various social roles and identities attributed to individuals and groups on the basis of their biological sex.

genealogical method The method of focusing ethnographic fieldwork on kinship, pioneered by British social anthropologists, notably William H. R. Rivers.

generalized exchange According to Claude Lévi-Strauss, the exchange of women among more than two kinship groups, promoting greater social solidarity than restricted exchange.

general systems theory A cybernetic model for culture used in the New Archaeology.

gestalt A psychological configuration, attributed by some psychological anthropologists to an entire culture.

globalization The expansion of Western institutions and lifeways into non-Western cultures and the emergence of new forms of cultural practice that are global in scope.

global village Marshall McLuhan's term for an increasingly interconnected global society.

glocalization A term popularized by Roland Robertson to describe the coexistence of globalizing and particularizing tendencies in a society.

Great Chain of Being A medieval philosophical schema that ranked all cosmic and earthly elements, including people, in a single ascending line of importance.

great man theory of history The theory that individuals affect the course of history more than do historical circumstances.

great tradition Robert Redfield's term for cultures characterized by literacy, industrialization, and rational religions; contrasted with little tradition.

group mind According to Émile Durkheim, the source of collective representations of social facts, sometimes called collective consciousness.

group selection A form of natural selection in which individuals behave altruistically, helping their group, and thereby helping themselves; contrasted with kin selection.

habitus Pierre Bourdieu's term for the capacity of individuals to innovate cultural forms based on their personal histories and positions within the community.

hegemony A term for the capacity of one social group to impose particular beliefs or political and economic conditions upon another group.

heliocentrism Literally sun-centredness, the diffusionist view that world civilizations arose from sun worship in Egypt and then spread elsewhere.

hereditarian Pertaining to the idea that differences among human beings can be accounted for primarily in terms of differential gene distribution.

hermeneutics The study of meaning, especially in literary texts, applied by interpretive and postmodern anthropologists to the study of culture.

historical linguistics The study of language consisting in the reconstruction and descriptive tracking of language genealogies over time.

historical particularism The theoretical orientation of Franz Boas and many of his students who focused on the particular histories of particular cultures.

holistic Pertaining to an overarching or integrated outlook, often associated with the broad scope of anthropological inquiry.

human biogram A term used in human ethology to describe the alleged suite of inherited predispositions of *Homo sapiens*.

human ethology A hereditarian approach to the study of human behaviour, derived in part from Darwinism and employing the analytical constructs of fixed action pattern, innate releasing mechanism, and key stimulus.

hypothetico-deductive model A philosophical model for scientific explanation used in the New Archaeology.

hysteria The clinical condition of calm hallucination that got Sigmund Freud interested in psychology.

id Or libido, according to Sigmund Freud, the part of the human psyche that expresses natural desires.

idealistic Pertaining to idealism, a perspective that looks to ideas and meanings, rather than material conditions, as the wellspring of culture.

idealists According to Marvin Harris, followers of cultural idealism, the misguided belief that culture change usually begins in the emic superstructure.

ideology A term used by Karl Marx and Marxist scholars denoting a system of beliefs that influences the outlooks of individuals and groups.

idiographic Pertaining to a particularizing approach to description and explanation; contrasted with nomothetic.

The Imperial Synthesis A name for the nineteenth-century synthesis of archaeology, racism, and colonialism.

incest Culturally proscribed inbreeding that, according to Sigmund Freud, is an act that led to the primal patricide.

inclusive fitness In sociobiology, the measure, or result, of kin selection.

independent invention The doctrine linked to psychic unity that cultural innovation can occur independently in more than one place; contrasted with diffusionism.

indirect rule The British colonial policy of co-opting Native leaders in order to avoid having to govern by force.

induction In scientific epistemology, the process of arriving at generalizations about particular facts; contrasted with deduction.

informant In anthropological fieldwork, someone who provides information.

infrastructural determinism In Marvin Harris's theory of cultural materialism, the name for the belief that culture change usually begins in the etic infrastructure.

inheritance of acquired characteristics The mechanism of biological evolution proposed by Jean Lamarck whereby traits acquired in one generation can be transmitted to subsequent generations.

innate releasing mechanism As conceived by human ethologists, the mechanism that, when triggered by a key stimulus, releases a fixed action pattern.

inner-worldly asceticism According to Max Weber, the ethical demand of Calvinist Protestantism that Christians not retreat from the world in order to live piously.

instrumental symbols Victor Turner's term for those symbols that can be consciously wielded in ritual as a form of technology in order to achieve particular ends.

interpretive anthropology The anthropological school, associated with Clifford Geertz, espousing the view that culture is lived experience integrated into a coherent, public system of symbols that renders the world intelligible.

invented tradition A phrase describing the modern invention of historical events and personages, often with the goal of legitimizing contemporary political or religious ideologies by linking them directly to Antiquity.

Ivory Tower A euphemistic and usually pejorative term for the Academy, or universities.

key stimulus As conceived by human ethologists, the device that triggers an innate releasing mechanism, thus releasing a fixed action pattern.

kinesics The scientific study of human body motion.

kin selection In sociobiology, reproductive success via genes shared with relatives; sometimes called the biology of nepotism.

Kuhn, Thomas The American historian and philosopher of science who represented science as paradigmatic.

GLOSSARY

kulturkreis Translated "culture circle"; according to certain theorists, the pattern of diffusion of cultural traits.

labour theory of value The proposition of Karl Marx that commodities should be valued in terms of the human labour required to produce them.

Lamarckism The evolutionary philosophy of Jean Lamarck, notably his mechanism of the inheritance of acquired characteristics.

landscape archaeology Archaeology that considers artifacts and features to be expressions of culture, both incorporating and modifying elements of the natural world.

langue In Ferdinand de Saussure's linguistics, reference to language as an abstract system that can be studied independently of actual speech, or parole.

law of universal gravitation Isaac Newton's scientific explanation of universal planetary and earthly motion.

layer-cake model of culture Leslie White's model of culture, with technology and economy at the bottom, ideology at the top, and social and political organization in between.

liminal An ephemeral psychosocial space in which social arrangements are subject to transformation, inversion, and affirmation.

lineages Multi-generational kinship groups with membership determined by ties to common ancestors.

little tradition According to Robert Redfield, cultures characterized by illiteracy, preindustrial economies, and "irrational" supernatural beliefs; contrasted with great tradition.

Lono In pre-colonial Hawaii, a god responsible for fertility and fecundity.

maintenance systems In the psychological anthropological model of John Whiting and Irvin Child, the equivalent of Abram Kardiner's primary cultural institutions without Freudian components.

Manchester School A coterie of anthropologists trained under Max Gluckman at Manchester University in the 1950s and 1960s.

Marxism A collection of views derived from Karl Marx and Friedrich Engels and their theory of dialectical materialism.

Marxist archaeology Archaeology conducted in accordance with the principles of Marxism.

material culture Cultural meaning expressed in the products of human artifice, or artifacts.

materialism In dialectical materialism, the belief that human existence determines human consciousness; in cultural materialism, the equivalent of the principle of infrastructural determinism.

matrilateral cross-cousin marriage Marriage to a child of one's mother's brother; contrasted with patrilateral cross-cousin marriage.

matrilineal Unilineal kinship systems reckoned through the female line.

means of production In dialectical materialism, how people make a living in the material world.

mechanical philosophy The philosophy inspired by the law of universal gravitation, portraying the universe as a complex machine with fine-tuned, interacting parts.

mechanical solidarity According to Émile Durkheim, social cohesion maintained by similarities among individuals; contrasted with organic solidarity.

mechanics The medieval science of motion.

medical anthropology The cross-cultural, pan-historical study of sickness and health.

Midwestern Taxonomic Method The archaeological classification used in culture-historical archaeology.

missing links Perceived gaps in the evolutionary record.

modernization The Western practice of transforming non-capitalist, preindustrial economies into capitalist, industrial economies.

monogenesis The doctrine that human races constitute a single biological species with a common origin and with differences produced over time; contrasted with polygenesis.

monotheism The belief in a single deity; contrasted with polytheism.

Moundbuilder Myth The myth that a mysterious people other than Native Americans built impressive earthen mounds throughout the American Midwest.

multilineal According to Max Weber, culture change occurring in fits and starts in different historical contexts; according to Julian Steward, "branching" cultural evolution; contrasted with universal and unilineal cultural evolution.

multivocal The quality of having more than one possible meaning or interpretation.

museological Pertaining to museology, the academic discipline focusing on museum organization, management, and cultural representation.

naked apery A disparaging term used to describe unfounded assertions about the inheritance of human behaviour.

national character According to certain psychological anthropologists, the dominant personality of a nation.

natural children The early theological conception of "primitive" peoples as capable of "improvement" and conversion to Christianity.

natural selection Charles Darwin's mechanism for biological evolution, involving struggle for existence and survival of the fittest.

natural slaves The early theological conception of "primitive" peoples as innately imperfect and subservient to European Christians.

naturwissenschaften Translated "natural sciences"; contrasted with *geisteswissenschaften*.

neo-evolutionists Twentieth-century anthropologists who revived and reformulated nineteenth-century classical cultural evolutionism.

neoliberal economics A form of political-economic ideology in which governments promote competition among businesses within a capitalist market theoretically free of state oversight.

Neolithic Or New Stone Age, the period of prehistory characterized by polished stone tools and the domestication of animals and plants.

Neptunists Geologists who proposed that the principal agent of major geological change was the subsidence of water; contrasted with Vulcanists.

New Archaeology The nomothetic archaeology advocated by Lewis Binford; also called processual archaeology.

GLOSSARY

New Ethnography A name for cognitive anthropology focusing on the methodologies of ethnoscience and ethnolinguistics.

New Physical Anthropology The name for physical anthropology committed to the synthetic theory of evolution.

New Stone Age Or Neolithic, the period of prehistory characterized by polished stone tools and the domestication of animals and plants.

nihilism The perspective that traditional values and beliefs are fundamentally uncertain and that existence is at base nonsensical.

noble savagery The romanticization of "primitive" life.

nomothetic Generalizing; contrasted with idiographic.

Oedipus complex According to Sigmund Freud, the troublesome psychological state of boys induced by their sexual desire for their mothers; contrasted with the Electra complex.

Old Stone Age Or Paleolithic, the period of prehistory characterized by chipped and flaked stone tools and hunting and gathering subsistence.

ontogeny The biological growth of an individual.

organic solidarity According to Émile Durkheim, social cohesion maintained by differences and interdependence among individuals; contrasted with mechanical solidarity.

organismic analogy Likening society to an organism.

original sin The Christian idea that early sin resulted in the expulsion of humanity from the Garden of Eden.

orthogenesis The idea that biological evolution operates in one direction, usually leading to *Homo sapiens*.

oscillating equilibrium Edmund Leach's term for the continuing existence of social structure, even against the backdrop of constant social change.

Paleolithic Or Old Stone Age, the period of prehistory characterized by chipped and flaked stone tools and hunting and gathering.

paradigm According to Thomas Kuhn, an intellectual framework for "normal" science, which is superseded by another paradigm in a scientific "revolution."

parole In Ferdinand de Saussure's linguistics, reference to language as actually used in speech, often deviating from the abstract structural system of language, or langue.

participant-observation The style of anthropological fieldwork requiring the fieldworker to see things from both the "native" and the fieldworker's points of view.

patriarchy A social group governed exclusively by males or groups of males.

patrilateral cross-cousin marriage Marriage to a child of one's father's sister; contrasted with matrilateral cross-cousin marriage.

patrilineal Unilineal kinship systems reckoned through the male line.

periphery In world-system theory, non-Western regions dominated economically and politically by Western regions; contrasted with core.

personality variables In the psychological anthropological model of John Whiting and Irvin Child, the equivalent of Abram Kardiner's basic personality structure without Freudian components.

phenotype The product of gene action, often affected by environment.

philosophical anarchist Following Paul Feyerabend, someone who believes that all scientific paradigms are logically equivalent, with no logical way to choose among them.

phonemes Minimally contrasting pairs of sounds that create linguistic meaning.

phonemics The study of linguistic meaning created by sounds.

phonetics The study of linguistic sounds that create meaning.

phylogeny The evolutionary growth of a species.

pietistic Pertaining to piety, or religious reverence and devotion.

Pioneer Fund A philanthropic organization dedicated to advancing the "scientific study of heredity and human differences," said by its detractors to be tinged with biological determinism and racism.

pleasure principle According to Sigmund Freud, living libidinously, as directed by the id; contrasted with reality principle.

political economy An anthropological perspective viewing sociocultural form at the local level as penetrated and influenced by global capitalism.

pollution According to Mary Douglas, aspects of the world unexplained by a society's basic categories of understanding, thereby threatening the social order; contrasted with purity.

polyandry Mating or marriage involving one woman and more than one man.

polygenesis The doctrine that human races constitute separate species with separate origins and innate differences; contrasted with monogenesis.

polygenic Variation in phenotype affected by the action of many genes.

polysemous Having more than one meaning or significance.

polytheism The belief in multiple deities; contrasted with monotheism.

positivism The view that science is objective and value-free.

Positivism The scientific philosophy of Auguste Comte.

postcolonialism A distinctive body of research and theory within anthropology that seeks to better understand the historical and cultural interconnections between colonizers and the colonized.

postmodernism A movement within the social sciences and humanities that questions the possibility of impartiality, objectivity, or authoritative knowledge.

post-processualists Archaeologists critical of the New Archaeology; also called contextual archaeologists.

poststructural An adjective that expresses disenchantment with static, mechanistic, and controlling models of culture, with a consequent interest in social process and agency.

potlatch A Pacific Northwest Native ceremony characterized by conspicuous exchange and consumption of goods.

practice Or praxis; according to Pierre Bourdieu, the concept that society is constructed by purposeful, creative agents who bring society to life through talk and action.

Prague School A school of linguists based in Prague that pioneered the analysis of phonemes.

praxis Or practice; according to Pierre Bourdieu, the concept that society is constructed by purposeful, creative agents who bring society to life through talk and action.

prehistory The period of human existence before writing.

primal patricide In Sigmund Freud's hypothetical primeval family, the killing of the father by his sons.

primary cultural institutions In psychodynamic anthropology, institutions that affect how children are raised and that shape basic personality structure.

primeval family In Sigmund Freud's reconstruction of human history, the first family form—monogamous, nuclear, and patriarchal.

primitive communism In some versions of Marxism, the view that past primitive peoples lived in a state to which future communism will, in a fashion, return.

processual archaeology A name post-processual archaeologists use for the nomothetic New Archaeology.

profane According to Émile Durkheim, that which is routine, mundane, impure, and "of the world"; contrasted with the sacred.

projective systems In the psychological anthropological model of John Whiting and Irvin Child, the equivalent of Abram Kardiner's secondary cultural institutions without Freudian components.

proletariat In the lexicon of Marxism, the working class.

proxemics The scientific study of posture as a form of non-verbal communication, which is sometimes called "body language."

psyche According to Sigmund Freud, the subconscious, comprising the id, ego, and superego.

psychic unity The doctrine that all peoples have the same fundamental capacity for change.

psychodynamic Pertaining to the school of psychological anthropology that adopted certain elements of the psychology of Sigmund Freud; often called Freudian anthropology.

psychological anthropology Anthropology concerned with the relationship between cultures and personalities.

pundit A person deemed to be authoritative who renders opinions publically, frequently by way of the mass and electronic media.

purity According to Mary Douglas, the ideal of a seamless social order symbolically excluding that which threatens a society's basic categories of understanding; contrasted with pollution.

racial memory According to Sigmund Freud, the subconscious awareness of the history of the human psyche.

rationalized According to Max Weber, evolved through the systematization of ideas, corresponding norms of behaviours, and motivational commitment to those norms.

reality principle According to Sigmund Freud, the principle of realizing that acting on the pleasure principle is dangerous and immature.

reciprocal altruism In sociobiology, the "Biological Golden Rule," said to account for altruistic behaviour among non-relatives.

reciprocity According to Marcel Mauss, the elementary principle of exchanging gifts; according to Claude Lévi-Strauss, the elementary principle of exchanging women.

reflexivity A popular postmodern analytical strategy of reflecting on the biases and assumptions that inform one's own theories and perspectives.

relatively non-privileged A phrase coined by Max Weber to describe those socioeconomic classes in complex societies most prone to the creation of new social forms.

religion An integrated system of meanings and practices that seeks to connect humankind with a divine or metaphysical order.

restricted exchange According to Claude Lévi-Strauss, the exchange of women between two kinship groups.

revitalization movement A term coined by Anthony F.C. Wallace to describe the spontaneous evolution of culture that occurs when communities experience conditions of extreme social and economic duress or marginalization.

Rhodes-Livingstone Institute A research institute in Zambia that conducted much ethnographic research in the final years of British colonialism, later called the Zambian National Research Institute.

ritual Any form of prescribed behaviour that is periodically repeated and links the actions of the individual or group to a metaphysical order of existence.

ritual process Arnold van Gennep's term for the tripartite nature of ritual, involving separation from society, transition to a new social status, and a new incorporation into society.

rituals of rebellion A phrase coined by Max Gluckman to describe the socially constructive role of ritual in helping to avoid real conflict.

ruling class In the theory of dialectical materialism, the class that controls the means of production.

sacred According to Émile Durkheim, that which is pure, powerful, and supernatural; contrasted with the profane.

salvage ethnography Ethnography motivated by the need to obtain information about cultures threatened with extinction or assimilation.

salvation According to Max Weber, escape from worldly capriciousness and evil through social arrangements rationalized in accordance with a divine plan, typically revealed by charismatic prophets.

Sapir-Whorf hypothesis The proposition of Edward Sapir and Benjamin Whorf that the structure of language conditions the nature of cultural meaning.

savagery, barbarism, and civilization Lewis Henry Morgan's tripartite schema for the universal evolution of humanity.

scientific racism Improper or incorrect science that actively or passively supports racism.

secondary cultural institutions In psychodynamic anthropology, social institutions that are projections of basic personality structure and help people cope with the world.

second law of thermodynamics The scientific proposition that the universe is running down, thereby increasing disorder, or entropy.

secularization theory A body of research and theory within sociology and political science that assumes the demise of religion in a modernizing world.

GLOSSARY

semantic domain A mental domain of cultural meaning that is the focus of inquiry in cognitive anthropology.

semiotic Pertaining to the relationship between symbols and what they represent.

seriationally According to the archaeological principle of seriation, or relative dating by the evolution of artifact style.

sexual selection Charles Darwin's evolutionary mechanism whereby members of one sex compete for the attention of members of the opposite sex.

shamans Magico-religious specialists who communicate with ancestral ghosts and souls.

sign In Ferdinand de Saussure's linguistics, the pair formed in the relation of a signifier to a signified, the essence of relations among meaningful units in a language.

signified In Ferdinand de Saussure's linguistics, one of two units making up the sign, the concept generated in our minds when represented by a sound or image, the signifier.

signifier In Ferdinand de Saussure's linguistics, one of two units making up the sign, the word or image that represents a concept, the signified.

social constructionism The theory that sociocultural phenomena are products of historically-situated interpersonal negotiation accomplished through patterned language and activity.

Social Darwinism A loosely used term referring to social philosophies based on Darwinian evolutionism, especially the mechanism of natural selection.

social dynamics In Positivism, the study of social change.

social facts Émile Durkheim's name for social phenomena, his units of sociological analysis.

social function In British social anthropology, the contribution of a part of society to the whole of society; sometimes called social physiology.

social morphology In British social anthropology, according to the organismic analogy, the study of social structure.

social physiology In British social anthropology, according to the organismic analogy, the study of social function.

social process According to late structural-functionalism, social change as the ongoing creation of a fluid, dynamic social structure.

social statics In Positivism, the study of social stability.

social structure In British social anthropology, the social matrix of behaviour; some times called social morphology.

sociobiology An investigation of the biological basis of social behaviour using the evolutionary principles of kin selection and inclusive fitness.

solipsism The idea that the individual self is the only reality and that the external world exists only in one's imagination.

Southwest School A group of German philosophers who differentiated human sciences, or *geisteswissenschaften*, and natural sciences, or *naturwissenschaften*.

species A group of organisms whose members can reproduce only with one another.

status societies In the schema of Henry Maine, societies that are family-oriented, hold property in common, and maintain control by social sanctions; contrasted with contract societies.

Stone Age The Old Stone Age, or Paleolithic, and the New Stone Age, or Neolithic.

stratigraphy The archaeological dating of artifacts relative to their placement in systematically layered earth.

structural-functionalism In British social anthropology, the synchronic concern with social structure and social function.

structuralism In British social anthropology, the synchronic concern with social structure, sometimes called social morphology, and in French structural anthropology, the concern with the elementary forms of minds and cultures.

structure of the conjuncture Marshall Sahlins's phrase describing the space of intersection between different cultural structures, where contingency produces historical change.

structural Marxists Proponents of a theoretical blend of Marxism, dialectical philosophy, and French structural anthropology.

struggle for existence Charles Darwin's view that evolution by natural selection involves competition for limited resources and results in survival of the fittest.

subconscious According to Sigmund Freud, the part of the mind that is the seat of the psyche, of which people are aware only unconsciously.

sublimate According to Sigmund Freud, to rechannel libidinous desires into culturally acceptable thoughts and behaviours.

substantivists Economic anthropologists who maintained that Western economic concepts do not apply to non-Western economies; contrasted with formalists.

superego According to Sigmund Freud, the part of the psyche, sometimes called conscience, that monitors the id and mediates between the ego and the outside world.

superorganic The idea that culture is distinct from and "above" biology.

survival of the fittest In Charles Darwin's theory of evolution by natural selection, the adaptive outcome of the struggle for existence.

survivals Edward Burnett Tylor's name for nonfunctional cultural traits that are clues to the past.

swamping effect The observation in Charles Darwin's time that small variations would always be diluted by heredity and therefore could not increase or intensify through natural selection.

symbolic anthropology The anthropological school, associated with Victor Turner, espousing the view that social solidarity is a function of the systems of symbolic logic that connect people.

symbolic capital According to Pierre Bourdieu, the body of meanings, representations, and objects held to be prestigious or valuable to a social group.

symbolic domination According to Pierre Bourdieu, the tendency of dominant social groups to create and sustain a world view in which all members of a society, including subjugated members, participate.

sympathetic magic Magic that can affect an object through a similar object.

synchronic Concerned with the present more than the past; contrasted with diachronic.

synthetic philosophy The all-encompassing philosophy of Herbert Spencer based on the premise that homogeneity is evolving into heterogeneity everywhere.

GLOSSARY

Synthetic Theory of Evolution The twentieth-century theoretical synthesis of Darwinian evolutionism and Mendelian genetics.

taboos Culturally sanctioned prohibitions.

tabula rasa Translated "blank slate," the idea that the mind acquires knowledge through experience rather than recognizes knowledge that is innate.

teleology The idea that biological evolution adheres to a long-term purpose or goal.

text In the interpretive anthropology of Clifford Geertz, the equivalent of culture, interpreted through a process of thick description.

theistic Pertaining to theism, the view that God created the universe and remains active in its day-to-day operations; contrasted with deistic.

theodicy A Christian term used by Max Weber to describe the explanation of evil in the world despite the existence of an omnipotent, just, and loving God.

thermodynamic law $E \times T > P$, or energy times technology yields cultural product, the nomothetic basis of Leslie White's culturology.

thermodynamics The study of conversion of energy in the universe, a fundamental part of culturology as expressed in the second law of thermodynamics.

thesis-antithesis-synthesis In dialectical materialism, Friedrich Hegel's form for dialectical change.

thick description In the interpretive anthropology of Clifford Geertz, the process of interpreting culture as text.

Three Age System The archaeological ages of Stone, Bronze, and Iron.

totems Objects of collective cultural veneration, according to several anthropological theorists, that are central to the maintenance of social stability.

transmigrate To pass into another body after death, as do spirits and ghosts.

truthy A satirical phrase coined by television personality Stephen Colbert to describe the implicit acceptance of a proposition where logic dictates otherwise or where there is a seeming lack of supporting evidence.

typological thinking Thinking of biological groups as homogeneous or pure when in fact they are heterogeneous and mixed.

Umma An Arabic word for "community," often used to designate the global diasporic Islamic "nation," a community of the faithful.

uniformitarianism The doctrine that gradual geological agents of change have operated throughout the past; contrasted with catastrophism.

unilineal Pertaining to the view that cultural evolution proceeds along the same lines everywhere, as in classical cultural evolution; contrasted with multilineal and universal evolution.

unilineal kinship systems Kinship systems reckoned through one parental line, either matrilineal or patrilineal.

universal Pertaining to a single schema for global cultural evolution; contrasted with unilineal and multilineal evolution.

universal historians Enlightenment thinkers who promulgated laws of human history.

universal pattern In cultural materialism, the levels of culture-infrastructure, structure, and superstructure—with emic and etic and mental and behavioural dimensions.

variables Carefully defined units of analysis that can be manipulated statistically and yield correlations.

vitalism The idea that biological evolution is self-motivated or willed.

volksgeist Translated "spirit of the people," according to some early theorists, the ethnographic essence of a people.

Vulcanists Geologists who proposed that major geological changes were caused by the elevation of land brought about by volcanic heat; contrasted with Neptunists.

vulgar materialists A label for cultural materialists who, according to their critics, ignore dialectical thinking.

weapons of mass destruction Or WMDs, the euphemistic term for weapon technologies with the potential to cause casualties on a massive scale, for example, biological, chemical, and nuclear weapons.

world system According to political economists, the global expansion of Western capitalism creating a world system of unequal commodity exchange.

world-system theory Immanuel Wallerstein's theory that core nation-states are engaged in the systematic exploitation of peripheral nation-states for labour and natural resources.

xenophobic Pertaining to xenophobia, the fear and dislike of foreigners.

Yoruban Pertaining to the Yoruba, an ethnolinguistic African society whose historic homeland is in southwest Nigeria and eastern Benin.

Sources and Suggested Reading

This list of sources and suggested reading comprises citations of books (and a very few articles) culled from a vast literature in the history of anthropological theory. The list concentrates on secondary sources, or sources written *about* the past, but includes some primary sources, or sources written *in* the past (in a few instances near the present). Readers may wish to search the Internet for additional sources. If, at the time of preparing the list, a book was in print, its latest published citation was used. If a book was out of print, its citation was derived from another book or from the source itself. Although many books are relevant to more than one part of *A History of Anthropological Theory 3/e*, they are listed only once. Some original or earlier dates of publication appear in square [ ] brackets. For certain reprint editions, dates appear in brackets only.

Part One: The Early History of Anthropological Theory

ANTHROPOLOGY IN ANTIQUITY

Cole, Thomas. (1967). *Democritus and the Sources of Greek Anthropology*. Cleveland, OH: Western Reserve University Press.

A study of the roots of anthropology in Antiquity focusing on an early Greek philosopher of materialism.

Darnell, Regna (Ed.). (1974). *Readings in the History of Anthropology*. New York, NY: Harper and Row.

A collection of primary sources including some from ancient times.

Edelstein, Ludwig. (1967). *The Idea of Progress in Classical Antiquity*. Baltimore, MD: The Johns Hopkins University Press.

An examination of the ancient foundations of an idea intertwined with the history of anthropological theory.

Gernet, Louis. [1981]. *The Anthropology of Ancient Greece*. Ann Arbor, MI: Books on Demand.

An informative study of the ancient roots of anthropology.

Humphreys, S.C. (1981). *Anthropology and the Greeks*. New York, NY: Routledge.

A book of anthropology in and about Greece.

Kluckhohn, Clyde. [1961]. *Anthropology and the Classics*. Ann Arbor, MI: Books on Demand.

A study of the ancient roots of anthropology by a distinguished American anthropologist.

Malefijt, Annemarie de Waal. (1974). *Images of Man: A History of Anthropological Thought*. New York, NY: Alfred Knopf.

An intellectual and social history of anthropological theory beginning in classical times.

Sassi, Maria Michela. (2001). *The Science of Man in Ancient Greece*. Chicago, IL: University of Chicago Press.

An examination of ancient Greeks' attempts to answer questions about human nature, especially questions about human differences.

Snowden, Frank M., Jr. (1991). *Before Color Prejudice: The Ancient View of Blacks*. Cambridge, MA: Harvard University Press.

An historical study of the cultural contexts of race and racism.

Voget, Fred W. (1975). *A History of Ethnology*. New York, NY: Holt, Rinehart and Winston.
A compendium of ethnological developments beginning in Antiquity and extending into the twentieth century.

THE MIDDLE AGES

Boas, George. (1966). *Essays on Primitivism and Related Ideas in the Middle Ages*. New York, NY: Octagon Books.
Analyses of ideas that have influenced—and, in turn, been influenced by—anthropology.

Brehaut, Ernest. (1964). *An Encyclopedist of the Dark Ages, Isidore of Seville*. New York, NY: B. Franklin.
A biographical account of the life and times of one of the most influential early Christian historians.

Friedman, John B. [1963]. *The Monstrous Races in Medieval Art and Thought*. Ann Arbor, MI: Books on Demand.
An historical account of the anthropologically exotic.

Lovejoy, Arthur O. (1936). *Great Chain of Being: A Study of the History of an Idea*. Cambridge, MA: Harvard University Press.
An analysis of a philosophical schema that prevailed during the Middle Ages and shaped anthropology.

Mahdi, Muhsin. (1957). *Ibn Khaldûn's Philosophy of History: A Study in the Philosophic Foundation of the Science of Culture*. London: G. Allen and Unwin.
An analysis of the work of a medieval Islamic historian who described Arab and Bedouin culture "scientifically."

THE RENAISSANCE

Allen, Don C. [1963]. *The Legend of Noah: Renaissance Rationalism in Art, Science and Letters*. Ann Arbor, MI: Books on Demand.
An analysis of Renaissance thought that highlights Christianity.

Davis, Thomas W. (2004). *Shifting Sands: The Rise and Fall of Biblical Archaeology*. Oxford: Oxford University Press.
A history of archaeology and archaeologists interested in Biblical scholarship.

Dudley, Edward J., and Maximillian E. Novak (Eds.). [1972]. *The Wild Man Within: An Image in Western Thought from the Renaissance to Romanticism*. Ann Arbor, MI: Books on Demand.
The history of an image incorporated into many anthropological portrayals of non-Western peoples.

Levin, Harry. (1969). *The Myth of the Golden Age in the Renaissance*. Bloomington, IN: Indiana University Press.
An examination of the Renaissance discovery of Greco-Roman glories.

Penrose, Boies. (1955). *Travel and Discovery in the Renaissance, 1420-1620*. Cambridge, MA: Harvard University Press.
An account of the early phases of European global exploration.

Piggott, Stuart. (1989). *Ancient Britons and Antiquarian Imagination*. New York, NY: Thames and Hudson.
A distinguished British archaeologist writes about the development of antiquarianism in the Renaissance.

Trigger, Bruce. (1990). *A History of Archaeological Thought*. New York, NY: Cambridge University Press.
A comprehensive history of archaeology beginning with classical Renaissance historicism.

VOYAGES OF GEOGRAPHICAL DISCOVERY

Banton, Michael. (1998). *Racial Theories*. 2nd ed. New York, NY: Cambridge University Press
A revised edition of a study that demonstrates how eighteenth- and nineteenth-century scientists viewed races as permanent "types," featuring a new chapter on race as a social construct.

Berkhofer, Robert F., Jr. (1979). *The White Man's Indian: Images of the American Indian from Columbus to the Present*. New York, NY: Random House.
A history of American Indians as seen through the eyes of "whites."

Bieder, Robert E. (1986). *Science Encounters the Indian, Eighteen Twenty to Eighteen Eighty: The Early Years of American Ethnology*. Norman, OK: University of Oklahoma Press.
A history of early American ethnology shaped by interactions between aboriginal and non-aboriginal populations.

SOURCES AND SUGGESTED READING

Burgaleta, Claudio M. (1999). *Jose de Acosta, S.J. (1540-1600): His Life and Thought*. Chicago, IL: Loyola Press.

A biography of the Jesuit humanist and missionary, who, according to the author, helped establish the foundation for later "liberation" theologies.

Campbell, Mary B. (1988). *The Witness and the Other World: Exotic European Travel Writing, 400-1600*. Ithaca, NY: Cornell University Press.

An examination of the early phase of European geographical exploration.

Cohen, William B. [1980]. *The French Encounter with Africans: White Response to Blacks, 1530-1880*. Ann Arbor, MI: Books on Demand.

A history of French attitudes toward Africans in the early colonial period.

Curtin, Philip D. [1964]. *The Image of Africa: British Ideas and Action, 1780-1850*. Ann Arbor, MI: Books on Demand.

A history of British attitudes toward Africans in the early colonial period.

Dickason, Olive Patricia. (1984). *The Myth of the Savage and the Beginnings of French Colonialism in the Americas*. Edmonton, AB: University of Alberta Press.

An account of how early French perceptions of aboriginal Americans influenced French colonialism.

Dussel, Enrique. (1995). *The Invention of the Americas: Eclipse of "The Other" and the Myth of Modernity*. New York, NY: Continuum.

An account of the origin of an anthropological image of America.

Garbarino, Merwyn S. (1983). *Sociocultural Theory in Anthropology: A Short History*. Prospect Heights, IL: Waveland Press.

A concise history of major sociocultural theories beginning with the period of European geographical exploration.

Hammond, Dorothy, and Alta Jablow. [1992]. *The Africa that Never Was: Four Centuries of British Writing about Africa—An Anthropological View Contrasting the Africa of Fact and the Africa of Fiction*. Rev. ed. Prospect Heights, IL: Waveland Press.

A revisionist history of the British depiction of Africa.

Hanzeli, Victor E. (1969). *Missionary Linguistics in New France: A Study of Seventeenth and Eighteenth Century Descriptions of American Indian Languages*. The Hague: Mouton.

An assessment of the linguistic writings of early French missionaries in America.

Hodgen, Margaret T. (1964). *Early Anthropology in the Sixteenth and Seventeenth Centuries*. Philadelphia, PA: University of Pennsylvania Press.

Accounts of anthropology in the early modern period.

Huddleston, Lee Eldridge. (1967). *Origins of American Indians: European Concepts, 1492-1729*. Austin, TX: University of Texas Press.

A history of early European attempts to explain the origin of American Indians.

Moore, Sally Falk. (1994). *Anthropology and Africa: Changing Perspectives on a Changing Scene*. Charlottesville, VA: University Press of Virginia.

An account of how changes in Africa have interacted with changing anthropological views of Africa.

Pagden, Anthony. (1987). *The Fall of Natural Man: The American Indian and the Origins of Comparative Ethnology*. New York, NY: Cambridge University Press.

An account of how Europeans' early perceptions of American Indians affected both populations.

Schwartz, Stuart B. (Ed.). (1994). *Implicit Understandings: Observing, Reporting and Reflecting on the Encounters Between Europeans and Other Peoples in the Early Modern Era*. New York, NY: Cambridge University Press.

Analyses of early encounters between Europeans and non-Europeans.

Stocking, George W., Jr. (Ed.). (1993). *Colonial Situations: Essays on the Contextualization of Ethnographic Knowledge*. Madison, WI: University of Wisconsin Press.

Analyses of anthropology in the context of colonialism.

Wauchope, Robert. [1962]. *Lost Tribes and Sunken Continents: Myth and Method in the Study of American Indians*. Ann Arbor, MI: Books on Demand.

An account of early theories linking American Indians to Europeans.

THE SCIENTIFIC REVOLUTION

Hall, Marie Boas. (1962). *Scientific Renaissance, 1450-1630.* New York, NY: Harper.
A history of key developments in the Scientific Revolution.

Henry, John. (1997). *The Scientific Revolution and the Origins of Modern Science*. Old Tappan, NJ: Macmillan.
A concise history of the Scientific Revolution.

Hull, David. (1990). *Science as Process: An Evolutionary Account of the Social and Conceptual Development of Science*. Chicago, IL: University of Chicago Press.
An account of how science develops in social contexts.

Kuhn, Thomas S. (1970). *The Structure of Scientific Revolutions*. 2nd ed. Chicago, IL: University of Chicago Press.
An influential history of the Scientific Revolution as a shift of paradigms.

THE ENLIGHTENMENT

Berry, Christopher J. (1997). *Social Theory of the Scottish Enlightenment*. Edinburgh: Edinburgh University Press.
An examination of cultural and historical theorizing in Scotland between 1740 and 1790, updating Gladys Bryson's *Man and Society: The Scottish Inquiry of the Eighteenth Century* (1945).

Bryson, Gladys. (1968) [1945]. *Man and Society: The Scottish Inquiry of the Eighteenth Century*. New York, NY: Augustus M. Kelly.
An examination of Scottish Enlightenment contributions to anthropology.

Cloyd, E.L. (1972). *James Burnett, Lord Monboddo*. Oxford: Clarendon Press.
A biography of an Enlightenment thinker who thought that a properly conditioned ape could learn to talk like a human being.

Daiches, David, Peter Jones, and Jean Jones (Eds.): (1986). *A Hotbed of Genius: The Scottish Enlightenment, 1730-1790*. Edinburgh: Edinburgh University Press.
An intellectual history of the Scottish Enlightenment.

Danesi, Marcel (Ed.). (1995). *Giambattista Vico and Anglo-American Science: Philosophy and Writing*. Berlin: Mouton de Gruyter.
An assessment of the contributions of the influential Italian Enlightenment thinker.

Faull, Katherine M. (Ed.). (1995). *Anthropology and the German Enlightenment: Perspectives on Humanity*. Lewisburg, PA: Bucknell University Press.
A volume of essays about eighteenth-century German views on human nature, including essays on Johann Herder and Immanuel Kant.

Harris, Marvin. (1968). *The Rise of Anthropological Theory: A History of Theories of Culture*. New York, NY: Harper Collins.
Theories of culture critiqued from the perspective of cultural materialism, beginning with the Enlightenment.

Jones, Peter (Ed.). (1991). *The Science of Man in the Scottish Enlightenment: Hume, Reid and their Contemporaries*. New York, NY: Columbia University Press.
Assessments of the anthropological relevance of key Scottish Enlightenment figures.

Locke, John. (1994) [1690]. *An Essay Concerning Human Understanding*. Amherst, NY: Prometheus Books.
An essay setting forth Locke's concept of *tabula rasa*, an intellectual foundation of the Enlightenment.

Mali, Joseph. (1992). *The Rehabilitation of Myth: Vico's New Science*. New York, NY: Cambridge University Press.
An appraisal of the work of Giambattista Vico.

Miller, Cecilia. (1993). *Giambattista Vico: Imagination and Historical Knowledge*. New York, NY: St. Martin's Press.
Another account of Vico's life and times.

Rousseau, George Sebastian, and Roy Porter (Eds.). (1990). *Exoticism in the Enlightenment*. Manchester: Manchester University Press.
European conceptualizations of "exotic-looking" peoples.

Saiedi, Nader. (1992). *The Birth of Social Theory: Social Thought in the Enlightenment and Romanticism*. Lanham, MD: University Press of America.
The origins of social theory in the eighteenth and early nineteenth centuries.

SOURCES AND SUGGESTED READING

Zammito, John H. (2002). *Kant, Herder, and the Birth of Anthropology*. Chicago, IL: University of Chicago Press.
An examination of the relationship between philosophers Immanuel Kant and Johann Herder, aimed at demonstrating how anthropology originated in philosophy.

THE RISE OF POSITIVISM

Comte, Auguste. [1830-1842]. *Positive Philosophy*. Trans. Harriet Martineau. New York, NY: AMS Press.
Auguste Comte's explication of Positivism.

Pickering, Mary. (1993). *Auguste Comte: An Intellectual Biography, Vol. I*. New York, NY: Cambridge University Press.
A partial intellectual biography of the architect of nineteenth-century Positivist philosophy.

MARXISM

Archibald, W. Peter. (1992). *Marx and the Missing Link: Human Nature*. Atlantic Highlands, NJ: Humanities Press International.
An evaluation of Karl Marx's anthropological thinking.

Berlin, Isaiah. (1996). *Karl Marx: His Life and Environment*. 4th ed. New York, NY: Oxford University Press.
A biographical account of the life and times of Karl Marx.

Engels, Friedrich. (1972) [1884]. *Origin of the Family, Private Property, and the State*. 2nd ed. Ed. Eleanor B. Leacock. New York, NY: International Publishers Company.
Engels's views on cultural evolution.

Marx, Karl, and Friedrich Engels. (1992) [1848]. *The Communist Manifesto*. Ed. David McLellan. New York, NY: Oxford University Press.
Marx's and Engels's exposition of dialectical materialism.

Price, David. (1997). *Anthropologists on Trial: The Lessons of McCarthyism*. Paper presented at the Annual Meeting of the American Anthropological Association, Washington, DC, November.
Price describes the trials and tribulations of five Fellows of the American Anthropological Association.

—. (2000). The AAA and the CIA? *Anthropology News* 41(9): 13-14.
Price recounts interactions between the CIA and the American Anthropological Association in the 1950s.

—. (2003). The Spies Who Came in From the Dig. *The Guardian*. 4 September.
Price describes episodes of spying and alleged spying by twentieth-century archaeologists.

—. (2003). *Threatening Anthropology: McCarthyism and the FBI's Surveillance of Activist Anthropologists*. Durham, NC: Duke University Press.
An investigative report on anthropologists as victims and perpetrators of spying in the era of the Cold War.

Wakin, Eric. (1992). *Anthropology Goes to War: Professional Ethics and Counterinsurgency in Thailand*. Madison, WI: University of Wisconsin Press.
An analysis of ethical and political considerations surrounding anthropologists working for the American government in Thailand in the 1960s.

Woolfson, Charles. (1982). *The Labour Theory of Culture: A Re-Examination of Engels' Theory of Human Origins*. London: Routledge.
An evaluation of Engels's writings on anthropology.

CLASSICAL CULTURAL EVOLUTIONISM

Ackerman, Robert. (1990). *J.G. Frazer: His Life and Work*. New York, NY: Cambridge University Press.
A biography of the classical cultural evolutionist who studied myth, folklore, and religion.

Barnard, Alan. (2000). *History and Theory in Anthropology*. New York, NY: Cambridge University Press.
A survey of some of the great theoretical debates in anthropology, organized thematically and chronologically with emphasis on the shifting interests of theoreticians.

Bowler, Peter J. (1990). *The Invention of Progress: The Victorians and the Past*. Cambridge, MA: Blackwell.
An examination of the relationship between the ideas of progress and the past in Victorian times.

Burrow, J.W. (1966). *Evolution and Society: A Study in Victorian Social Theory*. London: Cambridge University Press.
A study of evolutionism as an expression of Victorian themes.

Coombes, Annie E. (1994). *Reinventing Africa: Museums, Material Culture, and Popular Imagination in Late Victorian and Edwardian England*. New Haven, CT: Yale University Press.
An evaluation of the role of museums in shaping and reflecting European attitudes toward Africans.

Diamond, Alan (Ed.). (1991). *The Victorian Achievement of Sir Henry Maine: A Centennial Appraisal*. New York, NY: Cambridge University Press.
Assessments of the lesser-known British classical cultural evolutionist.

Erickson, Paul A., and Liam D. Murphy (Eds.). (2006). *Readings for a History of Anthropological Theory*. 2nd ed. Peterborough, ON: Broadview Press.
A collection of original writings by anthropological theorists from the nineteenth to the twentieth century and beyond.

Eriksen, Thomas Hylland, and Finn Sivert Nielson. (2001). *A History of Anthropology*. Herndon, VA: Pluto Press.
A history of social and cultural anthropology from the nineteenth century onward, focusing on themes and controversies after World War I.

Fortes, Meyer. (1970). *Kinship and the Social Order: The Legacy of Lewis Henry Morgan*. Chicago, IL: Aldine.
Evaluation of a nineteenth-century American cultural evolutionist by a twentieth-century British social anthropologist.

Frasen, Robert. (1990). *The Making of The Golden Bough: The Origins and Growth of an Argument*. New York, NY: St. Martin's Press.
A book about the evolution of James Frazer's *magnum opus*.

Frazer, James G. (1985) [1890]. *The Golden Bough*. Abr. and rev. ed. Old Tappan, NJ: Macmillan.
An abbreviated version of Frazer's monumental multivolume work on the evolution of myth, folklore, and religion.

Hinsley, Curtis M., Jr. (1994). *The Smithsonian and the American Indian: Making a Moral Anthropology in Victorian America*. Washington, DC: Smithsonian Institution Press.
A study of the role a leading museum played in the development of nineteenth-century American anthropology.

Ihanus, Juhani. (1999). *Multiple Origins: Edward Westermarck in Search of Mankind*. Frankfurt: Peter Lang.
An appraisal of the Victorian-era anthropologist who studied the history of marriage and had ties to cultural evolutionists, social anthropologists, and psychologists.

Judd, Neil Merton. (1967). *The Bureau of American Ethnology: A Partial History*. Norman, OK: University of Oklahoma Press.
A history of one of the most influential institutions of anthropology in the United States.

McGee, R. Jon, and Richard Warms (Eds.). (2007). *Anthropological Theory: An Introductory History*. 3rd ed. Mountain View, CA: Mayfield Publishers.
A collection of writings by key anthropological theorists from the nineteenth century to the present, with introductions and pedagogical aids.

Moore, Jerry D. (1997). *Visions of Culture: An Introduction to Anthropological Theories and Theorists*. Walnut Creek, CA: Altimira Press.
Introductions to numerous influential cultural theorists, including some from the nineteenth century.

Morgan, Lewis Henry. (1985) [1877]. *Ancient Society*. Tucson, AZ: University of Arizona Press.
Morgan's *magnum opus*.

Rumney, Jay. (1966). *Herbert Spencer's Sociology: A Study in the History of Social Theory*. New York, NY: Atherton Press.
An account of Spencer as a social evolutionist.

Sanderson, Stephen K. (1992). *Social Evolutionism: A Critical History*. Cambridge, MA: Blackwell.
A critique of social evolutionism encompassing the Victorian era.

Spencer, Herbert. [1967]. *The Evolution of Society: Selections from Herbert Spencer's Principles of Sociology*. Ed. Robert L. Carneiro. Ann Arbor, MI: Books on Demand.
A collection of Spencer's writings on social evolution.

Stocking, George W., Jr. (1987). *Victorian Anthropology*. New York, NY: The Free Press.
A masterful history of anthropology in the Victorian era.

SOURCES AND SUGGESTED READING

—. (Ed.). (1988). *Objects and Others: Essays on Museums and Material Culture*. Madison, WI: University of Wisconsin Press.
A collection of writings on the roles of museums in anthropology.

—. (1994). *The Collected Works of E.B. Tylor*. New York, NY: Routledge.
A compendium of the writings of the Victorian "father" of British anthropology.

Trautman, Robert R. (1987). *Lewis Henry Morgan and the Invention of Kinship*. Berkeley, CA: University of California Press.
A biography of Morgan that places him on the foundation of the anthropological study of kinship.

Tylor, Edward Burnett. (1873) [1871]. *Primitive Culture*. New York, NY: Gordon Press.
Tylor's summation of anthropological knowledge.

—. (1898) [1881]. *Anthropology: An Introduction to the Study of Man and Civilization*. New York, NY: D. Appleton.
The first anthropology "textbook."

Zimmerman, Andrew. (2001). *Anthropology and Anti-Humanism in Imperial Germany*. Chicago, IL: University of Chicago Press.
An account of how nineteenth-century German imperialism allowed anthropology to challenge humanism in intellectual battles that resembled the "culture wars" of today.

EVOLUTIONISM VS. DIFFUSIONISM

Elkin, A.P., and N.W.G. Macintosh (Eds.). (1974). *Grafton Elliot Smith: The Man and His Work*. Sydney: Sydney University Press.
A collection of articles about a pioneering Australian anthropologist who espoused diffusionism.

Perry, William J. (1968) [1923]. *Children of the Sun: A Study in the Early History of Civilization*. Saint Clair Shores, MI: Scholarly Press.
The book that explains why Perry believed civilization arose in Egypt and then spread elsewhere.

ARCHAEOLOGY COMES OF AGE

Bahn, Paul G. (Ed.). (1996). *The Cambridge Illustrated History of Archaeology*. Cambridge: Cambridge University Press.
A history of worldwide archaeology focusing on Europeans' interactions with non-Europeans, introduced by a survey of the "archaeology of archaeology."

Bowden, Mark. (1991). *Pitt Rivers: The Life and Archaeological Work of Lieutenant-General Augustus Henry Lane Fox Pitt Rivers, DCL, FRS, FSA*. New York, NY: Cambridge University Press.
An intellectual biography of a pioneering British archaeologist.

Brunhouse, Robert Levere. (1974). *In Search of the Maya: The First Archaeologists*. New York, NY: Ballantine Books.
A lively account of the excitement surrounding early Mayan archaeology.

Claassen, Cheryl (Ed.). (1994). *Women in Archaeology*. Philadelphia, PA: University of Pennsylvania Press.
A collection of articles by and about women archaeologists.

Cordell, Linda, and Don Fowler (Eds.). (2005). *Southwest Archaeology in the Twentieth Century*. Salt Lake City, UT: University of Utah Press.
A wide-ranging collection of appraisals of archaeology in the American Southwest, some historical and others personal.

Daniel, Glyn E. (Ed.). (1981). *Towards a History of Archaeology*. New York, NY: Thames and Hudson.
A collection of essays on the history of archaeology, edited by a distinguished British prehistorian.

Daniel, Glyn E., and Colin Renfrew. (1988). *The Idea of Prehistory*. 2nd ed. Edinburgh: Edinburgh University Press.
An account of developments leading to acceptance of the idea of prehistory in nineteenth-century Europe.

Diaz-Andreu, Margarita, and Marie Louise Stig Sorensen (Eds.). (1998). *Excavating Women: History of Women in European Archaeology*. New York, NY: Routledge.
A collection of "engendered" accounts of European national archaeological traditions.

Drower, Margaret S. (1995). *Flinders Petrie: A Life in Archaeology*. Madison, WI: University of Wisconsin Press.
A biography of the famous Egyptologist.

Fowler, Don D. (2000). *A Laboratory for Anthropology: Science and Romanticism in the American Southwest, 1846-1930*. Albuquerque, NM: University of New Mexico Press.
A history of the idea of "The Southwest" in American anthropology and archaeology from the Mexican-American War to the New Deal.

Givens, Douglas. (1992). *Alfred Vincent Kidder and the Development of Americanist Archaeology*. Albuquerque, NM: University of New Mexico Press.
A biography of a well-known early archaeologist of the American Southwest.

Gräslund, Bo. (1987). *The Birth of Prehistoric Chronology: Dating Methods and Dating Systems in Nineteenth Century Scandinavian Archaeology*. New York, NY: Cambridge University Press.
A history of archaeological dating techniques and chronologies, including the chronology of Three Ages.

Grayson, Donald K. (Ed.). (1983). *The Establishment of Human Antiquity*. Orlando, FL: Academic Press.
Perspectives on the origins of the idea of human antiquity in nineteenth-century anthropology.

Hawkes, Jacquetta Hopkins. (1982). *Adventurer in Archaeology: The Biography of Sir Mortimer Wheeler*. New York, NY: St. Martin's Press.
A biography of one of the best known and most colourful twentieth-century British archaeologists.

Kehoe, Alice B., and Mary Beth Emmerichs (Eds.). (1999). *Assembling the Past: Studies in the Professionalization of Archaeology*. Albuquerque, NM: University of New Mexico Press.
A collection of essays exploring the transition from antiquarianism to professionalism in American archaeology in the decades around 1900.

Lubbock, John. (1977) [1865]. *Pre-Historic Times*. North Stratford, NH: Ayer.
Lubbock's summation of mid-nineteenth-century prehistoric archaeology.

Lyell, Charles. [1863]. *Geological Evidence of the Antiquity of Man*. 4th ed. New York, NY: AMS Press.
Lyell's landmark summation of the evidence for human prehistoric antiquity.

Meltzer, David (Ed.). (1998) [1848]. *Ancient Monuments of the Mississippi Valley, by E.G. Squier and E.H. Davis, with an Introduction by David Meltzer*. Washington, DC: Smithsonian Institution.
An edited edition of the landmark evaluation of evidence for prehistoric Mississippi Valley mound builders.

Murray, Tim. (1999). *Encyclopedia of Archaeology: The Great Archaeologists*. 2 vols. Santa Barbara, CA: ABC-Clio.
A collection of biographical sketches of "the greatest archaeologists ever" arranged chronologically from the Renaissance to the present.

O'Brien, Michael J., and R. Lee Lyman. (1998). *James A. Ford and the Growth of Americanist Archaeology*. Columbia, MO: University of Missouri Press.
An account of Ford's role in the development of the "culture history" approach to archaeology during the heyday of Boasian anthropology in the United States.

Robertshaw, Peter (Ed.). (1990). *A History of African Archaeology*. Portsmouth, NH: Heinemann.
A collection of perspectives on the history of archaeology in the formerly colonized continent.

Rupke, Nicholas A. (1983). *The Great Chain of History: William Buckland and the English School of Geology (1814-1849)*. Oxford: Clarendon Press.
A history of the early exploration of British caves with prehistoric human remains.

Silverberg, Robert. (1986). *The Mound-Builders*. Athens, OH: Ohio University Press.
A history of the myth that mysterious people other than Indians built prehistoric earthen mounds throughout the Midwestern United States.

Smith, Pamela Jane, and Donald Mitchell (Eds.). (1998). *Bringing Back the Past: Historical Perspectives on Canadian Archaeology*. Hull, QC: Canadian Museum of Civilization.
A collection of histories of archaeology in Canada divided into sections on people, institutions, regions, and "toward the present."

SOURCES AND SUGGESTED READING

Thomas, David Hurst. (2000). *Skull Wars: Kennewick Man, Archaeology, and the Battle for Native American Identity*. New York, NY: Basic Books.
Inspired by the 1996 discovery of "Kennewick Man," a history of relationships among American archaeologists, governments, and Native Americans.

Van Riper, A. Bowdin. (1993). *Men Among the Mammoths: Victorian Science and the Discovery of Human Prehistory*. Chicago, IL: University of Chicago Press.
A detailed history of scientific developments in the 1850s and 1860s leading to acceptance of the idea of prehistory in Britain.

Willey, Gordon R., and Jeremy A. Sabloff. (1995). *A History of American Archaeology*. 3rd ed. New York, NY: W.H. Freeman.
A comprehensive history of American archaeology.

CHARLES DARWIN AND DARWINISM

Bannister, Robert C. (1988). *Social Darwinism: Science and Myth*. Rev. ed. Philadelphia, PA: Temple University Press.
An analysis of scientific and extrascientific rationalizations for a Darwinian interpretation of society.

Bowler, Peter J. (1983). *The Eclipse of Darwinism: Anti-Darwinian Evolution Theories in the Decades Around 1900*. Baltimore, MD: Johns Hopkins University Press.
An explanation of how Darwin's theory of evolution by natural selection fell out of scientific favour by 1900.

—. (1986) *Theories of Human Evolution: A Century of Debate, 1844-1944*. Baltimore, MD: Johns Hopkins University Press.
A history of ideas about human evolution in the pre- and post-Darwinian periods.

—. (1989). *Evolution: The History of an Idea*. Rev. ed. Berkeley, CA: University of California Press.
A history of the complex idea of evolution.

—. (1989). *The Mendelian Revolution: The Emergence of Hereditarian Concepts in Modern Science and Society*. Baltimore, MD: Johns Hopkins University Press.
An examination of "nature versus nurture" in the nineteenth and twentieth centuries.

—. (1996). *Charles Darwin: The Man and His Influence*. New York, NY: Cambridge University Press.
A scientific biography of Darwin.

Burckhardt, Richard W., Jr. (1990). *The Spirit of System: Lamarck and Evolutionary Biology*. Cambridge, MA: Harvard University Press.
A scientific biography of the famous pre-Darwinian evolutionist Jean Lamarck.

Clements, Harry. (1983). *Alfred Russel Wallace: Biologist and Social Reformer*. London: Hutchinson.
A biography of the co-discoverer of the idea of natural selection.

Darwin, Charles. (1964) [1859]. *On the Origin of Species: A Facsimile of the First Edition*. Cambridge, MA: Harvard University Press.
Darwin's *magnum opus*.

—. (1981) [1871]. *The Descent of Man and Selection in Relation to Sex*. Princeton, NJ: Princeton University Press.
Darwin's explanation of human evolution.

Degler, Carl. (1992). *In Search of Human Nature: The Decline and Revival of Darwinism in American Social Thought*. New York, NY: Oxford University Press.
An examination of the ebb and flow of Social Darwinism in the United States.

Desmond, Adrian. (1994). *Huxley: The Devil's Disciple*. London: Michael Joseph.
The first of a two-part biography of Darwin's "bulldog" Thomas Henry Huxley.

—. (1997). *Huxley: Evolution's High Priest*. London: Michael Joseph.
The second of a two-part biography of Darwin's "bulldog" Thomas Henry Huxley.

Eckman, Paul. (1973). *Darwin and Facial Expression: A Century of Research in Review*. Orlando, FL: Academic Press.
A book that traces the history of human ethology back to Charles Darwin.

Eiseley, Loren C. (1958). *Darwin's Century: Evolution and the Men Who Discovered It*. Garden City, NY: Doubleday.
A non-technical history of key developments in Darwinism.

Fichman, Martin. (2004). *An Elusive Victorian: The Evolution of Alfred Russel Wallace*. Chicago, IL: University of Chicago Press.
An examination of the work and controversial intellectual views of the man who, with Charles Darwin, came up with the idea of evolution by natural selection.

Gillispie, Charles C. (1996) [1951]. *Genesis and Geology.* Cambridge, MA: Harvard University Press.
A study of the influence of Christian theology on geology in the decades leading up to *Origin of Species*.

Gilman, Nicholas Wright. (2001). *A Life of Sir Francis Galton: From African Exploration to the Birth of Eugenics*. New York, NY: Oxford University Press.
An informative biography of Charles Darwin's cousin and the recognized founder of eugenics.

Glick, Thomas F. (Ed.). (1988). *The Comparative Reception of Darwinism*. Chicago, IL: University of Chicago Press.
A collection of articles examining the early reception of Darwinism in several countries.

Gould, Stephen Jay. (1987). *Time's Arrow, Time's Cycle: Myth and Metaphor in the Discovery of Geological Time*. Cambridge, MA: Harvard University Press.
A book about influences on the geological conceptualization of time in the nineteenth century.

—. (1996). *The Mismeasure of Man*. New York, NY: W.W. Norton.
An examination of the use and abuse of anthropometric measurements by nineteenth-century racial anthropologists.

Greene, John C. (1959). *The Death of Adam: Evolution and its Impact on Western Thought*. Ames, IA: Iowa State University Press.
An eloquent history of Darwinism and its implication for anthropology.

Haller, John S., Jr. (1995) [1971]. *Outcasts from Evolution: Scientific Attitudes of Race Inferiority, 1859-1900*. Champaign, IL: University of Illinois Press.
An account of the persistence of racist views in post-Darwinian anthropology.

Hawkins, Mike. (1997). *Social Darwinism in European and American Thought, 1860-1945: Nature as Model and Nature as Threat*. New York, NY: Cambridge University Press.
An interpretive history of Social Darwinism in Euro-American culture.

Himmelfarb, Gertrude. (1959). *Darwin and the Darwinian Revolution*. London: Chatto and Windus.
An analysis of Darwinism as an expression of its social time and place.

Hofstadter, Richard. (1992) [1944]. *Social Darwinism in American Thought*. Boston, MA: Beacon Press.
An analysis of Social Darwinism in America in the decades after *Origin of Species*.

Lyell, Charles. (1970) [1830]. *Principles of Geology.* Forestburgh, NY: Lubrecht and Cramer.
Lyell's landmark treatise on uniformitarian geology.

Mayr, Ernst. (1990). *The Growth of Biological Thought: Diversity, Evolution, and Inheritance*. Cambridge, MA: The Belknap Press of Harvard University.
A masterful history of biology by one of the architects of the twentieth-century synthetic theory of evolution.

—. (1991). *One Long Argument: Charles Darwin and the Genesis of Modern Evolutionary Thought*. Cambridge, MA: Harvard University Press.
An exposition of the Darwinian origins of evolutionism.

McCown, Theodore D., and Kenneth A.R. Kennedy (Eds.). (1972). *Climbing Man's Family Tree: A Collection of Major Writings on Human Phylogeny, 1699-1971*. Englewood Cliffs, NJ: Prentice-Hall.
A collection of interpretations of human evolution spanning three centuries.

Millhauser, Milton. (1959). *Just Before Darwin: Robert Chambers and Vestiges*. Middletown, CT: Wesleyan University Press.
A scientific biography of one of the most notable pre-Darwinian evolutionists.

Olby, Robert C. (1995). *The Origins of Mendelism*. Chicago, IL: University of Chicago Press.
A history of early modern genetics and hereditarian outlooks in science.

SOURCES AND SUGGESTED READING

Oldroyd, David R. (1996). *Thinking About the Earth: A History of Ideas in Geology*. Cambridge, MA: Harvard University Press.
An intellectual history of geology by a respected historian of science.

Ruse, Michael. (1997). *Monad to Man: The Concept of Progress in Evolutionary Biology*. Cambridge, MA: Harvard University Press.
A history of biology linked to the idea of progress.

Schiller, Francis. (1992). *Paul Broca: Founder of French Anthropology, Explorer of the Brain*. New York, NY: Oxford University Press.
An intellectual biography of the leading French physical anthropologist of the nineteenth century.

Shipman, Pat. (2000). *The Man Who Found the Missing Link: Eugene Dubois and his Lifelong Quest to Prove Darwin Right*. New York, NY: Simon and Schuster.
A biography of the Dutch scientist who set out to find the "missing link" and in 1890 discovered "Pithecanthropus erectus," or "Java Man."

Spencer, Frank (Comp.). (1986). *Ecce Homo: An Annotated Bibliographic History of Physical Anthropology*. Westport, CT: Greenwood.
A major sourcebook compiled by a leading historian of physical anthropology.

—. (Ed.). (1997). *History of Physical Anthropology: An Encyclopedia*. New York, NY: Garland.
A comprehensive two-volume encyclopedic history of physical anthropology.

Stanton, William Ragan. (1960). *The Leopard's Spots: Scientific Attitudes Toward Race in America, 1815-1859*. Chicago, IL: University of Chicago Press.
A history of American anthropology in the first half of the nineteenth century, highlighting the "American School."

Stocking, George W., Jr. (1982). *Race, Culture and Evolution: Essays in the History of Anthropology*. Chicago, IL: University of Chicago Press.
An analysis of important themes in nineteenth- and twentieth-century anthropology.

—. (Ed.). (1990). *Bones, Bodies, and Behavior: Essays on Biological Anthropology*. Madison, WI: University of Wisconsin Press.
A collection of articles on a wide range of topics in the history of physical anthropology.

Young, Robert M. (1985). *Darwin's Metaphor: Nature's Place in Victorian Culture*. New York, NY: Cambridge University Press.
An examination of the conceptualization of "nature" in nineteenth-century science and culture.

SIGMUND FREUD

Freud, Sigmund. (1960) [1913]. *Totem and Taboo*. Trans. Abraham A. Brill. New York, NY: Random House.
Freud's anthropological speculations on the origin of the conflict between culture and the human psyche.

—. (1973) [1928]. *The Future of an Illusion*. Rev. and ed. James Strachey. London: Hogarth Press and the Institute of Psycho-Analysis.
Freud's further thoughts on the conflict between culture and the human psyche.

Gilman, Sander L. (1993). *Freud, Race, and Gender*. Princeton, NJ: Princeton University Press.
An examination of anthropological themes in Freudianism.

Kardiner, Abram, and Edward Preble. (1961). *They Studied Man*. Cleveland, OH: World Publishing Company.
Biographical sketches of prominent early anthropologists accompanied by an essay on the contributions of Sigmund Freud.

Ritvo, Lucile B. (1990). *Darwin's Influence on Freud: A Tale of Two Sciences*. New Haven, CT: Yale University Press.
Histories of nineteenth- and twentieth-century Darwinian biology and Freudian psychology.

Spiro, Melford E. (1992). *Oedipus in the Trobriands*. New Brunswick, NJ: Transaction.
An account of Bronislaw Malinowski's investigation of Freudian psychology in the Trobriand Islands.

Wallace, Edwin R., IV. (1983). *Freud and Anthropology: A History and Reappraisal*. Madison, CT: International Universities Press.
A critical examination of the relationship between Freudian psychology and anthropology.

ÉMILE DURKHEIM

Allen, N.J., W.E.S. Pickering, and W. Watts Miller (Eds.). (1998). *On Durkheim's Elementary Forms of Religious Life*. New York, NY: Routledge.
A collection of essays on Durkheim's "masterpiece" examining his views on religion and society from contemporary and historical perspectives.

Besnard, Philippe (Ed.). (1983). *The Sociological Domain, the Durkheimians and the Founding of French Sociology*. Cambridge: Cambridge University Press.
Examinations of Durkheim's role in shaping French sociology.

Durkheim, Émile. (1966) [1897]. *Suicide*. New York, NY: The Free Press.
Durkheim analyzes suicide from his sociological perspective.

—. (1982) [1895]. *The Rules of Sociological Method*. New York, NY: The Free Press.
Durkheim explains the importance of social facts.

—. (1984) [1893]. *The Division of Labor in Society*. Trans. W.D. Hall. New York, NY: The Free Press.
Durkheim explains the distinction between mechanical and organic solidarity.

—. (1995) [1912]. *The Elementary Forms of the Religious Life*. Trans. Karen E. Fields. New York, NY: The Free Press.
Durkheim analyzes the collective conscious and the sacred role of religion.

Jones, Robert A. (1986). *The Sociological Theories of Émile Durkheim*. Thousand Oaks, CA: Sage Publications.
An assessment of Durkheim's sociology.

Jones, Susan Stedman. (2001). *Durkheim Reconsidered*. Oxford: Polity.
A reinterpretation of Durkheim's contributions in historical perspective.

Lukes, Steven. (1985). *Émile Durkheim: His Life and Work: A Historical and Critical Study*. Stanford, CA: Stanford University Press.
An interpretation of Durkheim's intellectual life and times.

Parkin, Frank. (1992). *Durkheim*. Oxford: Oxford University Press.
A biographical account of Durkheim.

Turner, Stephen P. (1993). *Émile Durkheim: Sociologist and Moralist*. New York, NY: Routledge.
An evaluation of Durkheim as a moralist.

MAX WEBER

Weber, Max. (1993) [1922]. *The Sociology of Religion*. Boston, MA: Beacon Press.
Weber's classic formulation of religion, paying special attention to the ways in which religion effects social change in a variety of cultural and historical settings.

—. (1996) [1920]. *The Protestant Ethic and the Spirit of Capitalism*. Ed. Randall Collins. Los Angeles, CA: Roxbury.
Written before *The Sociology of Religion*, this book looks at the dialectical relationship between Calvinist Protestantism as an ideology and the expansion of capitalism in the Renaissance and beyond.

FERDINAND DE SAUSSURE

Culler, Jonathan. (1976). *Ferdinand de Saussure*. Harmondsworth, UK: Penguin Books.
An engaging biographical introduction to Saussure and concise discussion of his contribution to social science, linguistics, and semiology.

Harris, Roy. (1991). *Reading Saussure: A Critical Commentary on the "Cours de Linguistiques Generale."* Chicago, IL: Open Court Publishing.
A relatively sophisticated discussion and critique of Saussurian theory by a distinguished philosopher of language and specialist on Saussure.

Holdcroft, David. (1991). *Saussure: Signs, System, and Arbitrariness*. New York, NY: Cambridge University Press.
A sophisticated introduction to Saussurian theory that scrutinizes his linguistics from the perspective of a philosopher of language and science and offers some important insights into the relative value of Saussure for contemporary scholars.

Saussure, Ferdinand de. (1998) [1916]. *Course in General Linguistics*. Trans. Roy Harris. Chicago, IL: Open Court Publishing.
Saussure's *magnum opus*, redacted after his death from his own lecture notes and those of his students, including all his contributions to language theory.

SOURCES AND SUGGESTED READING

Part Two: The Early Twentieth Century

AMERICAN CULTURAL ANTHROPOLOGY

Baker, Lee. (1998). *From Savage to Negro: Anthropology and the Construction of Race, 1896-1954*. Berkeley, CA: University of California Press.

A history of American anthropology and African-American experiences in the years between two landmark United States Supreme Court decisions affecting race relations.

Barrett, Stanley R. (1996). *Anthropology: A Student's Guide to Theory and Method*. Toronto, ON: University of Toronto Press.

An exposition of major twentieth-century theories and methods accompanied by ethnographic examples derived from the author's own fieldwork.

Bateson, Mary C. (1994) [1984]. *With a Daughter's Eye: A Memoir of Gregory Bateson and Margaret Mead*. New York, NY: Harper Collins.

A biography of Mead and her third husband by their daughter.

Benedict, Ruth. (1977). *An Anthropologist at Work: The Writings of Ruth Benedict*. Ed. Margaret Mead. Westport, CT: Greenwood.

A collection of key writings by Benedict edited by her long-time friend and colleague.

—. (1989) [1934]. *Patterns of Culture*. Boston, MA: Houghton Mifflin.

Benedict's classic analysis of three cultures, for decades an anthropology best-seller.

Boas, Franz. (1989). *A Franz Boas Reader: The Shaping of American Anthropology, 1883-1911*. Ed. George W. Stocking, Jr. Chicago, IL: University of Chicago Press.

A book that places major works of Boas in historical perspective.

Caffrey, Margaret M. (1989). *Ruth Benedict: Stranger in this Land*. Austin, TX: University of Texas Press.

A biography of Benedict that explores her sense of personal and cultural alienation.

Cassidy, Robert. (1982). *Margaret Mead: A Voice for the Century*. New York, NY: Universe Books.

A biography of Mead highlighting her ability to communicate with the public.

Chasdi, Eleanor H. (Ed.). (1994). *Culture and Human Development: The Selected Papers of John Whiting*. New York, NY: Cambridge University Press.

Key papers of an anthropologist who advanced psychological anthropology in the post-World War II period.

Cole, Douglas. (1999). *Franz Boas: The Early Years, 1858-1906*. Seattle, WA: University of Washington Press.

The first of a projected two-part scholarly biography, profiling Boas from his childhood in Germany to his departure from the American Museum of Natural History.

Cole, Sally Cooper. (2004). *Ruth Landes: A Life in Anthropology*. Lincoln, NE: University of Nebraska Press.

A biography of a student of Franz Boas and Ruth Benedict who pioneered anthropological studies of race and gender.

Cote, James E. (1994). *Adolescent Storm and Stress: An Evaluation of the Mead-Freeman Controversy*. Mahwah, NJ: Laurence Erlbaum Associates.

A contribution to the anthropological debate about Mead's ethnographic work in Samoa.

Cressman, Luther S. (1988). *A Golden Journey: Memoirs of an Archaeologist*. Ann Arbor, MI: Books on Demand.

A book in which Cressman shows why he should be remembered as more than Margaret Mead's first husband.

Darnell, Regna. (2001). *Invisible Genealogies: A History of Americanist Anthropology*. Lincoln, NE: University of Nebraska Press.

A reinterpretation of American anthropology aimed at counteracting postmodern anthropologists' efforts to set themselves apart from their Boasian predecessors.

Darnell, Regna, and Frederic W. Gleach (Eds.). (2002). *Celebrating a Century of the American Anthropological Association: Presidential Portraits*. Lincoln, NE: University of Nebraska Press.

A history of American anthropology as revealed in the contributions of past presidents of the American Anthropological Association.

Deacon, Desley. (1997). *Elsie Clews Parsons: Inventing Modern Life*. Chicago, IL: University of Chicago Press.

A biography of a pioneering American social theorist who was a patron of Boasian anthropologists.

Driver, Harold Edson. (1962). *The Contribution of A.L. Kroeber to Culture Area Theory and Practice*. Baltimore, MD: Waverly Press.
An American Indianist anthropologist recounts Kroeber's contributions to American Indian anthropology.

Du Bois, Cora. (1944). *The People of Alor: A Social-Psychological Study of an East-Indian Island*. Minneapolis, MN: University of Minnesota Press.
A classic monograph in the tradition of psychodynamic anthropology.

Fagan, Kevin. (2000). Ishi's Kin to Give Him Proper Burial. *San Francisco Chronicle*, 10 August.
A newspaper reporter's account of the Ishi affair.

Foerstel, Lenora, and Angela Gilliam (Eds.). (1991). *Confronting the Margaret Mead Legacy: Scholarship, Empire and South Pacific*. Philadelphia, PA: Temple University Press.
Examinations of Mead's legacy to anthropology.

Freeman, Derek. [1982]. *Margaret Mead and Samoa: The Making and Unmaking of an Anthropological Myth*. Ann Arbor, MI: Books on Demand.
The book that began a protracted anthropological debate about Mead's ethnographic work in Samoa.

—. (1997). *Margaret Mead and the Heretic: The Making and Unmaking of an Anthropological Myth*. New York, NY: Penguin Putnam, Inc.
An updated version of Freeman's book *Margaret Mead and Samoa* (1982).

—. (1998). *The Fateful Hoaxing of Margaret Mead: A Historical Analysis of Her Samoan Research*. Boulder, CO: Westview Press.
An expansion of Freeman's argument that Mead was misled by the mischievous joking of her native informants.

Gacs, Ute, *et al.* (Eds.). (1988). *Women Anthropologists: A Biographical Dictionary*. New York, NY: Greenwood Press.
Biographical sketches of numerous women in all fields of modern anthropology, including their backgrounds and professional accomplishments.

Grinanger, Patricia. (1999). *Uncommon Lives: My Lifelong Friendship with Margaret Mead*. Latham, MD: Rowman and Littlefield Publishers.
Recollections of a lifelong confidante of Mead, revealing Mead's opinions about her supporters and detractors.

Grosskurth, Phillis. (1988). *Margaret Mead: A Life*. London: Penguin Books.
A biography of Mead written to appeal to the public.

Handler, Richard (Ed.). (2000). *Excluded Ancestors, Inventable Traditions: Essays Toward a More Inclusive History of Anthropology*. Madison, WI: University of Wisconsin Press.
A collection of essays on "little-known scholars" who have contributed to the history of anthropology, featuring an essay on the anthropological "canon."

Hare, Peter H. (1985). *A Woman's Quest for Science: A Portrait of Anthropologist Elsie Clews Parsons*. Amherst, NY: Prometheus Books.
Another biography of Parsons.

Harrison, Ira E., and Faye V. Harrison (Eds.). (1999). *African-American Pioneers in Anthropology*. Urbana, IL: University of Illinois Press.
Portraits of African-American anthropologists, including W. Montague Cobb, Zora Neale Hurston, and Elliot Skinner, written to "critically reconstruct" and "decolonize" anthropology.

Helm, June (Ed.). (1988). *Pioneers of American Anthropology: The Uses of Biography*. New York, NY: AMS Press.
Biographical accounts of early American anthropologists.

Hemenway, Robert E. (1980). *Zora Neale Hurston: A Literary Biography*. Urbana, IL: University of Illinois Press.
A biography of an African-American student of Boas and acclaimed author and folklorist.

Herskovits, Melville J. (1953). *Franz Boas*. New York, NY: Scribner.
A biography of Boas by an accomplished Boasian anthropologist.

SOURCES AND SUGGESTED READING

Hill, Lynda Marion. (1996). *Social Rituals and the Verbal Art of Zora Neale*. Washington, DC: Howard University Press.
An appraisal of the writings of Zora Neale Hurston, a student of Franz Boas who believed that folklore was an important means of transmitting African-American culture.

Holmes, Lowell D. (1986). *Quest for the Real Samoa: The Mead-Freeman Controversy and Beyond*. Westport, CT: Greenwood.
A contribution to the anthropological debate about Mead's ethnographic work in Samoa.

Honigmann, John J. [1975]. *The Development of Anthropological Ideas*. Ann Arbor, MI: Books on Demand.
A history of anthropology with an emphasis on psychological anthropology.

Howard, Jane. (1984). *Margaret Mead: A Life*. New York, NY: Simon and Schuster.
A biography of Mead written to appeal to the public.

Hyatt, Marshall. (1990). *Franz Boas, Social Activist: The Dynamics of Ethnicity*. New York, NY: Greenwood Press.
A biographical account of Boas's involvement with social issues pertaining to the anthropological understanding of ethnicity.

Janiewski, Dolores. (2004). *Reading Benedict/ Reading Mead: Feminism, Race, and Imperial Visions*. Baltimore, MD: Johns Hopkins University Press.
Another account and interpretation of the life and times of Ruth Benedict and Margaret Mead.

Kroeber, A.L. (1944). *Configurations of Cultural Growth*. Berkeley, CA: University of California Press.
Kroeber's *magnum opus*.

Kroeber, A.L., and Clyde Kluckhohn. (1952). *Culture: A Critical Review of Concepts and Definitions*. Cambridge, MA: Peabody Museum of American Archaeology and Ethnology.
A compendium of conceptualizations of culture by two anthropologists who conceptualized culture as shared values.

Kroeber, Theodora. (1961). *Ishi in Two Worlds: A Biography of the Last Wild Indian in North America*. Berkeley, CA: University of California Press.
Alfred Louis Kroeber's wife recounts the saga of Ishi and her husband's involvement with him.

—. (1970). *Alfred Kroeber: A Personal Configuration*. Berkeley, CA: University of California Press.
A loving biography of Kroeber by his wife.

Lapsley, Hilary. (1999). *Margaret Mead and Ruth Benedict: The Kinship of Women*. Amherst, MA: University of Massachusetts Press.
An examination of the lifelong friendship between two of the most eminent Boasian-era anthropologists, highlighting personality, sexuality, and professional accomplishments.

Linton, Adelin, and Charles Wagley. (1971). *Ralph Linton*. New York, NY: Columbia University Press.
A biography of an accomplished Boasian-era anthropologist.

Lipset, David. (1980). *Gregory Bateson: The Legacy of a Scientist*. Englewood Cliffs, NJ: Prentice-Hall.
A biography of Mead's third husband and the scientist responsible for the "double-bind" theory of schizophrenia.

Lowie, Robert H. (1937). *History of Ethnological Theory*. New York, NY: Rinehart and Company.
Lowie contrasts Boasian ethnology with the ethnology of his nineteenth-century predecessors.

—. [1959]. *Robert H. Lowie, Ethnologist: A Personal Record*. Ann Arbor, MI: Books on Demand.
Lowie's autobiography.

—. (1960) [1920]. *Primitive Society*. London: Routledge and Kegan Paul.
Lowie's summation of anthropology contrasted with the summations of nineteenth-century evolutionists.

Lurie, Nancy. (1999). *Women and the Invention of American Anthropology*. Prospect Heights, IL: Waveland Press.
Profiles of women who helped anthropology achieve recognition as an academic discipline in the early twentieth century, including Alice Fletcher, Zelia Nuttalls, and Elsie Clews Parsons.

Manson, William C. (1988). *The Psychodynamics of Culture: Abram Kardiner and Neo-Freudian Anthropology*. Westport, CT: Greenwood.
An examination of the life and work of the chief architect of psychodynamic anthropology.

Mead, Margaret. (1974). *Ruth Benedict*. New York, NY: Columbia University Press.
A biography of Benedict by her long-time friend and colleague.

—. (1990) [1972]. *Blackberry Winter*. Magnolia, MA: Peter Smith.
The first volume of Mead's projected multi-volume autobiography.

—. (1990) [1928]. *Coming of Age in Samoa*. Magnolia, MA: Peter Smith.
The book that launched Mead's career.

Modell, Judith Schachter. (1983). *Ruth Benedict: Patterns of a Life*. Philadelphia, PA: University of Pennsylvania Press.
A biography of Benedict that explores her personal interest in cultural patterns.

Murphy, Robert Francis. (1972). *Robert H. Lowie*. New York, NY: Columbia University Press.
A biography of Lowie by an accomplished American anthropologist.

Murra, John V. (Ed.). (1976). *American Anthropology: The Early Years*. St. Paul, MN: West.
A collection of articles about pioneering American anthropologists.

Orans, Martin. (1996). *Not Even Wrong: Margaret Mead, Derek Freeman, and the Samoans*. Ed. L.L. Langness and Robert B. Edgerton. Novato, CA: Chandler and Sharp.
A contribution to the anthropological debate about Mead's ethnographic work in Samoa.

Parezo, Nancy J. (Ed.). (1993). *Hidden Scholars: Women Anthropologists and the Native American Southwest*. Albuquerque, NM: University of New Mexico Press.
A collection of articles highlighting contributions of women anthropologists working in the American Southwest.

Patterson, Thomas. (2001). *A Social History of Anthropology in the United States*. Oxford: Berg Publishers.
A history of American anthropology in the context of wider currents in American society, including colonialism and territorial expansionism.

Rice, Edward. (1979). *Margaret Mead: A Portrait*. New York, NY: Harper and Row.
A biography of Mead written to appeal to the public.

Rigdon, Susan M. (1988). *The Culture Facade: Art, Science, and Politics in the Work of Oscar Lewis*. Champaign, IL: University of Illinois Press.
A biography of a twentieth-century anthropologist who studied the culture of poverty.

Silverman, Sydel (Ed.). (2003). *Totems and Teachers: Key Figures in the History of Anthropology*. Rev. ed. Lanham, MD: Rowman and Littlefield.
Accounts of the history of anthropology shaped by the relationship between prominent students and teachers.

Simpson, George Eaton. (1973). *Melville J. Herskovits*. New York, NY: Columbia University Press.
A biography of a Boasian-era anthropologist who studied African-American culture.

Spindler, George Dearborn (Ed.). (1978). *The Making of Psychological Anthropology*. Berkeley, CA: University of California Press.
Assessments of the foundations of psychological anthropology.

Starn, Orin. (2004). *Ishi's Brain: In Search of America's Last "Wild" Indian*. New York, NY: Norton.
The saga of losing and then finding the brain of the famous California Indian befriended by Alfred Louis Kroeber.

Steward, Julian Haines. (1973). *Alfred Kroeber*. New York, NY: Columbia University Press.
A biography of Kroeber by a distinguished cultural ecologist and evolutionist.

Stocking, George W., Jr. (Ed.). (1985). *Observers Observed: Essays on Ethnographic Fieldwork*. Madison, WI: University of Wisconsin Press.
A collection of articles about the history of ethnographic fieldwork.

—. (Ed.) (1986). *Malinowski, Rivers, Benedict and Others: Essays on Culture and Personality*. Madison, WI: University of Wisconsin Press.
A collection of articles exploring themes in psychological anthropology.

—. (Ed.). (1996). *Volksgeist as Method and Ethic: Essays on Boasian Ethnography and the German Anthropological Tradition*. Madison, WI: University of Wisconsin Press.
A collection of essays highlighting Boasian anthropology, evolutionary anthropology, and institutions and national traditions of anthropology from the eighteenth century to the present.

SOURCES AND SUGGESTED READING

—. (2001) *Delimiting Anthropology: Occasional Inquiries and Reflections*. Madison, WI: University of Wisconsin Press.
A collection of essays by the eminent historian of anthropology, highlighting Boasian anthropology, evolutionary anthropology, and numerous institutions and national traditions from the eighteenth century to the present.

Taylor, Walter W., John Fischer, and Evon Z. Vogt (Eds.). (1973). *Culture and Life: Essays in Memory of Clyde Kluckhohn*. Carbondale, IL: Southern Illinois University Press.
Commemorations of the work of an American anthropologist interested in cross-cultural values.

Textor, Robert T. (Ed.). (2005). *Margaret Mead: The World Ahead: An Anthropologist Anticipates the Future*. New York, NY: Berghahn Books.
A collection of Mead's writing on the future of humanity as shaped by purposeful human action.

Thoresen, Timothy H. (Ed.). (1975). *Toward a Science of Man: Essays in the History of Anthropology*. Hawthorne, NY: Mouton de Gruyter.
A collection of articles highlighting the contributions of Boas and his students.

Valentine, Lisa Philips, and Regna Darnell (Eds.). (1999). *Theorizing the Americanist Tradition*. Toronto, ON: University of Toronto Press.
A collection of "state-of-the-art" appraisals of American and Canadian anthropology designed to challenge the notion that the Boasian tradition lacks theory.

Whiting, John W., and Irvin I. Child. (1984) [1953]. *Child-Training and Personality: A Cross-Cultural Study*. Westport, CT: Greenwood.
A landmark cross-cultural study of culture and personality.

Williams, Vernon J., Jr. (1996). *Rethinking Race: Franz Boas and His Contemporaries*. Lexington, KY: University Press of Kentucky.
Assessments of the efforts of Boas and his contemporaries to overcome an anthropological legacy of racism.

Winters, Christopher (Ed.). (1991). *International Dictionary of Anthropologists*. New York, NY: Garland.
A source book of information on American and other national anthropologists of the modern era, including backgrounds and professional accomplishments.

FRENCH STRUCTURAL ANTHROPOLOGY

Bertholet, Denis. (2003). *Claude Lévi-Strauss*. Paris: Plon.
A biographical account of the life and contributions of the architect of French structural anthropology.

Boon, James A. (1972). *From Symbolism to Structuralism: Lévi-Strauss in a Literary Tradition*. New York, NY: Harper and Row.
An analysis of Lévi-Strauss as a literary figure.

Champagne, Roland. (1987). *Claude Lévi-Strauss*. Old Tappan, NJ: Scribner's Reference.
A biographical study of Lévi-Strauss.

Douglas, Mary. (1966). *Purity and Danger: An Analysis of Concepts of Pollution and Taboo*. New York, NY: Praeger.
Douglas's ground-breaking study of the meaning and structuring of social boundaries.

Fardon, Richard. (1999). *Mary Douglas: An Intellectual Biography*. London: Routledge.
An examination of five decades of writing by the eminent British social anthropologist and Africanist whose work was informed by French structuralist theory.

Godelier, Maruice. (1999). *The Enigma of the Gift*. Trans. Nora Scott. Chicago, IL: University of Chicago Press.
A new interpretation of Mauss's theory of gift-giving from one of the gurus of structural Marxism.

Henaff, Marcel. (1991). *Claude Lévi-Strauss*. Paris: Belfond.
The life and work of Lévi-Strauss.

—. (1998). *Claude Lévi-Strauss and the Making of Structural Anthropology*. Minneapolis, MN: University of Minnesota Press.
An explication of Lévi-Strauss's structuralism, with emphasis on kinship systems, classification systems, and mythology.

Hugh-Jones, Stephen, and James Laidlaw (Eds.). (2001). *The Essential Edmund Leach*. 2 vols. New Haven, CT: Yale University Press.
A selection of numerous writings by Leach, in the first volume on anthropology and society, and in the second volume on culture and human nature.

James, Wendy, and N.J. Allen (Eds.). (1998). *Marcel Mauss: A Centenary Tribute*. New York, NY: Berghahn Books.
A collection of essays re-evaluating the work and influence of Mauss.

Jenkins, Alan. (1979). *The Social Theory of Claude Lévi-Strauss*. London: Macmillan.

An account of key theoretical elements of French structural anthropology.

Johnson, Christopher. (2003). *Claude Lévi-Strauss: The Formative Years*. Cambridge: Cambridge University Press.

Another biography of Lévi-Strauss, this one concentrating on his youth and early adulthood.

Leach, Edmund R. (1989) [1970]. *Claude Lévi-Strauss*. Chicago, IL: University of Chicago Press.

An assessment of the work of Lévi-Strauss by a distinguished British social anthropologist.

—. (1976). *Culture & Communication: The Logic by which Symbols are Connected*. New York, NY: Cambridge University Press.

In this concise text, Leach introduces French structuralism to an anglophone readership.

Lévi-Strauss, Claude. (1969). *Elementary Structures of Kinship*. Ed. James Harlebell *et al*. Boston, MA: Beacon Press.

Lévi-Strauss's seminal structural analysis of kinship.

—. (1974) [1963]. *Structural Anthropology*. New York, NY: Basic Books.

Lévi-Strauss's exposition of structuralism.

—. (1992) [1955]. *Tristes Tropiques*. Trans. John Weightman, and Doreen Weightman. New York, NY: Penguin Books.

Lévi-Strauss's autobiographically based reflections on fieldwork and theory.

Mauss, Marcel. (1990) [1924]. *Gift: The Form and Reason for Exchange in Archaic Societies*. New York, NY: W.W. Norton.

The book from which Lévi-Strauss derived part of his theory of reciprocity.

Obeyesekere, Gananath. (1992). *The Apotheosis of Captain Cook: European Mythmaking in the Pacific*. Princeton, NJ: Princeton University Press.

Obeyesekere challenges Marshall Sahlins's structural analysis of the Hawaiian colonial encounter, offering an alternative explanation for Cook's death based on miscommunication and antagonism between Natives and explorers.

Pace, David. (1978). Structuralism in History and the Social Sciences. *American Quarterly* 30,3: 282-97.

A comprehensive discussion of Lévi-Strauss's work and influence on various disciplines through the late 1970s.

Price, David H. (2001). "The Shameful Business": Leslie Spier on the Censure of Franz Boas. *History of Anthropology Newsletter* 27(2): 9-12.

Price reflects on the 1919 censure of Franz Boas by the American Anthropological Association.

Rossi, Ino (Ed.). (1974). *The Unconscious in Culture: The Structuralism of Claude Lévi-Strauss in Perspective*. New York, NY: Dutton.

Expositions of Lévi-Strauss's structuralism.

Sahlins, Marshall. (1985). *Islands of History*. Chicago, IL: University of Chicago Press.

Sahlins promulgates his view that "structure" is the historically objectified relations of cultural order.

—. (1995). *How "Natives" Think: About Captain Cook, for Example*. Chicago, IL: University of Chicago Press.

Sahlins's book-length rejoinder to Gananath Obeyesekere's criticisms contained in *The Apotheosis of Captain Cook*.

Stocking, George W., Jr. (Ed.). (1996). *Romantic Motives: Essays on Anthropological Sensibility*. Madison, WI: University of Wisconsin Press.

Accounts of anthropological styles, some French.

Tambiah, Stanley. (2002). *Edmund Leach: An Anthropological Life*. Cambridge: Cambridge University Press.

A biography of the distinguished British anthropologist who helped anglophone readers understand Claude Lévi-Strauss.

BRITISH SOCIAL ANTHROPOLOGY

Douglas, Mary. (1980). *Edward Evans-Pritchard*. New York, NY: Viking Press.

A biography of a distinguished British social anthropologist known for his ethnographic work among the Nuer and Azande of eastern Africa.

Ellen, Roy, *et al*. (Eds.). (1989). *Malinowski: Between Two Worlds: The Polish Roots of an Anthropological Tradition*. New York, NY: Cambridge University Press.

Investigations of the Polish background of Bronislaw Malinowski.

SOURCES AND SUGGESTED READING

Evans-Pritchard, E.E. (1976) [1937]. *Witchcraft, Oracles, and Magic Among the Azande*. Oxford: Clarendon Press.
In this seminal ethnography, Evans-Pritchard infuses structural-functional analysis with a concern for the meaning and logic of non-Western beliefs and practices.

—. (1940) *The Nuer: A Description of the Modes of Livelihood's Political Institutions of a Nilotic People*. Oxford: Clarendon Press.
An influential structural-functional text combining the study of empirical social relations with a concern to understand the cultural logic informing social life among the Nuer of southern Sudan.

Gellner, Ernst. (1998). *Language and Solitude: Wittgenstein, Malinowski, and the Habsburg Dilemma*. Cambridge: Cambridge University Press.
A comparison of two seemingly different thinkers who shared assumptions derived from common childhood experiences in the Habsburg Empire.

Gluckman, Max. (1955). *Custom and Conflict in Africa*. Glencoe, IL: Free Press.
In one of his most influential texts, Gluckman examines the political and contested nature of social structures and the rituals in which these are expressed.

—. (1963). *Order and Rebellion in Tribal Africa*. New York, NY: Free Press.
An examination of the influence of cultural norms on the decisions taken by tribal courts in Africa.

Goody, Jack. (1995). *The Expansive Moment: The Rise of Social Anthropology in Britain and Africa, 1918-1970*. New York, NY: Cambridge University Press.
A history of British social anthropology highlighting its African connection.

Handler, Richard (Ed.). (2004). *Significant Others: Interpersonal and Professional Commitments in Anthropology*. Madison, WI: University of Wisconsin Press.
A collection of articles about anthropologists and their relationships with spouses, partners, friends, and informants.

Henson, Hilary. (1974). *British Social Anthropologists and Language: A History of Separate Development*. Oxford: Clarendon Press.
An examination of the relationship between social and linguistic anthropology in Britain.

Herle, Anita, and Sandra Rouse (Eds.). (1998). *Cambridge and the Torres Strait: Centenary Essays on the 1898 Anthropological Expedition*. Cambridge: Cambridge University Press.
A collection of illustrated assessments of the multi-disciplinary expedition to the Torres Strait that helped shape twentieth-century British social anthropology at Cambridge University.

Hiatt, L.R. (1996). *Arguments about Aborigines: Australia and the Evolution of Social Anthropology*. New York, NY: Cambridge University Press.
An introduction to the anthropology of Australian aborigines that examines their role as exemplars of early humanity in the work of influential social theorists such as Émile Durkheim, Sigmund Freud, and E.B. Tylor.

Kuklik, Henrika. (1992). *The Savage Within: The Social History of British Anthropology, 1885-1945*. New York, NY: Cambridge University Press.
A contextual history of British social anthropology in its heyday.

Kuper, Adam. (1983). *Anthropology and Anthropologists: The Modern British School*. Rev. ed. New York, NY: Routledge.
An informative history of British social anthropology.

—. (1999). *Among the Anthropologists: History and Context in Anthropology*. London: Athlone Press.
An analysis of some of the central theoretical arguments in anthropology by an anthropologist especially interested in British social anthropology.

Langham, Ian G. (1981). *The Building of British Social Anthropology*. Norwell, MA: Kluwer Academic Publishers.
A history of the foundations of British social anthropology.

Malinowski, Bronislaw. (1984) [1922]. *Argonauts of the Western Pacific*. Prospect Heights, IL: Waveland Press.
Malinowski's critically acclaimed ethnography of Trobriand Islanders.

—. (1989) [1967]. *A Diary in the Strict Sense of the Term*. Stanford, CA: Stanford University Press.
Malinowski's personally revealing diary of his fieldwork experiences.

Marcus, Julie (Ed.). (1993). *First in Their Field: Women and Australian Anthropology*. Concord, MA: Paul and Company Publishers Consortium.
Assessments of the importance of female Australian anthropologists.

Radcliffe-Brown, A.R. (1964) [1922]. *The Andaman Islanders*. New York, NY: Free Press.
Radcliffe-Brown's highly regarded ethnography using a structural-functionalist framework.

—. (1965) [1952]. *Structure and Function in Primitive Society*. New York, NY: Free Press.
Radcliffe-Brown's exposition of structuralism and functionalism.

Slobodin, Richard. (1978). *W.H.R. Rivers*. New York, NY: Columbia University Press.
A biography of the British anthropologist who pioneered the genealogical method of fieldwork.

Stocking, George W., Jr. (1992). *The Ethnographer's Magic and Other Essays in the History of Anthropology*. Madison, WI: University of Wisconsin Press.
A collection of essays about fieldwork and related anthropological topics.

—. (1995). *After Tylor: British Social Anthropology, 1888-1951*. Madison, WI: University of Wisconsin Press.
An authoritative history of British social anthropology in the first half of the twentieth century.

—. (Ed.). (1984). *Functionalism Historicized: Essays on British Social Anthropology*. Madison, WI: University of Wisconsin Press.
A collection of essays on British social anthropology highlighting functionalism.

Strenski, Ivan. (1992). *Malinowski and the Work of Myth*. Princeton, NJ: Princeton University Press.
An assessment of Malinowski's contributions to the anthropological study of myth.

Urry, James. (1993). *Before Social Anthropology: Essays on the History of British Anthropology*. Newark, NJ: Gordon and Breach.
A collection of essays on early modern British anthropology.

Vermeulen, Han, and Artura A. Roldan (Eds.). (1995). *Fieldwork and Footnotes: Studies in the History of European Anthropology*. New York, NY: Routledge.
A collection of articles about the history of anthropological traditions in Europe.

Young, Michael. (2004). *Malinowski: Odyssey of an Anthropologist, 1884-1920*. New Haven, CT: Yale University Press.
A biography of Malinowski's early years, including his famous fieldwork in the Trobriand Islands.

Part Three: The Later Twentieth and Early Twenty-First Centuries

COGNITIVE ANTHROPOLOGY

Aarsleff, Hans. (1982). *From Locke to Saussure: Essays on the Study of Language and Intellectual History*. Minneapolis, MN: University of Minnesota Press.
A history of linguistics beginning in the late seventeenth century.

Carroll, J.B. (Ed.). (1956). *Language, Thought and Reality: Selected Writings of Benjamin Lee Whorf*. New York, NY: John Wiley and Sons.
A collection of key writings by the co-formulator of the Sapir-Whorf hypothesis.

D'Andrade, Roy. (1995). *The Development of Cognitive Anthropology*. New York, NY: Cambridge University Press.
An exposition of cognitive anthropology in historical perspective.

Darnell, Regna. (1990). *Edward Sapir: Linguist, Anthropologist, Humanist*. Berkeley, CA: University of California Press.
A biography of the distinguished Boasian anthropologist and co-formulator of the Sapir-Whorf hypothesis.

Hall, Robert A. (1987). *Leonard Bloomfield: Essays on His Life and Work*. Philadelphia, PA: John Benjamins.
Evaluations of the work of a twentieth-century linguist who pioneered phonemic analysis.

Hymes, Dell. (1983). *Essays in the History of Linguistic Anthropology*. Philadelphia, PA: John Benjamins.
A distinguished anthropological linguist writes about the history of his subject.

—. (Ed.). (1974). *Studies in the History of Linguistics: Traditions and Paradigms*. Ann Arbor, MI: Books on Demand.
A major collection of articles about themes in the history of linguistics.

Joseph, John. (2002). *From Whitney to Chomsky: Essays in the History of American Linguistics*. Philadelphia, PA: John Benjamins.
A varied collection of essays on theorists and theories in American linguistics in historical perspective.

Pike, Eunice. (1981). *Ken Pike: Scholar and Christian*. Dallas, TX: Summer Institute of Linguistics, Academic Publications.
A biographical account of the linguist who helped formulate the distinction between emics and etics.

Sapir, Edward. (1958). *Culture, Language, and Personality: Selected Essays*. Ed. David Mandelbaum. Berkeley, CA: University of California Press.
A collection of essays on the relationships among language, culture, and personality by the leading anthropological linguist of the Boasian era.

Sebeok, Thomas Albert (Ed.). (1966). *Portraits of Linguistics: A Biographical Source Book for the History of Western Linguistics, 1746-1963*. Bloomington, IN: Indiana University Press.
A valuable source of information about linguists of the last two centuries.

Tyler, Stephen. (1969). *Cognitive Anthropology*. New York, NY: Holt, Rinehart, and Winston.
A book about cognitive anthropology written in its heyday.

CULTURAL NEO-EVOLUTIONISM

Binford, Lewis R. (1983). *In Pursuit of the Past*. London: Thames and Hudson.
An exposition of the New Archaeology by the leading New Archaeologist.

Bohannan, Paul, and Mark Glazer (Eds.). (1989). *High Points in Anthropology*. 2nd ed. New York, NY: McGraw-Hill.
A collection of writings by influential anthropologists of the nineteenth and twentieth centuries.

Carneiro, Robert L. (2003). *Evolutionism in Cultural Anthropology: A Critical History*. Boulder, CO: Westview Press.
A prominent follower of cultural evolutionism recounts its broad history.

Clemmer, Richard O., Daniel Myers, and Mary Elizabeth Rudden (Eds.). (1999). *Julian Steward and the Great Basin: The Making of an Anthropologist*. Salt Lake City, UT: University of Utah Press.
A critical assessment of Steward's influence on American anthropology linking his career to changes in anthropological theories, including cultural ecology.

Fried, Morton H. (1967). *The Evolution of Political Society: An Evolutionary View*. New York, NY: McGraw-Hill.
Variation in political organization explained in evolutionary terms.

Green, Sally. (1981). *Prehistorian: A Biography of V. Gordon Childe*. Bradford-on-Avon: The Moonraker Press.
A biography of the maverick "Marxist" archaeologist who described Neolithic and urban "revolutions."

Harris, David R. (Ed.). (1994). *The Archaeology of V. Gordon Childe*. Concord, MA: Paul and Company Publishers Consortium.
A collection of articles evaluating Childe's contributions to archaeology.

Kearns, Virginia. (2003). *Scenes from the High Desert: Julian Steward's Life and Theory*. Urbana, IL: University of Illinois Press.
An intellectual and personal biography of the eminent cultural neo-evolutionist and ecologist.

Manners, Robert Alan (Ed.). (1964). *Process and Pattern in Culture, Essays in Honor of Julian Steward*. Chicago, IL: Aldine Publishing Company.
Examinations of Julian Steward's role in the development of cultural ecology and evolution.

McNairn, Barbara. (1980). *The Method and Theory of V. Gordon Childe*. Edinburgh: Edinburgh University Press.
An intellectual biography of Childe.

Patterson, Thomas C. (1994). *Toward a Social History of Archaeology in the United States*. Ed. Jeffrey Quilter. Orlando, FL: Harcourt Brace College Publishers.
A history of American archaeology in social contexts.

Peace, William J. (2004). *Leslie A. White: Evolution and Revolution in Anthropology*. Lincoln, NE: University of Nebraska Press.
An intellectual and political biography of one of the key theorists of cultural neo-evolutionism.

Pinsky, Valerie, and Alison Wylie (Eds.). (1995). *Critical Traditions in Contemporary Archaeology: Essays in the Philosophy, History and Socio-Politics of Archaeology*. Albuquerque, NM: University of New Mexico Press.
Critical archaeological perspectives.

Reyman, Jonathan E. (Ed.). (1992). *Rediscovering Our Past: Essays on the History of American Archaeology*. Avebury, England: Aldershot.
A collection of articles representing new views on the history of American archaeology.

Sabloff, Paula L.W. (1998). *Conversations with Lew Binford: Drafting the New Archaeology*. Norman, OK: University of Oklahoma Press.
A series of interviews with Binford recounting in personal terms the origins of the New Archaeology in the 1960s.

Sahlins, Marshall D., and Elman R. Service (Eds.). (1960). *Evolution and Culture*. Ann Arbor, MI: University of Michigan Press.
Sahlins and Service reconcile the evolutionary theories of Julian Steward and Leslie White.

Service, Elman R. (1962). *Primitive Social Organization: An Evolutionary Perspective*. New York, NY: Random House.
Variation in social organization explained in evolutionary terms.

—. (1985). *A Century of Controversy*. Orlando, FL: Academic Press.
A history of ethnology written by a prominent cultural neo-evolutionist.

Steward, Julian. (1972) [1955]. *Theory of Culture Change: The Methodology of Multilinear Evolution*. Champaign, IL: University of Illinois Press.
Steward's explanation of cultural evolution contrasted with the explanations of Leslie White and others.

ger, Bruce G. (1980). *Gordon Childe: Revolutions in haeology*. New York, NY: Columbia University Press.
graphy of Childe by a respected historian of gy.

White, Leslie A. (1949). *The Science of Culture*. New York, NY: Grove Press.
A collection of seminal essays on culturology.

—. (1959). *The Evolution of Culture: The Development of Civilization to the Fall of Rome*. New York, NY: McGraw-Hill.
White's explanation of cultural evolution in terms of thermodynamics and the principles of culturology.

CULTURAL MATERIALISM

Harris, Marvin. (1979). *Cultural Materialism: The Struggle for a Science of Culture*. New York, NY: Random House.
Harris's cultural materialist manifesto.

—. (1990) [1974]. *Cows, Pigs, Wars, and Witches: The Riddles of Culture*. New York, NY: Random House.
One of several popular books written by Harris to demonstrate the explanatory power of cultural materialism.

—. (1998). *Theories of Culture in Postmodern Times*. Walnut Creek, CA: Altimira Press.
A restatement of the tenets of cultural materialism in the anthropological environment three decades after *The Rise of Anthropological Theory* (1998).

Koznar, Lawrence A., and Stephen K. Sanderson (Eds.). (2007). *Studying Societies and Cultures: Marvin Harris's Cultural Materialism and its Legacy*. Boulder, CO: Paradigm Publishers.
A collection of appraisals and examples of cultural materialism in anthropology.

Murphy, Martin F., and Maxine L. Margolis (Eds.). (1995). *Science, Materialism, and the Study of Culture*. Gainesville, FL: University Press of Florida.
Several essays by anthropologists committed to understanding culture from a materialist point of view.

BIOLOGIZED ANTHROPOLOGY

Ardrey, Robert. (1961). *African Genesis: A Personal Investigation into the Animal Origins and Nature of Man*. New York, NY: Atheneum.
Ardrey's "popular" views on human evolution and the "innateness" of human aggression.

SOURCES AND SUGGESTED READING

Cravens, Hamilton. (1988). *The Triumph of Evolution: The Heredity-Environment Controversy, 1900-1941*. Baltimore, MD: Johns Hopkins University Press.
Historical background for exploring "nature versus nurture" in anthropology.

Dawkins, Richard. (1989) [1976]. *The Selfish Gene*. 2nd ed. New York, NY: Oxford University Press.
Dawkins's "ultra-Darwinist" exposition of evolution and contribution to sociobiology.

Dunn, Leslie C. (1991). *A Short History of Genetics: The Development of Some of the Main Lines of Thought, 1864-1939*. Ames, IA: Iowa State University Press.
A history of genetics and genetics issues.

Kevles, Daniel J. (1995) [1985]. *In the Name of Eugenics: Genetics and the Uses of Human Heredity*. Cambridge, MA: Harvard University Press.
A history of genetics, eugenics, and related scientific and social issues.

Kuhl, Stefan. (1994). *The Nazi Connection: Eugenics, American Racism, and German National Socialism*. New York, NY: Oxford University Press.
An examination of the scientific and social underpinnings of German National Socialism.

Larson, Edward J. (1996). *Sex, Race, and Science: Eugenics in the Deep South*. Baltimore, MD: Johns Hopkins University Press.
An examination of eugenics in the American South.

Leakey, L.S.B. (1966). *White African: An Early Autobiography*. Cambridge, MA: Schenkman.
Louis Leakey's early life in Africa.

Leakey, Mary. (1984). *Disclosing the Past: An Autobiography*. New York, NY: Doubleday.
Mary Leakey's account of her life with and without Louis.

Leakey, Richard E. (1984). *One Life: An Autobiography*. Salem, NH: Salem House.
Richard Leakey's account of his life written while he was critically ill.

Maasen, Sabine. (1995). *Biology as Society, Society as Biology: Metaphors*. Ed. Everett Mendelsohn, *et al*. Norwell, MA: Kluwer Academic Publishers.
An examination of the interplay among biological and sociological conceptualizations.

Marks, Jonathan. (2002). *What It Means to Be 98% Chimpanzee: Apes, People, and Their Genes*. Berkeley, CA: University of California Press.
A provocative anthropological critique of biological assertions and activities.

McLaren, Angus. (1990). *Our Own Master Race: Eugenics in Canada, 1885-1945*. Toronto, ON: McClelland and Stewart.
A history of Canadian eugenics in the late nineteenth and early twentieth centuries.

Morrell, Virginia. (1995). *Ancestral Passions: The Leakey Family and the Quest for Humankind's Beginnings*. New York, NY: Simon and Schuster.
Biographies of Louis, Mary, and Richard Leakey.

Morris, Desmond. (1980). *The Naked Ape*. New York, NY: Dell.
The book that spawned the phrase "naked apery."

Neel, James V. (1994). *Physician to the Gene Pool: Genetic Lessons and Other Stories*. New York, NY: John Wiley and Sons.
The autobiography of a leading human geneticist.

Nisbet, Alec. (1977). *Konrad Lorenz*. New York, NY: Harcourt Brace Jovanovich.
A biography of the pioneering European ethologist.

Poliakov, Leon. (1974). *The Aryan Myth: A History of Racist and Nationalist Ideas in Europe*. Trans. Edmund Howard. London: Chatto and Windus.
A critical history of Aryanism.

Provine, William B. (1987). *The Origins of Theoretical Population Genetics*. Chicago, IL: University of Chicago Press.
For the mathematically inclined, a history of the early phase of population genetics.

Ruse, Michael. (1984). *Sociobiology: Sense or Nonsense?* Rev. ed. Norwell, MA: Kluwer Academic Publishers.
A critique of sociobiology by a well-known philosopher of science.

Sahlins, Marshall. (1976). *The Use and Abuse of Biology: An Anthropological Critique of Sociobiology*. Ann Arbor, MI: University of Michigan Press.
An early negative critique of the sociobiological perspective in anthropology.

Schafft, Gretchen E. (2004). *From Racism to Genocide: Anthropology in the Third Reich*. Urbana, IL: University of Illinois Press.
An analysis of the troubled relationship between anthropological science and politics in the era of the Holocaust.

Shipman, Pat. (1994). *Evolution of Racism: The Human Difference and the Use and Abuse of Science*. New York, NY: Simon and Schuster.
A scientific critique of racism by a respected physical anthropologist.

Spencer, Frank. (1990). *Piltdown: A Scientific Forgery*. New York, NY: Oxford University Press.
The story of a famous whodunit.

—. (Ed.). (1982). *A History of American Physical Anthropology, 1930-1980*. New York, NY: Academic Press.
Histories of American physical anthropology in the mid-twentieth century.

Thorpe, W.H. (1979). *The Origins and Rise of Ethology*. Westport, CT: Greenwood.
A history of ethological approaches to the study of animal and human behaviour.

Weikart, Richard. (2004). *From Darwin to Hitler: Evolutionary Ethics, Eugenics, and Racism in Germany*. New York, NY: Palgrave Macmillan.
A history of the interplay of scientific, social, and political themes in the emergence of policies leading to the Holocaust.

Wilson, Edward O. (1975). *Sociobiology: The New Synthesis*. Cambridge, MA: Belknap Press of Harvard University.
The book that introduced sociobiology to science and society.

—. (1994). *Naturalist*. Washington, DC: Island Press.
An autobiography of the founder of sociobiology.

—. (1994). *On Human Nature*. Cambridge, MA: Harvard University Press.
A discussion of the relevance of sociobiology to *Homo sapiens*.

Wolpoff, Milford, and Rachel Caspari. (1997). *Race and Human Evolution: A Fatal Attraction*. New York, NY: Simon and Schuster.
examination of historical relationships among ies of race and human evolution.

SYMBOLIC AND INTERPRETIVE ANTHROPOLOGY

Comaroff, Jean, and John L. Comaroff. (1991). *Of Revelation and Revolution, Vol. 1: Christianity, Colonialism, and Consciousness in South Africa*. Chicago, IL: University of Chicago Press.
Part one of an influential "historical ethnography" and Weberian study of the colonial inscription of European culture on the native Tswana and landscape of South Africa, focusing on the eighteenth and nineteenth centuries.

—. (1997). *Of Revelation and Revolution, Vol. 2: The Dialectics of Modernity on a South African Frontier*. Chicago, IL: University of Chicago Press
Part two of an influential "historical ethnography" and Weberian study of the colonial inscription of European culture on the native Tswana and landscape of South Africa, focusing on the nineteenth and twentieth centuries.

Geertz, Clifford. (1968). *Islam Observed: Religious Development in Morocco and Indonesia*. New Haven, CT: Yale University Press.
A comparison of the diversity of beliefs and practices among Muslims in two different societies.

—. (1977) [1973]. *Interpretation of Cultures*. New York, NY: Basic Books.
The classic treatise of American "interpretive anthropology," which contains Geertz's influential essays about "thick description," religion as a "cultural system," and the analysis of a Balinese cockfight.

—. (1996). *After the Fact: Two Countries, Four Decades, One Anthropologist*. Cambridge, MA: Harvard University Press.
Geertz's autobiography.

Hodder, Ian. (1986). *Reading the Past: Current Approaches to Interpretation in Archaeology*. Cambridge: Cambridge University Press.
An exposition of post-processual archaeology by a leading post-processualist.

Schneider, David M. (1980). *American Kinship: A Cultural Account*. Chicago, IL: University of Chicago Press.
A well-known "interpretive" account of kinship advocating a more "structuralist" approach to understanding symbols and looking to the coherence and logic behind the symbolic "system" first described by Clifford Geertz.

SOURCES AND SUGGESTED READING

Turner, Victor. (1967). *The Forest of Symbols: Aspects of Ndembu Ritual*. Ithaca, NY: Cornell University Press.
In this prototypical ethnography of the symbolic "school," Turner employs an instrumental theory of Ndembu symbols to show how they are effective in producing certain ritual transformations, which ultimately result in social cohesion.

—. (1969). *The Ritual Process: Structure and Anti-Structure*. Hawthorne, NY: Aldine de Gruyter.
In this work, Turner presents his influential reworking of van Gennep's thesis concerning ritual transformation.

Van Gennep, Arnold. (1961) [1959]. *The Rites of Passage*. Trans. Monika B. Vizedon and Gabrielle L. Caffee. Chicago, IL: University of Chicago Press.
Van Gennep's original formulation of the "liminal" transition from one social state to another, as accomplished in and by religious ritual.

Wallace, Anthony F. (1966). *Religion: An Anthropological View*. New York, NY: Random House.
Wallace develops his theoretical perspective on religion, and in particular its capacity to effect personal psychological "mazeway transformation" and social "revitalization" in response to cultural stress or dissonance.

—. (1972). *The Death and Rebirth of the Seneca*. New York, NY: Random House.
Wallace's classic study of colonization and social change among the Seneca nation of eastern North America, combining Durkheimian and Weberian perspectives.

Worsley, Peter. (1968). *The Trumpet Shall Sound*. New York, NY: Schocken Books.
In this classic account of "cargo cults" in the South Pacific, Worsley writes from a distinctly Weberian perspective.

TRANSACTIONALISM

Bailey, Frederick George. (1996). *The Civility of Indifference: On Domesticating Ethnicity*. Ithaca, NY: Cornell University Press.
An ethnographic study of a village in eastern India in which individuals and ethnic groups compete with one another for moral and political authority.

Barth, Fredrik. (1959). *Political Leadership Among Swat Pathans*. London: Athlone Press.
An ethnographic classic about the contested nature of political and economic organization in the Swat valley of Pakistan.

—. (1993). *Balinese Worlds*. Chicago, IL: University of Chicago Press.
An ethnographic study of village culture and social organization in northern Bali.

—. (Ed.). (1969). *Ethnic Groups and Boundaries: The Social Organization of Culture Difference*. Boston, MA: Little, Brown, and Company.
A classic volume of essays on the processes involved in the construction of ethnic identities and boundaries in which individual social actors are shown to maximize their own economic advantage.

Paine, Robert. (1994). *Herds of the Tundra: A Portrait of Saami Reindeer Pastoralism*. Washington, DC: Smithsonian Institution Press.
An ethnographic account of Saami pastoralism in Norway and the effects of government efforts to control it.

FEMINISM AND ANTHROPOLOGY

Behar, Ruth, and Deborah A. Gordon (Eds.). (1995). *Women Writing Culture*. Berkeley, CA: University of California Press.
Taking its name from the successful deconstructionist volume *Writing Culture*, this edited collection explores the "poetics" of ethnography as viewed through the lens of feminist theory.

Boddy, Janice. (1989). *Wombs and Alien Spirits: Women, Men, and the Zâr Cult in Northern Sudan*. Madison, WI: University of Wisconsin Press.
This feminist ethnography looks at how Islamic ideals of feminine purity conflict with local women's desire for empowerment, as manifested in spirit possession.

Di Leonardo, Micaela. (1991). *Gender at the Crossroads of Knowledge: Feminist Anthropology in the Postmodern Era*. Berkeley, CA: University of California Press.
A broad range of essays that examine the effects of feminist scholarship on the study of race, biology, language, culture, and economy.

Geller, Pamela L., and Miranda K. Stockett (Eds.). (2006). *Feminist Anthropology: Past, Present, Future*. Philadelphia, PA: University of Pennsylvania Press.
An edited collection in which contributors explore the contentious history and current state of feminist anthropology, attempting to break new epistemological ground.

Keohane, Nannerl O., Michelle Z. Rosaldo, and Barbara C. Gelpi (Eds.). (1982). *Feminist Theory: A Critique of Ideology*. Chicago, IL: University of Chicago Press.
A collection of essays that examine the relations between feminist theory, science, language, nationality, and other social institutions.

Lewin, Ellen (Ed.). (2006). *Feminist Anthropology: A Reader*. Malden, MA: Blackwell.
A compendium of classic and contemporary ethnographic essays that traces the history of feminist scholarship within anthropology.

Moore, Henrietta L. (1988). *Feminism and Anthropology*. Minneapolis, MN: University of Minnesota Press.
A theoretical study of the engendered character of kinship, domestic life, and the state.

Olson, Gary A., and Elizabeth Hirsch (Eds.). (1995). *Women Writing Culture*. Albany, NY: State University of New York Press.
A collection of interviews with leading feminist scholars who view language and literature as "sites" for the social construction of engendered knowledge.

Ortner, Sherry B. (1997). *Making Gender: The Politics and Erotics of Culture*. Boston, MA: Beacon Press.
A collection of essays in which social differences and hierarchy between men and women are explored in relation to broader ideas about "nature" versus "culture."

—. (2006). *Anthropology and Social Theory: Culture, Power, and the Acting Subject*. Durham, NC: Duke University Press.
The well-known feminist scholar and theoretician presents her views on critical anthropological issues.

Ortner, Sherry B., and Harriet Whitehead (Eds.). (1981). *Sexual Meanings: The Cultural Construction of Gender and Sexuality*. New York, NY: Cambridge University Press.
Essays on political and cultural contexts for the social construction of gender difference in Western and non-Western societies.

Oyewùmí, Oyèrónké. (1997). *The Invention of Women: Making an African Sense of Western Gender Discourses*. Minneapolis, MN: University of Minnesota Press.
Oyewùmí deconstructs the Western category of "women," arguing that its underlying biological determinism does not feature in the social organization of Yoruban society.

Reiter, Rayna R. (Ed.). (1975). *Toward an Anthropology of Women*. New York, NY: Monthly Review Press.
A key text in feminist anthropology in which contributors criticize androcentric epistemology and look to develop new models that reconceptualize the place of women across various societies.

Rosaldo, Michelle Zimbalist, and Louise Lamphere (Eds.). (1974). *Woman, Culture and Society*. Stanford, CA: Stanford University Press.
A seminal collection of essays that explore the structural contexts and constraints underpinning gender differences.

Strathern, Marilyn. (1987). An Awkward Relationship: The Case of Feminism and Anthropology. *Signs* 12(2): 276-92.
A theoretical essay exploring the boundaries between feminism as a discrete discipline and anthropology as a Western field of scholarship that ostensibly promotes, but simultaneously homogenizes, diversity.

—. (1988). *The Gender of the Gift: Problems with Women and Problems with Society in Melanesia*. Berkeley, CA: University of California Press.
An ethnographic study of the politics of gift-exchange and gender relations in Melanesia.

Visweswaran, Kamala. (1997). Histories of Feminist Ethnography. *Annual Review of Anthropology* 26: 591-621.
An historical overview of the development of feminist anthropology from the late nineteenth through the end of the twentieth centuries, paying special attention to the changing conceptual relationship between "gender" and "sex."

SOURCES AND SUGGESTED READING

POLITICAL ECONOMY

Asad, Talal (Ed.). (1974). *Anthropology and the Colonial Encounter*. Atlantic Highlands, NJ: Humanities Press International.
A history of anthropology in the context of European colonialism.

Dirks, Nicholas B., Geoff Eley, and Sherry B. Ortner (Eds.). (1993). *Culture/Power/History: A Reader in Contemporary Social Theory*. Princeton, NJ: Princeton University Press.
A collection of essays on the recent history of anthropology, including one by Ortner that is very useful for situating the theoretical developments that led to the rise of political economy in the 1970s.

Mintz, Sidney W. (1986). *Sweetness and Power: The Place of Sugar in Modern History*. New York, NY: Penguin Books.
A fascinating historical study of the powerful effect that sugar and the sugar-trade have had in forming new European cultural meanings and political and economic relationships.

Redfield, Robert. (1971) [1956]. *Peasant Society and Culture: An Anthropological Approach to Civilization*. Chicago, IL: University of Chicago Press.
Redfield's proto-political economy looks at the continuum between "folk" and "urban" traditions in Mexico.

Roseberry, William. (1989). *Anthropologies and Histories: Essays in Culture, History, and Political Economy*. New Brunswick, NJ: Rutgers University Press.
A well-known collection of essays in which Roseberry looks at the relationship between capitalism and the historical formation of social and political power, as well as the role power has played in shaping cultural meaning and practice.

Schneider, Peter, and Jane Schneider. (1986). *Culture and Political Economy in Western Sicily*. Orlando, FL: Academic Press.
The Schneiders explore the way in which rural Italian underdevelopment and alienation of the south from the north produced local conditions in which new forms of local economy could flourish, in particular the Sicilian Mafia.

Taussig, Michael T. (1980). *The Devil and Commodity Fetishism in South America*. Chapel Hill, NC: University of North Carolina Press.
A widely-read ethnography in anthropological political economy that explores how Columbian peasants use locally meaningful symbolism and ritual to critique the powerful capitalist economic system in which they live.

Wallerstein, Immanuel. (1974). *The Modern World System: Capitalist Agriculture and the Origins of the World Economy in the Sixteenth Century*. Orlando, FL: Academic Press.
Wallerstein's influential exposition of the expansive capitalist "world system," cast in terms of a "core" of consumers who control and exploit the labour and resources of a poor "periphery."

Wilcox, Clifford. (2006). *Robert Redfield and the Development of American Anthropology*. Lanham, MD: Rowman and Littlefield.
A biography of the anthropologist who distinguished between "great" and "little" traditions.

Wolf, Eric R. (1982). *Europe and the People Without History*. Berkeley, CA: University of California Press.
A well-known study drawing on the ideas of Immanuel Wallerstein and André Gunder Frank to argue that local cultures around the world are not self-contained, but develop in a dialectical relationship with the expansive forces of global capitalism.

POSTMODERNITY

Anderson, Benedict. (1991). *Imagined Communities: Reflections on the Origin and Spread of Nationalism*. London: Verso.
An influential work examining the broad historical conditions, notably the development of print-capitalism and the post-medieval voyages of discovery, that allowed nation-states to become "imagined" as new forms of community in Europe and its colonies.

Berger, Peter L., and Thomas Luckmann. (1967). *The Social Construction of Reality: A Treatise in the Sociology of Knowledge*. New York, NY: Doubleday.
An exposition of sociology that views the "real" as being the non-objective product of constructive processes, mainly language-related, in which people participate during daily life.

Bourdieu, Pierre. (1977). *Outline of a Theory of Practice*. Trans. Richard Nice. New York, NY: Cambridge University Press.
Bourdieu's best-known formulation of his theory of "practice" in which social unity and diversity are produced by creative, historically situated agents who actively structure and re-structure their worlds of experience.

Clifford, James. (1988). *The Predicament of Culture: Twentieth-Century Ethnography, Literature, and Art*. Cambridge, MA: Harvard University Press.
Clifford's reflections on how the possibility of an "objective" description of culture, and even its very definition or identification, are undermined by the powerful insight that ethnographies are textual artifice.

Clifford, James, and George E. Marcus (Eds.). (1986). *Writing Culture: The Poetics and Politics of Ethnography*. Berkeley, CA: University of California Press.
The highly influential collection of essays that alerted anthropologists to the problematic character of "objectivist" research, proposing instead that ethnographies are cultural "texts" in which the ethnographer's own subjectivities are deeply embedded.

Comaroff, John, and Jean Comaroff. (1992). *Ethnography and the Historical Imagination*. Boulder, CO: Westview Press.
An influential call to re-think basic tenets of the concepts of structure and function by focusing ethnographic attention on historical process and political-economic transformation.

Foucault, Michel. (1973) [1965]. *Madness and Civilization: A History of Insanity in the Age of Reason*. Trans. Richard Howard. New York, NY: Pantheon Books.
Foucault's landmark investigation into the contingent nature of, and historical trajectory behind, Western beliefs about the condition of "insanity" and treatment of the "insane."

—. (1982). *The Archaeology of Knowledge*. New York, NY: Pantheon Books.
Foucault's outline of his argument that "knowledge" and "truth" are inexorably linked to social and political power, and that buried beneath the official discourse of modernity and civilization are to be found echoes of dissenting "voices."

Giddens, Anthony. (1979). *Central Problems in Social Theory: Action, Structure, and Contradiction in Social Analysis*. Berkeley, CA: University of California Press.
A sophisticated theoretical treatment of the interrelations among power, social structure, and subjective agency.

Gramsci, Antonio. (1992). *Prison Notebooks, Vol. 1*. New York, NY: Columbia University Press.
Gramsci's perspectives on power, written while he was a prisoner, describing the ways in which power inscribes itself on and insinuates its way into social life.

—. (1996). *Prison Notebooks, Vol. 2*. Ed. and trans. Joseph A. Buttigieg. New York, NY: Columbia University Press.
A continuation of Gramsci's study of power and hegemony.

—. (2007). *Prison Notebooks. Vol. 3*. Ed. and trans. Joseph A. Buttigieg. New York, NY: Columbia University Press.
The third volume of Gramsci's study of power and hegemony.

Hobsbawm, Eric J., and Terence Ranger (Eds.). (1992). *The Invention of Tradition*. New York, NY: Cambridge University Press.
A collection of essays looking at the historical process behind the recent production of "ancient" traditions—such as Hugh Trevor-Roper's study of the Scottish kilt—and the general problem of what social purposes might be served by "inventing" history in this way.

Johnson, Thomas M., and Carolyn F. Sargent (Eds.). (1990). *Medical Anthropology: A Handbook of Theory and Method*. New York, NY: Greenwood Press.
A review of theory and method in medical anthropology and ethnomedicine, and a survey of different ethnomedical systems.

Landy, David (Ed.). (1977). *Culture, Disease, and Healing: Studies in Medical Anthropology*. New York, NY: Macmillan.
A comprehensive textbook that introduces readers to emic and etic dimensions of medical anthropology.

Lindenbaum, Shirley, and Margaret Lock. (1993). *Knowledge, Power & Practice: The Anthropology of Medicine and Everyday Life*. Berkeley, CA: University of California Press.
A collection of essays that examine the cultural production of ethnomedical knowledge in different societies.

SOURCES AND SUGGESTED READING

Lutz, Catherine. (1988). *Unnatural Emotions: Every Day Sentiments on a Micronesian Atoll and Their Challenge to Western Theory*. Chicago, IL: University of Chicago Press.
A thought-provoking postmodern ethnography of the "emotional" world of a small island in Micronesia, illuminating the cultural basis of emotions and highlighting inadequacies in how Western "scientific" theorists have divided the world into the categories of, among other dichotomies, "self" versus "other."

Sankar, Andrea. (1999). *Dying at Home: A Family Guide for Caregiving*. Baltimore, MD: Johns Hopkins University Press.
A cultural history of death and care-giving at home, combined with an anthropologically informed guide for primary caregivers on how to look after patients in the home.

Scheper-Hughes, Nancy. (1992). *Death Without Weeping: The Violence of Everyday Life in Brazil*. Berkeley, CA: University of California Press.
A widely read postmodern ethnography in which Scheper-Hughes examines the cultural construction of knowledge about health and illness in a poor Brazilian community.

GLOBALIZATION

Appadurai, Arjun. (1996). *Modernity at Large: Cultural Dimensions of Globalization*. Minneapolis, MN: University of Minnesota Press.
An ethnographically-based deconstruction of the concept of modernity.

Coleman, Simon. (2000). *The Globalization of Charismatic Christianity*. Cambridge: Cambridge University Press.
A contribution to the globalization-focused literature, in which Coleman looks at the cultural, political, and economic dimensions of a transnational religious movement.

Escobar, Arturo. (1995). *Encountering Development: The Making and Unmaking of the Third World*. Princeton, NJ: Princeton University Press.
An examination of the role of Western development policy—in Escobar's view, the heir to colonial regimes—in creating, naturalizing, and economically subjugating the "Third World."

Featherstone, Mike (Ed.). (1990). *Global Culture: Nationalism, Globalization, and Modernity*. London: Newbury Sage.
Various essays on the relations among culture, nation, the world system, and globalization.

McLuhan, Marshall, and Bruce R. Powers. (1989). *The Global Village: Transformations in World Life and Media in the 21st Century*. New York, NY: Oxford University Press.
Posthumous essays on the effects of media and technology in a globalizing world.

Robertson, Roland. (1992). *Globalization: Social Theory and Global Culture*. London: Sage.
A wide-ranging introduction to the political, economic, and cultural debates that characterize the study of globalization.

PUBLIC ANTHROPOLOGY

Besteman, Catherine, and Hugh Gusterson (Eds.). (2005). *Why America's Top Pundits Are Wrong: Anthropologists Talk Back*. Berkeley, CA: University of California Press.
A collection of essays in which leading scholars join the conversation on important and highly charged public issues such as poverty, racism, violence against women, and American foreign policy.

Feinberg, Ben. (2006). The Promise and Peril of Public Anthropology. *Human Rights & Human Welfare* 6: 165-77.
A thoughtful review essay that examines key themes and perspectives in several recent texts in public anthropology.

Forman, Shepard (Ed.). (1995). *Diagnosing America: Anthropology and Public Engagement*. Ann Arbor, MI: University of Michigan Press.
A collection of essays advocating anthropological engagement in the formulation of American public policy, challenging assumptions regarding the morally neutral character of anthropology.

Gonzãlez, Alberto J. (Ed.). (2004). *Anthropologists in the Public Sphere: Speaking Out on War, Peace, and American Power*. Austin, TX: University of Texas Press.
Several dozen examples of recent anthropological editorializing in non-academic publications, especially concerning the exercise of American military power.

Purcell, Trevor W. (2000). Public Anthropology: An Idea Searching for a Reality. *Transforming Anthropology* 9,2: 30-33.
A short editorial summarizing some of the main ambitions of public anthropology.

Rhodes, Lorna A. (2004). *Total Confinement: Madness and Reason in the Maximum Security Prison*. Berkeley, CA: University of California Press.
A recent contribution to the University of California Press "Public Anthropology" series in which Rhodes explores the complex world and fragile politics of the supermaximum security prison.

Smith, Gavin. (1999). *Confronting the Present: Towards a Politically Engaged Anthropology*. New York, NY: Berg.
An invitation to dialogue among anthropologists and other social scientists about the role of political engagement in a globalizing, postmodern world.

Conclusion

Darnell, Regna, and Frederic W. Gleach. (2002). Introduction. *American Anthropologist* 104(2): 417-22.
An introductory essay to a centennial year edition of *American Anthropologist*, in which various contributors consider their perspective on the history of anthropological scholarship.

Davis, Wade. (2002). For a Global Declaration of Interdependence. *The Globe and Mail*. (Toronto): 6 July.
A sobering post-9/11 essay concerning the contribution of gross inequities in power and wealth to the rise of Islamic extremism and jihad.

Lewis, Herbert S. (1998). The Misrepresentation of Anthropology and Its Consequences. *American Anthropologist* 100(3): 716-31.
Lewis asserts that in its eagerness for deconstruction, postmodern anthropological theory has misrepresented and effectively demonized disciplinary ancestors, in the process reducing their use in current undergraduate and graduate curricula.

—. (1999). A Response to Sandy Toussaint's Commentary: "Honoring Our Predecessors: A Response to Herbert Lewis's Essay on 'The Misrepresentation of Anthropology and Its Consequences.'" *American Anthropologist* 101(3): 609-10.
In Lewis's rejoinder to Toussaint's review essay on his paper, he dismisses her criticisms on the grounds that they do not relate to the intent of his thesis concerning the misrepresentation of anthropological ancestors.

Mascia-Lees, Fran. (2006). Can Biological and Cultural Anthropology Coexist? *Anthropology News* 47(1): 9-13.
A brief article in which Mascia-Lees proposes that unity among the four fields will be achieved only if new paradigms are developed and questions asked that invite collaboration across diverse types of research.

Segal, Daniel A., and Sylvia J. Yanagisako (Eds.). (2005). *Unwrapping the Sacred Bundle: Reflections on the Disciplining of Anthropology*. Durham, NC: Duke University Press.
A provocative collection of essays in which contributors interrogate the value of and alternatives to the reigning "four-field" model of anthropology within the North American academy.

Smith, Eric Alden. (2002). Anthropological Schisms. *Anthropology News* 47(1): 8-11.
A brief article in which Smith calls on anthropologists to recognize the value of a four-field anthropology, especially in terms of the potential contributions of the subfields to one another.

Thomas, R. Brooke. (2006). Anthropology for the Next Generation. *Anthropology News* 47(1): 9-11.
A brief article in which Thomas champions the eclecticism of a four-field approach, arguing that current disunities will be undetermined as pressing global environmental problems demand research that spans anthropological scholarship.

SOURCES AND SUGGESTED READING

Toussaint, Sandy. (1999). Honoring Our Predecessors: A Response to Herbert Lewis's Essay on "The Misrepresentation of Anthropology and Its Consequences." *American Anthropologist* 101(3): 605-10.

Toussaint's review essay of Lewis's paper, in which she takes him to task for selectively eliminating early women anthropologists from his canon of ancestors and for reifying the relative contributions of "old-time" versus "young" anthropologists.

Wolf, Eric R. (1982). Introduction. In *Europe and the People Without History*. Eric Wolf. 3-23. Berkeley, CA: University of California Press.

In this introductory chapter to a classic study in anthropological political economy, Wolf discusses the rise of distinctive social sciences and humanities disciplines as the outcome of structural developments within European and North American universities.

SPEAKING ABOUT ANTHROPOLOGICAL THEORY

Boddy, Janice. 1982. Womb as Oasis: The Symbolic Context of Pharaonic Circumcision in Rural Northern Sudan. *American Ethnologist* 9 (4): 682-98. Revised and reprinted in *The Gender/Sexuality Reader: Culture, History, Political Economy.* Ed. Roger N. Lancaster and Micaela di Leonardo. 309-24. New York: Routledge, 1997.

—. 1988. Spirits and Selves in Northern Sudan: The Cultural Therapeutics of Possession and Trance. *American Ethnologist* 15 (1): 4-27. Reprinted (abridged) in *Reader in the Anthropology of Religion*. Ed. M. Lambek. 398-418. Oxford: Blackwell, 2001.

—. 1989. *Wombs and Alien Spirits: Women, Men, and the Zar Cult in Northern Sudan.* Madison, WI: University of Wisconsin Press.

—. 1998. Remembering Amal: On Birth and the British in Northern Sudan. In *Pragmatic Women and Body Politics*. Ed. Margaret Lock and Patricia Kaufert. 28-57. Cambridge, UK: Cambridge University Press.

—. 2007. *Civilizing Women: British Crusades in Colonial Sudan*. Princeton, NJ: Princeton University Press.

Bourdieu, Pierre. 1990. *The Logic of Practice*. Trans. Richard Nice. Stanford, CA: Stanford University Press.

Collier, Jane, and Sylvia Yanagisako (Eds.). 1987. *Gender and Kinship: Essays Toward a Unified Analysis*. Stanford, CA: Stanford University Press.

Geertz, Clifford. 1973. *The Interpretation of Cultures*. New York, NY: Basic Books.

National Film Board of Canada. 1973. *Behind the Masks*. Tom Shandel, producer.

Ortner, Sherry, and Harriet Whitehead (Eds.). 1981. *Sexual Meanings: The Cultural Construction of Gender and Sexuality*. New York, NY: Cambridge University Press.

Said, Edward. 1979. *Orientalism*. New York, NY: Vintage.

Illustration Sources

Cover Image and Page 29: DÜRER, Albrecht. "Adam and Eve," from *The Fall of Man*. Nuremburg, Germany, engraving. Copyright © Historical Picture Archive/CORBIS. Reprinted by permission of Corbis, Inc.

Page 31: WINSOR, Justin. "New World," from *Narrative and Critical History of America*. Volume I. Boston: Houghton Mifflin, 1889. Copyright © 1889 by Houghton Mifflin Company.

Page 33: TLAXCALLA, Lienzo de. "The Old World Meets the New. Attack on Great Temple," from *Antiguedades Mexicanas*. Plate 16. Negative no. 330879. Reprinted by permission of the Library, American Museum of Natural History.

Page 55: "Sir James Frazer (1854–1941)." Image is a photograph of the original drawing. Accession number **PRM 1998.271.2**. Reprinted by permission of the Pitt Rivers Museum, University of Oxford.

Page 57: DRIVER, Harold E. "Culture Areas of North America," from *Indians of North America*. Chicago: University Of Chicago Press, 1961. Copyright © 1961 by the University of Chicago Press. Reprinted by permission of the University of Chicago Press.

Page 61: SQUIER, Ephraim G. and E.H. Davis. "Grave Creek Burial Mound, West Virginia," from *Ancient Monuments of the Mississippi Valley*. Volume 1. Washington, DC: Smithsonian Contributions to Knowledge, 1848.

Page 64: LINNAEUS, Carolus. "Carolus Linnaeus' Biological Classification of Humanity," from *Systema Naturae*, 1735. Reprinted by permission of the Library, American Museum of Natural History.

Page 66: HUXLEY, Thomas H. "Comparison of Ape and Human Skeletons," from *Man's Place in Nature*. Ann Arbor: The University of Michigan Press. Copyright © 1959 by The University of Michigan Press.

Page 67: HAIG, Axel H. "Charles Darwin's Study at Down House, Kent, England." Negative no. 326814. Reprinted by permission of the Library, American Museum of Natural History.

Page 91: "Janice Boddy." Reprinted by permission of the Royal Society of Canada.

Page 95: "Franz Boas (1858–1942)." Photograph by Blackstone Studios, New York, American Anthropological Association. Reprinted by permission of the American Anthropological Association.

Page 99: "Robert Lowie (1883–1957)." Courtesy of the Phoebe Apperson Hearst Museum of Anthropology and the Regents of the University of California. Reprinted by permission of the Phoebe A. Hearst Museum of Anthropology.

Page 101: "Alfred Kroeber (1876–1960)." Photograph by Blackstone Studios, New York, American Anthropological Association. Reprinted by permission of the American Anthropological Association.

Page 103: "Margaret Mead (1901–1978)." Photograph by Blackstone Studios, New York, American Anthropological Association. Reprinted by permission of the American Anthropological Association.

Page 105: "Ruth Benedict (1887–1948)." Photograph by Blackstone Studios, New York, American Anthropological Association. Reprinted by permission of the American Anthropological Association.

Page 109: DU BOIS, Cora. "Alorese Youth Drawings," from *The People of Alor, Volume II*. Minneapolis: The University of Minnesota Press, 1944. Copyright © 1944 by the University of Minnesota Press. Reproduced by permission of the University of Minnesota Press.

Page 114: LÉVI-STRAUSS, Claude. "The Totemic Operator," from *The Savage Mind*. Chicago: University of Chicago Press, 1962. Copyright © 1962 by Librarie Plon, 8 rue Granciere, Paris-6e. Copyright © 1966 George Weidenfield and Nicholson Ltd. Reprinted by permission of the University of Chicago Press.

Page 127: KEESING, Roger M. "The Kula Ring," from *Cultural Anthropology, a Contemporary Perspective*, First Edition. Copyright © 1976 by Holt, Richart and Winston. Reprinted by permission of Wadsworth, a division of Thomson Learning: www.thomsonrights.com. Fax: 800-730-2215.

Page 129: EVANS-PRITCHARD, E. "Neur Seasonality," from *The Neur: A Description of the Modes of Livelihood's Political Institutions of a Nilotic People*. New York: Oxford University Press, 1960. Reprinted by permission of Oxford University Press.

Page 135: "Lee D. Baker." Photograph by Yaa Asantewaa Thomas Baker. Reprinted by permission of Yaa Asantewaa Thomas Baker.

Page 139: CARROLL, John B. "The Sapir-Whorf Hypothesis," from *Language, Thought and Reality: Selected Writings of Benjamin Lee Whorf*. Cambridge: The MIT Press. Copyright © 1971 by MIT. Reprinted by permission of the Massachusetts Institute of Technology.

Page 143: "Leslie White (1900–1975)." Photograph by Blackstone Studios, New York, American Anthropological Association. Reprinted by permission of the American Anthropological Association.

Page 165: LOCOCK, Martin. "Formal Gardens at Castle Bromwich Hall, West Midlands, England," from *Meaningful Architecture: Social Interpretations of Buildings*. London: Ashgate Publishing. Copyright © 1994 by Martin Locock.

Page 169: "Louise Lamphere (President of the American Anthropological Association 1999–2001)." Photograph by Blackstone Studios, New York, American Anthropological Association. Reprinted by permission of the American Anthropological Association.

Page 176: "Robert Redfield (1897–1958)." Photograph by Blackstone Studios, New York, American Anthropological Association. Reprinted by permission of the American Anthropological Association.

Page 203: HUTCHINSON, Sharon. "Abu-Lughod Interviewing Bedouin Women in West Egypt." ID#0935. Reprinted by permission of Anthro-Photo.

The publisher has endeavored to contact the rights holders of all copyrighted illustrations published in this text and would appreciate receiving any information regarding errors or omissions so that we may correct them in future reprints and editions of the work.

Index

INDEX

INDEX

INDEX

INDEX

INDEX

INDEX

INDEX